D1116477

Preface

This book is a study of the presentation of the martyrs as Christ figures in the early church, both the way that the martyr acts interpret the person and death of Jesus and the manner in which this interpretation can inform our understanding of martyrdom in early Christianity. As such it has a dual focus: the reception history of traditions about Jesus and views of martyrs in the ancient churches. Yet despite the breadth of these subjects, this book focuses upon the presentation of the martyrs in a single generic source: the acts of the martyrs, or *passiones*. The focus on this particular type of narrative might be interpreted by some as either myopic or anachronistic—myopic in that it appears to disregard the wealth of other ancient sources for the cult of the saints in antiquity, and anachronistic in that it appears overly committed to the genre of the martyrdom account itself. While this present study takes the martyrdom accounts as its focus, other literary, artistic, and architectural sources are not ignored. Indeed, they play a vital role in contextualizing these narratives. In placing the martyrdom accounts at the forefront of my work, I am attempting to treat them seriously as interpretative, rhetorically powerfully, and theologically constructive literature. Rather than read the stories about the martyrs as supporting evidence for the ideas of patristic authors, I treat them as individual documents produced by anonymous but *no less valuable* authors and communities. As texts, the martyrdom accounts are shaped by their readings, but we should not assume that this interpretative process was always constrained by the views of Tertullian, Cyprian, or Origen. Instead, we should treat these narratives individually and try to imagine the various ways that they were understood by the communities that produced and used them.

This project is in many respects an exercise in the history of interpretation and ideas. I am interested in the way that the death of Jesus is constructed in the context of martyrological traditions. An exhaustive study of the interpretation of the death of Jesus would have been impossible. Given my interest in *imitatio*, I have focused on martyr traditions whose narrative form mirrored that of extant traditions about the death of Jesus. This interest led me to focus upon martyr narratives that generically are considered part of the acts of the martyrs.

In terms of form, these narratives are drawn together by their common interest in presenting biographical accounts of the deaths of martyrs. As a result, scholars have treated these stories not only as generically united but as ideologically homogeneous. Yet whatever formal similarities we can identify on a micro, narrative level is undercut by the variety of ways in which they functioned in the early church. Some accounts appear in apologetic or heresiological treatises, others as part of collections of martyrdom accounts, and others still as part of histories of the church. While we can imagine that many of these narratives were used in similar social settings, we cannot assume that they had identical functions. In an inversion of the maxim "divide and conquer," my collection and use of these texts is intended to problematize the genre of the martyrdom still further. I strive to show the different views of the martyr at play in the ancient churches and the interpretative richness and diversity in ancient martyrdom accounts. I have retained a commitment to the "genre" of the martyr act only insofar as it enables me to demonstrate the diverse ideas about martyrs held by ancient Christians. We should not speak of an ideology or theology of martyrdom in the ancient Church. Just as we speak of ancient Christianities, we should speak of ancient ideologies of martyrdom.

Writing about martyrdom in the early church is made difficult by the elusive task of identifying and delineating martyrdom accounts composed in this period. While I have attempted to collect those *passiones* and *acta* that can most reliably be dated before the reign of Constantine, slipperiness and uncertainty are an inherent part of this practice. Rather than brush over difficult questions of dating and provenance, I have tried to be as transparent as possible in handling these sources and the evidence for their dating. I remain convinced that the dating of the *passiones* and, more particularly, the *difficulty* in dating these texts remain an important precursor to their use by historians and theologians of the early church. My own views on the dating of the *passiones* are laid out in the appendix to this work; I invite the reader to decide for him- or herself whether or not my arguments are sound. I only hope that, even if readers disagree with my dating of individual martyr acts, they will accept my argument that sensitivity to detail and the diverse arguments of these accounts are an integral part of their study.

Acknowledgments

One of the joys of finishing this work is that it offers me the opportunity to thank those to whom I am greatly indebted. This book is a revision of my dissertation, completed at Yale University. During the final stages of my work on the dissertation, I was fortunate to receive financial assistance not only from the Graduate School but also from the Charlotte W. Newcombe Foundation and the Catholic Biblical Association. The Institute for Scholarship in the Liberal Arts in the College of Arts and Letters at the University of Notre Dame provided financial assistance as I completed the project. I am indebted to the librarians and staff of the Yale Divinity School Library, the British Library, and the Bodleian for their wisdom and patience. I am grateful to Cynthia Read, Jennifer Kowing, Susan Ecklund, and the editorial team at Oxford University Press for their help and guidance and to the Clarendon Press for granting me permissions to use texts and translations from Herbert Musurillo, *Acts of the Christian Martyrs* (Oxford: Clarendon Press, 1972).

My thanks go to Harold Attridge, for his support and exemplary model of rigorous biblical scholarship; Stephen Davis, for giving freely of his research, time, and friendship; Bentley Layton, for his high standards and judicious criticism; Dale Martin and Ludger Viefhues, for deconstructing my world; my colleagues in the Program of Liberal Studies for their support during my first year here at Notre Dame; and Kenneth Wolfe, who set me on the path of biblical scholarship.

I am particularly indebted to Adela Yarbro Collins, my doctoral adviser, without whom this book would never have been written. Her careful criticisms, advice, exemplary scholarship, and marvelous instruction—for all of which she is well known—are but the very least of the things for which I am grateful. She has been the finest mentor and most unfailing friend, and without her support I would surely be less of a scholar and person than I am today.

Thanks are due to Stephanie Cobb, Adela Colins, Jim Kelhoffer and Wolfgang Wischmeyer for making their work available to me in prepublication form and to Max Johnson for enthusiastically reading my work. There are numerous friends, teachers, and colleagues whose support, expertise, and collegiality have greatly improved this work; most notable among them are Joel Baden, David Eastman, Timothy Luckritz Marquis, Brent Nongbri, Michael Peppard, Tudor Sala, and Diana Swancutt. Christine Luckritz Marquis and Meghan Henning deserve special thanks for sharing their papers, ideas, and passions with me. Eric Prister and Jessica Shaffer have served as exemplary and tireless research assistants, embracing every task happily and with good humor.

To my family—my four parents and my sisters, grandparents, uncles, aunts, and cousins—I must extend my gratitude for their support and love, especially during my final year of graduate school. My husband, Kevin McCarthy, has been a source of unfailing and unquestioning support and love. A debt of an entirely different kind is owed to my uncle James Fairbairn, whose humble, loving *imitatio Christi* I am grateful for every day.

Contents

Abbreviations

Aristotle, *Poet.*	*Poetics*
Ascen. Isa.	*The Ascension of Isaiah*
Augustine, *Conf.*	*Confessions*
Augustine, *Enarrat. Ps.*	*Enarrations on the Psalms*
Augustine, *Faust.*	*Against Faustus the Manichaean*
Augustine, *Serm.*	*Sermones*
Augustine, *Serm. Dom.*	*Sermon on the Mount*
Augustine, *Tract. ep. Jo.*	*Tractates on the First Epistle of John*
Augustine, *Tract. Ev. Jo.*	*Tractates on the Gospel of John*
Augustine, *Unit. eccl.*	*The Unity of the Church*
BHO	*Biblioteca hagiographica orientalis*
Clement of Alexandria, *Paed.*	*Christ the Educator*
Clement of Alexandria, *Strom.*	*Miscellanies*
Cyprian, *Fort.*	*To Fortunatus: Exhortation to Martyrdom*
Cyprian, *Test.*	*To Quirinius: Testimonies against the Jews*
Cyprian, *Unit. eccl.*	*The Unity of the Catholic Church*
Cyprian, *Zel. liv.*	*Jealousy and Envy*
Did.	*Didache*
Ep. Apos.	*Epistle to the Apostles*
Epictetus, *Diatr.*	*Dissertationes*
Euripides, *Iph. taur.*	*Iphigeneia at Aulis*
Eusebius, *Hist. eccl.*	*Ecclesiastical History*
Gos. Thom.	*Gospel of Thomas*
Gos. Truth	*Gospel of Truth*
Herm., *Vis.*	Shepherd Hermas, *Vision*
Herm., *Sim.*	Shepherd of Hermas, *Similitude*
Hippolytus, *Haer.*	*Refutation of All Heresies*
Hippolytus, *Trad. ap.*	*The Apostolic Tradition*
Homer, *Od.*	*Odyssey*
Ign., *Eph.*	Ignatius, *To the Ephesians*
Ign., *Phld.*	Ignatius, *To the Philadelphians*
Ign., *Pol.*	Ignatius, *To Polycarp*
Ign., *Rom.*	Ignatius, *To the Romans*
Ign., *Smyrn.*	Ignatius, *To the Smyrnaeans*
Ign., *Trall.*	Ignatius, *To the Trallians*
Irenaeus, *Haer.*	*Against Heresies*
Jerome, *Vigil.*	*Adversus Vigilantium*
John Chrysostom, *Ign.*	*In sanctum Ignatium martyrem*

Josephus, *J.W.*	*Jewish War*
Justin Martyr, *1 Apol.*	*First Apology*
Justin Martyr, *2 Apol.*	*Second Apology*
Justin Martyr, *Dial.*	*Dialogue with Trypho*
Lucian, *Demon.*	*Demonax*
Lyons	*Letter of the Churches of Lyons and Vienne*
Mart. Agape	*Martyrdom of Agape, Irene, Chione, and Companions*
Mart. Apaioule	*Martyrdom of Apaioule*
Mart. Arcadius	*Martyrdom of Arcadius*
Mart. Barsamya	*Martyrdom of Barsamya*
Mart. Caecilia	*Martyrdom of Caecilia*
Mart. Conon	*Martyrdom of Conon*
Mart. Crisp.	*Martyrdom of Crispina*
Mart. Dasius	*Martyrdom of Dasius*
Mart. Fruct.	*Martyrdom of Fructuosus and Companions*
Mart. Iren.	*Martyrdom of Irenaeus Bishop of Sirmium*
Mart. Isa	*Martyrdom of Isaiah*
Mart. Mar.	*Martyrdom of Marian and James*
Mart. Marculus	*Martyrdom of Marculus*
Mart. Marinus	*Martyrdom of Marinus*
Mart. Maximilian	*Martyrdom of Maximilian*
Mart. Maximian	*Martyrdom of Maximian*
Mart. Mont.	*Martyrdom of Montanus and Lucius*
Mart. Palestine	*Martyrs of Palestine*
Mart. Pasius	*The Martyrdom of Pasius*
Mart. Pion.	*Martyrdom of Pionius*
Mart. Pol.	*Martyrdom of Polycarp*
Mart. Pot.	*Martyrdom of Potamiaena and Basilides*
Mart. Pusai	*Martyrdom of Pusai*
Mart. Simeon	*Martyrdom of Simeon*
Minucius Felix, *Oct.*	*Octavius*
NPNF	*Nicene and Post-Nicene Fathers*
Origen, *Cels.*	*Against Celsus*
Origen, *Comm. Matt.*	*Commentary on the Gospel of Matthew*

Origen, *Hom. Lev.*	Homily on Leviticus
Origen, *Mart.*	Exhortation to Martyrdom
Origen, *Princ.*	First Principles
Pass. Dorothea	Passion of Dorothea
Pass. Maxima	Passion of Maxima, Donatilla, and Secunda
Pass. Perp.	Passion of Perpetua and Felicitas
Pass. Serge	Passion of Serge and Bacchus
Philo, *Mos.* 1	On the Life of Moses 1
Philo, *Opif.*	On the Creation of the World
Pirqe R. El.	Pirqe Rabbi Eliezer
PL	Patrologia Latina
Plato, *Leg.*	Laws
Plato, *Phaed.*	Phaedrus
Plato, *Symp.*	Symposium
Plato, *Theaet.*	Theaetetus
Plato, *Tim.*	Timaeus
Pliny the Younger, *Ep.*	Epistulae
Plutarch, *Aem.*	Aemilius Paullus
Plutarch, *Quaest. conv.*	Quaestionum convivialium libri IX
Pol., *Phil.*	Polycarp, To the Philippians
Quintillian, *Inst.*	Institutio oratoria
SC	Sources chrétiennes
T. Benj.	The Testament of Benjamin
T. Levi	The Testament of Levi
Tertullian, *Apol.*	Apology
Tertullian, *Bapt.*	Baptism
Tertullian, *Fug.*	Flight in Persecution
Tertullian, *Idol.*	Idolatry
Tertullian, *Marc.*	Against Marcion
Tertullian, *Mart.*	To the Martyrs
Tertullian, *Nat.*	To the Heathen
Tertullian, *Or.*	Prayer
Tertullian, *Scorp.*	Scorpiace

The Other Christs

Introduction

In a letter to the Christian community in Rome, written around the turn of the second century, the bishop martyr Ignatius implores his addressees not to intervene with the Roman authorities to save him.[1] He longs, he says, "to be an imitator of my suffering God."[2] His ardent desire for a Christly death exemplifies the early Christian preoccupation with mimetic suffering. Out of the host of gory accounts of torture and triumphant manly battles with Satan, a seemingly innocuous theme emerges; the martyrs are imitators of their Lord. Indeed, the characterization, conceptualization, and depiction of the martyrs are grounded in the premise that in their death they imitate Jesus. From the proclamations of the churches to the footnotes of the academy, all agree: the martyr follows Christ both literally and literarily.[3] In the words of Judith Perkins, "The one thing everyone knows about Christianity is that it centers on suffering in the exemplar of the crucified Christ."[4] Despite, or perhaps because of, its ubiquity in the ancient and medieval churches, the mimetic relationship between the martyr and Christ remains unexplored in its cadences, nuances, and significance. The relationship is everywhere assumed but nowhere dissected.[5] The scholarly trend is to refer to the fact that the martyr imitates Christ, but never to examine the details and function of this imitation. What is this imitation? What does it mean to lay martyrs on the literary scaffold of the crucifixion?

The answers, of course, are anything but simple. Language of imitation is interwoven with ideals of discipleship and Pauline notions of "putting on" Christ. Christ suffers *in* the martyrs and shares a particular intimacy with them. The elaborate way in which imitation is constructed complicates the picture but does not, as some have argued, negate the fact that imitation is at work in ideologies of martyrdom.[6] That Christ lives in the martyrs does not exclude the possibility that they also imitate him. Our understanding of imitation is further augmented by the diversity of its representation. In some narratives, such as the famous *Martyrdom of Polycarp*, the martyr is explicitly identified both as an imitator of Jesus and as a model for other Christians. In other accounts the presentation of the martyr as Christly imitation is subtler. The martyrs imitate Christ in their words and gestures, mouthing scripture and retreading the path blazed by Christ. But the imitation is never explicitly identified in the account; Christ is, in a sense, "invisible." In the same way as the apostles in the apocryphal *Acts of the Apostles*, the martyrs fill the vacancy left by Jesus at the executioner's block.[7]

The presentation of the martyr as imitator of Christ was a delicate theological balancing act. Even in the case of Polycarp the author of the account is careful to distinguish between Polycarp's martyrdom "according to the gospel" and the unevangelical enthusiasm of Quintus, who eagerly offers himself for martyrdom. Only certain kinds of martyrdom are to be emulated.[8] At the same time, the author is keen to differentiate between Polycarp and Christ. In order to guard against the misconception that Christians worship their martyrs, the author notes, "For him [Christ] we reverence as the Son of God, whereas we love the martyrs as the disciples and imitators of the Lord" (*Mart. Pol.* 17). Regulating the imitation of Christ is, in this text, a question of defining what should be imitated and what imitation is. Does following in Christ's footsteps mean standing in his place?

To simply state that the martyrs imitate Christ does not exhaust what the imitation of Christ can tell us about either martyrdom or the history of ideas. Imitating something or someone involves an understanding of what that thing or person is, an interpretation of his or her significance. In the case of ancient communities presenting their martyrs as Christly imitators, this involves a particular reading of traditions about Jesus, his death, his significance, and his work. By presenting martyrs as Christly imitators, the authors of the early martyrdom accounts provide scholars with a window into early Christian understandings of scripture, Christology, and soteriology.

The ways that ancient literature can serve as sources for the history of interpretation is not limited to the martyrdom accounts. In recent years there has been in a surge of scholarly interest in the reception history of the New Testament. The interpretative moves of the early church, in particular, are the subject of numerous studies seeking to understand the ways in which the canonical texts were understood by the first generations of Christian readers. In the past, reception histories of the canonical New Testament have adhered to one of two approaches. The first is found in the numerous studies dedicated to biblical interpretation in the work of a particular author.[9] This approach seeks to identify the exegetical strategies and interpretative eccentricities of a particular author and is useful for identifying the way in which an individual church father utilizes and interprets scripture. The confines of the evidence are such, however, that these patristic authors are often later fourth- or fifth-century writers.

The second approach is found in works that attempt to trace out the reception of a particular canonical work in the writings of the early church.[10] These studies offer valuable insights into the reception history of canonical texts, yet their contribution is hampered by the narrow manner in which they identify scriptural intertexts. Both focus on authors and works that employ explicitly and self-consciously interpretative genres such as commentary, allegory, or citation. If a biblical text is not explicitly "cited," then it is not included. This criterion has meant that there is little, if any, discussion of more ambiguous forms of biblical intertextuality such as "allusion."[11] Consequently, these approaches are inherently limited, both temporally, in that the majority of studies focus on later patristic authors, and generically, in that the material examined is confined to citation and commentary.[12]

In the study of martyrdom accounts the use of scriptural texts is acknowledged but rarely analyzed. Scholarly discussions of the use of the New Testament in the martyr acts are limited almost entirely to the italicization and identification of canonical quotations.[13] With the exception of Victor Saxer's magnificent work on the use of the Bible in early hagiography and a handful of exceptional articles on the *Martyrdom of Polycarp*, early writings about the saints are rarely regarded as appropriate sources for reception history.[14] Yet as evidence for the history of ideas, the acts of the martyrs present a number of opportunities. To begin with, they are early, with a number of texts being dated to the mid-second century, a period largely inaccessible for those interested in reception history. Furthermore, as a literary tradition, the martyr acts stem from a variety of social settings.[15] Unlike other forms of early Christian narrative, such as the *Apocryphal Acts of the Apostles*, the martyr acts can often be reliably tied to specific geographic locations. As a result, they not only provide us with a view of specific churches but also allow us to construct a geographical picture of the diverse forms of Christianity in the early church.

Last, the form of interpretation contained in the *acta* offers a number of advantages over more "traditional" interpretative formats like commentary. In order for the presentation of the martyr to be effective, the rereading of Jesus must necessarily remain in close contact with those Jesus traditions with which it assumes its audience to be familiar. This does not mean that the implied understanding of Jesus traditions is guileless. Martyr acts do not simply reproduce biblical narrative, they "interpret" and offer a "reading" of it.[16] There are very specific agendas at work here; rather, the *manner* in which the rereadings relate to the scriptural texts they reimagine differs from the manner of relationship in more self-consciously interpretative genres.

This book endeavors to show how the martyr acts can illuminate our understanding of the interpretation of writings and ideas about Jesus until the conversion of Constantine.[17] It asks both what does the imitation of Christ in the acts of the martyrs tell us about martyrs and also what does the martyrs' imitation of Christ tell us about early views of Christ? It is impossible to give a full account of the martyr's imitation of Christ and the myriad ways that this functioned in different places, times, and settings. Yet, I hope to offer a window into the ways in which the martyr's imitation can be instructive for our understanding of the early church. Imitation, for this study, means both the way that the genre of the martyr act—problematic as it is—imitates and interprets the gospel account, and also the way that the martyr is portrayed as or presumed to imitate Christ. These two aspects are clearly related; each fosters and nurtures the other, and we cannot really speak of one without the other. It is worth parsing them here because they highlight different ways in which the study of martyrdom in valuable. In the first place, the imitation of the narrative form of the death of Jesus extends the Gospels into the lives of early Christians. It forges a concrete connection between individual Christians in the early church and the scriptural narrative and enables them to construct their lives within the scriptural world. In the case of the presentation of the martyr as an *alter Christus*, we can see both the rereading of the person of Jesus and the construction of the martyr as Christ figure.

This book will follow the path of the martyr from trial and imprisonment, to death, the heavens, and the throne of God. This journey and its focus on imitation will allow us to see a variety of ways in which the martyr's imitation of Jesus can enlighten our understanding of martyrdom, the reception of traditions about the death of Jesus, the construction of heaven in the early church, and historical theology. We will see the passion of Jesus renarrated in the bodies of the martyrs. These traditions are examples both of scriptural interpretation and of embodied biblical hermeneutics. Rhetorically, the narrative reenactment of Jesus traditions clothed Christ in ecclesiastical attire. The martyrs served to demonstrate the Christly response to persecution, communal conflicts, perceived heresies, and oppression. By reincarnatating Christ in the tortured flesh of martyrs, Christian communities empowered the authors of the martyr acts to speak the message of the divine son through martyr mimes.

The imitation of the martyrs is not only a question of biblical hermeneutics or rhetorical elegance. The acts of the martyrs cast light on the development of historical doctrines about the status and nature of Christ, on anthropology in the early church, and on the mechanics of salvation. Chapter 3 will explore how death was made meaningful through association with the death of Jesus and, moreover, the meaning ascribed to the saving death of Jesus. It will challenge the conventional view of the martyr's death as sacrifice and the death of Christ as unique.

The presentation of martyrs as "other Christs" was transformative for the status of the martyrs in their own communities. Whereas previously they had been slaves, women, artisans, bishops, deacons, aristocrats, and foreigners, they had ascended—through Christly death—to the upper ranks of the Christian hierarchy. The benefits of this kind of Christian social climbing are most discernible in portrayals of martyrs in heaven. The activities, roles, and functions of the martyrs in heaven suggest that they occupied a privileged position there.

The martyrs' emulation of Christ, the salvific function of their deaths, and their promotion in the heavenly hierarchy raise questions about their relative status vis-à-vis Christ. Imitation itself is rather more complicated than mere "copying," particularly when associated with language of "putting on" and "possessing" Christ. For all its ubiquity, the question of what it means to imitate Christ is largely overlooked. Imitation involves the recognition of the superior status and power of someone or something else. In choosing to imitate another individual, a person first admires the abilities, person, influence, and status of the other individual. There is an implicit acknowledgment that the other outranks or outstrips oneself. This recognition creates a chain or hierarchy in which lower imitates higher. There are a variety of ways in which imitation is used and what the copy hopes to achieve. To use one brief example, an athlete may imitate the style and accomplishments of another athlete. These efforts reinforce a hierarchy in which the model is superior to the copy, but the ambitions of the mimetic athlete are to acquire for him- or herself the status and acclaim of the model. Depending on its use, therefore, imitation can appropriate, subvert, or reinforce the power and status of the model.[18]

There is a certain ambiguity to the imitation of the martyr. Ignatius both longs to imitate Christ and claims to bear Christ inside himself. What does taking hold of Christ mean? Does the imitation of the martyrs alter their status? Idealized in death, did the martyr rise in the mimetic hierarchy to share the status of Jesus? Leaving aside post-Nicean and post-Chalcedonian assumptions about the uniqueness and transcendence of the ontologically divine Christ, chapters 4 and 5 will examine the ways in which the charisma of the exalted martyr disrupted the mimetic hierarchy that separated martyr from Messiah. This disruption will be revealed through an examination of both the martyrs' functions in heaven and their status in the divine hierarchy.

The division of these chapters into function and status is in some respects a mimetic reproduction of the traditional division between function and ontology in discussions of Christology.[19] These are the scholarly categories used to ascertain who Christ is in relation to God. Similarly, in martyrological scholarship it is the assumption that martyrs share the same roles and functions as angels that has contributed to view that they *are*, in fact, angels.[20] The former category, therefore, is preserved in order to demonstrate the absence of functional similarity with angelic beings. The selection of "status" rather than "essence" is an important and deliberate attempt to avoid anachronistic and inappropriate discussions of ontology—inappropriate not only to martyrdom literature, which does not utilize this language, but also to the period as it would anachronistically assume an interest in essence. If, as Castelli has shown, imitation is about hierarchy and status, then hierarchy and status are the appropriate lenses through which to view the martyr's ascent.

In chapter 5, the examination of distinctively Christological language of enthronement, reign, divine sonship, and inheritance will be used to tease out the martyrs' status—to examine the extent to which the mimetic hierarchy that placed Christ above the martyrs was disrupted by the mimesis itself. The elevation of the martyr's status does not make claims about divine essence or deification, but it did prove troublesome for some church fathers. The charisma of the memorialized martyrs proved hard to control, and it was necessary to produce and police a doctrinal, ontological divide between Christ and the martyrs.

Before turning to the specifics of the interpretation of Jesus traditions, we must first review the history of scholarship on martyrdom that has shaped the way that martyrdom literature is treated and viewed by the scholarly community. Martyrdom is not just mimesis, and an understanding of the broader ways in which martyrdom functioned is an important precursor to this work.

Intellectual Influences and Historical Origins

In the history of scholarship, the twin aims of identifying the historically "reliable" martyrdom account and locating the origins of martyrdom have been the primary focus of scholarly interest. From the beginnings of scientific inquiry in the period of the Enlightenment, scholars of martyrdom have attempted to categorize the acts of the martyrs according to historical value. Value in this instance is defined as the extent to which the martyrdom account accurately records the words and events surrounding the death of a particular early Christian. The Société des Bollandistes was founded with the express aim of sorting the fraudulent chaff from the historically dependable wheat.[21] Its historical analyses, recorded in more than seventy volumes of the *Acta Sanctorum*, have laid the foundation for subsequent generations of scholars to debate the historical veracity of the martyrdom accounts.[22] The work of the Bollandistes, combined with the efforts of scholars like Ruinart,[23] von Harnack,[24] and von Gebhardt,[25] established a small canon of martyrdoms that are deemed historically reliable. Despite the seismic methodological shifts in the study of the early church, the historical reliability and authenticity of this canon of martyrdom accounts have remained relatively secure. Even though modern scholars are less concerned with the historical martyr and more interested in the communities that produce texts, the canon has remained largely unaltered.[26]

Toward the beginning of the twentieth century, scholars began to probe the origins of martyrdom itself. The great ecclesiastical scholar Hans Freiherr von Campenhausen proposed that the notion of martyrdom originated within Christianity itself as a distinctive feature of this new religious group.[27] For Campenhausen and his followers, the Greek term *martys* describes a particular kind of death in which an individual dies as a result of his or her religious confession or witness. This view was supported by the linguistic studies of a cohort of German scholars, most notably Norbert Brox, whose *Zeuge und Märtyrer* (1961) demonstrated that the term *martys* does not become a *terminus technichus* until the *Martyrdom of Polycarp* in the mid-second century.[28] More recently, Campenhausen's argument has been reasserted by the classicist Glenn Bowersock, who locates the origins of martyrdom in second-century Asia Minor.[29]

In contrast to Campenhausen's sui genesis theory of martyrdom, a number of scholars have attempted to trace the conceptual basis of martyrdom—if not the terminology—to a variety of Jewish and Greco-Roman accounts. This work was begun by W. H. C. Frend, whose *Martyrdom and Persecution in the Early Church* argued for a strongly Jewish background and located the origins of martyrdom within the history of the suffering of the Jewish people.[30]

For Frend, narratives that described the unjust suffering and sometimes death of righteous individuals are interpreted as early examples of martyrdom. While the oldest Jewish stories involving the actual death of the hero are found in 2 Maccabees, the theme of the righteous sufferer is traced back further to the psalms of lament, the accounts of the three young men in the furnace (Daniel 3), and the story of Daniel in the lion's den (Daniel 6). This theme is greatly amplified in the accounts of the noble deaths of Elieazar and the seven sons in the writings of the Maccabees. In recent scholarship, the influential role of 2 and 4 Maccabees on the development of ideologies of martyrdom has been more fully parsed out in a number of works by Jan Willem van Henten, who argues that thes Maccabees are the antecedents of Christian martyrs.[31]

The genesis of martyrdom is further complicated when scholars look outside Jewish sources, to examples from the Greco-Roman world. There are a number of startling literary and thematic similarities between Jewish and Christian martyrdoms and Greco-Roman narratives that are more usually termed "noble deaths." The figure of Achilles, Athenian funeral orations, the tragedies of Euripides, and the deaths of the philosophers, most notably the iconic figure of Socrates, played an instrumental role in shaping ideas of self-sacrifice and noble death. These noble deaths served as paradigms for imitation; the death of Socrates, for instance, served as the model for Tacitus's description of the deaths of Seneca and Thrasea Paetus. Such examples serve to foreshadow the way in which the suffering and death of an exemplary figure can serve as a model for his followers and admirers. Not only "martyrdom" but the idea of the suffering exemplar predate the deaths of early Christians.[32]

Even if parallels to martyrdom are found in contemporary literature, a number of scholars are reluctant to term the deaths of the Maccabees or Greek philosophers "martyrdoms." The absence of language of witness is a critical part of this reticence. The task of locating the origin of martyrdom often hinges on scholarly definitions of "martyr" and "martyrdom" and the extent to which these definitions rest upon semantic or conceptual foundations. While scholarly consensus maintains that the term *martys* only begins to resemble our own term "martyr" in the second century, the majority of scholars have moved away from linguistic definitions toward broader conceptualist notions of martyrdom. To be sure, the linguistic focus of Brox and Campenhausen *is* limited in scope, yet it draws our attention to the distinctive ways that the term "martyr" was discursively shaped by various Christian communities. There is chronological development, but there are also geographic distinctions and cultural nuances. The term was employed differently in different social, geographic, and chronological moments, and describing these nuances should be the task of the scholar.

The construction of the linguistic category "martyr" took place alongside and in dialogue with the construction of the category "Christian." Nowhere is this more evident than in the martyrdoms themselves, where the declaration "I am Christian" is inextricably tied to the process of becoming a martyr.[33] This is not to say that, as linguistic and conceptual categories, *martys* and *Christianismos* are not constantly being produced; rather, in their *initial* production they were constantly being coproduced.[34] This point is critical because it illustrates that—for those individuals we categorize as ancient Christians—the ideology of martyrdom and the status of the martyr did not stand outside and beyond the realms of ordinary self-definition.

Whether or not the origins of martyrdom can be located in Jewish or Christian traditions, there are a number of early church writings that lend themselves well to martyrological interpretation. Once again, in the case of these examples scholarly attention has focused on the intersection of particular linguistic and conceptual definitions of *martys* and the presence of these concepts in the writings of New Testament authors. For us, it is not particularly relevant whether the authors of these texts themselves worked with an understanding or definition of the term *martys* that can be directly mapped onto our own. What is relevant, however, is the way that these cultural and intellectual influences served to construct ideologies of martyrdom in which martyrdom becomes inextricably linked to the notion of imitating Christ.

Social Contexts

While twentieth-century New Testament and patristic scholarship was preoccupied with the intellectual origins of martyrdom, late antique scholars have gravitated toward the social contexts in which martyrdom texts were produced and performed. An audience or members of an audience understand texts using the generic categories and intellectual and cultural information available to them, but this understanding is equally shaped by the context in which the text is heard or read. A biblical text read aloud in a congregation as part of a liturgical service is understood differently from a text studied in the classroom of a university.

It is not only bold contextual differences that affect the way that a text is received; seemingly narrow contexts such as "the liturgy" leave room for multiple modes of presentation. Within modern liturgy, for instance, biblical texts are presented in distinct ways, and the particular form and mode of presentation greatly affect the text's reception. The reading of scriptural passages as part of modern Catholic Eucharistic performance uses scripture in a number of discrete ways.[35] On the one hand, some texts are presented as "scriptural readings" and as texts that will be explicitly used as the basis of the homily. Within this group, Gospel readings are marked as particularly special; only the priest may read from the Gospel, and the reading of Gospel passages is marked by physical signs—such as the sealing of one's forehead, lips, and chest with a cross—that further mark out the Gospel reading as "special." The receptions of the Gospel readings and the Old Testament readings are not the same; they are received differently, and we must be attentive to this. In addition to scriptural readings, the words of Jesus in the Gospels form the structure and framework for the preparation and consecration of the gifts, the bread and wine used in the ceremony. In consecrating the gifts, the priest refers to the words that Jesus spoke "on the night before he died" to provide the context, justification, and grounds upon which the consecration takes place. The explicit mentions of scripture are further augmented by the subtle unmarked quotation of the words of Jesus during the mass.

During the consecration of the gifts, the congregation kneels and says, "Lord I am not worthy to receive you but only say the words and I shall be healed." The words are a near-perfect quotation from the story of the healing of the centurion's servant in Matthew 8:8, yet they are not marked as such in the performance of the liturgy. Whether or not this response is understood as scripture by the congregation is completely unclear. These brief examples illustrate the ways that scripture can be received and understood within the context of the liturgy of the Eucharist in the Catholic Church. Scripture is used, presented, and received in a variety of ways. There is no singular "liturgical setting" for the reception of biblical texts; there are instead many liturgical contexts, and an understanding of the use and reception of a scriptural text can vary *even within a single liturgical performance.* This is to say nothing of different liturgical performances such as baptismal or funerary liturgies that color the presentation of scripture differently.

The same attention to detail and thirst for specificity should be applied in scholarship seeking to locate the social contexts in which the martyr acts were performed. In identifying the loci in which martyrdom literature was produced, we must bear in mind the specific manner in which the account is presented. The martyrdom of Saint Stephen, as it comes to be read, is part of the canon of scripture. The canonical status of this account is undoubtedly part of the driving force behind the particularly popular cult of Saint Stephen.[36] In the later period, canonicity assures that the martyrdom of Saint Stephen is read differently from other accounts.[37] Developing a more sophisticated understanding of the contexts in which martyrdom accounts are read, therefore, is an essential part of understanding how they functioned.

A number of patristic writers and ancient sources refer to the public reading of the martyrdom accounts on the anniversary of the martyr's death, also referred to as the martyr's birthday, or *dies natales.* This practice appears to have been widespread, particularly at sites associated with the martyrs such as their tombs, churches dedicated to them, or their places of execution. The decision of the Third Council of Carthage, in 397 C.E., to permit the reading of the "Passiones Martyrum cum anniversarii dies eorum celebrentur" indicates that in Carthage at least the practice was supported by church authorities.[38]

The public reading of martyr acts in churches or other communal gather-
ings endowed the accounts with authority and power. The degree of authority
apportioned to the account was related to both the premortem and the postmortem status of the martyr—who they were in life and who they were in
death. Apostles, the protomartyr Stephen, and the famed bishop Cyprian are
examples of martyrs whose premortem identity and status guaranteed them
authority and fame in death. In the case of other powerful martyrs, their status
and importance were derived from the prominence of their cults and enormity
of their shrines. The cults of the martyr Demetrios in Thessaloniki[39] and of
Serge and Bacchus in Syria[40] are examples of martyrs made famous through
the dissemination of their cult. In the minds of both ancient and modern readers (although perhaps more in the minds of the latter), the prominence of
a particular saint was further bolstered by the homilies of important
church thinkers like Augustine, John Chrysostom, and Gregory of Nyssa.[41] The
admiration of esteemed church thinkers elevated the status of the individual
martyr.

The location of the reading of the martyrdom account is critical to understanding its importance. The *acta* were read aloud in small shrines, in catacombs, and in cathedrals, and the reception and function of the accounts are
augmented by each of these settings. The reading of the martyr acts in tombs
orients the attention of the audience on the themes of death and resurrection.
The presence of other tombs reminds them of the contrast between the fate of
the martyr and the fates of the ordinary dead and the unsaved. In his *Confessions*, Augustine refers to the celebration of the martyr's birthday with meals
and libations.[42] If the reading of the martyrdom account took place in conjunction with a meal for the dead or other kind of refreshment, then the reception
of the account would be different than it would be in a cathedral.[43] All of this is
to say that we should be wary of generalizing about the "social settings" in
which martyrdom accounts were received.

A number of scholars have argued that the acts of the martyrs were composed for liturgical performance.[44] The evidence for liturgical readings of the
acta is manifold. Ancient records suggest that the martyrdom accounts were
read aloud on the feast day of the martyr, and we possess a slew of patristic
homilies delivered on these occasions. The homilies, which frequently refer
to the stories about the martyrs, suggest that the martyr acts were read aloud
as part of the liturgy. Scholars who argue that the martyrdom accounts were
a part of Eucharistic liturgy invariably read the deaths of the martyrs through
sacrificial understandings of the liturgy.[45] Such readings are productive and
offer valuable insights into the performance of *acta* in the context of sacrificial interpretations of the Eucharist. We should not assume, however, that the

liturgical setting and function of the *acta* were stagnant and fixed, that the martyrdom accounts were used in a single fashion, and that "liturgical function" itself refers to something homogeneous and uniform. Recent studies of the Eucharist, for example, have demonstrated the diverse practices in operation in the ancient world, to say nothing of the unregulated baptismal practices in the early church.[46] Given that liturgical practices varied from location to location, we must assume that heterogeneity, not uniformity, was the rule and as a result resist the temptation to draw broad generalizations about liturgical function.

At the same time as we recognize the influence that social setting has upon the reading of the martyrdom account, we must also embrace the manner in which the readings of martyrdom accounts can alter the understanding of the social performance itself. The liturgical performance of a particular account is altered by the content of the specific account. The legends surrounding Saint Lawrence, for example, have a particular resonance with Eucharistic liturgical performance. As his bishop is led away to execution, the deacon Lawrence protests, exclaiming that they "always celebrate the sacrament" together. Read within a Eucharistic liturgy, the performance of this account identifies the priestly officiants and Eucharistic liturgy with the performance of martyrdom. The more mundane liturgical sacrifice and the extraordinary offering of the deacon Lawrence are aligned and compared.

The Eucharistic focus of writings about Lawrence can be compared to the baptismal imagery of the *Passion of Perpetua and Felicitas*, which understands martyrdom as a kind of "second baptism."[47] The reading of these texts in identical liturgical settings would color their performances differently, the former lending a sacrificial flavor to the proceedings, the latter providing a baptismal wash. Situating a text or genre of texts within the context of "liturgical performance" is more complicated than it may at first seem.

Scholarly imagination has leaned toward the Eucharist as the touchstone of liturgical practice, but can we imagine other liturgical settings in which the *acta* could have functioned? Martyrdom accounts and practices of martyrdom are frequently described as tools in the conversion and promulgation of Christianity. In the words of Tertullian, "the blood of the martyrs is the seed of the church."[48] The conversion of the bystander is a topos of the genre itself, the accounts frequently noting the effect that martyrdom had on the audience of the execution. Given the prevalence of this phenomenon, it seems possible that martyrdom accounts were read in the context of baptismal liturgies.[49] The *Passion of Perpetua and Felicitas*, for example, with its catechumen protagonists and frequent references to baptism, would appear to be a prime candidate for this kind of reading.[50] A number of patristic authors describe martyrdom as a form of baptism, endowing martyrdom with a kind of sacramental quality and baptism with a martyrological significance.[51] Even if the *acta* were not read as part of baptismal liturgies, there is considerable evidence to suggest that they were used in catechetical contexts to encourage initiation into Christianity and to exhort the faithful to great endurance and virtue.[52]

In addition to their liturgical or catechetical life span, a number of the martyr acts functioned as epistolary communiqués and thus as part of a program of intra-ecclesial dialogue.[53] The *Martyrdom of Polycarp* and the *Letter of the Churches of Lyon and Vienne* are but two early examples of this phenomenon. The exchange of stories about martyrs certainly served as a means of communicating events, as well as a form of consolation and communal bonding among the churches.[54] The reading of narratives of persecution and endurance in far-flung lands served to inspire Christians to greater endurance, to produce camaraderie and a sense of "being in it together." A church enduring persecution in Antioch, for example, did not suffer alone; its brethren in Gaul suffered with it in solidarity and reality. Yet the exchange of martyrdoms accomplished other things, serving to propagate a particular image of an individual church as especially virtuous, persecuted, and enduring. The persecuted church in Gaul, for example, appears successful, brave, and exemplary, and this presentation sets up an implicit hierarchy among the churches. When the *Letter of the Churches of Lyons and Vienne* is read aloud in Asia Minor, the congregants and the church in Asia Minor are implicitly encouraged to behave *like* the churches of Gaul. Seeking to imitate the behaviors of others sets up a mimetic hierarchy in which the object of imitation is elevated above the imitator. For the churches of Lyons and Vienne, communities that otherwise lacked distinction, the presence of a strong martyrological tradition, a tradition grounded in the imitation of Christ, served to bolster their status among readers of their letter in Asia Minor. The dissemination of martyrdom accounts, therefore, enabled individual churches to claim authority and power and to rise up the hierarchy of churches even as the martyrs themselves were elevated above the general Christian populace.

Even if the majority of martyr acts were composed with liturgical or catechetical functions in mind, the earliest accounts conform to the genre and function of apologetics. Discounting Polycarp, to the dating of which we will return in the appendix, the earliest accounts of the deaths of Christians were composed as part of the literary program of the "apologist" Justin Martyr. The *Acts of Ptolemaeus and Lucius* forms part of Justin's second apology and was directed to the emperor Marcus Aurelius. The account of Justin's own martyrdom, the *Acts of Justin and his Companions*, follows the same philosophical and apologetic conventions. There is considerable debate as to whether "apologetic literature" in the early church was truly composed with an imperial audience in mind.[55] Tessa Rajak, for example, has argued that apologetic literature was composed with a Christian audience in view as part of a strategy of boundary making.[56] The composition of the acts of the martyrs within the context of rhetorically styled philosophical apologetics provides us with another social location in which the *acta* were read.

The writings of the apologists are particularly concerned with issues of identity and boundary making. They focus on the continuity between the Jewish scriptures and the beliefs and practices of Christianity, and on the superior morality of the Christians over and against their pagan neighbors. Such arguments are as useful for self-definition within a Christian community as they are for defending Christianity from external attack. Writers of texts intended for insiders invariably had to contend with questions and anxieties from members who were schooled in the cultural milieu of the outsiders, and the apologetic "genre" filled this void. Apologetic literature replied to the unspoken and invisible critique that lingered in the minds of the philosophically educated.[57] The textual overlap between apologetic and martyrological discourse, particularly in the writings of Justin, confirms the proposition that martyrdom and apologetic occasionally served as overlapping genres in the early church. Like apologetic literature, martyrdom accounts are concerned with the construction of Christian identity and establishing boundaries between the Christian family and those outside it. Defining what it means to be Christian in intra-ecclesial dialogue was as important as establishing boundaries with outsiders.[58]

Whether or not apologetic literature was as internally directed as Rajak suggests, is critically important for our understanding of how martyrdom literature functioned in this setting. We can still, however, draw some conclusions about the role of martyrdom literature in the arena of apologetics. As apologetic literature, the martyrdom accounts functioned to answer external critique (be it real or imagined). Even if apologetic missives were actually sent to emperors, we can assume that they were read in public Christian settings in which they served pedagogical and exhortatory functions. These readings were not catechetical, but they were instructive. Justin himself ran a Christian school in which he taught his students the tenets of Christianity. We can imagine, therefore, that some early martyrdoms were read aloud to Christian students as part of their schooling in the new Christian philosophy.

A related function of the martyr acts is the role that martyrs played in the promulgation of particular doctrines and the suppression of perceived heresies. The charisma and authority of the martyr were such that they rivaled even the most powerful bishops and Christian thinkers. As articulate and brilliant as he was, Augustine struggled with the competing power of the martyrs and—more specifically—those who controlled their veneration. Religious leaders were wise to the authority of the saints, seeking to cast themselves as "friends of the martyrs" in attempts to harness their power for political and theological gain.[59] At the same time, the communities responsible for the production and editing of martyrdom accounts realized their potential for disseminating their own theological views and ideas about Christian life. By placing doctrinal statements on the lips of the martyr, an author or community could authorize its position using the martyr's seal of authority—an authority connected to the martyr's association with Christ.

Just as the writers of the apocryphal acts sought to harness the authority of an apostle to endow their writing with power, so the editors of the martyrdom accounts attempted the same feat using the persona of the martyr. The increasing theologization of the martyrdom accounts can be traced through the redaction and translations of accounts. An addendum to the *Martyrdom of Polycarp* found only in the Moscow codex follows Irenaeus in portraying Polycarp's condemnation of the followers of Marcion.[60] Over time, references to the Trinity, references to the status of Mary as "mother of God," and anti-Donatist language of unity crept into the martyrdom accounts. Even though the social location of the accounts' performances may have remained the same, there was now an added layer of functionality. The martyrdom accounts acted as heresiology, as literature that sought to eliminate the heterodox and subtly promote the doctrinal statements of the dominant group.

The social context of martyrdom is by no means more secure than the intellectual contexts. We can imagine and have evidence for a variety of locations in which martyrdom texts functioned: liturgical, catechetical, intraecclesial, pedagogical, apologetic, and heresiological. Even these functions are broadly conceived—liturgical settings vary according to the grandeur of the church, the personality of the homilist, and the purpose of the gathering. We should be wary of exclusively assigning martyrdom literature to the realm of the liturgical. Even if in the majority of cases martyrdom accounts were composed with this setting in mind, they were used in a variety of settings and in a number of different ways.[61]

As much as these diverse social settings limit our ability to speak with certainty about the reception of a text, they open multiple avenues of inquiry about the ways in which martyrdom literature is relevant to the early church. These texts can shed light upon every aspect of Christian life, from the preparation and instruction of the initiate, to liturgical rituals, the Christian family, doctrine, and death. It would be impossible to consider the interpretation of each individual instance of *imitatio Christi* in every possible social location. Nonetheless, the concatenization of the various ways in which martyr acts functioned here serves to illustrate a number of contexts in which the presentation of martyr as Christ type was rhetorically powerful for those producing these texts. I leave it to the reader to imagine for him- or herself the many ways in which the following individual examples of Christological mimesis resonated within these different contexts.

With these diverse intellectual and social contexts lingering in our minds, we return now to the object of the martyr's ambitions: the person of Jesus. It is in the earliest formulations of what it meant to follow Jesus—the writings of the Jesus movement—that the premise of imitating Christ through suffering was first established. The idea of imitating a suffering exemplar may not have been unique, but the precise articulation of this concept is critical to our understanding of the martyr's imitation. We will begin, therefore, with an examination of the formation of the Jesus follower in the literature of the nascent church. We will see the ways in which suffering like Jesus was a foundational element of membership in the communities of Jesus followers and an essential component of Christian identity. Rather than taking for granted the fact that suffering was important for the first followers of Jesus, we will explore the ways in which this idea was expressed in terms of imitation and the manner in which it became foundational for early Christian martyrdom.

I

Suffering Like Christ

To the modern reader, martyrdom literature has an alien quality. Even in communities where martyrdom is viewed as admirable, it frequently assumes the role of something foreign and historically distant. Martyrdom is extreme and removed, necessitated by dire historical circumstances that arise in far-flung places and times. We assume that it is an exceptional form of Christian behavior, a practice that can only exist in these extraordinary historical moments, outside of normal Christian practices and realms of being. It is a grounding premise of the early church, however, that suffering and death could serve a redemptive and transformative function for early Christians.

The ideology of martyrdom did not emerge—creation-style—out of an intellectual vacuum. Long before the persecutions of Decius and Diocletian, Christians had begun to identify their own sufferings, be they "real" or "perceived," with those of their suffering Messiah. The close association and indeed identification of communal and personal afflictions with those of Christ played an instrumental role in shaping and defining emerging Christian identities.

The identification of personal suffering with the sufferings of Christ, however, is part of a larger complex of practices in which members of the Jesus movement and early Christians sought to imitate Christ in aspects of their daily life. The association of personal with Christological suffering, therefore, was not solely the by-product of theodicy; it was part of a web of mimetic practices that writers and church leaders sought to inculcate in their audiences and congregations. Patient endurance and righteous suffering became part of a set of Christly moral virtues that early Christians were exhorted to emulate. Suffering as Christological imitation was not just a passive interpretative move; it was an active practice to which Christians were constantly encouraged.

Both the association of individual suffering with the sufferings of Jesus and the promotion of mimetic practices predate the emergence of martyrdom literature. These ideas were present in the literature of the Jesus movement and early church. The prevalence of these ideas was so great that by the time of the composition of the *acta martyrum*, the interpretation of individual suffering as a means of emulating Christ was assumed. This chapter discusses the New Testament and early church texts that contributed to the emergence of this view.[1] The inclusion of a particular text does not indicate either that this kind of reading was the original intent of the author or that this is the only or dominant interpretation of that text. Although in many cases it may have been true that the author him- or herself viewed suffering in this manner, it is less the original intent of the author than the possible readings that their work may have elicited that are of interest.

Imitatio Christi in New Testament Scholarship

The exhortation to imitate Christ is one of the earliest themes in the literature of the Jesus movement. From the Pauline to Ignatian epistles, imitating the actions of Christ is a pervasive theme for early Christian writers. For early Christians, the activities and teaching of Jesus became the template for the Christian life. Jesus was the model for calling disciples (Mark 3:13–19; Matt 28:18–20), prayer (Mark 1:35–39; Matt 6:9–13), performing healings (Matt 8:1–17), answering the charges of opponents (Mark 2:1–3:27), and relating to one's family (Mark 3:31–35). In the absence of a codified ethical system, the person and teachings of Jesus became the guiding principle for Christian behavior.

The importance of imitation in moral discourse was not the product of Christian invention; on the contrary, it was well established in ancient discourse and particularly in the writings of Greco-Roman moralists.[2] In his classic study of mimesis in antiquity, Hermann Koller argues that the word group arrived in Greece as an accompaniment to the Dionysiac cult.[3] Mimetic language functioned in a number of ways as means of describing artistic production,[4] the relationship between the sensible and intelligible worlds,[5] the correct attitude toward God,[6] as well as its use in an ethical sense as a means of exhorting individuals to behave in a certain manner.

In exhorting their students to live virtuous lives, Greco-Roman moralists utilized the language of mimesis and ethical exempla as a powerful rhetorical tool. While living models were to be preferred, the study of the *bioi* of distinguished individuals had great pedagogical benefit.[7] Through the imitation of the words and deeds of great figures, it was possible to become like them. The same idea was present in Jewish writers in the Hellenistic period, who used the language of mimesis to inspire their readers to live more virtuous lives. These writers found inspiration in biblical figures such as Moses or Joseph, whose outstanding achievements as deliverers of the Israelite people made them eminently qualified for the role of ethical model.[8]

In the writings of the Jesus movement, exhortations to imitate the behavior and actions of Jesus abound. The canonical New Testament overflows with the idea that its readers should seek to imitate the actions of the savior. Yet New Testament scholars have exhibited an astonishing and often unjustified reluctance to speak of the imitation of Christ as a theme in the earliest Christian literature. *Imitatio* anxiety among scholars is grounded in one of three underlying motivations: the almost proprietorial hold that Roman Catholicism has over the term, the Christological convictions threatened by the concept, and the inescapable but repugnant conclusion that dying for Christ may be a central, rather than peripheral, part of the Christian experience.

An underlying current in the rejection of imitation is the importance of *imitatio Christi* in later Roman Catholicism and a latent anti-Catholicism in scholarly treatments of the issue.[9] In addressing the question of *imitatio Christi* in the literature of the earliest Christians, it is important not to import the later, more refined, technical use of the term in medieval Roman Catholicism. More often than not, the term *imitatio Christi* calls to mind the manual of spiritual devotion composed by the fourteenth-century German monk Thomas à Kempis.[10] Unfortunately, the close association of the term *imitatio Christi* with the writings of Kempis and practices of medieval Catholics has led many scholars to reject its applicability to early Christian literature and to force an unnatural dichotomy between *imitatio Christi* in its later manifestation and New Testament notions of imitation and discipleship.[11]

The polarization of discipleship or following after Christ over against the imitation of Christ is inappropriate in a number of respects. First, despite their linguistic distinctiveness, the terms are used in similar and occasionally interchangeable ways. Discipleship is frequently assumed to entail imitation of things that Jesus did, imitation often implies ethical imitation, and both terms are used to describe suffering in imitation of Christ.[12] It is not the case, therefore, that discipleship is an ethical exhortation and imitation a performative practice. Conceptually, the terms function in interlocking and mutually enlightening ways.[13] Second, the division between the two is often performed on canonical terms. Discipleship is constructed as a New Testament concept used by Jesus himself while imitation is relegated to the province of the early church.[14] From the perspective of the historian, separating these ideas on the basis of canonicity involves importing the later theological category of "canon." The anachronistic introduction of canon by scholars into the first century reveals that what is really at stake here is a latent vulgar Catholic and Protestant divide. Canonicity in the first century is not the concern of the historian; it is the anxiety of the believer.

To the theologian, *imitatio Christi* is inherently troubling; the Christian audaciously eyes the divine throne and attempts to claw him- or herself onto it. In doing so the Christian threatens the stability of modern Christian ideas of soteriology and Christology. It would be more convenient, then, if soteriologically orientated imitation could be assigned to the early church period and thereby dismissed as just another mistaken tradition in the sticky theological mess of patristic theological controversy. Post-Chalcedonian Christological assumptions, therefore, are the second motivation behind the rejection of *imitatio Christi*. The extent to which individual scholars see a particular Christly action as imitable is directly connected to their own Christological views. As caveats to their own discussions of *imitatio Christi*, many scholars will express their belief in the inability of the Christian to imitate Jesus in terms of his uniqueness, that is to say, in his "preexistent life" or his postmortem exaltation.[15]

These arguments are essentially religious and stem from a commitment to Jesus' identity as the second person of an unattainable trinity. Such theological commitments stem from a period much later than the New Testament texts, and it is anachronistic to impose them here. This theological unpalatability is handled in one of two ways. Either *imitatio Christi* is sanitized so as to refer to a somewhat wishy-washy ethical concept. This trend is exemplified by the work of Gerald Hawthorne, who envisions *imitatio Christi* as an exhortation to allow the thinking and actions of Jesus to permeate and influence the lives of everyday Christians.[16] Or, if at all possible, a critique of the theology of *imitatio Christi* is offered. This approach is particularly evident in discussions of Ignatius of Antioch, who is frequently condemned for his "abortive Christology" and "misunderstanding" of the theme of imitation in Paul.[17] In these instances, *imitatio Christi* is rejected either because it simply will not fit within the theological framework of the scholar or because if it did, it would bankrupt the theological economy of modern Christianity.

The final objection to *imitatio* is the unnerving idea that martyrdom is not an optional extra in the Christian experience. If Christians are exhorted to imitate the actions of Christ, if discipleship entails suffering like Christ, and if

Christ the true martyr blazes the way for his followers, then dying for Christ was not just a possibility; it was an obligation. For moderns, martyrdom lies on the periphery, outside the scope of normal Christian experience. Bringing martyrdom inside the vibrant and living New Testament makes for uncomfortable reading.[18]

In dealing with the literature of the Jesus movement and early Christian churches it is, to my mind, both anachronistic and inappropriate to use the term *imitatio Christi* in its expanded medieval sense. At the same time, it is inappropriate to discard the notion of imitating Christ completely, merely because it conjures up bad memories in the Protestant collective unconscious. In its basic meaning, *imitatio Christi* refers to actions or words that imitate those of Christ, not complicated ethical and spiritual systems of thought. For the purposes of this work, I will employ the term to describe the idea that Jesus' followers should seek to imitate him. This idea can be expressed both linguistically using the mimesis word group and conceptually in passages that propose mimicry of Jesus' behavior but do not explicitly use this terminology.

Having explored the dearth of scholarship on *imitatio* in the literature of the Jesus movement, we can now turn to those texts that reveal an interest in imitation and mimesis. The function of exhortations to imitate the behavior of another is as much rhetorical as it is ideological. With respects to these early texts, we are interested in the manner in which they began to construct followers of Jesus as suffering imitators.

Pauline Epistles

From the beginning of the Jesus movement, the imitation of Christ was a focal point in the literature of the churches. Throughout his epistles, Paul frequently exhorts his audiences to imitation of himself and Christ. In her work on this theme, Elizabeth Castelli has drawn attention to the rhetorical function of mimetic language.[19] She shows that it functions as part of a larger rhetorical strategy that enables Paul to establish a particular set of societal relations. Paul constructs a hierarchy of imitation in which he invites his audience to participate. He places Christ at the top of the hierarchy and himself as the mediator between Christ and the congregation. The effect of mimetic language is to regulate behavior and draw together Paul's rebellious and disorderly communities in obedient mimesis not just of Jesus, but of Paul himself.

Regardless of the rhetorical aim of Paul's use of mimetic language, he inaugurates a tradition within Christian communities in which the suffering of Christians is understood in terms of mimesis. Even if, as Castelli has proposed,

Paul's commands are a means of eliciting unity and conformity in his communities, his exhortations to imitate were reread in Christian communities as ethical injunctions and practical admonitions. For our purposes we will focus on those passages that are particularly concerned with suffering, persecution, and death.

Paul's interest in mimesis is apparent as early as 1 Thessalonians, which is considered by most scholars to be the earliest of his extant epistles.[20] Unlike some of his other letters, there is little sense that Paul is responding to any reports of unrest or discord in the Thessalonian congregation. He writes instead that his anxiety and desire to strengthen their faith (2:17–3:5) have occasioned the letter.[21]

Paul's use of Christological mimesis begins in the first thanksgiving section (1 Thess 1:6–7, 2:14), where he describes the Thessalonians as "imitators" ($\mu\mu\eta\tau\alpha\acute{\iota}$) of himself and Christ in their receipt of the word despite much affliction. The notion of imitation through suffering resurfaces in the second thanksgiving section in 1 Thess. 2:14, where the community at Thessaloniki are exhorted to "become imitators" ($\mu\mu\eta\tau\alpha\grave{\iota}\ \dot{\epsilon}\gamma\epsilon\nu\acute{\eta}\theta\eta\tau\epsilon$) of the churches in Judea. The basis for the exhortation is that the Thessalonians suffered the same thing from their countrymen as the church in Judea did from the Judeans. The Thessalonians are inserted into what Castelli calls the "mimetic economy" in which they imitate Paul, the Lord, and the Judean churches:[22] "For you, brothers and sisters, became imitators of the churches of God in Christ Jesus that are in Judea, for you suffered the same things from your own compatriots as they did from the Jews."[23] Paul grounds his exhortation in the shared experience of persecution felt by the churches. The common experience of suffering ties the churches together. The same rationale reappears in later Pauline epistles where the readers are exhorted to imitate the endurance of Paul and Christ in the face of suffering. If we, somewhat unhistorically, imagine Paul as anticipating his language of the body of Christ in 1 Corinthians, we might say that the body of Christ dispersed throughout the world is a body held together by the common experience of persecution.

In his letter to the Philippians, Paul uses mimetic language as a call to unity within the community. He exhorts the brethren ($\dot{\alpha}\delta\epsilon\lambda\phi o\iota$) to come together in like-mindedness in their imitation of him:

> Brothers and sisters, join in imitating me, and observe those who live according to the example you have in us. For many live as enemies of the cross of Christ; I have often told you of them, and now I tell you even with tears. Their end is destruction; their god is the belly; and their glory is in their shame; their minds are set on earthly things.

But our citizenship is in heaven, and it is from there that we are
expecting a Savior, the Lord Jesus Christ. He will transform the body
of our humiliation that it may be conformed to the body of his glory,
by the power that also enables him to make all things subject to
himself.[24]

In this passage in particular, Paul's language encourages unity among those he
calls brethren. His use of the unusual form συμμιμητής underscores this call
to unity and coming together. It is not mimesis alone but mimesis that establishes union and agreement.[25] At the same time as he invites unification, he
sets up a clear distinction between those brethren who are invited to join in
mimesis, and the enemies of the cross of Christ (τοὺς ἐχθροὺς τοῦ σταυροῦ
τοῦ Χριστου). The implication is that those who fail to imitate Paul are enemies of the cross of Christ. The dichotomy is unforgiving; come together in
imitation of the figure of Paul or find yourself an enemy of the cross of Christ.

For our purposes, the most interesting instance in which Paul exhorts his
readers to imitate Christ is found in the so-called Christological hymn of Philippians 2:5–11. Since the groundbreaking work of Lohmeyer, the majority of
scholars have maintained that this pericope was a pre-Pauline liturgical hymn
that was inserted into the epistle by Paul for exhortatory ends.[26] The passage
begins with Paul expressing the desire that the Philippians have the same mind
as did Christ. He then proceeds to qualify what having "this mind" would mean
by inserting a hymn that illustrates the humility and obedience of Christ:

Let the same mind be in you that was in Christ Jesus, who, though he
was in the form of God, did not regard equality with God as something to be exploited, but emptied himself, taking the form of a slave,
being born in human likeness. And being found in human form, he
humbled himself and became obedient to the point of death—even
death on a cross. Therefore God also highly exalted him and gave
him the name that is above every name, so that at the name of Jesus
every knee should bend, in heaven and on earth and under the earth,
and every tongue should confess that Jesus Christ is Lord, to the
glory of God the Father.[27]

While many elements of this hymn fascinate its readers, one clause is particularly striking for our interest in the relationship between suffering and imitation of Christ: "ἐταπείνωσεν ἑαυτὸν γενόμενος ὑπήκοος μέχρι θανάτου,
θανάτου δὲ σταυροῦ." (2:8). For Lohmeyer, Christ's obedience unto death was
the focal point of the hymn and the rationale behind Paul's inclusion of it.
Christ's obedience became the supreme example for the believer and was even

the model for martyrdom.[28] Following Lohmeyer, we can see Paul as exhorting his readers to imitate Christ (v. 5) in obedience and humility (v. 8). The supreme illustration of this self-effacing obedience is found in Christ's readiness to accept a shameful death. Even if Paul's intention is to exhort the Philippians to follow his advice, he ends up encouraging his readers to mimic the death of Christ. If Christ could obediently accept such a death, says Paul, so too should you.

Not all are convinced that Paul's inclusion of the Philippians hymn is an attempt to establish Christ as an example.[29] Ralph P. Martin argues that emulation of the life and person of Christ is an impossible task: "The Apostolic summons is not: Follow Jesus by doing as He did—an impossible feat in any case, for who can be a 'second Christ' who quits his heavenly glory and dies in shame and is taken up into the throne of the universe?"[30] Martin's argument here rests, as we have already noted, on a number of basic post-Chalcedonian Christological assumptions. He assumes that no one can be a "second Christ" because he is certain both that Philippians 2:5–11 describes a unique preexistent heavenly being and that exaltation to the throne of God was a glory accorded only to Christ. In the Christological controversies Martin's theological assumptions become standardized, yet in the first four centuries of the Christian church these assumptions were by no means set. It is wholly possible, therefore, that for members of the earliest churches the imitation of Christ could include exaltation on the heavenly throne. Evidence of this is found in the Apocalypse of John where those who "overcome" current persecution are promised a seat on the throne of God (Rev 3:21).

In 1 Corinthians Paul twice exhorts his readers to a life of imitation (1 Cor 4:16–17 and 11:1).[31] The by now familiar call to imitate Paul's conduct as he imitates Christ's is grounded in his appeal to the parental role he assumes in the Corinthian community: "For though you might have ten thousand guardians in Christ, you do not have many fathers. Indeed, in Christ Jesus I became your father through the gospel. I appeal to you, then, be imitators of me. For this reason I sent you Timothy, who is my beloved and faithful child in the Lord, to remind you of my ways in Christ Jesus, as I teach them everywhere in every church."[32] The inclusion of the phrase "to remind you of my ways" suggests that Paul proposes something more particular than just "live a good life."[33] The specific referent of this *imitatio* has been variously identified as Paul's attempt to inculcate a particular value in the lives of Corinthians, be it personal qualities of humility and self-sacrifice,[34] communal or relational values of unity,[35] or a life of suffering.[36]

All these suggestions base themselves on internal evidence within the Corinthian correspondence. In 1 Corinthians 4:11, Paul references his own self-sacrifice and humility as an apostle who forgoes food, clothing, and shelter.[37]

Paul's understanding of imitation is further qualified later in the letter in 11:1 where he again exhorts the Corinthians to "imitate me as I imitate Christ" (μιμηταί μου γίνεσθε καθὼς κἀγὼ Χριστοῦ). Castelli is correct to direct us to the implicit power structure here. Paul is elevated above the Corinthians, and the disjointed community is directed to look to him as their model.[38] At the same time, however, it is clear that there is something about Christ's behavior or actions that is being identified as worthy of imitation. Paul intends *imitatio Christi* to include a variety of ethical stances and practical actions, not least of which is Christ's self-sacrificial obedience unto death.[39]

In 2 Corinthians, Paul reorients his ethical instructions to focus on the example offered in Jesus. Here, perhaps more than anywhere else in his correspondence, Paul focuses on traditional material about Jesus and uses this as a means to exhort the Corinthians to mimic the exemplary behavior of Jesus.[40] Of special importance to our study is Paul's focus on the sufferings of Christ and the relationship between Christly suffering, apostolic suffering, and communal and individual suffering. The theme of suffering lingers under the surface of the entire work and forms the basis for Paul's apostleship. It legitimizes him as an apostle, serves as the cornerstone of his missionary activity, and is a marker of his special relationship to Christ. Indeed, it is these sufferings that validate and confirm his vocation, and "it is in these circumstances that Paul's union with Christ is expressed."[41] Paul's accounts of his sufferings for Christ permeate this epistle (2 Cor 6: 4–10; 11:23–33) and are expressed as evidence of his apostleship (2 Cor 11:23).

The theme of imitation reappears in Galatians. The most confrontational of Paul's letters, Galatians is widely considered to be Paul's response to an increasing preoccupation with circumcision on the part of the community there.[42] Paul's heated rebuke of the Galatians requires that he justify his position as an apostle and a figure of authority for the church he himself founded. In doing so he invokes the marks of his suffering as a source of authority. In Galatians 6:17, Paul authenticates his mission on the basis of "the marks" (τὰ στίγματα) of Jesus that he has borne: "From now on, let no one make trouble for me; for I carry the marks of Jesus branded on my body."[43] The term στίγματα is a *hapax legomenon* in the New Testament.[44] It is probable that τὰ στίγματα are those scars Paul received as a result of the persecutions inflicted upon him during his missionary campaigns.[45] This language is connected to his interest in imitating Christ, a theme alluded to throughout Galatians without explicit use of mimetic language (cf. Gal 2:19; 4:13; 5:24; 6:14).[46] It is, however, through the replication of Christ's suffering, through being "crucified with Christ" (Gal 2:20), that Christ lives in Paul. Suffering as Christ suffered is precisely what enables Paul to "have" Christ within himself. It is suffering that binds them together. This idea resurfaces in martyrdom accounts in which, in moments of extreme torture, Christ dwells within the martyr's body (*Lyons* 1.23).

Claims to have suffered and exhortations to others to expect suffering were a means of gaining authority and respect in early Christian communities, allowing Paul to connect himself to Jesus using the rhetoric of imitation and, in doing so, to authenticate his mission. For Paul exhortations to imitate the sufferings of others serve a valuable rhetorical purpose. Within the "mimetic economy" of the early church, suffering like Christ was "cultural capital."[47] Read in conjunction with Paul's language of putting on Christ and being reborn in Christ, exhortations to imitate the sufferings of Christ resonated in a particular way. Life in Christ was read as assuming a life lived individually and communally within the suffering body of Christ. The rhetorical power of suffering like Christ transfigured participation in Christ into suffering.

Gospels

In the Gospels we encounter, for the first time, attempts to catalog and record *narratively* the life and teachings of Jesus.[48] The generic difference between the epistles of Paul and the *bioi* of the Gospels means that the presentation of Jesus as a model for imitation takes on a different shape.[49] On the one hand, the model is clearer and more defined as the words and actions are explicitly described. The accounts of the teachings and activities of Jesus provide a template for the disciples in the narrative and the would-be disciples in the audience. On the other hand, the language of mimesis is absent. In its stead, we find discussion of the nature of discipleship and how to "follow" Jesus. As a theme, the nature and demands of discipleship permeate the gospel accounts, and for some scholars there is an essential difference between following Christ and imitating him.[50] As we shall see, however, there are plenty of instances in which "following Christ" entails suffering in the same manner as he did.[51] In these instances, whether or not the term "mimesis" is used, the practice of following Christ effectively is embodied imitation.

Mark

The earliest Gospel, and thus the first to discuss suffering for Christ, is the Gospel of Mark.[52] A variety of locations have been suggested for its composition, but the majority of scholars agree that it was composed between 65 and 73 C.E. in the midst of the Jewish War.[53] Regardless of the precise place of composition, a number of characteristics of the text suggest it was an encyclical composed for the purpose of widespread circulation.[54]

Throughout the Gospel, the theme of following Christ is prevalent. From the beginning, Mark describes the activity and journeying of Christ as "the way." He begins his gospel by appealing to the "way of the Lord" (1:1–3) and repeatedly describes the journey from Caesarea Philippi to Jerusalem in the same fashion (8:27; 9:33f.; 10:32).

Structurally, the overall shape of Mark's account offers a paradigm for discipleship. As noted by Philip Davis, in Mark the teachings of Jesus take a backseat to the exhortations to follow the example of Jesus.[55] For Davis, Mark's Gospel "can be read as a blueprint for the Christian life: it begins with baptism, proceeds with the vigorous pursuit of ministry in the face of temptation and opposition, and culminates in suffering and death orientated toward an as-yet unseen vindication."[56] Similarly, Larry Hurtado argues that Mark lacks a resurrection appearance, not because he has no knowledge of such accounts but because Mark intends to focus his readers' attention on Jesus' life as exemplar. The abrupt ending to the Gospel, therefore, encourages the reader to follow Jesus' example despite fear and uncertainty.[57] For Hurtado and Davis, the structure of Mark represents the path of discipleship from baptism to death, Jesus himself is the "true model of Christian discipleship" and the narrative is shaped to make the story of Jesus the road map for the lives of his followers.[58]

This leitmotif is further distilled in 8:22–10:52, where the role of the disciple and the true nature of discipleship become preoccupying themes for the evangelist. Toward the beginning of this section, Jesus instructs the disciples in what it means to follow him:

> And he called to him the multitude with his disciples, and said to them, "If any man would come after me, let him deny himself and take up his cross and follow me. For whoever would save his life will lose it; and whoever loses his life for my sake and the gospel's will save it. For what does it profit a man, to gain the whole world and forfeit his life? For what can a man give in return for his life? For whoever is ashamed of me and of my words in this adulterous and sinful generation, of him will the Son of man also be ashamed, when he comes in the glory of his Father with the holy angels.[59]

Scholarly attention to this passage has focused upon the opening verse and the meaning of the dramatic phrase "ἀράτω τὸν σταυρὸν αὐτοῦ." Should we understand this phrase literally, as a kind of exhortation to martyrdom? Or should it be read figuratively as a cipher for mistreatment or abuse? On a literal reading, given the additional exhortation to "follow" Jesus, it seems that Jesus exhorts his disciples to follow him to crucifixion and death.[60]

Yet despite its apparent straightforwardness, this literal interpretation has been rejected by a number of scholars in favor of spiritualized or figurative readings of the phrase. Gundry argues that the instruction could not have been intended literally because Jesus had not predicted his own death in terms of crucifixion, and the disciples would have been unable to orchestrate events so that they would be condemned to death in this manner.[61] Instead, Gundry proposes that the phrase "take up one's cross" is meant figuratively to imply will-fully subjecting oneself to the shame and ridicule of following Christ. Gundry's argument seems overly labored in his attempt to resist the notion that the disciples are being invited to follow Jesus to their deaths.

If we assume that this passage has been reworked by Mark, it is neither here nor there that Jesus did not predict his own passion in terms of crucifixion.[62] The information that Jesus was crucified and resurrected was the most publicized element of the Jesus story in the early days of the Jesus movement. Thus, if Mark could assume any knowledge about Jesus on the part of his audience, it was that he was crucified.[63] Furthermore, if we give credence to the early Christian tradition that links the Gospel of Mark with Petrine traditions, we can safely assume that Mark was familiar with traditions about the crucifixion of Peter.[64] If we read this statement in light of the Petrine tradition, it can be seen as an allusion to the crucifixion of the most prominent apostle in Mark.

Even apart from traditions relating to Peter, the phrase "take up your cross and follow me" can be read as a literal instruction that employs the image of the cross as a figure for death. For first-century readers familiar with the narrative of the death of Jesus, it seems difficult to imagine that the barbaric image of the cross could *not* have conjured up the image of the brutal death of Jesus. As for Gundry's objection that the disciples would not have been able, logistically speaking, to ensure that they were crucified, this seems to assume on the part of the historical Jesus an interest in and knowledge of the machinations of Roman law courts for which we lack evidence entirely.[65]

Perhaps the most convincing evidence that we should read verses 34–36 literally is their connection to verses 37–38. The latter portion of this section deals explicitly with the comparable rewards of losing or saving one's physical life. Unquestionably, in the verses that immediately follow the exhortation to "take up one's cross," we have a discussion of the significance of dying for Christ.

Although it is the language of discipleship and following (ὀπίσω μου ἀκολουθεῖν and ἀκολουθείτω μοι) that is prominent here, it is clear that following after Jesus involves imitating him. A literal reading of the instruction to "take up the cross" (ἀράτω τὸν σταυρὸν αὐτοῦ) implies that following Christ involves following a death like his. Death *for* Christ is aligned with the death *of* Christ. Even if the phrase "take up his cross" is read in a purely figurative manner, the function of the saying remains the same; it equates the experience of the disciple with the death of Jesus.

Regardless of Mark's own intent, early readers of Mark were aware of and in some cases supported literal interpretations. A rejection of the literal interpretation is found in Luke's redaction of this pericope: "Then he said to them all, 'If any want to become my followers, let them deny themselves and take up their cross daily and follow me.'"[66] The addition of the phrase "every day" (καθ' ἡμέραν) here transforms the saying so that it cannot be read martyrologically. The redaction betrays a Lukan anxiety about the demands of discipleship. Clearly Luke intends that the idea of taking up the cross must be read figuratively, not literally. By inserting this phrase, Luke resists the literal interpretation of taking up one's cross as a call for martyrdom and directs his readers toward a more pedestrian ethical interpretation. That Luke needs to alter his source indicates that there were those at the time who read Mark as a call for suffering and death. Apparently Luke was aware of the potential for a literal reading of Mark and was consciously trying to suppress it in his version of the story.

A more positive approach to the literal interpretation is found in the writings of the early church. In his *Exhortation to Martyrdom*, the third-century Alexandrian Origen uses this passage to support his argument that the work of Jesus is continued through the deaths of the early Christian martyrs. In addressing Ambrosius, his bishop, he writes: "You go in procession bearing the cross of Jesus and following him when he brings you before governors and kings."[67] Here, Origen interprets Mark 8:34–38 in a literal sense as an instruction to members of his Christian community to prepare for arrest and martyrdom.[68] The cross that they were to bear is meant to refer to *at least* persecution and arrest and—given the context of this passage within an exhortation to martyrdom—most probably death. In one sense, Origen understands the phrase "bearing the cross" figuratively, in that he does not take it to mean actual wooden crosses, but he also reads the instruction literally as he clearly expects his addressees to meet with death.

For our purposes, perhaps the clearest indication that this passage was read literally is found in the *Acts of Euplus*.[69] In this turn-of-the-fourth-century account the martyr Euplus enters the courtroom with scriptures and is instructed to read aloud from the text. The passages he elects to read are Matt 5:10 and Mark 8:34–38//Matt 16:24: "The martyr opened [the book] and read: 'Blessed are they who suffer persecution for justice sake, for theirs is the kingdom of heaven' and in another place 'He that will come after me, let him take up his cross and follow me.'"[70] When the judge asks Euplus what this statement means he replies, "'It is the law of my Lord, which has been given to me'"(*Ac. Euplus*, 1.5) The selection of these two passages, and his description of them as law indicate that for some members of the early church, these passages were read as instructive and even legislating. Clearly, martyrdom was understood as the proper response to Jesus' request to take up the cross and follow him. This statement, however, was viewed as more than a simple request or suggestion. In the words of Euplus, these texts were understood as a *law*, as proscriptive, legislating texts, as mandates for martyrdom in the lives of Christians.

Toward the end of his section on discipleship, Mark again returns to the question of the harsher demands of discipleship, this time with a specific interest in the fate of the sons of Zebedee:

> And they said to him, "Grant us to sit, one at your right hand and one at your left, in your glory." But Jesus said to them, "You do not know what you are asking. Are you able to drink the cup that I drink, or to be baptized with the baptism with which I am baptized?" And they said to him, "We are able." And Jesus said to them, "The cup that I drink you will drink; and with the baptism with which I am baptized, you will be baptized; but to sit at my right hand or at my left is not mine to grant, but it is for those for whom it has been prepared."[71]

Here, James and John, part of the inner circle of Jesus' disciples, request seats at Jesus' right and left hand. Their request to sit "in glory" ($\dot{\epsilon}\nu\ \tau\hat{\eta}\ \delta\acute{o}\xi\eta$) rouses images of messianic kingship.[72] Evidently, the sons of Zebedee have misunderstood the nature of Jesus' kingdom.[73] Jesus' response is veiled and provocative. Again, it is an ambiguous but suggestive image that forms the critical point for interpreting this passage; what exactly should we understand by "the cup" that Jesus drinks?

The mention of a cup in connection with baptism prompted Patrick Henry Reardon to argue that this passage should be read sacramentally as a symbolic reference to baptism and the Eucharist.[74] This explanation is particularly curious given Jesus' question about the capabilities of James and John to drink from the cup. The disciples in Mark may be foolish, but we should not assume they have problems drinking out of everyday containers. Furthermore, the sacraments would appear to be "out of order" because Jesus would be placing the Eucharist before baptism.[75] Moreover, if Mark is alluding symbolically to the sacraments, he assumes on the part of his readers a detailed knowledge of Pauline sacramental theology.[76] This kind of an assumption does not fit well with other passages in the Gospel where Mark goes to great lengths to ensure that his readers understand him.[77]

More probably, the cup in Mark 10:37–40 refers to the Hebrew Bible image of the cup of wrath or suffering.[78] This image is employed unambiguously in the Gethsemane agony when Jesus begs that the cup pass from him (Mark 14:36). That in chapter 10 Jesus explicitly refers to the cup as the cup that he himself must drink indicates that we must take the two scenes together. Jesus asks James and John if they are able to face the same suffering that he will endure in the crucifixion.[79] The death of Jesus and the death of those who are invited to follow are presented in identical terms. Again, Mark extends the possibility of suffering like Christ to the disciples and his audience; he revels in the paradox of the suffering Messiah and challenges his readers to consider the possibility that they themselves might follow Jesus to their deaths.

A number of scholars have endeavored to push their interpretation of Mark 10:37–40 further, toward a martyrological reading. In the second century the image of "drinking a cup" becomes a metaphor for martyrdom.[80] Likewise, in the acts of the martyrs, martyrdom is presented as a kind of "second baptism" and becomes an alternate form of baptism for catechumens.[81] According to this reading, this passage casts the death of Jesus as a kind of martyrdom and offers a prophecy about the eventual martyrdom of the sons of Zebedee.[82] It is more probable that Mark 10:37–40 served as a key text in the development of various ideologies of martyrdom and that this use of cup and baptismal imagery in the *acta martyrum* emerged out of readings of this passage.[83] This is an invitation to follow Jesus to death, but the focus here is on the synonymous nature of the death of Jesus and the death of those who follow him, not on notions of witness or confession.

Throughout the Gospel of Mark, "Jesus is both the basis for and the pattern of discipleship."[84] Following Jesus entails suffering and dying in a manner that is not just "like Jesus" but is described in identical terms that are explicitly linked to Jesus' own death. The focus is on the synonymity of the death of the follower with that of Jesus. The necessity of this death may be described in terms of discipleship, but practically it involves reenactment of the same suffering.

Luke-Acts

Written roughly twenty years after the Gospel of Mark, the Gospel of Luke tends to shy away from interpretations of Mark that promote following Christ to the death. The author of Luke-Acts is not interested in imitation. As C. K. Barrett has remarked, "The language of imitation is wanting."[85] At the same time, however, the conduct of the Lukan Jesus becomes the template for subsequent martyrs. This includes the death of his first imitator, Stephen, the protomartyr in Acts 7.[86] Conzelmann argues that the literary seams in the account indicate that Luke is using a source document.[87] If so, this source may have been generically similar to the early Christian *acta*.

Throughout the account of the arrest, "witness," and execution, Luke labors to present Stephen in the same way as he narrated the passion of Jesus. The attack on Stephen is precipitated by the same accusation made of Jesus. In Acts 6:14 he is he accused of saying that "Jesus will destroy this place and change the customs that Moses delivered to us," a reference back to the sayings of Jesus that predict the destruction of the Temple. Like Jesus, Stephen appears before and is interrogated by the high priest. Both Jesus and Stephen refer to the Son of Man at the right hand of God (Acts 7:55; cf. Luke. 22:69) and cry out at the moment of their deaths. Finally, at the point of death, Stephen commends his spirit to Jesus just as Jesus commended his to his father in Luke 23:46. And in the same spirit of magnanimity, both Stephen and Jesus beg forgiveness for those who cause their deaths (Luke 23:34; cf. Acts 7:60).[88]

The similarities between the deaths of Jesus and Stephen can hardly be coincidental, particularly when we consider the evangelist's penchant for parallelism and structure. Yet the narrative does more than simply illustrate the idea that the deaths of Christians can and do imitate the death of Christ. This is not just a prime example of *imitatio Christi* at play in ancient literature; it is itself a model for imitation. Irrespective of the author's intent, the death of Stephen serves an exhortatory purpose for the subsequent generations of readers who looked to it as a model of the good Christian death. Stephen becomes the protomartyr, the first to die the exemplary death for Christ, and a pattern—in his own right—for those who come later. The patterning of Stephen's death on that of Jesus is of great significance here. It is precisely *because* Stephen imitates Christ so well that he becomes a paradigm for those who follow him.

1 Peter

Of all the texts associated with the apostles, the most explicit association of personal suffering with that of Christ is found in the pseudonymous epistle known as 1 Peter. Traditionally, the document has been associated with Simon Peter of Galilee, the chief apostle of the synoptic tradition and apparent author of the text (cf. 1 Pet 1:1).[89] The fine quality of Greek employed by the author of the text, the knowledge of rhetorical conventions, and the absence of references to the life of Jesus make Petrine authorship highly unlikely.[90]

Despite the widespread rejection of Petrine authorship, the majority of scholars maintain that the letter originated in Rome.[91] The dating of the letter is more complex. External attestation of 1 Peter in later sources is only partially helpful, for while there are clear citations of the letter in the writings of Tertullian (*Scorp.* 12) and Clement of Alexandria (*Paed.* 1.6.44), earlier "citations" in Justin Martyr (e.g., *Dial.* 116, 119) or the *Epistle of Barnabas* (6.2, 6) are inconclusive. 1 Peter may have been cited in Polycarp's *Letter to the Philippians*, but the evidence for this is ambiguous and ultimately inconclusive. Comparisons between 1 Peter and *First Clement* are equally unfruitful and yield ambiguous results.[92] For Beare the most damming evidence against an early dating is Ignatius of Antioch's apparent lack of acquaintance with the document.[93] If 1 Peter was written and circulated throughout Asia Minor before Ignatius's travels through the region, we might expect to find some reference to it.

With Petrine authorship largely discounted, a number of scholars have attempted to use the references to suffering and persecution in 1 Peter as a means for determining the date and place of its composition. From the epistle it is clear that Christians are suffering (1:6; 3:14; 4:12, 16, 19; 5:10) and that this suffering is widespread (5:9) but sporadic (1:6; 5:10). The form of persecution appears to be more rejection by society than martyrdom (3:9, 16; 4:14). The sporadic nature of the persecution envisaged in the text coupled with the absence of severe or lethal punishments suggest that 1 Peter was not composed during one of the "periods of persecution" attributed to Nero, Domitian, or Trajan.[94] The situation appears to be more one of unofficial local harassment than a widespread coordinated persecution.[95] While it is impossible to pinpoint the precise dating of the letter, the absence of explicit references to martyrdom seems to presuppose that 1 Peter was written prior to Pliny's persecutions in Bithnyia circa 112–114 C.E. This would place the composition of the letter circa 80–100 C.E.[96] The geographic location of the addressees of the letter is fairly certain. The opening words of the prescript indicate that the epistle is addressed to five Roman provinces (Pontus, Galatia, Cappadocia, Asia, and Bithnyia) located in the region of Asia Minor.[97] That the addressees are repeatedly described as "strangers" and "resident aliens" suggests that they were located in an unstable sociopolitical region.

While the dating, provenance, and authorship of 1 Peter remain keenly debated, the role of suffering as one of the predominant themes of the letter is universally agreed upon. The themes of submission to higher authorities and acceptance of suffering are deftly intertwined throughout the letter. The author of 1 Peter exhorts his audience to accept unjust suffering and to submit to those who persecute them in the same way as Christ accepted his sufferings. The analogy is drawn further, however, as the author not only makes Christ the model for the suffering Christian but adds that this suffering allows the individual to share in the sufferings of Christ. This comparison is particularly noticeable in 1 Peter 2:20–25, where the author joins a Christological hymn (2:21–25) to the preceding verse about the suffering of members of the congregation: "If you endure when you are beaten for doing wrong, what credit is that? But if you endure when you do right and suffer for it, you have God's approval. For to this you have been called, because Christ also suffered for you, leaving you an example, so that you should follow in his steps."[98] Throughout 1 Peter the author stresses the importance of submission to authority and willful acceptance of suffering. This forms part of a program of discouraging the audience from active or violent responses to alienation. Suffering unjustly is to be commended, and the audience should look to the model provided in Christ as its pattern for behavior: "Beloved, do not be surprised at the fiery ordeal which comes upon you to prove you, as though something strange were happening to you. But rejoice in so far as you share in Christ's sufferings, that you may also rejoice and be glad when his glory is revealed. If you are reproached for the name of Christ, you are blessed, because the spirit of glory and of God rests upon you."[99] Here in 1 Peter 4, innocent suffering is explicitly identified with the suffering of Christ. It enables the sufferer to participate in the identity of Christ and is a sign of special favor, as the glory of God rests upon them.

Hebrews

The much neglected and poorly named Epistle to the Hebrews presents an entire line of succession of faithful examples of endurance for imitation.[100] Chapters 11–12 begin with a catalogue of *exempla virtutis*, drawn from the Hebrew Bible and apocrypha, who faithfully bore witness and endured violent sufferings. The list extols the virtue of faithful endurance in the heroes of the past and occasionally locates this fidelity in their endurance of sufferings and persecutions (11:26, 35–40). The catalog reaches a climax at the beginning of chapter 12, where the author of Hebrews turns to the ultimate model, Christ:

> Therefore, since we are surrounded by so great a cloud of witnesses,
> let us also lay aside every weight and the sin that clings so closely, and
> let us run with perseverance the race that is set before us, looking to
> Jesus the pioneer and perfecter of our faith, who for the sake of the
> joy that was set before him endured the cross, disregarding its shame,
> and has taken his seat at the right hand of the throne of God. Consider him who endured such hostility against himself from sinners,
> so that you may not grow weary or lose heart. In your struggle against
> sin you have not yet resisted to the point of shedding your blood.[101]

Here the model of Jesus crucified is held up as the supreme model for fidelity. It is the image of crucifixion that should hold the audience's attention and inspire them to persevere in their race. The paranetic purpose of invoking the example of Jesus is an attempt to rouse them to greater perseverance. The author invites them to compare their sufferings to those of Jesus, to keep the image of the crucified Christ utmost in their minds, and to seek to follow the "ἀρχηγὸς." The notion of "looking toward" (ἀφορῶντες) a model recalls Hellenistic notions of the virtuous imitating God and is applied to the Maccabean martyrs in 4 Maccabees 17:10. Here the object of their attention is not God transcendent but Jesus. That it is the human and humbled Jesus rather than the exalted Christ is significant. This proper name is also used in connection with human sufferings in Hebrews 2:9 and here identifies the model as the human preexaltation Jesus. While the community had not yet experienced hostile opposition to the point of death, the author envisions this as a reasonable expectation (v. 4). He encourages his audience to think of their sufferings in terms of the suffering Jesus and supplies an implicit promise of exaltation like Christ at the hand of God.

Unlike other New Testament authors, however, Hebrews' understanding of imitating Christly suffering is more directly connected to the author's Christology. In Hebrews, Christ is presented as a new high priest who establishes a new and better covenant with God. He occupies the position of high priest, sacrificial offering, and trailblazer. Chapters 8 through 10 develop and explore the analogy between Jesus and the high priest. In 9:15–22 this priestly role is further explored in the new covenant-inaugurating sacrifice made by Christ in conformity with God's will.[102] The exposition of Christ's priestly role is not merely an exercise in theological discourse; the actions of Christ have practical implications for the lives of the reader. The ramification of Christ's status as the pioneer and perfecter (ἀρχηγὸς καὶ τελειότης) of the faith is that other Christians must follow the supreme example of faith. In the words of Harold Attridge, "The existential, practical consequence is that because his death is a covenant-inaugurating act, it is to be followed, to be lived out in the lives of the addressees."[103] The standard set by Christ, the ἀρχηγὸς, are standards the author of Hebrews expects his readers to meet, to imitate, and to follow.

Revelation

In the Apocalypse of John we begin to see, for the first time, what is commonly referred to as a "theology of martyrdom." Revelation not only offers detailed words of encouragement and instruction for those dealing with persecution; it goes further, offering a theodicy for the existence of persecution and a vision of the future in which those persecuted would be vindicated and rewarded. If we were to track the development of theologies of martyrdom on some kind of evolutionary scale, the Apocalypse would offer a far more detailed and considered approach than the other New Testament books we have examined. The theology of martyrdom present in the book of Revelation is deserving of its own exposition and cannot be fully explored here. Here we will merely deal with the way in which the suffering and death of Christ are related to the suffering and death of the characters and audience of the book of Revelation.

Revelation was composed sometime between the end of the first and the beginning of the second century C.E. during a period in which Christians suffered various forms of opposition. Until recently it was generally maintained that the Johannine Apocalypse emerged out of a period of persecution instigated by the emperor Domitian (81–96 C.E.).[104] While the majority of scholars would continue to date the work during this period, the existence of a Domitianic persecution has been called into question. G. E. M. De Ste. Croix, in particular, has questioned the existence of organized persecution of Christians before Decius and revealed the dearth of evidence for Domitianic persecution.[105] It appears, therefore, either that the author addressed a situation of localized unofficial opposition, or that he perceived the community to be persecuted. The Apocalypse is written as a response to this situation of opposition and marginalization, whether actual or perceived. The author describes Rome and its rulers as emissaries of Satan who labor to destroy God's people. Rome will meet its end in a series of divinely ordained punishments (Rev 6:1–8:1; 8:2–11:19; 15:1–16:21) as retribution for the persecution of the people of God (cf. 6:12–17; 16:5–6; 18:4–8). The enemies of God will be crushed in grand eschatological battles (19:11–21; 20:7–10), the final judgment will ensue, and the New Jerusalem will descend.

As already noted in the introduction, the development and use of *martys* terminology is a point of contention among scholars who write on martyrdom.[106] For those seeking to trace the development of the language of martyrdom, the Apocalypse has been a key text because it is the first to use the term "ὁ μάρτυς" in a titular sense. Some have gone so far as to argue that in the Apocalypse we see for the first time the use of ὁ μάρτυς to designate someone who dies on account of his or her religious beliefs. Regardless of its precise meaning, the term is used by the author of Revelation for both Christ and other individuals who are tried and executed. The Apocalypse opens with an epistolary prescript in which greetings are conveyed "from Jesus Christ the faithful witness (ὁ μάρτυς, ὁ πιστός), the firstborn of the dead and the ruler of the kings of the earth" (Rev 1:5). The first titular use of the term μάρτυς, therefore, is as one of a string of Christological titles. The use of μάρτυς in this way occurs only here and, in an expanded form, in Revelation 3:14, where Jesus is called "the faithful and true witness" (ὁ μάρτυς ὁ πιστὸς καὶ ἀληθινός).[107] By beginning with a Christological use, the author of Revelation introduces the term μάρτυς as it relates to Christ and then expands its range of meaning to include those who suffer and die on his account.

The phrase "faithful witness" reappears in the letter to the church in Ephesus, where Antipas, a man who was executed, is described in the same manner: "I know where you are living, where Satan's throne is. Yet you are holding fast to my name, and you did not deny your faith in me even in the days of Antipas my witness, my faithful one, who was killed among you, where Satan lives."[108] Evidently, Antipas was a member of the church who held fast to the name and was executed as a result. As only the actions of holding fast to the name and the faith and subsequent execution are mentioned, we can assume that it is on account of these that Antipas is accorded the honor of being named "my faithful witness" (cf. Rev 11:3; 17:6). Whether or not we take μάρτυς to mean either "witness" or "martyr," the use of the same theologically loaded term for both Christ and members of the seven churches is significant. It identifies Christ's status of martyr with that of members of the churches. The distinction between lord and followers is elided by their shared status and role. The concept that in his death Christ blazes a trail for his followers becomes central in subsequent martyrological traditions. As Lucy Grig notes, "Christ was the first, archetypal, proto-martyr. The mimetic importance of the martyr acting out the *imitatio Christi* in his or her own death would be of key importance."[109] Christ may have been the true and first martyr, but this remains a status to which members of the community could aspire.

The same correlation between the activity and status of Christ and his followers is made elsewhere in Revelation 3:21, where the exalted Christ says: "To the one who conquers I will give a place with me on my throne, just as I myself conquered and sat down with my Father on his throne."[110] The term νικῶν in the Apocalypse, paradoxically, refers to a victory achieved through humiliation and death. In this respect Jesus is the paradigm for his followers, having achieved a great victory and ransomed his people through his death (Rev 5:9). In Revelation 3:21 the activity of Christ as victor, that is to say, the one who suffered and died, is held up for the church as an example. Members of the Jesus movement can emulate the conquest of Christ in their own sufferings and death and receive the same heavenly reward as a result.[111]

Clement

Looking beyond the modern Christian canon, we can see the theme of exemplary endurance and suffering further illustrated in the early Christian document commonly referred to as *First Clement*. Outside of those works preserved in the canonical New Testament, *First Clement* or Clement's *Letter to the Corinthians* is generally considered the earliest extant church writing. It was composed in the final years of the first century and is attributed to Clement, the third bishop of Rome. The opening sentences of the letter refer to "sudden and successive calamitous events" (1.1), events that conventionally have been taken to refer to a general persecution of Christians from 81 to 96 C.E. during the reign of the emperor Domitian. The ambiguity of this phrase and the dearth of evidence for a Domitianic persecution make the precision of this dating uncertain.[112] Even if the precise date of the work's composition is unclear the references to *First Clement* toward the end of the second century and the ecclesiastical structure presumed in the text support a late first-century date.

The letter itself appears to have been occasioned by intra-ecclesial conflict within the Corinthian community between presbyters and younger members of the congregation (40.1–59.2). In a brief section toward the beginning of the letter Clement discusses the role of noble death in the life of the church. His discussion of the fallen heroes of the church immediately follows a list of heroic figures from Israel's past who suffered because of envy (4.1–6.2). In 5.1–6.2 the focus shifts to Peter and Paul and from there to other anonymous Christians who suffered and died on account of envy.

In *First Clement*, it is not Christ but Peter and Paul who serve as the "greatest example" for the audience of the letter. The presentation of the "two pillars" as part of a history of suffering heroes is reminiscent of the list of faithful examples in Hebrews 11. Here in *First Clement*, Peter and Paul serve a clear rhetorical function. Clement draws upon their status as chief apostles and the close personal ties between Paul and the Corinthians as a means of calling the community to order. It is their status as "athletes" who "contended unto death" (5.2), however, that is the focal point and the subject of his repeated calls for imitation (5.4; cf. Heb 12:1–3). The suffering and endurance of Peter and Paul are more than a rhetorical flourish; they are the model for Clement's readers. What we see is a further development in the creation of *imitatio* hierarchies in which the martyred Peter and Paul are transformed into the models for imitation. Their successful imitation of the suffering and death of Christ ensures that they themselves become models. This is more than just an insertion into the mimetic economy; it is *itself* a form of imitation. Just as Peter and Paul imitated the obedient suffering and death of Christ, they imitate Christ's function as the *model* for suffering and death. The assumption of the exemplary role is a form of *imitatio* that begins here in *First Clement* and flourishes in the production of martyrological literature in the subsequent centuries.[113]

Ignatius of Antioch[114]

The letters of Ignatius, bishop of Antioch in the early part of the second century, which were written as he journeyed toward his trial and eventual martyrdom, have provoked strong, almost visceral, reactions in his readers. For some, Ignatius is a source of inspiration and a model martyr whose letters provide a glimpse into the mind of someone eagerly anticipating martyrdom. For others, Ignatius appears arrogant, crazed, and self-obsessed. In this respect he has the singular talent of being able to turn historians into psychoanalysts. Irrespective of our estimation of him, Ignatius was widely admired as a martyr in the early church, and his bold language about suffering with God became particularly important for later Monophysite interpreters.[115] Ignatius's letters are valuable both as interpretations of earlier now-canonical texts about suffering and as influential literature that helped to shape early Christian understandings of suffering.

For any study of Ignatius, the authenticity of the letters and the textual difficulties they pose present an unavoidable quagmire. Traditionally, three recensions of Ignatius's letters are identified: a short, middle, and long. The short recension is an abridgment of the letters to Polycarp, Ephesians, and Romans together with a brief excerpt of Trallians, and is preserved only in Syriac. To the standard seven letters of the middle recension, the long recension adds several others, including letters to and from Mary, the mother of Jesus, and a one to the disciple John. The modern scholarly consensus regarding the letters of Ignatius was established by the exhaustive work of Zahn and Lightfoot.[116] Their thoroughgoing examination of the textual problems led them to propose the authenticity of the middle recension and a date between 100 and 118 C.E. A number of challenges to the work of Lightfoot have been raised, but, as Schoedel notes, there are no clear anachronisms in the middle recension: the "cumulative weight of arguments against its authenticity is not sufficient to dislodge it from its place in the history of the early church."[117]

The seven letters of the middle recension (the letters to the Ephesians, Magnesians, Trallians, Romans, Philadelphians, and Smyrnaeans and to Polycarp) chronicle the course of Ignatius's journey from Antioch to Rome. Throughout these letters he reflects upon the purpose of his suffering and probable death and discourages outsiders from seeking to intervene to prevent his death. He describes this journey as triumphal (*Rom.* 5.1), possessing a kind of mythic quality (*Rom.* 2.2). For Ignatius, his suffering and imminent martyrdom are viewed through the lens of imitation, discipleship, and attaining to God.

In the expressions of praise that open his letters, Ignatius frequently describes his addressees as imitators of God (*Eph.* 1.1, 10.3; *Trall.* 1.2). In the context of exhorting the Philadelphians to greater harmony, he reminds them of a proclamation of the spirit that they should "be imitators of Jesus Christ as he himself is of the Father" (*Phld.* 7.2). He proposes that Christians themselves function as models for the pagans to imitate (*Eph.* 10.1–3) and that individual Christians serve as models for others (*Smyrn.* 12.1). This idea of imitation and serving as models is used in conjunction with his discussion of discipleship. In *Eph.* 10.1–3, both concepts are referenced as Ignatius prays that others may "learn at least from your deeds to become disciples" while we are "imitators of the Lord":

> But pray on behalf of other people unceasingly, for there is hope for
> repentance in them that they may attain God. Let them learn at least
> from your deeds to become disciples. Before their anger be gentle,
> before their boastfulness be humble, before their slanderings offer
> prayers, before their deceit be fixed in faith, before their fierceness be
> mild, not being eager to imitate them in return. Let us be found their
> brothers in gentleness; let us be eager to be imitators of the Lord.[118]

Ignatius's description of the proper response to hostility may well have served as a kind of preparation for martyrdom. The virtues of humility, faithfulness, and gentleness coupled with the instruction to pray serve as a kind of template for the behavior of the martyrs in *acta martyrum*.[119] For Ignatius, as for these later Christians, this behavior is tied to an *imitatio Christi*. Interestingly enough, he qualifies his hopes that the Christians serve as models for the pagans by reminding his readers not to become imitators of the pagans in return. The clear implication of verse 2 is that learning to be a disciple from the deeds of the Christians involves imitation. In Ignatius, discipleship and imitation are intertwined with one another.

On a personal level, both discipleship and imitation are ultimately tied to martyrdom.[120] Discipleship for Ignatius personally will be attained at martyrdom, where he will finally "attain to God."[121] In *To the Ephesians* 3.1, he addresses his own discipleship: "I do not command you as being someone; for even though I have been bound in the name, I have not yet been perfected in Jesus Christ. Indeed, now I have but begun to be a disciple, and I speak to you as my fellow learners; for I must be anointed by you with faith, admonition, endurance, patience."[122] For Ignatius, discipleship was merely inaugurated by his arrest and awaits completion in his martyrdom. That discipleship is fully realized in martyrdom becomes abundantly clear in the famous passage from his letter *To the Romans* where he asks to become food for the wild beasts: "Let me be the food of wild beasts through whom it is possible to attain to God. God's wheat I am, and by the teeth of wild beasts I am to be ground that I prove

Christ's pure bread. Better still, coax the wild beasts to become my tomb, and to leave no part of my person behind; once I have fallen asleep I do not wish to be a burden to anyone. Then I shall truly be a disciple of Jesus Christ."[123] True discipleship is realized in martyrdom (cf. *Pol.* 7.1). Up to this point in his life, Ignatius has described his discipleship as unfulfilled. He becomes more of a disciple through mistreatment and enslavement (*Rom.* 5.1), but his discipleship is merely beginning (*Eph.* 3.1; *Rom.* 5.3). Here, as he anticipates his martyrdom, he looks forward to death, to become a true disciple ($\mu\alpha\theta\eta\tau\grave{\eta}s$ $\dot{\alpha}\lambda\eta\theta\hat{\omega}s$) of Jesus and therefore to attain to God. Repugnant though it seems, the conclusion is inescapable; for Ignatius, discipleship *is* martyrdom.

The explicit identification of discipleship with martyrdom made by Ignatius is picked up in the Latin version of the *Acts of Phileas.* Moments before his beheading, the protagonist Phileas gives a speech that closely follows Ignatius's *Letter to the Romans:* "Before we did not suffer; but now we begin to suffer; now we begin to become disciples of Christ" (9. 1–2).[124] Like Ignatius, Phileas identifies the moment of his death as the beginning both of suffering and of discipleship. For both martyrs, martyrdom is not only equated with discipleship; it is the *beginning* of discipleship. It is not clear, therefore, if it is possible to *be* a disciple without enduring suffering that leads to death.

In the same way, the theme of imitating God or Christ, in Ignatius, finds its expression most properly in the experience of martyrdom. This idea is clearest in *To the Romans* 6.3, where he asks his audience not to seek to prevent his martyrdom: "Indulge me, brothers: do not prevent me from living, do not want my death, do not give to the world one who wants to be God's, nor deceive him with matter; let me receive pure light—when I am there, I shall be a human being; allow me to be an imitator of the suffering of my God."[125] This passage is illustrative of the way in which Ignatius sees the life of the Christian generally, and the death of the martyr particularly, as modeled on the pattern of Christ crucified. This may be the only instance in which the imitation of Christ is connected with his own suffering and death, but it is strikingly unambiguous in viewing the death of the believer as an imitation of the death of Christ.

Discomfort with martyrdom as a part of discipleship or Christly imitation permeates scholarly discussions of Ignatius, as it does elsewhere. In his commentary, Schoedel seeks to draw the attention of the reader to the manifold instances where imitation of Christ does not involve martyrdom (e.g., *Eph.* 1.1; 10.3; *Trall.* 1.2; *Phld.* 7.2; *Smyrn.* 12.1). He writes, "The fact that the theme does not always have in view Christ's death or does so only to draw attention to the love of God of Christ's endurance also indicates how improbable it is to regard imitation in Ignatius as linked with the idea of cultic reenactment of the Lord's passion."[126] Whether or not *imitatio Christi* in Ignatius is cultic, it is clear that for himself, at least, martyrdom was the forum in which his discipleship would be realized and his imitation of Christ perfected.

Conclusion

From the beginning of the literary production of the early church, apostolic, ecclesiastical, and individual suffering was rendered meaningful by the image of the crucified Christ.[127] The pervasive theme of suffering like, in participation with, or in imitation of Christ resonates beneath the surface of almost all the earliest Christian writings. Jesus movement and early church authors augmented and adapted this theme in different ways to address the needs of their audiences and the rhetorical program of their work. The suffering savior provided a model for endurance in the face of perceived hostility and aggression. For some writers, the possibility that Christians would have to endure and suffer the same fate and suffering as Jesus seems to have been expected as part of either the nature of discipleship or the new covenant inaugurated by Christ. For others, suffering and dying like Christ will serve as a transformative and perfecting experience, one in which discipleship and imitation of Christ are fully realized. The preponderance of this theme in the literature of the early church created an environment in which the suffering, persecution, and death of an individual were understood Christologically, in terms of the sufferings of the savior. Identification with the sufferings of Christ was a commonplace even in the embryonic communities of the Jesus movement and even before official or widespread persecution began. The prevalence of this idea formed part of the intellectual climate out of which the practices, literature, and theologies of martyrdom emerged.

2

The Martyr as *Alter Christus*

If originality is the hallmark of good writing, then the acts of the martyrs are deserving of their traditional scholarly label *Kleinliteratur.*[1] It is no great feat of ingenuity to read the deaths of early Christians through the lens of the Jesus story. The similarities with the Gospels are so overt that the *acta* have an almost plagiaristic quality; their characters and plots are derivative and predictable and—with some notable exceptions—fail to grasp the attention of the literary critic.

What it lacks in narrative ingenuity, however, the martyrdom genre makes up for in its capacity to use scripture to construct a world of latter-day biblical characters. Superimposing the narrative of the martyr's death upon the Gospel structure has a particular rhetorical impact. Not only are martyrs elevated to positions of almost untouchable authority, but their executioners and guards are reread against a cast of biblical actors. As a result, the attributes of the canonical antagonists overshadow the individual personalities of the characters in the martyrdom literature. Roman judges and guards are tarnished by the same brush that painted the Sadducees and Herod.

For the scholar, the deafening scriptural echoes strewn about the *acta* provide a mine of information about the ways in which ancient readers understood narrative events. Literary reworkings of the passion narratives function like ancient commentaries on scripture, providing valuable insights into how the earliest Christians interpreted stories about Jesus. The *acta* offer another opportunity to see Christ crucified and to understand the interpretative possibilities that this event yielded in the minds of ancient readers.

Though it is rhetorically powerful and interpretatively useful, *imitatio Christi* in the *acta* is more than a neat literary or rhetorical trick. Assimilating the martyr to Christ affected more than the literary imagination; it fundamentally altered the status of the martyrs in the eyes of the audience. It endowed them with Christly authority, authority that could be manipulated by those controlling the memory, legacy, and cults of the saints, but an authority that could never quite be harnessed. By presenting a martyr as an *alter Christus*, an author or homilist unwittingly created the potential for the complete assimilation of the martyr to Christ. Such assimilation encompassed not only the manner of death but also Christ's saving function and divine status. Reining in this interpretative tradition and limiting its theological possibilities proved difficult with a genre of literature that was wildly popular and unregulated.

In the previous chapter we examined how various scriptural passages point to the idea that following and imitating Christ involved suffering and death. This chapter will probe more deeply into the specifics of how the martyrs are modeled on Jesus; our task is not solely to create an inventory of the ways in which this happens but to ask what it accomplishes. If scripture is, in the words of Richard Hays, the "determinative subtext"[2] for the production of the *scriptores martyrum*, how does it function, rhetorically and theologically, to reshape the world of the audience? How does it manipulate, reinforce, and subvert particular scriptural texts? Before proceeding to the minutiae of *imitatio Christi* in the *acta*, we will first discuss the various ways in which the *acta* themselves use scripture to justify martyrdom. How is martyrdom viewed as part of a biblically mandated lifestyle?

Martyrdom as *Imitatio* and Biblical Command

Martyrdom as Imitatio

For ancient audiences of the *acta*, the observation that martyrs imitate Christ is obvious. The preponderance of allusions, quotations, and statements explicating martyrdom's value as an *imitatio Christi* render this statement banal; it is everywhere implied and frequently stated. Among scholars, the idea is most closely associated with the *Martyrdom of Polycarp*, a text that has become a staple among students of early Christian martyrdom. Polycarp's *imitatio* is explicitly stated from the outset, where his conduct is compared to that of Jesus.[3] Polycarp is part of a mimetic chain, one that connects the audience of the martyrdom to Christ himself.[4]

Despite its well-earned position as the sine qua non of martyrological *imitatio Christ*, the *Martyrdom of Polycarp* is not alone among the *acta* in emphasizing this theme. The same idea is found in the late second-century account of *Carpus, Papylus and Agathonice*, in which Carpus gives thanks that in death he has a share in Christ. Likewise, the sophisticated Gallic *Letter of the Churches of Lyons and Vienne* goes to elaborate lengths to underscore this point, describing the martyrs as "eager to pursue and imitate Christ."[5]

Crossing the Mediterranean and the linguistic divide, a number of Latin North African *acta* continue the theme, explicitly stating that the martyr's death is an imitation of the words and actions of Christ. The *Martyrdom of Montanus and Lucius*, for instance, takes for granted that the martyr's death imitates the death of Jesus and celebrates the ability of the martyr to imitate even Jesus' words.[6] The same idea extends into Syriac literature; the author of the *Martyrdom of Barsamya* writes that the sufferings of Christ are indelibly portrayed in martyrs.[7] These are but a few examples of instances in which the martyr's death is explicitly aligned with that of Christ; to these can be added the myriad statements by patristic authors regarding the status of martyrs as Christly imitators. A closer examination of the differences and nuances of the martyr's *imitatio Christi* will follow; the point to note for the time being is the ubiquity of this theme among the linguistically and geographically disparate communities that produced these *acta*.

Martyrdom as the Fulfillment of Law or Gospel

For some, martyrdom was viewed not only as a means of imitating Jesus but as the fulfillment of a biblical command. Traces of this idea surface in martyr acts from early Christian Smyrna to Diocletian martyrdoms from southern Italy and Thessaloniki. As noted in the previous chapter, the martyr Euplus interprets the Matthean beatitudes and the Synoptic imperative to "take up the cross" not only as exhortations to martyrdom but as prescriptive commands, as laws.[8]

The idea first appears in the opening to the *Martyrdom of Polycarp*, where Polycarp's martyrdom is described as taking place in accordance with the gospel: "For nearly everything that happened before took place so that the Lord might show us a martyrdom in accordance with the gospel.[9] Just as the Lord did, he too waited that he might be delivered up, that we might become his imitators, not thinking of ourselves alone, but of our neighbors as well. For it is a true and solid love, to desire not only one's own salvation but that of all the brothers and sisters."[10] The legitimacy and efficacy of Polycarp's martyrdom are offset against those of another character, Quintus, who of his own volition approaches the authorities in order to secure his martyrdom (*Mart. Pol.* 4).

Quintus, a Phrygian and perhaps also a Montanist, gave himself up and forced others to do likewise but is unable to follow through with the martyrdom itself and sacrifices to the gods. The narrator informs the reader that it is for this reason "that we do not approve of those who come forward of themselves, since this is not the teaching of the gospel."[11] From this we can infer that a certain kind of martyrdom is the "teaching of the gospel," but that the author thinks it must be carefully delineated and adjudicated. If Polycarp is anything to go by, a measured approach to death is an *imitatio Christi* and a sign that Polycarp's death is "in accordance with the gospel." This measured approach extends, it seems, only to the arrest itself. The gospel-worthy martyr does not offer him- or herself for martyrdom but eagerly embraces it once the sentence is passed. Evidence can be seen in Polycarp's eagerly disembarking the carriage and scratching himself and Germanicus pulling the beast on top of him in his haste to greet death.[12] Polycarp's death is "in accordance with the gospel" both literally in that it imitates the passion narratives and abstractly in the sense that it coheres with the author's idea of how to behave "in accordance with the gospel." The author overlays the rhetorical power of *imitatio* with the more commonplace appeal to what is "in accordance with scripture" to great effect.

Toward the end of the narrative, the author sums up the accomplishments of Polycarp by again using language of *imitatio* and the gospel. Here, though, the focus of the mimesis has shifted; it is now not Christ but Polycarp who is the model for our testimony: "He was not only a great teacher but also a conspicuous martyr, whose martyrdom, following the Gospel of Christ, everyone desires to imitate."[13] The shift in focus is significant; it articulates the way in which Polycarp appropriates the position of honor previously occupied by Christ. Just as at the beginning of the narrative Jesus was a teacher and model for imitation, now the pedagogue Polycarp's death is the model. The author is cautious not to stray too far from the person of Jesus even though the focus of the reader has shifted to Polycarp, so the emphasis on the gospel foundations of martyrdom remains. The martyrdom of Polycarp as model is still construed as sanctioned by and part of the gospel of Christ.

The notion of martyrdom as behavior mandated by the gospel is found in the fourth century Thessalonian account of the *Martyrdom of Agape, Irene and Chione*. Toward the beginning of the account the author describes how the three women "following the gospel laws"[14] abandoned their family, friends, country, and city and took refuge in the mountains. They fled their persecutors, "according to the commandment,"[15] and took refuge on a mountain. The alternative lifestyle taken up by the women has much in common both with the practices associated with the cult of Dionysos in Thessaloniki and also with early monasticism, a burgeoning phenomenon by the time of the narrative's composition.[16] In the narrative, however, the practice of abandoning one's family and taking refuge in the hills is connected to "gospel laws" and "commandments" and thus presented as a kind of biblically grounded *vita Christiana*. It seems probable that such practices were supported by, if not derived from, Markan passages praising the abandonment of family and wealth (Mark 10:29–31) and exhorting the audience to retreat to the hills in times of persecution (Mark 13:14). Given that the mountainous area near Thessaloniki cannot be identified, it would seem that the activities of the martyrs are symbolic narrative constructions.[17] The behavior of the women, therefore, represents a kind of ideal *vita Christiana* derived from a reading of the Gospel of Mark.[18] This ideal life of eschewing family, city, and wealth in favor of persecution is presented in legal terms as the fulfillment of "gospel law." While the author never explicitly calls their martyrdoms a fulfillment of written law, this assessment of their conduct appears to extend throughout the narrative and incorporates all of their actions from before their arrest to the moment of their deaths. As in the case of Polycarp, their conduct leading up to their martyrdom is based upon a particular understanding of how best to fulfill gospel commandments.

Martyrdom as the Fulfillment of the Command to Love

In comparison to Levitical codes or rabbinic *mishnoth*, early Christian literature is frustratingly devoid of ethical specificity. The synoptic command to love one's neighbor is vague and ambiguous, and only John ventures so far as to give specifics. For the Johannine author, love is defined in terms of Christly imitation and self-sacrifice. In John 13–15 the author repeatedly discusses the nature of love. In the initial occurrence, Jesus commands his disciples to love one another as he has loved them: "I give you a new commandment, that you love one another. Just as I have loved you, you also should love one another.[19] By this everyone will know that you are my disciples, if you have love for one another."[20] In understanding what it means to love one another, Jesus presents himself as a model. We should love others as Jesus loves us. A simple enough command, to be sure, except that to love as Jesus does means self-sacrifice and death. Later, in the Last Supper discourse, the Johannine Jesus explicitly identifies voluntary death on behalf as others as the supreme example of love:

> As the Father has loved me, so I have loved you; abide in my love. If you keep my commandments, you will abide in my love, just as I have kept my Father's commandments and abide in his love. I have said these things to you so that my joy may be in you, and that your joy may be complete. "This is my commandment, that you love one

another as I have loved you. No one has greater love than this, to lay down one's life for one's friends."[21]

In John, the command to love is redefined in terms of imitation, discipleship, and self-sacrifice. The readers must love imitatively, following the example of Jesus, by laying down their lives for his or her friends (cf. 1 John 3:16). It is as a consequence of their act of love that they will be recognized by others as disciples (13:35) and by Jesus as friends (15:14).[22] The Johannine community certainly does not have a monopoly on the idea of love as self-sacrifice. The Pauline (Rom 5:8) and Deutero-Pauline (Eph 5:2) epistles also connect love with self-offering, perhaps drawing upon the famous statement of Plato in the *Symposium* that "only those who love wish to die for others."[23]

In the context of the early church, the Johannine command to love provided the ethical grounding for the martyr's death.[24] Clement of Alexandria, a church father known for his somewhat more moderate position on martyrdom, consistently portrays martyrdom for Christ as an act committed on account of love.[25] This idea is more forceful in the *acta*; Vettius Epagathus in *Lyons* exemplifies the idea that martyrdom is an expression of love. Vettius is a young rhetorician who, seeing the injustice of the charges brought against the Christians, offers a speech in their defense. Predictably, his *apologia* is rejected and he himself is martyred. The description of Vettius's actions fuses the Johannine notion of discipleship with the language of Revelation: "He [Vettius] possessed the Advocate within him, the Spirit that filled Zachary, which he demonstrated by the fullness of his love, consenting as he did to lay down his life in defense of his fellow Christians. He was and is a true disciple of Christ, following the lamb wherever he goes."[26] The description of Vettius combines typically Johannine concern for the Spirit and love with Markan ideas of discipleship (Mark 8:34) and Revelation's language of following the lamb (Rev 14:4). As we saw in Ignatius, discipleship is predicated upon imitation. That is to say, it is by imitating Christ that one is truly his disciple.[27] The idea of discipleship is more nuanced than merely imitating what Jesus did; in true Johannine style Vettius imitates the ethic of love that underlies the act of laying down one's life.

The interpretation of John 15:13 as an exhortation to martyrdom reverberates in the language of numerous other martyr acts. The Thessalonian martyr Irene almost nonchalantly defends her decision to retain sacred writings as the fulfillment of this command: "The Prefect Dulcitius said: 'Who was it that advised you to retain those parchments and writings up to the present time?' 'It was almighty God,' said Irene, 'who bade us to love him unto death.'"[28] While Irene's statement seems to be an allusion to John 15:13 or 1 John 3:16, she designates God almighty as its author. Given that in John it is Jesus who instructs the disciples to love one another, we might question whether this text would arise in the mind of either the author or potential audiences of the text. The allusion is clouded by the discrepancy in the presumed speaker. If we situate the martyrdom within the church at Thessaloniki, the situation is partially resolved. In her analysis of Christian architecture and mosaics in Thessaloniki, Laura Nasrallah draws attention to the rhetoric of imperialism and empire that lies behind the construction of Christian artwork there.[29] The depiction of Christ *pantokrator* in the mosaic of Hosios David/Moni Latomou, for example, reveals the Thessalonian preoccupation with positing a new triumphal emperor Christ in the place of a Roman emperor. The language of God *pantokrator* used in the *Martyrdom of Agape, Irene and Chione* ties in with this program of anti-imperial rhetoric and co-opting of imperial ideology.[30] For a community that already identified Jesus as the *pantokrator*, Irene's statement would have been easily understood as a reference to Jesus and, therefore, as an allusion to John. Here again we find that the command to love resurfaces as an explanation for Christian martyrdom.

An interesting twist on the command to love is found in the North African account of the martyrdom of Montanus and Lucius. Flavian, a deacon and the final martyr to die in the narrative, exhorts his audience to preserve the bonds of love and unity in the church. Flavian's citation of the Johannine command to love is directed toward disharmony in the Carthaginian church; he does not so much call the church to martyrdom as to unity. His use of the Johannine command, however, relies upon the implied similarities between Jesus' and Flavian's final commands. Just as Jesus commanded the disciples to love one another, so Flavian commands them to love one another in unity: "Most beloved brothers, he said, you will keep peace with me, if you acknowledge the peace of the church and preserve the bond of love. Do not think that what I have said is insignificant. Our Lord Jesus Christ himself, when he was close to death, left us these last words: 'This is my commandment, he said, that you love one another as I have loved you.'"[31] By noting that Jesus gave his command to love "when he was close to death," the narrative Flavian is able tease out the similarities between Jesus and himself. Here, he uses the command not so much to exhort others to martyrdom but to bolster his position in the eyes of his audience. Like Jesus, he leaves a parting command to the church, and like Jesus this is a command to love. Whereas the Johannine author may have sought to urge his readers on to discipleship and friendship with Christ, the author of the martyrdom pushes the audience toward harmonious conduct.

The language of *unitas* so prominently featured here is best understood against the backdrop of the historical circumstances that led to the composition of the martyrdom. Language of unity was an important part of the rhetorical program of "orthodox" Christians in Carthage who sought to combat schismatic elements in the church there.[32] It was an important feature in the writings of Cyprian and Augustine, in their efforts to deal with the confessors and Donatist controversies.[33] In the case of both Cyprian and Augustine, the rhetorical impact of their message was met with the supremely persuasive charismatic power of the persecuted confessors and martyrs. Bishops were persuasive, but martyrs outstripped them in sheer dynamism. Donatist writers responded to ecclesiastically grounded calls for unity by composing martyrdom accounts in which *unitas* was demonized. In the *Martyrdom of Montanus and Lucius* the charismatic power of the martyr's words is coupled with the orthodox desire for unity to great effect. The demands of Flavian for unity are here compared to the parting commands of Jesus to love and his prayer for unity (John 17:20–23). In this passage, the unity called for by the orthodox episcopate is bolstered by the words of the martyr and the implicit analogy between the martyr's words and those of Jesus. By drawing together the farewell discourse of Jesus with the swan song of the martyr, the *imitatio Christi* serves to strengthen the rhetorical claims of the orthodox church.[34]

A final theme among ancient Christian commentators on martyrdom is the idea that Jesus predicted the future martyrdom and persecution of Christians during his lifetime. Although this is not strictly speaking an instance of *imitatio Christi*, it is another example of the manner in which martyrdom was shaped by a particular scriptural reading tradition. This idea is by no means exclusive to the martyrdom genre itself. In letters and homilies exhorting people to martyrdom, both Clement of Alexandria and Cyprian of Carthage assembled lists of passages from the Gospels that they understood as prophecies of martyrdom.[35] In the *Letter of the Churches of Lyons and Vienne*, the author comments that persecution was the fulfillment of prophecy: "Thus the Lord's saying was proved true: The time is coming when whoever kills you will think he is doing a service to God."[36] The prophecy, taken from john 16:2, is interpreted as a prediction of persecution in the early church. Readings like this helped to create a sense that persecution was preordained and unavoidable.

As we have seen, members of the early Jesus movement valued suffering as a means of imitating Jesus. The same principle applied for the authors of the *acta* themselves, but they developed more nuanced and sophisticated ways of communicating this idea.[37] Martyrdom was valuable as *imitatio*, but this idea was further refined so that it became an imitation of a particular characteristic, attribute, or function of the Savior. In this way, martyrdom became an expression of love, an instructional tool, and a fulfillment of law. We should note, however, the rhetorical function of reading martyrdom as the fulfillment of biblical command. In the case of Polycarp, his martyrdom is described as being "in accordance with gospel" in order to exclude practices of martyrdom that the author deemed unsuitable. Similarly, the reading of the Johannine command to love is used by the author of the *Martyrdom of Montanus and Lucius* to bring about congregational cohesion and unity. The interpretation of key biblical commands as exhortations to martyrdom, therefore, is a strategic practice that utilizes both the authority of sacred text and the charismatic power of the figure of the martyr. Invoking *imitatio Christi* as a means of combining and manipulating these two sources of discursive power was a valuable rhetorical strategy for the authors of the *acta*.

Narrative Mirroring of the Passion Narrative

In the writings of the church fathers, interpretations of events in the life and death of Jesus are self-consciously presented. Interpretative methods may vary and may or may not be specified, but more often than not, biblical texts are referred to, identified, and occasionally cited.[38] Rewriting the deaths of the martyrs within this biblical world is not less strategic than the exegesis of church fathers but is necessarily closer to popular understandings of the meaning of the biblical narrative. In order for the martyr to appear to be imitating Christ, he or she must be portrayed in as Christly a fashion as possible. The presentation of the martyr must cohere with the generally held presentation of Jesus in the passion narratives insofar as is possible. For the presentation to be effective, the author cannot drift too far from his or her audience's understanding of scripture even as he or she seeks to reimagine and control it. The relationship between the narrative reworking and standard interpretation, therefore, is closer than in the commentary of the church fathers. In some respects, therefore, the *acta* provide a clearer picture of some of the interpretations of the passion narratives.[39]

With the notable exception of the account of the death of Stephen in Acts and the *Martyrdom of Polycarp*, which we will treat separately, few *acta* follow the entire story line of the passion narrative in its entirety. To be sure the general structure of the *acta* is the same—arrest, trial, confession, judgment (insert optional tortures and visions here), execution—but the authors felt under no compulsion to follow the precise sequence of the passion narrative, and it did not appear to affect the quality of their allusions. Fructuosus, for example, is offered wine mixed with myrrh while in prison. The scene is an obvious allusion to the drugged wine offered to Jesus on the cross, but Fructuosus is still imprisoned.[40] A more unusual example is found in the Donatist martyr Victoria, who

throws herself off a cliff but is miraculously saved from bodily dismember-
ment. Her deliverance is an allusion, perhaps, to the Synoptic temptation
accounts in which angels will bear up Jesus in such circumstances. That these
allusions appear "out of place" in no way detracts from their potency. Narrative
mirroring of the passion narratives in the *acta*, therefore, does not rely upon
following the sequence of events precisely but upon a generally similar structure into which certain biblical elements are interspersed.

The somewhat haphazard manner in which different accounts incorporate
motifs of the passion narratives makes it difficult to speak in general terms about
the *acta*. Only certain Jesus traditions are alluded to in the *acta*, frequently out of
order, and rarely in the kind of systematic manner beloved by scholars. Instead
of seeking to generalize about the *acta* or provide an exhaustive catalog of every
possible allusion here, we will attempt to analyze those motifs or elements that
appear most frequently. We will begin with an examination of the accounts of
Stephen and Polycarp in their entirety before proceeding to a discussion of the
utilization of certain individual elements in other acts of the martyrs.

Stephen

The use of narrative mirroring to portray a martyr as particularly Christlike
begins with the composition of Acts. The death of Stephen in Acts 7 is a carefully constructed narrative in which the events of Stephen's death shadow those
of Jesus. While there are notable differences between the accounts—the lengthy
speech that prompts Stephen's death, the sequence in which Stephen quotes
the words of Jesus, and, of course, the manner of Stephen's death—the close
relationship between the two is undeniable. In the early church Stephen came
to attract attention as the great protomartyr,[41] the first of many thousands who
die for Christianity.

The practice of reading Stephen as an imitator of Jesus may even have
influenced the textual history of the Gospel of Luke itself. Among New Testament textual critics there is considerable debate surrounding Luke 23:34, in
which Jesus asks for the forgiveness of those involved in his crucifixion. The
scene is paralleled in Acts 7 where Stephen prays for the forgiveness of those
stoning him. In Luke, the phrase is absent in a number of key textual witnesses,
leading to considerable debate regarding its authenticity.[42]

External evidence suggests that the phrase is not original. It is omitted in a
wide variety of documents dated from the second to thirteenth centuries, including examples from the Alexandrian, Western, Byzantine, and Caesarean text
types. Additionally, these documents are geographically diverse, originating in
Egypt, Europe, Syria, and Byzantium. In contrast, evidence for the inclusion of

the phrase may include a number of early manuscripts, but—prior to the fourth century—is found only in the Western text type.[43] External evidence suggests that while both readings can be dated to the second century, only the omission of the logion is attested in geographically and textually diverse manuscripts.

Additionally, internal evidence has been supplied in favor of the authenticity of the logion. Thomas Bolin has argued that the language used in the logion is Lukan.[44] As Whitlark and Parsons note, this argument is hardly compelling because such vocabulary is in fact stock New Testament language.[45] Furthermore, Luke 23:34 interrupts the flow of the narrative, breaking up the description of the dividing of Jesus' garments with the prayer.[46] Delobel argues that given the similarities between the characterizations of the deaths of Jesus and Stephen, one narrative was copying the other.[47] Given the "logical" directional flow of influence from Jesus to Stephen, Stephen's prayer must have been derived from that of Jesus. The logion must, according to Delobel, be original.[48] If, as Delobel, Brown, and others have concluded, the logion is authentic, then we must account for its omission in so many early manuscripts.[49]

A number of scholarly explanations have been formulated;[50] first, a scribe felt the statement contradicted either Jesus' previous prediction of judgment (Luke 23:29–31) or the destruction of Jerusalem.[51] Second, the anonymous scribe felt that because this was addressed to the authorities, they could hardly be judged ignorant.[52] And, most popularly, the omission is part of a trend of anti-Jewish redaction in the early church. The removal of the phrase eliminates the possibility that the Jews are exonerated from guilt on account of ignorance.[53] Such explanations, however, cannot account for the nature of the textual evidence. The omission is widely and diversely attested, and the inclusion is found only in the Western text type, which is known for its theological reflection.[54] The external evidence speaks overwhelmingly for Luke 23:34a as a later addition to the text.

If, as we have argued, the logion is secondary, what is the reason for its interpolation? Whitlark and Parsons provide an ingenious solution to this question, suggesting that the inclusion has numerical significance.[55] As the Gospels were read collectively as parts of a single narrative, the logion was added to bring the number of sayings from the cross to seven, not six. To support this argument, Whitlark and Parsons assemble an impressive list of examples of the numerical significance of the number seven in Judeo-Christian literature. Taken in conjunction with evidence from the Diatessaronic tradition, they conclude that Luke 23:34a was a floating tradition incorporated into the Gospel in order to bring the sayings of Jesus from the cross to seven. Impressive though their argument is, Whitlark and Parsons fail to account for the inclusion of this particular logion in this particular Gospel.[56]

The heightened parallelism that the inclusion of the phrase gives the death of Jesus with the death of Stephen can hardly be accidental. Is it possible, therefore, that contrary to the assumptions of Delobel and Brown, the logion was introduced into Luke under the influence of the account of Stephen? A similar argument is made by David Flusser with respect to the *Martyrdom of James*.[57] Flusser notes that, according to Hegesippus, James prays this logion for his persecutors at his execution.[58] Flusser goes on to argue that the narrative of the execution of James influenced the insertion of the logion into Luke 23:34. If Flusser's argument is at all convincing, we must consider the possibility that the account of Stephen's death also exerted influence over the textual transmission of Luke. After all, the two accounts are literarily related and often parallel one another. It seems most likely that the inclusion of the logion in Luke 23:34 was intended to harmonize the death of Jesus with that of subsequent martyr imitators, most particularly Stephen in Acts 7, but perhaps also—as Flusser argues—the *Martyrdom of James* and other martyrdom accounts that include this trope.[59]

If, as we have supposed, the phrase is a secondary addition to Luke under the influence of later martyrological accounts, this speaks volumes about the centrality of the martyr's imitation of Jesus. The reading of Stephen as an *alter Christus* is so strong that his prayer for forgiveness is read as an example of his Christliness, and this behavior is in turn retrojected into the life of Jesus. The belief that Stephen is a perfect imitator of Jesus has led to the assumption that Jesus must have uttered these words.

This example is indicative of the centrality and vital importance of *imitatio Christi* in the early church. Commitment to this idea shaped, quite literally, the narrative of the death of Jesus. Given the choice between excising Stephen's request and altering the words of Jesus, early church editors opted for the latter. In this instance, Stephen is judged the more Christly, and rather than assimilate Stephen to Jesus, they assimilate Jesus to Stephen. Consequently, we must conclude that the relationship between the death of Jesus and the death of Stephen is dialogical. Not only is Stephen modeled on Jesus, but the death of Jesus is edited to be more like that of Stephen. It is difficult to overstate the significance of *imitatio Christi;* here the death of the martyr shapes the death of Jesus, infiltrates the memory of his death, alters the perception of his character, and irreversibly changes the literary record. This phrase so often used to characterize the magnanimity of Jesus is, in actuality, plucked from the lips of one of his martyrs.

Polycarp

In the *Martyrdom of Polycarp*, allusions to the passion narrative reach an entirely new level. This sophisticated account is usually dated to the middle of the second century, but its complex textual history and developed theology of martyrdom may suggest that it was composed sometime later, in the third century.[60] In its extant form, the text makes overt and repeated references to the passion narratives.[61] The author deftly but overtly weaves references to the Gospels throughout the account, beginning with an outright declaration of Polycarp's imitation and proceeds to mirror the passion narratives from the garden of Gethsemane to the moment of death. The deliberate imitation of the generic and narrational qualities of the death of Jesus in this text is so pronounced that scholars are drawn into debate about the individual Gospel that most greatly influenced the author of the *Martyrdom of Polycarp*.[62]

Narrative mirroring in the *Martyrdom of Polycarp* begins long before the death or even trial of the martyr. The circumstances that bring Polycarp to trial are narrated in explicit detail, the author(s) taking care to note—in case you should miss it—the parallelism with the arrest of Jesus: "The police captain, who was called Herod, was eager to bring him to the amphitheatre: destiny had given him the same name, that Polycarp might fulfill the lot that was appointed to him, becoming a partaker of Christ and those who betrayed him might receive the punishment of Judas."[63] Long before Polycarp sets foot in the arena, the stage is set with biblical actors. The police captain is conveniently named Herod, and those who hand Polycarp over are identified with Judas, the betrayer of Christ.[64] The author seems to recognize that the identification of the opponents of Polycarp with the villains of the passion narrative demonizes them in the eyes of the reader and shores up the Christliness of Polycarp. The force of the allusion stretches further, however, reaching into the lives of the audience.

Those participating in Christian communities before the reign of Constantine lived under the shadow of persecution. The threat of betrayal to Roman authorities was a real one, one of which the audiences of the *Martyrdom of Polycarp* would have been well aware.[65] The alignment of the betrayers of Polycarp with Judas tarnishes all betrayers with the notoriety and fate of Judas and acts as a potential deterrent to those who might feel inclined to defect. It operates as an implicit threat to the audience: betray a fellow Christian and you betray Christ.

Like Jesus, upon arrest Polycarp exhibits a calm demeanor and admirable self-restraint. His acceptance of his arrest has a dignified prayerful tone. The author is keen to point out the timing of Polycarp's arrest and death in order to draw out parallels with the Fourth Gospel:

> With the slave then, the police and cavalry set out on Friday at the dinner hour with the usual arms as though against a brigand. It was late evening when they closed in: they found him reclining in a small

room upstairs. He could have left and gone elsewhere but he refused, saying: "May the will of God be done." And so, hearing that they had arrived he went downstairs to talk with them, while all those present were surprised at his composure and his old age, and why there should have been such concern to capture so elderly a man.[66]

Polycarp's serenity is further underscored in the following account of his Gethsemane-styled prayer. He extends hospitality to the soldiers who come to arrest him and asks only that he be permitted an hour of undisturbed prayer. Ever the overachiever, he eschews the opportunity for flight and instead prays for two hours, a feat the author terms "godlike":

> At any rate Polycarp immediately ordered food and drink to be set before them, as much as they wished, even at this hour, and only requested that they might grant him an hour to pray undisturbed. When they consented, he stood up and began to pray facing the east, and so full was he of God's grace that he was unable to stop for two hours, to the amazement of those who heard him, and many were sorry that they had come out to arrest such a godlike old man (θεοπρεπῆ πρεσβύτην).[67]

Even at this early stage in the proceedings, Polycarp's controlled behavior wins supporters, the guards appearing remorseful that they are forced into arresting him. His journey into the city continues the *imitatio* theme, his entrance into the city being a dark replication of Jesus' triumphal entry into Jerusalem.[68]

Polycarp's vision of his death is fulfilled, and he is sentenced to be burned alive. In its totality, the account of Polycarp's death follows the style and sequence of events found in the gospel passion narratives. Yet here at the moment of death, the critical event in the story, the pattern changes, and Polycarp is not nailed in his cruciform pose: "When they were on the point of nailing him to it, he said: 'Leave me thus. For he who has given me the strength to endure the flames will grant me to remain without flinching in the fire even without the firmness you will give me by using nails.' They did not nail him down then, but simply bound him."[69] The reader might be forgiven for thinking that here, at the crucial moment, the *imitatio* breaks down. Polycarp is not nailed to the stake; he is bound. This conclusion, while understandable, fails to account for the augmentation and adaptation of the allusion. The self-assured request to remain unnailed in Polycarp's crucifixion overshoots even the achievements of the crucified Jesus. Polycarp does not need nails; he has reservoirs of endurance.

At the same time, however, the augmentation of the crucifixion scene blends another biblically based allusion into the narrative; the *akedah* (binding) traditions surrounding Isaac. The account of Abraham's near sacrifice of his son Isaac in Genesis 22 was enormously influential in both early Christian and rabbinic circles.[70] For early Christians the *akedah* served as a prototype of the sacrifice of Jesus and as an example of faithfulness in God.[71] Interweaving *akedah* and crucifixion in this way, therefore, is part of a traditional Christian reinterpretation of the binding of Isaac as a prototype of God's sacrifice of Jesus. The reference to the binding of Isaac does not undermine the allusion to the crucifixion as the two accounts were linked in Christian typological constructions of history. The binding of Polycarp does not break down the *imitatio* but rather reinforces it; Polycarp is inserted into the cycle of history alongside Isaac and Christ as another *typos* of the innocent sacrificial victim. The rereading of the death of Jesus is here based not solely on the passion narratives but on a typological rereading of Genesis 22 popular among ancient Christians.

Incorporation of Elements of the Jesus Tradition

The Incident in the Temple (Mark 11:15//Matt 21:12–16)

In the life of the historical Jesus as constructed by scholars, the temple incident is considered to be the definitive event that led to his arrest and execution.[72] For the authors of the *acta* the significance of the event lay elsewhere, in what it revealed about the state of Jewish and pagan rituals in the eyes of God. The fourth-century Greek *Martyrdom of Dasius* offers a narrative reworking of this event in which a Roman soldier, Dasius, disrupts a festival dedicated to Saturn. Dasius is selected to play the role of king and human sacrificial victim in an otherwise unknown *pharmakos* ritual.[73] The macabre festival involves dressing up as the king, parading around the city, and then throwing oneself on a sword. Understandably, Dasius refuses, quickly calculating that if death is inevitable, then martyrdom would be the preferable mode, and finds himself in front of a Roman judge, who tries again to convince him to sacrifice, only this time to "unclean demons."

The shift from barbaric human sacrifice to the ordinary offerings of imperial cult is almost indiscernible. Because the author never notes a distinction between the human sacrifices performed for the feast of Saturn and the more mundane sprinkling of incense in the imperial cult, a cursory reader would be excused for thinking they were one and the same. The confusion is deliberate; no doubt, the author is less concerned with the legalities of the proceedings than with the portrayal of all pagan ritual as demonic and barbaric. The juxtaposition of the historically suspect human sacrifice with offerings of incense in imperial cults tarnished the latter with the moral impunity of the former. For Dasius, at least, they are the same; to the very end he refuses to participate in any of the rituals and, in imitation of the gospel accounts, disrupts the proceedings:

> As he was going in to his glorious martyrdom, he had someone preceding him with the forbidden censer. But when they tried to force Dasius to sacrifice to the unclean demons, taking it in his own hands he scattered all their incense about and threw about the profane and disgusting idols of the sacrilegious ones and trampled them into the ground, while he fortified himself on the forehead with the sign of the precious cross of Christ, by whose power he contested with the tyrant.[74]

The description of Dasius overturning the idols in the pagan temple recalls the scene in the Jerusalem temple (Mark 11:15–18//Matt 21:12). By overturning idols, Dasius's attack is not so much a disruption of the individual ritual as it is a rebellion against the cult itself. The implicit parallel between the Jerusalem temple and pagan worship has damaging effects for both parties. Not only are Jewish and pagan ritual practices grouped together by the allusion; they are then further condemned by the analogy with the practice of human sacrifice. For the author, the comparison with the feast of Saturn is not so far-fetched, since the immoral killing of human beings is exactly what the author of Dasius accuses both the Roman and (through use of parallelism) the Jewish authorities of doing. The Romans kill Christians just as the Jews killed Jesus, because both engage in impious cultic activities.

A twist on this idea occurs in a homily on the martyrdom of Theodore of Amasea in 306 C.E. Like Dasius, Theodore was a military man, a young recruit in the Roman army who belonged to the *cohors Tyronum* and was thus nicknamed "Tiro."[75] The account of his death is extremely unreliable but is supported in part by a homily delivered by Gregory of Nyssa on his feast day.[76] Theodore confessed to being a Christian but was nonetheless released by the judges that night, "on account of his youth," to think over his decision. Theodore used this time productively to burn down the Temple of Cybele, an act that led to his reimprisonment, torture, and death.

Descriptions of Christian martyrs disrupting temple activities serve a number of rhetorical purposes. They demonstrate the inability of pagan gods to defend themselves,[77] they align the martyr with Jesus, and they align pagan authorities with the much-vilified leaders of the Jews. In grouping Jews and pagans in this way, these martyrdoms anticipate a larger rhetorical trend in early Christianity in which Jews, heretics, and pagans were coproduced as a negative antitype to Christians.[78]

This trend is anticipated in accounts like the *Martyrdom of Dasius* and *Martyrdom of Polycarp*, which equate Roman and Jewish authorities both with one another and with Satan. As we saw earlier, the police captain who comes to arrest Polycarp is called Herod. The narrator remarks upon the parallel to the gospel passion narrative as a work of destiny that enables Polycarp to participate in Christ and the captain to receive the punishment of Judas. The alignment of the antagonists of the martyrs with Jewish authorities is not limited to pagans alone. The Donatist *Sermon on the Passion of Donatus and Advocatus* compares Roman—presumably Catholic—soldiers to Pharisees.[79] All these examples predate the pagan revival and Christian responses to Julian and newly renovated "paganism." It would appear, therefore, that the practice of aligning and comparing hostile authorities with the Jews did not begin as a response to the pagan revival, since it was imbedded in narratives of persecution long before.

Crucifixion

For early Christians, crucifixion became exclusively associated with the death of Jesus. The wooden cross was ideologically whittled into the *trophaeum* of the conquering redeemer. That crucifixion continued to be used as a form of execution after the death of Jesus meant that Christians were able to replicate the mechanics of the death of the Savior should the opportunity present itself. Whether or not the individual believed him- or herself worthy of the honor of Christ's manner of death was entirely a matter of personal conscience. The church historian Eusebius notes not only the famed inverted crucifixion of Peter but also the more run-of-the-mill execution of Symeon, bishop of Jerusalem circa 106.[80] Symeon was apparently betrayed to Roman authorities by nondescript heretics, withstood astonishing tortures, and eventually "suffered like the Lord" (τῷ τοῦ κυρίου πάθει παραπλήσιον τέλος ἀπηνέγκατο). In this instance, even the charges brought against him parallel those of Jesus, since Eusebius recounts that he was accused of being descended from David.[81] The accusation leveled against Symeon parallels, albeit roughly, the charge of royal lineage levied against Jesus in the Gospels.[82]

The best-known instance in which a martyr was crucified is described in the relatively late traditions associated with the martyrdom of the apostle Peter. In an event of penitent humility immortalized by the painters of the Renaissance, the apostle refuses to be crucified in the same way as Jesus and instead insists on being executed upside down. The textual tradition of the apocryphal *Acts of Peter* is decidedly complex, although the account of his martyrdom is preserved in not only the Latin text but also three Greek manuscripts as well as Coptic, Syriac, Ethiopic, Arabic, Armenian, and Slavonic versions.[83] Before and during his crucifixion Peter delivers a speech with a complex allegorical reading of the significance of the cross that is markedly different from the crucifixion of Jesus and other martyrs. Nonetheless, Peter remarks at length upon the significance of the form of the cross as a symbolic type of Jesus.

The symbolic importance of the cruciform pose is particularly pronounced in the case of Blandina the lowly slave girl of the *Letter of the Churches of Lyons and Vienne*. In the narrative the author goes to great pains to point out the low social status of Blandina, describing her as lowly, cheap, and ugly. Her low position in the ordinary social hierarchy is starkly contrasted with her exalted place in martyrological hierarchy embedded in the text:

> Blandina was hung on a stake[84] and set as food before the beasts
> driven in the arena. Because she was seen hanging in the form of a
> cross and on account of her energetic and unceasing prayer she
> stirred up great enthusiasm among the contestants. During the
> contest they looked with their eyes through their sister to the one
> who was crucified for them so that (s)he convinced those who believe
> in him that everyone who suffers for the glory of Christ will have
> eternal fellowship with the living God.[85]

In Blandina's case, the cruciform pose and the accompanying prayers have a startling narratological impact; the other martyrs instantly recognize Christ in her and are inspired and strengthened in their own martyrdoms. Even if the wooden beam upon which she is hung is *not* a cross, her crosslike form is particularly specified by the author as that which enables the other martyrs to look through her to Christ. The effect of the cruciform pose is almost mystical in its ability to transform the martyr into Christ. In the eyes of the other martyrs, Blandina herself disappears; in her place and in her physical form they see only Christ crucified. The transformative quality of her imitation of the crucifixion is so strong that the martyr herself vanishes; her identity is transformed into and is subsumed by that of Christ.

For those martyrs not (un)fortunate enough to be crucified, there was still the opportunity to assume the appropriate Christly position at the moment of death. An example of such self-actualization is found in Eusebius's account of the deaths of the Egyptian martyrs in Phoenicia, in which a young man replicates the sacred pose:

You could have seen a youth not twenty years of age standing unbound and stretching out his hands in the form of a cross, with unterrified and untrembling mind, engaged earnestly in prayer to God, and not in the least going back or retreating from the place where he stood, while bears and leopards, breathing rage and death, almost touched his flesh. And yet their mouths were restrained, I know not how, by a divine and incomprehensible power, and they ran back again to their place. Such a one was he.[86]

His deliberate reenactment of the cross and his "unhurried" prayers underscore the controlled nature of the martyr's actions; he is not distracted by pain and is instead completely absorbed in his prayers. The extension of the arms in a cruciform pose was reminiscent not only of the cross but also of the pose assumed by Christians during prayer.[87] This form was the predominant and usual method by which ancient Christians practiced prayer.[88]

For the art historian, the form of prayer with outstretched arms so frequently described in the *acta* appears in iconography as the *orans* or *orant*, a figure dominant in Greco-Roman art before its adoption by Christians in the late antique period.[89] The *orans* pose appears on the walls of the Roman catacombs, in conjunction with biblical scenes of deliverance such as the youths in the flames in Daniel 6, and Jonah and the whale.[90] This funerary context and the combination of the *orant* in paradisiacal settings led some to propose that the *orans* represents the already saved Christian soul in paradise.[91] Other scholars have argued more broadly that the image merely represents filial devotion or— given the feminine characteristics of the *orant*—the church.[92] The occasional specificity contained in the facial features (e.g., the image in the *donna velata* in the catacomb of Saint Priscilla in Rome), coupled with the existence of figures left with blank faces, suggests that some were portraits of individuals.[93]

Given that the *acta* depict prayer with outstretched arms as an allusion to the crucifixion, we might expect that the *orans* pose contains the same double reference. Yet the understanding of the *orans* pose as replicating the crucifixion is begrudgingly accepted only by some and then only because of the unequivocal statements of Minucius Felix and Tertullian.[94] In his *On Prayer*, Tertullian explains the *orans* pose, saying, "We, however, not only raise our hands, but even expand them; and, taking our model [*modulatum*] from the Lord's Passion, even in prayer we confess [*confitemur*] to Christ."[95] Tertullian's statement is interesting not only because he draws a clear connection between the *orans* pose of prayer and the cross but because he identifies this kind of *imitatio* as a confession. That he connects confession here with the formation of a cruciform pose indicates that he means confession as a form of witness rather than penitence. The *orans* pose is a self-conscious act of *imitatio* in which the suffering Christ is the model that the Christian must embody.[96]

Embodied *imitatio* of the suffering Christ is a foundational goal of Christian martyrdom. To find that the same concept was at work in the day-to-day activities of North African Christians demonstrates the widespread appeal of this idea. Transforming oneself into the *suffering* Christ was a mainstream ideal practiced in a wide variety of social locations. Further evidence for the *orans* pose as a means of performing the crucifixion is found in archaeological material in which the *orant* is overlaid on a cross in the place of the crucified Jesus, as if the saint is attached to "une croix invisible."[97] Such images attest to the commonplace identification of the iconographic depiction of the *orant* and the Christian practice of prayer with the crucifixion.[98] It would seem, therefore, that in praying at the moment of death martyrs physically reenact the crucifixion scene.

A somewhat augmented cruciform pose appears in the Spanish *Martyrdom of Fructuosus*. Here, the bishop-martyr kneels before stretching out his arms in prayer:[99] "When the bands that tied their hands were burnt through, recalling the Lord's prayer and their usual custom, Fructuosus knelt down in joy, confident of the resurrection, and stretching out his arms as a sign of the Lord's victory, he prayed to the Lord."[100] The description of the prayerful cruciform pose of the bishop Fructuosus is rich in meaning and an allusion that the author takes pains to explicate for the reader. Immediately preceding this account, the martyrs are compared to Ananias, Azarias, and Misael, the three men consigned to the fiery furnace in Daniel 6. The combination of the *orant* and this particular biblical account was, as we have already noted, typical in ancient Christian art. That the author interprets Fructuosus's assumption of the pose as a display of confidence in the resurrection is intriguing. It lends credence to Grabar's argument that the *orant* in art is a representation of the resurrected soul in paradise.[101] Read in light of this theory, then, Fructuosus's actions would be "confident" because he assumes the pose of the resurrected soul even before his actual death.

The significance of Fructuosus's actions goes further than merely affirming the readers' views of his chutzpah. In noting the cruciform pose of the martyrs, the author fuses the mundane with the extraordinary. The extension of the arms recalls both the cross of Jesus and the familiar *orans* pose employed by early Christians in prayer. In reciting the Lord's Prayer in an *orans* pose, the actions of the martyrs are starkly mundane, run-of-the-mill actions performed daily by Christians in the ancient world. This is, as the author stresses, "their usual custom." Simultaneously, the exceptional nature of the pose is underscored; in their execution the martyrs strike their Christly pose with a self-control that requires no physical constraints. Their *imitatio* oversteps even the achievement of Christ on the cross as they kneel with perfect self-control. The martyrdom draws together the cross of Christ with the liturgical performance of prayer, imbuing the latter with some of the imitative import of the former.

The multiplicity of meanings embedded here is unequivocal; the *orans* pose struck by the bishop recalls both the cross (the trophy of the Lord) and the practice of prayer. Given that Fructuosus is a bishop, the liturgical overtones in the work, and the potentially liturgical setting in which the work was read, the more precise referent might be recitation of the Lord's Prayer during the Eucharist. The text of his martyrdom indicates that it is Fructuosus alone who kneels with arms extended, not—as Musurillo would have it—Fructuosus and his deacons.[102] If we grant that liturgical undertones are at work here, then the death of Fructuosus mimics not only the death of Jesus but also the sacramental reenactment of his death. The martyr's death acquires a sacramental quality even as various ways of imitating Christ—martyrdom, prayer, and the Eucharistic liturgy—are layered upon one another, multiplying their imitative quality.

While the connection between prayer and the cross is made explicit in the *Martyrdom of Fructuosus*, the same double meaning can be read in the cruciform deaths of other martyrs. For example, in the case of martyrs we have already mentioned, the Egyptian martyrs and Blandina, we should note that both the unnamed young man and Blandina are described as praying at the moment of their deaths.[103] The *orans* style of prayer was recognized by both Minucius Felix and Tertullian as a bodily reenactment of the cross, indicating that from as early as the reign of Marcus Aurelius the *orans* pose was reinterpreted as a kind of reenactment of the cross. If this view was more widely held, then it stands to reason that early readers of the acts of the martyrs would recognize in their final prayer a double allusion to the death of Jesus and to their own day-to-day practice of prayer. By offering the martyrs as Christly imitators in death and models of good prayer, the double allusion reinforces the imitative quality and significance of the *orans* pose in Christian life.

Committal of the Spirit (Luke 23:46//Acts 7:50)

Arguably the most distinctive and undeniable aspect of *imitatio* in the *acta* is the manner in which martyrs speak the words of Jesus at their trials and execution. The *acta* are littered with martyrs who forgive their executioners and commend their spirits to their fathers. The sayings of Jesus lifted from scripture form the template and vocabulary for the martyr's final words. Their citation and reiteration of the *verbum Christi* have a dramatic effect in aligning the martyrs with Jesus and in imbuing them with his self-controlled and self-effacing characteristics.

In most *acta*, the final words of the martyr form the climax of the piece. In some *acta* the final words are uttered in the courtroom and are a last emboldened refusal to sacrifice or declaration of Christian identity. In other stories the martyrs' final words are comically dismissive of the proceedings. The famous parting shots of Pionius and Lawrence seem reminiscent of the death of Socrates.[104] While the reader soon tires of the details of the tortures, the final of words of the martyr never fail to leave an indelible imprint. Whether ironically humorous or boldly inspiring, the final words of the martyr are the most distinctive and memorable.

As we might expect, many authors use the passion narratives to supply the martyrs' final words. Of the many gospels—canonical and non-canonical—available, it is noteworthy that the majority of such citations are drawn from the Gospel of Luke The citations that proved to be the most popular were Jesus' appeal to God to forgive his executioners (Luke 23:34) and his final words: "and crying out in a loud voice Jesus said, 'Father into your hands I commend my Spirit!' and having said this he breathed his last."[105] The earliest and most deliberate reenactment of the Lukan passion is found, as already noted, in the account of the death of Stephen in Acts 7: "And as they were stoning Stephen, he prayed, 'Lord Jesus, receive my spirit.' And he knelt down and cried with a loud voice, 'Lord, do not hold this sin against them.' And when he had said this, he died."[106] The majority of scholars have taken references to the commissioning of the spirit in the *acta* as references to Stephen. This is because, like Stephen, martyrs place themselves in the hands of Jesus, not God. We should be wary, however, of concluding too quickly that Stephen is the sole or even primary point of reference. As noted earlier, both the sequence of proclamations and the vocabulary of Stephen's final statements are slightly different from those of the Lukan Jesus. Stephen's final request is for the forgiveness of his executioners, whereas Jesus' parting words serve as a self-commission of his spirit to God. Furthermore, we should note that Stephen addresses his prayers to Jesus, not God. In the interim between the ascension of Jesus to heaven and the martyrdom of Stephen, Jesus has assumed the role of the recipient of prayerful requests. Even though in the second instance Jesus has acquired a more powerful role, the similarities between the two accounts are painstakingly clear. Stephen's ability to embody the final moments of the death of Jesus only elevates him in the eyes of the reader.

Just as Stephen imitates Jesus, so also a slew of martyrs imitate Stephen's *imitatio*. The Latin version of the *Acts of Carpus, Papylus, and Agathonice* depicts Carpus as an *alter* Stephen. In the original Greek version both Carpus and Aga-thonice use the language of psalmody to cry out to God for help. The citation of psalms was a hallmark of the Markan Jesus who converses with his father almost exclusively using the language of psalms of lament. The Latin redactor rides roughshod over the subtle allusions in the Greek by replacing Carpus's poetic thanksgiving with a straightforward citation from Acts 7:59: "After he had said this, as the servants piled the fire high, he looked up to heaven and said: 'Lord Jesus Christ receive my spirit.' And with these words he gave up his soul."[107] In the same way, a number of other Latin martyrdoms pick up on this idea. The soldier Julius completes his martyrdom in a similar manner, requesting that the Lord "receive my spirit together with your holy martyrs."[108] The reference to the other martyrs is a neat touch. Julius's note of the other martyrs traces the ongoing expansion of heavenly occupants. Just as Stephen's prayer to Jesus acknowledges that he has ascended to heaven, here Julius alludes to the martyrs who preceded him, including, presumably, Stephen and others. The addition of this phrase serves to acknowledge the martyrological model that he himself utilizes, a subtle tribute to his spiritual mentor.

The dramatic impact of speaking the words of Jesus is not lost on the authors of the *acta*. The narrator of *Montanus and Lucius* remarks of the newly deceased Flavian: "This then is what it means to suffer for Christ, to imitate Christ's example even in his words, and to give the greatest proof of one's faith. What a wondrous model he was of belief!"[109] The ability of the martyr Flavian to replicate the words of Jesus demonstrates the extent to which he embodied and lived scripture in every aspect of his life and death. Flavian's *imitatio* permeates his whole person to the extent that he speaks Jesus.

It is often assumed that the commissioning of one's spirit to Jesus is modeled exclusively upon the death of Stephen. This is a logical assumption, as the martyr commissions him- or herself to Jesus, not to God. We should be wary, however, of removing Jesus from the equation altogether. The presentation of Stephen as a model is predicated on his status as perfect imitator of Christ. Imitation of Stephen, therefore, necessarily implies *imitatio Christi* and places the martyr in a mimetic chain (Christ-Stephen-martyr) with Christ.

Imitating the words of Jesus at their deaths is not only important for the reader's perception of the martyrs. We should entertain the possibility that this kind of imitation transforms both the martyr and the biblical text that is cited. It alters the audience's perception of the scriptural passage itself, supplying yet another layer of prophetic importance. The words of the psalmist that became prophecies of a dialogue between Jesus and God again become prophecies of the sufferings of the martyrs. The parting words of the Lukan Jesus foreshadow the words of the martyrs.

The Flow of Blood and Water (John 19:34)

In the Johannine account of the passion, a soldier passing by the body of Jesus on the cross idly slices through his side, causing a stream of blood and water to pour forth from his side. There is no shortage of scholarly discussion of the significance of blood and water in the Fourth Gospel, and many scholars note the significance of these fluids as symbols in the nascent church.[110]

The *Letter of the Churches of Lyons and Vienne* provides an interesting example of one way in which the flow of water was understood in the church in Gaul. The martyr Sanctus is tortured using burning plates of bronze, but despite the tortures the liquid flowing from the side of Christ acts as an analgesic and spiritually strengthening tonic: "And though these did burn him, he nonetheless remained unbending and stubborn, firm in his confession of faith, cooled and strengthened by the heavenly fountain of the water of life that flows from the side of Christ."[111] The flow that seeps from the passion narrative of John into the world of *Lyons* serves to unify the two accounts. Jesus and the martyr are connected by the stream of water, and the martyr's death is constructed inside the world of the Gospel of John. The biblical allusion is not pure; the author of the *Letter of the Churches of Lyons and Vienne* dilutes the Johannine image with the imagery of the book of Revelation. The author conflates the water streaming from the side of Jesus with the heavenly fountain mentioned in Revelation 21:6.[112] The conflation makes a certain kind of sense. The Johannine Jesus, now residing in heaven, continues to hemorrhage water, which functions to fortify the martyr Sanctus physically and spiritually. The effect of the allusion is to collapse the boundaries between heaven and earth, between the life of Jesus and the life of the church, and between scripture and *acta*.[113]

A more sacramental reading of the significance of John 19:34 emerges out of the North African *Martyrdom of Montanus and Lucius*. As Flavian approaches the place of martyrdom, it begins to rain. Flavian remarks that "it was raining that water might mix with blood in imitation of the Lord's passion."[114] Flavian has a demonstrated preference for the Johannine passion, for when he arrives at the place of execution he climbs up onto a high spot[115] and delivers a parting homily on John 15:12 and unity.[116] In both cases Flavian is portrayed as consciously viewing his words and actions as an *imitatio* of the passion narrative. Like other martyrs, his actual death is an exercise in self-control. Flavian himself walks down from the hill to the place of execution, binds the blindfold around his eyes, and kneels "as if in prayer." Assuming that this prayerful stance involved extended arms, it is not a stretch to suppose that this cruciform pose is also part of the *imitatio*. Flavian's self-controlled demeanor,[117] his farewell discourse based on the words of Jesus, his interpretation of his death in light of John 19:34, and his *orans* pose all suggest a strong affinity with the Johannine passion narrative.

Conversion of the Centurion at the Cross
(Mark 15:39//Matt. 27:54//Luke 23:47)

The conversion of the military bystander at the scene of the martyr's death becomes a trope in martyrological literature.[118] The preponderance of this motif is linked, in part, to the high proportion of military martyrs in the early church. For obvious reasons, military Christians were more likely than civilians to be called upon to swear oaths, offer sacrifice on behalf of the emperor, or engage in battle, all of which offered ample opportunity for conflict with authorities and execution.[119] The large numbers of military martyrs led, in turn, to the development of a specific ideal of military martyr, a characterization that was distinctive and differed from those of civilians.[120] This is particularly apparent in late antique hagiography, where the characterization of the military martyr becomes rarefied. Certain elements of the ideal emerge earlier and are found in the earliest strata of martyrdom literature where soldier bystanders feature as converts and secondary martyrs.[121] A close examination reveals that their characterization owes much to the centurion's proclamation in the Gospel of Mark, the criminal on the cross in Luke, and the depiction of Saul/Paul in Acts. In these military converts, therefore, we find a reading of the passion narrative in which a number of Jesus sympathizers are conflated into a single figure and portrayed as Christian converts.

Despite the large amount of scholarly interest in the late antique and Byzantine "soldier-martyr," early examples are often overlooked. For both Delehaye and von Harnack, the questions were the historicity of the soldier-martyr, Christian pacifism and the motivation for the martyr's behavior, and the development of the literary stereotype. The similarities between the soldier-martyr and the biblical prototypes are almost completely ignored. Harnack acknowledges the existence of the military convert *trope* but restricts his comments to the following: "The soldier who led a Christian to execution (or was the informer) and then became a Christian himself gradually became a stereotype in the Acts of the Martyrs."[122] This is all that Harnack has to say on the matter; the unhistorical nature of the stereotype is enough for him to lose interest. Even though the "military convert" is a literary trope, we should be wary of blanket interpretations that fail to appreciate the nuances in individual narratives or address the function of the trope. Given the abundance of examples, we will focus on only three: Clement of Alexandria's account of the soldier who accompanied James the son of Zebedee to his death, Besas of the *Martyrs of Alexandria*, and Basilides in the *Martyrdom of Potamiaena and Basilides*.[123]

Arguably the earliest example of the soldier-convert is found in a fragment of Clement of Alexandria's *Hypostases* preserved in Eusebius. It is not completely impossible that Clement may have preserved some oral tradition regarding the church in Jerusalem that is otherwise lost to us. It is worth noting however, that there is no external evidence corroborating this account.[124] According to the fragment preserved in Eusebius, an individual was present who was supposed to lead James to his death and, having seen James's witness, was moved and converted.[125] From the text alone, it is difficult to ascertain the identity of the convert. It would seem from his role as escort that he serves a professional function at executions. It is most tempting to conclude that he was a soldier, but we should be reluctant to do so decisively. What is clear is the motivation behind the conversion; he is shaken up by the witness of the apostle and confesses that he himself is Christian. Being sentenced to die alongside James, the convert implores the apostle for his forgiveness. James's response, "Peace be with you," is a citation of the words of Jesus.[126] It is reminiscent of the resurrection appearances (cf. Luke 24:36; John 20:19; 20:21; 20:26) and is the phrase that Jesus uses to address his disciples. By using this term, James is aligned with the resurrected Jesus, and the soldier moves into the role of disciple.

The combination of the phrase "peace be with you" and the forgiving kiss has a somewhat liturgical ring to it and might be another reference to Eucharistic practice.[127] Perhaps the author of the martyrdom means to imply that the convert undergoes a quasi-baptismal ritual in which sins are forgiven and the Christian initiate is purified. A similar event transpires in the *Passion of Perpetua and Felicitas* when the martyrs seal their "second baptism"—their martyrdom—with a ritual kiss of peace.[128] The use of liturgical gestures and formulas emphasizes the reality of the converts' entrance into the church at the point of death. An audience listening to this story would instantly recognize the kiss of peace as a reference to baptismal and eucharistic practice and understand this as a marker of Christian identity.

A brief reduplication of this theme comes in another Eusebian narrative, the so-called martyrs of Alexandria, which relays the appearance of a sympathetic soldier-convert named Besas. Besas attempts to protect the martyrs from the attacks of the crowd and is subsequently executed.[129] Like other soldier-converts, Besas inexplicably defends the innocent martyrs from the verbal insults of the crowds. As a result he is arraigned and tried, presumably in the same manner as the Christians. The details of his trial are not included, but he is tantalizingly described as a "warrior of God." Similarly, his death is labelled, using the terminology of martyrdom, as a "great contest for piety."[130] The reference to piety suggests that like other early Christian martyrs he refused to swear an oath, declared himself to be Christian, and was executed as such. The text surely portrays Besas as a Christian martyr. The point at which Besas changes allegiance, however, is

unclear. All that can be said is that, in the world of the text, Besas becomes suf-
ficiently swayed by Christian ideologies that he is prepared to forfeit his life.

The clearest early example of the military convert comes in the *Martyrdom
of Potamiaena* or, as it is sometimes known, *The Martyrdom of Potamiaena and
Basilides*. Basilides, the soldier-convert, is included only in Eusebius's account
of the martyrdom.[131] He is identified as the soldier who leads Potamiaena to
her execution and kindly fends off attacks and insults. After her execution,
Basilides is found to be a Christian and reveals that the martyr appeared to him
in a vision and placed a wreath on his head.

While scholars are unanimously agreed that the incident is a much later
addition to the text, none have tried to account for the insertion of the incident
into the text on either historical or literary grounds. The incident is of
vital importance, however, not only because it initiates a martyrological trend
but precisely because it is so unhistorical. The incident begins in the
following way:

> No sooner had she uttered the word and received the sentence of
> condemnation, when a man named Basilides, who was one of those
> in the armed services, seized the condemned girl and led her off to
> execution. The crowd then tried to annoy her and to insult her with
> vulgar remarks; but Basilides, showing her the utmost love and
> kindness, prevented them and drove them off. The girl welcomed the
> sympathy shown her and urged the man to be of good heart: when
> she went to her Lord she would pray for him, and it would not be
> long before she would pay him back for all he had done for her.[132]

Potamiaena's statement that she would repay the helpful soldier is at once an
expression of thanks, an offering of martyr intercession, and an allusion
to Jesus' words to the penitent thief in Luke 23:34. In the cult of the saints,
Christians made similar requests of the martyrs, asking that the martyrs intercede with God on their behalf. Here, Potamiaena not only offers intercession
but guarantees repayment. As it does for the penitent criminal in Luke, this
intercession comes in the form of entry into the heavenly kingdom. Basilides's
defection to Christianity is uncovered in the normal way. He is placed in a situation where he is asked to swear an oath to the emperor and naturally refuses:
"Not long afterwards Basilides for one reason or another was asked by his fellow soldiers to take an oath; but he insisted that he was not at all allowed to do
so, since he was a Christian and made no secret of it."[133] There are dozens of
martyrdoms in which the soldier-martyr protagonist refuses to swear an oath.
Basilides's response differs inasmuch as he replies that he is unable to swear
at all. His response is an allusion to the command not to swear in Matthew

5:34. In Matthew the phrase used is μὴ ὀμόσαι ὅλω.[134] The allusion creates symmetry in the text. In her words to Basilides, the martyr Potamiaena speaks using the vocabulary of scripture. Likewise, Basilides obeys and pronounces the ethical commands of the Gospels.

The *imitatio* here is not merely a matter of phraseology; it is also a question of activity. In a recent article on Jesus' use of the psalms, H. W. Attridge has argued that New Testament portraits of Jesus reveal a figure who spoke in scripture and, more specifically, the psalms.[135] Attridge's argument is particularly significant for the study of Christly imitation in the acts of the martyrs. By speaking the words of Jesus as recorded in scripture, the martyrs imitate both his vocabulary and his very *mode* of speaking. The art of imitation works on a number of levels. This phenomenon is not necessarily the product of a literary mind. In fact, it is likely that Christians facing execution would have identified with Christ at his crucifixion and have actually quoted his words as a means of identifying themselves with their savior.[136] In the practice of martyrdom as well as the narration of it, the imitation of Christ took both verbal and physical forms.

After his confession and imprisonment, Basilides is confronted by nervous Christians who inquire about his sudden change of heart: "His brothers in the Lord came to visit him, and when they questioned him about this strange and sudden turn, he is said to have replied that three days after her martyrdom Potamiaena appeared to him at night and put a crown on his head; she said that she had requested his grace from the Lord and had obtained her prayer, and that she would welcome him before long."[137] In itself Basilides's vision of the martyred Potamiaena is not particularly remarkable. Visions of deceased saints were commonplace in the cult of the saints, and a number of other martyrdoms recount how a young martyr continued to inspire and exhort her fellow Christians after her death.[138] Basilides's vision is said to have occurred three days after the death of Potamiaena. That Potamiaena makes her first postmortem visitation after three days is a thinly veiled reference to the three days that elapsed between Jesus' death and his resurrection.[139] Like Christ, Potamiaena intercedes on behalf of the generous stranger and gains his heavenly reward.[140]

In these examples the military bystanders are swayed by the dignified and courageous deaths of the martyrs and are "converted." This would seem to indicate that some early Christians understood the death of Jesus and the responses of those around him in the same way. This is to say that the centurion's declaration was read by some as a confessional statement. This would refute the assertion of R. H. Gundry that the centurion's statement *cannot* be understood in terms of conversion to Christianity.[141] The readings of the centurion contained in the *acta* provide evidence that it can and it could.[142] The medley of biblical characters—the penitent criminal, the centurion at the cross, and even Paul—alluded to in the conversion of soldiers in the *acta* indicates there was a strong tradition of reading these characters as converts and the death of Jesus as a prompt for conversion.

Postmortem

In the earlier martyrdom accounts, the narrative ends with the death of its protagonist.[143] Resurrection and vindication are confidently asserted by the martyrs throughout their trials and passages to execution but are never explicitly described by the author.[144] There are glimpses of resurrection here and there. Bishop Fructuosus and his deacons, for example, are seen in a vision ascending to heaven—crowned and still bound to their stakes—a double allusion to both the crucifixion and ascension narratives in the Gospels.[145] Likewise, Potamiaena, as noted, makes her first postmortem appearance after three days. For the most part, however, the *acta* follow the Gospel of Mark in focusing on the martyr's death.[146] With the passage of time, editors and hagiographers supplied additional liturgical conclusions,[147] narratives of visions or miracles,[148] and secondary martyrs[149] so that the martyr's afterlife became the focus of cultic activity. Examples of these can be seen even in some of the accounts we have examined. The supplementation of a visionary event to the conclusion of a martyrdom account again parallels the form and textual history of the Markan passion narrative.

With the addition of later material, the life and death of the martyrs are fleshed out. We begin to learn something more of their personalities, eccentricities, and sayings. The focus of the congregation shifts to the intercessory powers and ongoing activitives of the martyred saints on behalf of pious supplicants. In these early examples, however, the martyrs' accomplishment is—like Christ—their deaths. They perfect and are perfected by their martyrdom by drawing their witness to completion under the executioners' sword. It is the suffering and death of the martyrs that imbues them with power and propels them above the ranks of the angels. It is to this crowning point—the significance of the martyrs's deaths—that we now turn.

3

The Savior Martyr

Throughout the history of interpretation, readers of the *acta martyrum* have sought to answer the question, Why do martyrs die? This preoccupying question has been approached in a variety of ways. Critical readers such as Ste. Croix have used historical analysis in an attempt to uncover the historical and legal situation that brought so many Christians to their deaths.[1] Others, like Donald W. Riddle, have used sociological models in an attempt to understand the psychological and sociological pressures that would cause persons to lay down their life in this way.[2] In this chapter, we will address this question from the perspective of ancient audiences; what purpose does the death of the martyr have in the minds of ancient audiences? This is essentially an exercise in historical theology and ideology.[3] We seek to uncover the ideological structures that rendered the death of the martyr meaningful and important. How did ancient Christian communities describe the deaths of their members in these circumstances? And what purpose did this kind of death serve both for the individual who died and for other Christians?

As has been argued throughout, martyrs were Christly imitators. This basic premise leads us to consider the relationship between the significance of the death of a martyr and the significance of the death of Christ. If the death of the martyr is modeled on the death of Christ, surely the *meanings* of their deaths are also related? In theological, as well as biblical, accounts of salvation history, the death of Christ is the critical salvific moment. From Anselm's sacrifice to Abelard's moral exemplar to the *Christus Victor* of Aulén and the suffering companion of Moltmann, many have struggled to articulate the significance of the death of Christ.[4] While the terminology applied to this event varies and the mechanics of salvation are the subject of considerable debate, the cross is widely recognized as the defining moment in salvation history. Ambiguous, repulsive, and indescribable though it is, the crucifixion is the saving event in the history of humankind.[5] In this event, soteriology and Christology are tightly interwoven. Who Christ was and what he did are two sides of the same coin. Explaining how they relate to one another, however, and the mechanics of the saving act is rather more difficult.

This problem becomes even more complex when we turn to an early church torn apart by erudite discussions of Christology and soteriology. Whereas modern theologians might feel bound to doctrinal assumptions regarding the nature of Christ or his unique status as the preexistent son of God, we cannot presuppose that second- or third-century Christians subscribed to these beliefs. In short, in the second and third centuries, ideas about the purpose of Jesus' death were not clearly established or uniformly maintained. Instead of concrete descriptions of how Christ saves, early Christian literature is replete with unequivocal declarations that he does save and ambiguous images of how this salvation is brought about. The waters of soteriology, then, are clearly muddied.

The martyr acts offer one avenue of exploration into ancient views of the saving death of Christ. The preponderance of language of *imitatio* and statements indicating the martyrs' desire to die like Christ has not been lost on scholarly readers of the martyrdoms. Nor has their value as interpretations of the death of Christ gone unnoted. In her work on sacrifice in the ancient church, Frances Young insightfully notes the relationship between the martyr's death and the death of Christ: "It is highly probable that the tradition that a martyr's death could expiate sin was in fact the earliest means of understanding the death of Christ."[6] Her argument that a martyr's death could "atone" for sin may be too broad, but her observation that the deaths of martyrs offer a window into early understandings of the death of Christ could not be more apt. The deaths of the martyrs mirrored the death of Jesus in function as well as in form.

Our task in this chapter is to explore the language used to describe the deaths of the martyrs and the manner in which this language fits into a variety of soteriological models. While we will be exploring the ways that the martyrdom accounts fit with these models individually, it is important to remember that these are just conceptual models. In practice the communities responsible for the martyrdom accounts constructed the deaths of the martyrs using more than one model.[7] Imagery of sacrifice, cosmic battle, and moral exemplarity is weighted differently in different accounts. The effect is that we find a wide variety of highly nuanced views of the ways in which the deaths of the martyrs served a redemptive purpose.

At risk of belaboring the point, it is important to bear in mind the diversity of opinions that these accounts represent. Even though our examination is organized thematically using soteriological models, the martyr acts do not present a consistent view on salvation. This diversity is itself instructive and exciting; it destabilizes the way in which we want to construct theological "development" historically and resists compartmentalization into theological and exegetical "schools."

At the same time as we explore the different lenses through which the deaths of the martyrs were viewed, we will reflect upon the potential problems that the death of the martyr as an *alter Christus* poses for constructions of soteriologically grounded Christology. The death of Christ, be it victory, atonement, sacrifice, or otherwise, is consistently portrayed as something unique. It was, in the words of the author of the epistle to the Hebrews, a onetime event.[8] If we presuppose—which we need not—that members of the early church recognized the uniqueness of Christ, then the martyrs offer a certain theological puzzle; if the crucifixion is the turning point in salvation history, why are the deaths of martyrs characterized in the same terms as similarly important? What does it mean for the uniqueness of Christ to say that there are Christly imitators whose deaths achieve similar results? Is it possible that some ancient Christians viewed Christ's death as the *first*, rather than the *only*, salvifically valuable death?

Martyrdom as Sacrifice

In critical studies of the ancient world the predominant lens through which the deaths of Jesus and the martyrs are viewed is one of sacrifice. A number of scholars have explored the ways in which the death of Jesus was viewed as a sacrifice for sin.[9] In the same way, it is argued, the deaths of the martyrs were cast as sacrificial offerings. In approaching this question we should note the distinction between modern and ancient usage of the term "sacrifice." In modern parlance, the word is used to refer to the act of giving something up. In the ancient world, sacrifice implied a complex set of practices and discourses. Whereas we might be tempted to use the term "sacrifice" for martyrs as a way of communicating that they "gave up" their lives, the same could not be said of the ancient world. While the concept of "dying for" something existed, we should not confuse that notion with either the linguistic or the conceptual categories that sacrifice designated in ancient contexts.[10] Sacrifice was a socioreligious phenomenon that formed an important part of the lives of ancient Jews, Greeks, and Romans.[11] In the Hebrew Bible it has an illustrious and storied history both as the cornerstone of right relations with Yahweh and as the despicable underbelly of idolatrous worship.[12] Among Greek philosophers the practice of sacrifice had value in a traditional form but was likewise subject to abuse and therefore critique. In the Roman Empire the offering of libations or incense at civic or domestic shrines served as sacrifices within the imperial cult.[13] Within the context of Christianity, sacrificial language persisted not only in descriptions of the death of Jesus but in the application of sacrificial language to liturgical practice. In seeking to appreciate the martyr's death, scholars have turned to biblical, Roman imperial, and liturgical constructions of sacrifice to provide definition and meaning.

Sacrifice in Scripture

As in other ancient cultures, sacrificial practices were a vital component of ancient Israelite and Jewish religious life. Not only did such practices form the high point of important religious festivals, but they were thoroughly ingrained in ancient society; underwriting good relations with the deity and turning the cogs of day-to-day life. The Hebrew Bible is replete with descriptions of the different sacrifices offered to God, and a number of scholars have labored to organize and analyze these sacrifices into a more general taxonomy of sacrifice. In her analysis of sacrifice in the ancient world, Frances Young groups both Greek and Jewish sacrifices into one of three forms: communion sacrifices,[14] gift sacrifices,[15] and expiatory sacrifices.[16] Young's typology of sacrifice is a useful starting point, but her categorization can force an artificial divide between her categories. A sacrifice that expiates for sin could also serve to propitiate a wronged deity in the same manner as a gift sacrifice. The distinctions between her categories are overly forceful and concrete, and we should allow for fluidity and overlap between the different types.

From among Jewish practices, two feast days have been isolated as having particular significance for early Christian understandings of sacrifice: the feast of Passover and the Day of Atonement ritual. The feast of Passover was a cultic reenactment of the sacrifice of the lamb on the eve of Israel's deliverance from Egypt. With the construction of the temple, the Passover feast was transformed from a family affair to a national pilgrimage festival. The lambs were now slaughtered in the temple the afternoon before Passover and were eaten in homes that night.

In contrast, the Day of Atonement, or Yom Kippur, was a relatively late and complex festival. The ritual element was composed of two very disparate ceremonies. The first ritual was a sin offering involving the sacrifice of a bull on behalf of the priests and a goat on behalf of the people. These rituals followed the procedures laid out in Leviticus,[17] except that on this day the high priest entered the holy of holies to sprinkle blood from each of the offerings on the mercy seat itself. In the second ceremony, a second goat was brought, and the sins of the people of Israel were transferred onto it by the priest through the laying on of hands. The goat was then dispatched into the desert. The goats in both ceremonies were brought forward together, and lots were cast to determine which goat would be sacrificed to Yahweh and which would be dispatched into the desert "to Azazael."[18]

Moving to narratives accounts of the sufferings of the people, we can see the application of sacrificial language to personal suffering in prophetic works. The idea that innocent suffering served sacrificial functions may have developed out of the "Servant Poems" of Isaiah 42:1–9; 49:1–7; 50:4–11; 52:13–53:12. In these passages the "servant" is called by God to perform a mission but is ultimately rejected, persecuted, and killed. The servant is bruised, chastised, and wounded, apparently because of the transgressions of the people. The idea that the deaths of an individual or individuals can atone for the sins of a larger group of people becomes explicit in the Maccabean literature, most particularly the description of the deaths of the so-called Maccabean martyrs in 2 and 4 Maccabees. In 2 Maccabees 7:18, the deaths of the seven brothers are interpreted as punishment for their own sins (2 Macc 7:18). In 4 Maccabees 6:29 Eleazar's blood serves as the purifying cleanser for the people, and in 17:21 the blood of the martyrs serves to purify the land. There appears to be, as van Henten has argued, a dual notion of purification taking place; the blood of the martyrs both atones for the sins of the people and cleanses the land.[19] What is implied in 2 Maccabees and explicitly proclaimed in 4 Maccabees is that the deaths of righteous individuals can serve a purificatory sacrificial purpose in atoning for the sins of others and cleansing the land of their ancestors.

Turning to the writings of the Jesus movement, we immediately run into the death of Jesus and the description of his death using sacrificial language. The interpretation of Jesus' death as a sacrifice for sin is one of the foundational concepts in judicial and substitutionary theories of the atonement. The idea that Jesus' death served to expiate sins is attributed by some to the earliest strata of the Jesus movement, perhaps even to Jesus himself.[20] Sacrificial metaphors abound throughout the Pauline epistles.[21] Jesus is the "Paschal Lamb" (1 Cor 5:7), the one who knew no sin (2 Cor 5:21; cf. the sin offering in Lev 4:8, 20–21), and the ἱλαστήριον (Rom 3:25), an ambiguous term frequently used in connection with sacrifice.[22]

At every turn, the Johannine writings amplify the sacrificial interpretation of the death of Jesus. Jesus' death is rescheduled so that he suffers death on the cross the day before Passover at the same hour as the lambs were slaughtered in the temple. Jesus offers himself as a new Paschal Lamb of the new covenant.[23] In John's Gospel, the lamb is responsible for taking away the sins of the whole world, shaping, in Young's schema, the death of Jesus as expiatory sacrifice. The epistle known as 1 John describes how the "blood of Jesus" purifies us from sin (1 John 1:7), a statement that assumes the atoning effects of Jewish expiatory sacrifice. As in Paul, Jesus is the atonement for sins (ἱλασμός 1 John 2:1) whose death can only be understood as a sacrificial offering "for us" (3:16).

In Revelation, sacrificial language is extended from Christ the lamb to his followers. In Revelation 7:14, the author describes Christ's executed followers as those who had washed their robes and made them white in the sterilizing "blood of the lamb." In 6:9 the souls of Christians who died bearing witness to Christ take up residence under the altar in the heavenly sanctuary.[24] In 14:4 they are described as the first fruits, the ἀπαρχή, who were redeemed for God and the lamb. The term ἀπαρχή resonates within sacrificial traditions in which the first portion of an offering of produce was dedicated to God.[25] Just as the term "lamb" invokes sacrificial imagery to reference the death Christ, so also those who died for Christ are portrayed using sacrificial language.

The idea that Jesus died as a sacrifice receives its fullest treatment in Hebrews, where the blood of Jesus drips over the mercy seat in a decisive purificatory moment. Throughout chapters 9 and 10 the author of Hebrews weaves in and out of biblical texts about sacrifice, combining the liturgy of the Day of Atonement with the covenant sacrifice of Exodus 24:3–8 and the tabernacle in the wilderness. The supreme offering of Jesus, the one without sin (7:26), offered a permanent cleansing of sins (1:2; 7:27; 9:12, 26; 28:10). In a single decisive sacrifice (10:12, 14), access to God is restored for all time (1:3; 4:16; 10:19). This sacrifice involved obedience to God in life as well as suffering and death (5:7–8 cf. 10:9–10) and became programmatic for the lives of the readers of Hebrews.

In Paul, the Johannine literature, and Hebrews, redemption is most forcefully articulated through reference to the blood of Christ. The same idea appears in the Apostolic Fathers, for example, First Clement 8.4; where Clement writes that the precious blood of Christ was poured out for our salvation.[26] These texts present us with a view of Christ's death as spiritual detergent, as an expiatory sacrifice that washed away sin in a manner that some argue is "strictly analogous to the sacrifices of the Old Testament."[27] The understanding of the death of Jesus as a cleansing sacrifice is one way in which sacrificial imagery and language were interpreted in the early church.

Sacrifice in the Liturgical Practice of the Early Church

Within the liturgical life of early Christians, the definition of sacrifice was broadened to include activities that suggested but did not replicate or even adopt the meaning of earlier sacrificial practices. Communal meals, hymnody, and prayer came to be understood as bloodless sacrifices of prayer that mirrored and perhaps even participated in the heavenly praises of angelic choirs in heaven. As an extension of sacrificial interpretations of the death of Jesus, Paul and the author of Hebrews use sacrificial imagery to describe the activity of members of their churches. The Lord's Supper is described in sacrificial terminology (1 Cor 10:14–22). The use of sacrificial language in connection with the Eucharist serves the dual purpose of connecting it with the sacrificial practices of Israel and temple worship and creating a kind of communal worship that rules out the need to participate in pagan sacrifices. In 2 Corinthians 2:14–16, Paul again expands the language of sacrifice so that it incorporates the acts of evangelization and preaching: "But thanks be to God, who in Christ always leads us in triumphal procession, and through us spreads in every place the fragrance that comes from knowing him. For we are the aroma of Christ to God among those who are being saved and among those who are perishing; to the one a fragrance from death to death, to the other a fragrance from life to life. Who is sufficient for these things?"[28] Here Paul utilizes the sacrificial interest in the fragrance of the cultic offering and applies it to the act of preaching the gospel.[29] The same idea lies beneath Romans 15:16, where Paul is a priest performing the "priestly sacrifice" (*hierogounta*), transforming the gentiles into an acceptable sacrifice by converting them to Christ. Paul sees himself reflected in the activities of Christ; he envisions his own life and potential death as a sacrifice to God. Weaving together the language of sacrifice and cultic service, he casts his life as a libation poured out to God (Phil 2:17).[30] For Paul, communal meals, evangelization, and personal suffering could all be reconfigured as sacrificial activities.

The application of sacrificial language to various aspects of liturgical and communal life continued as the church expanded. Even after cultic sacrifice was rendered obsolete in Christ, Christians continued to offer sacrifices of praise and "thanks-offerings."[31] Evidence of this can be found in the description of spiritualized sacrifice of thanksgiving in *Second Clement* and in the application of the term "sacrifice" to elements of the liturgy. The Eucharist, in particular, is described using a variety of sacrificial models.[32] It is understood—to use Young's typology—as a kind of communal sacrifice,[33] an offering of thanks,[34] an expiatory sacrifice,[35] an avertive sacrifice,[36] and a propitiatory sacrifice.[37] The status of the Eucharist as a sacrifice, however, was closely bound up in its relationship to Christ. The Eucharist may have supplanted Jewish forms of sacrifice, but it was nonetheless connected to the typological reading of these sacrifices present in narratives about the sacrifice of Christ's death. These examples demonstrate the extent to which sacrificial language had permeated ideas about the death of Christ and the worship of the early church. This language served to reconfigure the Christian experience as one in which Christians were joined through their "sacrificial" offering of praise to the violent sacrifice of Christ.

Against this backdrop of Eucharistic sacrifice, Robin Darling Young has explored the ritual of martyrdom as a kind of "public and liturgical act of sacrifice," a performance.[38] In describing martyrdom as public liturgy, Young refers more to the practice of martyrdom itself than to the performance of the acts of the martyrs in particular social settings, but we can assume that she intends this reading to apply to understandings of the deaths of martyrs more broadly. Her observations about the intersection of martyrdom and liturgy rightly draw our attention both to the importance of liturgical practices in shaping Christian identities and to the ritualistic and performative nature of martyrdom. In certain contexts, such as the public reading of acts of the martyrs alongside rituals of the Eucharist, the martyr's death most likely functioned as part of a liturgical reenactment of the sacrifice of Jesus. Martyrdom, in this context, would add another stratum to the *mille feuille* of early Christian Eucharistic practices, in which Levitical laws were layered with Christly self-offering and liturgical celebrations.

Sacrifice in the Roman Empire

In addition to reading dearly beloved scriptural texts steeped in the language of sacrifice, early Christians gleaned their understanding of sacrifice from the Roman society of which they were a part. The audiences of the martyrdoms, in particular, were acutely aware of the mechanics of sacrifice to Roman deities or the genius of the emperor, as it was the refusal to participate in precisely these kinds of sacrifice that habitually led to their deaths. Roman imperial cult itself was not contained neatly within the arena of religious practice. Like other forms of religiosity, it was a practice in which political, social, and religious concerns intersected and blended.[39] Participation in the imperial cult meant not only the satisfaction of a deity but also political and social conformity. As a consequence, a number of scholars have hypothesized that the imperial cult served as a means by which the elite could control the populace both socially and politically.[40]

That the discourse of martyrdom responded to Roman sacrificial ideologies is patently clear; refusal to sacrifice was the point of contention between Roman judges and Christian martyrs. It was in responding to Roman sacrifice that Christian identity was forged and martyrs were born. We might expect, therefore, to find martyrdom couched in the language of sacrifice and to see martyrs presented as acceptable Christian sacrifice in apposition to the evil Roman ones, to see sacrifice as a contested term in Christian and Roman discourses of power. To be sure, we do see this. George Heyman's analysis of discourses of sacrifice and martyrdom in the writings of the early church demonstrates this discursive process of contestation beautifully.[41] In both the New Testament[42] and the writings of church leaders he demonstrates the way in which the idea of the martyr's death as sacrifice is more common in the writings of ancient commentators than in the acts of the martyrs themselves.[43] We shall turn now to the acts of the martyrs, before forming any conclusions.

Sacrificial Language and Imagery in the Acts of the Martyrs

The preponderance of sacrificial language and the breadth of its usage in the literature and liturgy of the early church have had profound implications for the study of the *acta martyrum*. Among scholars of Christianity the predominant model for explaining the function and purpose of the martyrs' death is one of sacrifice.[44] This view is confirmed by the writings of Cyprian and Origen, whose exhortations to martyrdom use sacrificial language and imagery to describe the deaths of the martyrs. The interpretation of the martyr's death as a sacrifice, however, is greatly altered by the underlying notions of sacrifice with which the individual scholar is working.

For Francis Young, the death of the martyr functioned like sacrificial offerings of ancient Israel and Greece, which atoned for the sins of the people.[45] She argues that both the death of Christ and the deaths of martyrs were viewed as expiatory sacrifices, that is to say, they eradicated or atoned for sin. For Robin Darling Young, the martyrs' deaths serve a liturgical function that mimics the praiseful sacrifices of Christian liturgy. For Heyman, the martyrs' sacrificial deaths serve as moments of resistance and definition in the midst of imperial oppression. These slightly nuanced takes on the nature and function of sacrifice naturally produce different readings of the martyrs' deaths. It is of primary importance, therefore, that we read the martyrdom stories carefully and evaluate both the extent to which they employ sacrificial language and imagery *and* the ways in which this language functions.

Within early martyrological literature, evidence for the expiatory effect of the death of the martyr is gleaned almost exclusively from the writings of Ignatius and the *Martyrdom of Polycarp*. In his letter to the Romans, Ignatius expresses his wish that he be poured out as a libation, an image that invokes both the hopes of the apostle Paul and pagan sacrificial practice.[46] He repeatedly asks that he might be able to be a "sacrifice to God" and even describes himself as a ransom ($\dot{\alpha}\nu\tau\dot{\iota}\psi\upsilon\chi\omicron\nu$) for his Christian audience.[47] In his own mind then, Ignatius's death was sacrificial in character and served a concrete atoning purpose not only for himself but for the members of his church in Antioch. As we saw in the first chapter, Ignatius speaks of his approaching death using the language of imitation; he yearns to suffer with Christ and in imitation of him. It is reasonable for us to suppose, therefore, that he viewed his death in sacrificial terms because this was the lens through which he interpreted the significance of the death of Christ.

The same use of sacrificial terminology is found in the *Martyrdom of Polycarp*. This account is considered by most scholars, despite its difficult and complex textual history, to be the earliest example of Christian martyrdom.[48] Given the connection between the *Martyrdom of Polycarp* and Ignatius in the literary tradition, it is unsurprising that they would use language of martyrdom in a similar way to describe his death. The description of the final moments of Polycarp's life explicitly characterizes his martyrdom as a sacrifice:

> They did not nail him down then, but simply bound him; and as he put his hands behind his back, he was bound like a noble ram chosen for an oblation from a great flock, a holocaust prepared and made acceptable to God. . . . "May I be received this day among them before your face as a rich and acceptable sacrifice, as you, the God of truth who cannot deceive, have prepared, revealed and fulfilled beforehand. Hence I praise you, I bless you and I glorify you above all things, through that eternal and celestial high priest Jesus Christ."[49]

Polycarp's unsettling eagerness to be sacrificed grows ever more sinister with the extension of sacrificial language so that it incorporates divine actors; he draws Christ into the event as the "eternal and celestial high priest." The author of Polycarp uncomfortably constructs his death so that he dies at the hand of Jesus as a preordained sacrifice to God.[50] The application of priestly language to Christ is a prominent feature of Hebrews in which Christ serves as both the sacrificial victim and the high priest. The use of the distinctive term "eternal and celestial high priest" indicates that Hebrews lingers beneath the surface of Polycarp's request. The unsettling image of Polycarp's Lord and Savior poised to slice open one of his bishops is softened by the gentle reminder that he underwent a similar sacrificial experience himself. The imagery is further sweetened by its parallels with the imagery of Eucharistic offerings.[51] Just as Polycarp offered the Eucharist as an "acceptable sacrifice," so too here he offers himself in the same way. The framing of biblical sacrificial imagery within the context of liturgical practice softens the grotesque idea of the bloodthirsty deity and draws together the liturgical sacrifical interpretation of the martyr's death with the liturgical context of the martyrdom's performance.

Whatever liturgical or biblical concepts reverberate beneath the surface of the text, it is critical that we attend to the narratological function of sacrificial metaphors and language within the account itself. Polycarp's prayer implies that he sees the sacrificial nature of his death as the means by which he will be brought into the company of God. He asks that he "be received . . . as a sacrifice," a statement that implies that it is his identity as a sacrificial offering that brings him into the presence of God. This same idea is found in the elegant *Martyrdom of Conon* where the narrator uses sacrificial language to describe Conon's journey to the heavenly realm, saying that he "was brought as an offering (προσφορα) to God the king of the ages."[52] The term προσφορα is used throughout Hebrews 10 to describe sacrificial offerings to God. In using such a distinctively sacrificial term, the *Martyrdom of Conon* alludes to this particular understanding of the death of Jesus and casts the execution of Conon in the same light.

In the case of both these martyrs their sacrifice serves a personal instrumental function as the means by which the martyr is translocated to heaven. It is as sacrifices that Polycarp and Conon are brought into the presence of God. In older scholarship, it was believed that the common element underlying Jewish sacrificial practices was the idea of the vicarious death of the victim. This idea was applied to biblical sacrifice by Gese in "Die Sühne."[53] In recent years, this has been challenged by Christian Eberhart, who has pointed to the importance of the burning ritual, and particularly the grain offering, in the Levitical codes.[54] Using a linguistic analysis of the terms used to describe offerings, Eberhart argues that the burning of the offering marked the climax of the approach to God. The transformed offering ascended to God in the form of smoke. According to this approach, then, the process of burning was "the constitutive element of sacrifice."[55] Eberhart's focus on the burning rite in preference to the blood of the victim is particularly relevant to the acts of the martyrs, in which sacrificial imagery explains the transference of the martyr to heaven. The martyr acts pick up on the biblical idea that burning translocates the sacrificial offering to the presence of God. We should further note that there is no mention of an expiatory or avertive function. The martyrs' deaths do not serve as sacrifices in the sense that they expiate sin.[56] In the *Martyrdom of Polycarp*, the sacrificial model that is employed is that of the holocaust or the burnt offering, and within the martyrdom account itself, sacrificial language serves only to explain the mechanics of the martyr's ascent to heaven.[57]

The use of sacrificial imagery and language does not always imply a positive assessment of sacrifice. In the *Letter of the Churches of Lyons and Vienne*, for example, the deaths of two martyrs invoke sacrificial imagery in order to demonstrate the savage character of the martyr's opponents. Following an intense contest, Alexander and Attalus were "sacrificed" in the amphitheater.[58]

As Attalus was burned on the pyre, a "sacrificial savour arose" from his body. The sweet smell of the martyrs comes to be a literary trope, but in this context, the sacrificial imagery serves to illustrate the barbarism of those killing the martyrs.[59] Attalus labels their enjoyment of his burning flesh "cannibalism" and chastises them for their sinful actions. The "sacrifice" of the martyrs here is not a sacrifice to God but a perverse twist on the culinary functions of ancient sacrifice. The use of sacrificial language serves to heighten the reader's sense of injustice and underscores the barbaric nature of the events described. It can hardly be said to represent a positive theological interpretation of the death of Attalus but rather serves to shock and condemn.

The negative use of sacrificial imagery as a form of social and political commentary reappears much later in the Greek fourth-century *Martyrdom of Dasius*. Rather than being given the stock choice between imperial sacrifice or death, Dasius faces the unusual and rather more simple task of choosing between two different kinds of death. He could either die as a sacrificial victim to the god Saturn, or he could declare himself a Christian and die for his illegally held religious position. Dasius frames his choice in sacrificial terms: "Seeing that you force me to such a despicable act, better it is for me to become a sacrifice to the Lord Christ by my own choice rather than immolate myself to your idol Saturn."[60] In the case of Dasius the significance of the sacrificial language is made unclear by the unusual circumstances in which he finds himself. Framing his potential death in the pagan ritual as a sacrificial one is not so much an act of interpretation as straightforward description. Here he places becoming a sacrifice to Christ in antithesis to becoming a sacrifice to Saturn. Juxtaposing pagan and Christian beliefs or activities is a frequent motif in *acta*. Worship, piety, and obedience to the God(s) are contested terms in exchanges between martyrs and prefects.[61] The use of language of sacrifice in the *Martyrdom of Dasius* might be similarly strategic.[62] It packs more rhetorical, than ideological, punch.

Sacrificial language continues to resurface upon occasion in Latin martyrdoms. In the Latin recension of the *Acts of Euplius*, the redactor adds a proclamation of self-sacrifice to the martyr's defiant refusal to sacrifice to the emperor.[63] The same motif recurs in later accounts such as the Donatist *Martyrdom of Felix the Bishop*. Felix declares that he bends his neck as a sacrifice to him who abides forever,[64] and the dismembered Arcadius, upon gazing at his scattered limbs, proclaims that his "happy members" now "truly belong to God, being all made a sacrifice to him."[65]

The use of sacrificial language and imagery in *Polycarp* is markedly different from the presentation of, say, Dasius in the *Martyrdom of Dasius*. Sacrificial imagery functioned in a variety of ways: as part of the mechanics of ascent, as a reenactment of liturgical practice, to condemn the martyr's opponents, and as a response to Roman ideologies of sacrifice. In discussing the interpretation of the martyr's death as sacrifice, it is critical that we are attentive to the different rhetorical functions of sacrificial language.

In particular, we should note the difference between the use of sacrificial language in the *passiones* and its use in other scriptural and early Christian contexts. In those few instances in the martyr acts when sacrificial language *is* employed, there is almost no mention of its expiatory or purificatory function. Sin, sinfulness, and the abatement of sin are almost never mentioned as explanations for the death of the Christian. Unlike 2 and 4 Maccabees, there is little sense that individual Christians die to atone for the accumulated sin or guilt of the people. There is simply no mention of collective sin as the cause of their deaths. This is a striking departure from the idea that the language of sacrifice in 2 and 4 Maccabees influenced Christian martyrdom.[66] If we wish to trace out the development of Christian martyrdom from its presumed roots in Jewish tradition, we should be careful to note the ways in which Christian instantiations differ from their predecessors. This is one such case. Here, in discussions of the "sacrifice" of the martyr, sin does not rear its ugly head.[67]

Given the relative dearth of evidence for sacrificial interpretations of martyrdom, it is striking that scholars have seized upon expiatory sacrifice as the model de rigueur.[68] To be sure, *Polycarp* was an important text in early Christian circles, but the interest in sacrifice exhibited therein is not enough to produce a totalizing narrative of martyrdom as sacrifice. For when we look beyond Polycarp and the texts directly dependent upon it, there is a paucity of this kind of sacrificial language. That the deaths of the martyrs were sometimes interpreted in sacrificial terms is clear; sacrifice and refusal to sacrifice played an important role in Christian identity formation and discursive practice. We should resist the temptation, however, to color our understanding of the martyr's death with one sacrificial coat, to subordinate our reading of the acts of the martyrs to the views of church fathers, and to generalize about the ideology of martyrdom as a whole. As we shall see, early Christian writers interpreting the deaths of the martyrs utilized a rich *variety* of images to explain the significance of their death. Sacrifice was just one part—and, perhaps, not even the most important part—of the complex of ideas about the function of the martyr's death.

Martyrdom as Cosmic Battle

In 1931 Gustaf Aulén published his enormously influential theological work *Christus Victor*.[69] Aulén's work was essentially an attempt to recapture a patristic soteriological theory, what he termed the "classical theory of the atonement."

According to this view, Aulén argued, God—in Christ—reconciled the world to himself by delivering it from the enemies that held them in bondage: sin, death, and the devil.[70] This theory he labeled *Christus Victor*, a phrase that summed up the victorious nature of Christ's defeat of the devil.[71] In tracing out the development of *Christus Victor* in the early church, Aulén relies upon highbrow theological treatises to illustrate his argument. The same idea, however, can be seen in the acts of the martyrs, where the deaths of the martyrs are consistently portrayed as victories over the devil and evil powers. Our purpose in this section is to draw out the development of *Christus Victor* in the martyrdom accounts and reflect on what this can tell us about views of the atonement in the early church.

The devil and his servants resurface throughout the *acta* as the instigators and causes of persecution.[72] In Greek and Latin martyr acts from the second century onward, the devil becomes increasingly popular as the cause of persecutions, seeking to corrupt the martyrs, and active in the work of those who seek to destroy them. Roman prosecutors and soldiers are characterized as servants or agents of the devil, who works through them to attack the church. Given their propensity for executing Christians, the vilification and demonization of the Roman authorities is unsurprising. The martyrs, conversely, are cast as soldiers of God. Consequently, the verbal and physical exchanges between the martyrs and their persecutors are portrayed as grand battles between God's emissaries and Satan. The devil is armed with torturous devices and cruel punishments, and the martyrs are armed with their Christian proclamation. Martyrdom is reconceived as cosmic battle.[73] In the end, however, the result is always the same; with their deaths the martyrs trample the devil and emerge victorious.

This construction of the deaths of the martyrs views them as warriors in the cosmic conflict between good and evil and as participants in God's conquest of the devil. The portrait of the martyrs as victors over Satan fits with Aulén's *Christus Victor* model and the apocalyptic idea that the witnesses to Christ assist him in triumphing over the devil.[74] This generalized picture of martyrs as participants in the cosmic battle requires further definition. While it is certainly true that the idea was prevalent among a variety of Christian groups throughout antiquity, the extent to which it resonated within these communities varied enormously. A wide spectrum of interpretative possibilities presented themselves to those authors who wanted to involve the devil in their account. Some *acta* merely refer to the Romans as agents of the devil; others reflect at length upon the triumph of the martyr over evil. In the subsequent section we will trace out the emergence of the *Christus Victor* theme in the *acta* and its significance for the history of ideas.

Greek Martyr Acts

While many Greek *acta* refer to the activity of the devil in the world, not all of these references are original. It is noteworthy that references to the devil in early Greek *acta* appear to be inserted largely by later redactors or translators. For example, while the devil is nowhere to be seen in the Greek, he becomes a motivating force in the Latin translation of the *Acts of Phileas*.[75] The original Greek version has no mention of the devil at all, but the Latin redaction—perhaps under the influence of 1 Peter 5:8—introduces a warning against the predatory devil.[76] The introduction of the devil into these accounts by later translators served to bring the martyrdoms into line with the taste and worldview of later Latin hagiographic audiences who become accustomed to this idea in their own martyrdom accounts.

The introduction of the devil in the editing of martyrdom accounts did not take place only in the context of translating stories for Latin audiences but also formed part of Greek editorial traditions. For example, the fifth-century editor of the philosophically styled *Acts of Apollonius* elaborates on the importance of the martyr's *dies natales* by describing it as the day of the martyr's conquest over the evil one.[77] Without the liturgical additions, the body of the account bears no traces of ideas about the devil.[78] Apollonius is presented as a rhetorician and philosopher in the tradition of Socrates and provides logical arguments for his refusal to sacrifice. The reference to conquest of Satan seems completely out of keeping with the tone and argumentation of the rest of the account. A similar incongruity presents itself in the redaction history of the *Acts of Justin*. The *acta* survive in three recensions—short, middle, and long—with each recension representing a later period of development.[79] The insertion of references to Satan and his involvement in the persecution into the opening of the account grows stronger through the series of redactions. In the earliest recension, A, there is no mention of Satan at all. The opening of the *acta* merely designates the decrees to sacrifice to the emperor as "wicked." This idea is somewhat expanded in the beginning of recension B to create an antithetical relationship between the "impious" Romans and "pious" Christians. Again, however, there is no mention of Satan or evil. It is only in the third recension, C, that Satan is named as the driving force behind the persecutions. The recension begins:

> While the wicked Antoninus wielded the scepter of the Roman
> empire, Rusticus happened to be the despicable prefect at Rome, a
> terrible man, a plague, and filled with all impiety. Once while he was
> sitting at the tribunal, a group of the saints was brought before him
> as prisoners, seven in number. For this was eagerly sought after by

the ministers of Satan, to arrest them, afflict them with cruel
torments, and thus deliver them to death by the sword.[80]

The hostility toward the Roman accusers and prefects escalates throughout the
three recensions, but it is only here in the latest edition of the *acta* that Satan is
named as the source of the attacks. A further allusion to personified evil is
added later in the account where Justin's philosophical maxim that no one of
sound mind turns from impiety to piety is edited so as to include a reference to
the "soul-destroying demons."[81] References to Satan seem out of keeping with
the tone of the philosophical first recension.[82] In the early editions of both the
Acts of Justin and *Acts of Apollonius*, it is the all-consuming judgment of God that
the martyrs seek to escape. This is in contrast to the fires of Gehenna and Satan
mentioned in later texts more concerned with evil and hell.[83] It seems likely,
therefore, that the references to Satan are later editorial additions. These redactions serve to "update" the ideology of the martyrdoms for later audiences
accustomed to the more dualistic, dramatic, and horror-filled accounts emerging out of the Latin West.

Curiously, the introduction of what is usually considered an "apocalyptic"
theme into some of the early Greek martyrdoms takes place—at the earliest—
during the latter part of the fourth century, a period of relative peace for Christians. Traditionally, scholars attribute "apocalyptic" themes such as battle with
Satan to a situation of social oppression or marginalization. Apocalypticism, it
is argued, is the product of persecution.[84] It is startling to observe that it was
only during a period of peace that apocalyptic themes made their way into the
Greek martyrdoms. The aesthetics of Christian audiences rather than struggle
or persecution in the church, therefore, motivated the introduction of "apocalyptic" elements into Greek martyrdoms in late antiquity. Such evidence seems
to undermine the scholarly assumption that apocalyptic literature is the daughter of oppression and forces us to consider the possibility that—*Kleinliteratur* or
not—apocalyptic themes were aesthetically pleasing to ancient audiences.

When it comes to the paucity of interest in the devil among early Greek
acta, the *Letter of the Churches of Lyons and Vienne* is the exception that proves
the rule. The battle between Christ and the devil motivates the actions of the
characters of the piece, the demonic and divine battling it out in the bodies of
the martyrs. The particular interest in the devil and cosmic battle we see in
Lyons can be accounted for in two ways. The first is the text's literary affinity
with the book of Revelation. Revelation is cited throughout and provides cosmic underpinnings to the whole work. The second factor is the geographic
origin of the document and its historical and theological context. It is preserved
in Eusebius but is apparently a transcript of a letter sent by two churches in

Gaul—Lyons and Vienne. This would place the document in close physical and temporal proximity to Irenaeus, the bishop of Lyons during this time. If we make the not unreasonable assumption that the content of Irenaeus's sermons corresponded to the content of his literary production (or at least a homiletical trend in second-century Lyons), then it stands to reason that his congregation was exposed to his budding *Christus Victor* soteriology.[85] As such, we would expect that an account of martyrdoms produced in the same region at roughly the same time as Irenaeus would reflect a similar interest in the cosmic battle, and it does. Or, to posit a more nuanced hypothesis, that Lyonnais Christianity— of which both *Lyons* and Irenaeus are representative—was apocalyptically inclined.

The narrative is replete with references to demonic interference in the world, so much so that the devil even becomes an actor in the narrative, complete with thoughts, suppositions, and assumptions. The role of Satan in the account is both general in the sense that he orchestrates the torture and execution of Christians and personal in the sense that he is embroiled in individual struggles with martyrs.[86] These individual encounters employ military and athletic imagery to describe the struggle and eventual victory of the martyr over the devil or adversary.

Sanctus is the first martyr to achieve victory over Satan. His witness is contained in the sufferings of his body, which is distorted and broken but is nonetheless the site of Christ's victory over Satan: "But his body bore witness to his sufferings, being all one bruise and one wound, stretched and distorted out of any recognizably human shape; but Christ suffering in him achieved great glory, overwhelming the Adversary, and showing as an example to all the others that nothing is to be feared where the Father's love is, nothing painful where we find Christ's glory."[87] The reference to Satan, and more precisely to conquest over Satan, is in this instance a victory of Christ. The crumpled body of the martyr is the locus of Christ's struggle with the adversary. All the same, he is an agent in Christ's victory, as it is his bodily sufferings that earn glory. The motif of Christ triumphing over Satan is also exemplary as Sanctus is described as a pattern, a ὑποτύπωσις.[88] In this instance the virtue to be imitated is courage, not, as is more usually supposed, obedience.[89] Courage resurfaces in the description of the torture of Biblis that follows immediately on the heels of Sanctus's torture. The devil mistakenly thinks that Biblis is a coward and tortures her in the hopes that she will slander the Christians. Again, the focus on courage, over and against cowardice, is a central motif. The devil feeds on the supposed cowardice of the martyr and is conquered by her courage.[90]

Throughout the narrative, the deaths of the martyrs are interpreted as both exemplary and inspirational and as victories over Satan. The language of victory

is occasionally tied to military or athletic imagery but is most consistently connected to the conquest of Satan. The death of Blandina, in particular, serves a
dual function as example and triumph. Her torture in a cruciform pose incites
the admiration and excitement of bystanders, and its efficacy is summed up in
the following way: "Thus for her victory in further contests she would make
irreversible the condemnation of the crooked serpent, and tiny, weak, and
insignificant as she was she would give inspiration to her brothers, for she had
put on Christ, that mighty and invincible athlete, and had overcome the Adversary in many contests and through her conflict had won the crown of immortality."[91] The fusion of athletic imagery and biblically derived elements of the
cosmic myth is apparent in the description of Blandina as putting on the "invincible athlete," Christ. The description of the devil as the "crooked serpent" can
be understood both as an allusion to the "Fall of Man" in Genesis and as a reference to the primordial beast Leviathan (cf. Isa 27:1).[92] In the case of the former,
this reading places the work of Christ in Blandina firmly within the scope of
salvation history. The curse brought about by the serpent is reversed by the
martyr's death. In the case of the latter, relating Blandina to the primordial sea
monster gives her death a kind of cosmic significance. In either reading, the
permanency of the effect of her death is highlighted as something of great cosmic importance.

The cosmic battle imagery endures to the end of the work. The devil himself is a voracious and gluttonous beast who eagerly seeks to consume the
Christians: "Because of the sincerity of their love this became the greatest of all
the contests which they waged against the Demon, to the end that the throttled
Beast might be forced to disgorge alive all those whom he at first thought he
had devoured."[93] The language of consumption is striking here; not only does
the beast consume the martyrs, but their love forces him to vomit them back
up. The image of the devil swallowing the martyrs may be familiar to readers of
Aulén; the idea of the devil being tricked into swallowing the Christological
fishhook is one of the most distinctive images of his work. Aulén explains the
consumptive trick as follows: "When the Godhead clothes itself in human
form, the devil thinks that he sees a uniquely desirable prey . . . therefore he
accepts the offered prey; as a fish swallows the bait on the fish-hook, so the
devil swallows his prey, and is thereby taken captive by the Godhead."[94]

Aulén attributes the fishhook metaphor to Gregory of Nyssa.[95] Traces of
this idea, he adds, are present in Irenaeus and Origen, but the image reaches
its fullest exposition in Gregory.[96] Yet, as we have seen, this image reverberates
strongly in *Lyons*, where the devil repeatedly and mistakenly attempts to devour
the Christians. Even though the fishhook itself is not mentioned, both the
account of Biblis and the summary of the events at the end of the letter describe

the devil as a greedy beast eager to swallow the martyrs and being forced to disgorge them alive when he realizes his mistake. This is the same image that later authors such as Gregory of Nyssa and John of Damascus apply to Christ. Both of these authors employ the same image of swallowing and disgorging in their summaries of Christ's victory. Gregory of Nyssa writes:

> For since, as has been said before, it was not in the nature of the opposing power [the devil] to come in contact with the undiluted presence of God, and to undergo His unclouded manifestation, therefore, in order to secure that the ransom in our behalf might be easily accepted by him who required it, the Deity was hidden under the veil of our nature, that so, as with ravenous fish, the hook of the Deity might be gulped down along with the bait of flesh, and thus, life being introduced into the house of death, and light shining in darkness, that which is diametrically opposed to light and life might vanish; for it is not in the nature of darkness to remain when light is present, or of death to exist when life is active.[97]

And again in John of Damascus: "Wherefore death approaches, and swallowing up the body as a bait is transfixed on the hook of divinity, and after tasting of a sinless and life-giving body, perishes, and brings up again all whom of old he swallowed up."[98] In Gregory of Nyssa's statement the "power" to which he refers is the "enemy" described in the previous chapter.[99] By the time we reach John of Damascus, who uses Gregory as his source, the satanic enemy of Gregory has morphed into death, if indeed they were ever truly separate. In both these formulations, the death of Christ becomes the trick that forces the opposing force to disgorge "all" whom he had previous swallowed.

Even though the *Letter of the Churches of Lyons and Vienne* does not mention the fishhook itself, the complex of ideas about the devil swallowing and disgorging Christians as a result of the victory of Christ underlies all these accounts. The similarity between these later soteriological treatises' views of the devil and the perspective of the *Letter of the Churches of Lyons and Vienne* is striking and can hardly be accidental. *Lyons* was composed circa 177, some 200 years before Gregory of Nyssa became bishop. Its composition as a letter to the churches in Asia indicates that it was intended to circulate outside of the province of Gaul and was thus highly likely to have been read by the Cappadocian Fathers. While some scholars have argued that references to the devil are the work of later redactors, they have consistently dated these passages to—at the latest—the third century.[100] Even the most skeptical view of the provenance of the *Letter of the Churches of Lyons and Vienne* would date it before the lifetime of Gregory of Nyssa.[101]

This is not to say, however, that the *Letter of the Churches of Lyons and Vienne* is either the literary or conceptual source for Gregory of Nyssa's formulation of the fishhook metaphor. Rather, both the martyrdom account and the church father draw upon a common homiletical trope of the devil as a predatory sea monster and Christ as the means by which Christians are disgorged. The myth of the devil as a sea monster can be traced back to the book of Revelation and the primordial sea monster of the Psalms, Job, and Isaiah. In early Christian circles the connection between the sea monster and death was also well attested, the large fish of Jonah serving as a cipher for death on the walls of Roman catacombs.[102] The mechanics of salvation present in the *Letter of the Churches of Lyons and Vienne*, therefore, are part of a particular construction of cosmology that was widely diffused throughout early Christian circles.

The ramification of this evidence for historical theology is quite startling. To begin with, the metaphor of Satan as the primordial sea monster who swallows and regurgitates Christ and Christians does not originate with Gregory of Nyssa. It would appear to be a traditional interpretative move derived from a reading of Satan as Leviathan. Gregory may have developed his articulate exposition of this theme from *Lyons* or merely as a part of the expository inheritance he gleaned from his predecessors. In either case, he is not the author of this idea; it began some 200 years earlier and was circulated widely. In addition, the evidence suggests that the origins of this motif lie within the realm of popular martyrological, homiletical, and artistic discourse, not erudite theological debate.[103] This is a significant observation, inasmuch as it demonstrates both the theological character of the *acta* and the intersection between the *acta* and theological discourse.

Moreover, it is in itself significant that the earliest extant example of this famous metaphor is used not of Christ but of his imitators. While Aulén himself certainly allows room for the extension of the *Christus Victor* model to the church, he describes this in vague terms, writing that "recapitulation . . . continues in the work of the Spirit in the church."[104] The *Letter of the Churches of Lyons and Vienne* provides concrete examples of the ways in which the triumph over Satan continued to be performed in the deaths of members of the church, yet there are no such examples in Aulén. This has left him open to critique by later scholars, who see in his model a cosmic drama in which there is no place for individual agency. If we read the classical model in light of the *Letter of the Churches of Lyons and Vienne*, however, it is clear that individual Christians could participate in the great cosmic drama. The triumph of good over evil includes the followers of Christ as well as Christ himself.

Once we turn to Decian martyrdoms, the devil becomes a major player in the events that bring the martyrs to their deaths. He becomes the architect and instigator of persecution and torture and begins to live up to his title "the Adversary." In the *Martyrdom of Polycarp*, some references to the devil are redactional.[105] The Moscow manuscript contains an incident in which Polycarp denounces Marcion as the firstborn of the devil.[106] On this occasion, the reference to Satan appears to be part of the heresiological interest of the redactor. Other references to the devil are built into the narrative itself. In the opening summary of the persecutions, the author labels the tortures stratagems of the devil (*Mart. Pol.* 3). The devil's primary focus, however, is on preventing the Christians from preserving the body of Polycarp:

> The jealous and evil one, who is the adversary of the race of the just, realizing the greatness of his witness, and his unblemished career from the beginning, seeing him now crowned with the garland of immortality and the winner of an incontestable prize, prevented us even from taking up the poor body, though so many were eager to do so and to have a share in his holy flesh. Hence he got Nicetes, Herod's father and Alce's brother, to petition the governor not to give up his body.[107]

The passage serves to explain why the Christians did not collect the body of Polycarp for posterity and thus fits with the interest in relics that preoccupied the late antique church. In the context of the cult of the saints, later writers felt that it was necessary to explain the absence of the physical remains of a saint in their community. Given the large number of stories relaying the miraculous recoveries of saints' bodies after the fact, a weighty excuse was required to account for the loss of the great Polycarp, and the devil served as a handsome scapegoat. In the *Martyrdom of Polycarp*, the devil manipulates the mind of Nicetes, son of the biblically named Herod, so that he arranges for the body's cremation. The passage is reminiscent of Luke 22:3, in which the devil plants the idea of betrayal into the mind of Judas Iscariot.[108] The function of the devil is primarily mechanistic; he thwarts the best efforts of Christians and serves as an explanatory device in the narration of the story.

The fourth-century Greek text the *Martyrdom of Dasius* is remarkable for a number of reasons, not least of which is its preoccupation with the martyr's battle with Satan. The account of the soldier Dasius's involvement in a festival of Saturn is strikingly different from the usual circumstances that brought Christian soldiers to their death.[109] The author of the *acta* goes to great lengths to portray the festival as demonic, even recounting how those Christians participating in the event dressed up like the devil:

For on the first day of January, foolish Greeks who call themselves
Christians march in a great procession disguised, wearing the
costume and appearance of the Devil. Having changed their features,
clad in goatskins, they renounce the grace in which they were reborn
and take hold of the evil in which they were born. Though they
confessed at the time of their baptism to renounce the Devil and all
his devices, they once again serve him by their wicked and shameful
actions.[110]

In contrast to the more usual task of demonizing the Roman accusers, this
story sets out to tarnish Christians who continued to participate in pagan festivals by branding them devil worshipers. The act of dressing up as the Devil is a
neat play on the baptismal concept of "putting on Christ" that further serves to
contrast the holy and profane. The implicit alignment of pagan festivals with
demons is a common feature in other *acta*, but it is at its most explicit here
where Christians renege on their baptismal promises and serve Satan instead.
It may well be that the narrative reflects a degree of religious syncretism among
Christians who believed that participation in this kind of festival was compati-
ble with Christianity. The lone opponent of the practice is Dasius, who finds
himself in the extraordinary position either of becoming a sacrificial offering to
Saturn or of declaring himself a Christian and being executed anyway. Placed
in a difficult situation, Dasius opts for the more pragmatic death of a Christian;
at least he can enjoy eternal life in heaven. Dasius's choice is framed in terms
of his rejection of the devil: "Having recognized this as a worthless custom, the
blessed Dasius had trodden upon the world with its deceptions, had spat upon
the Devil with his procession and had yoked himself to the crucified Christ and
came forth as a champion against the Devil's shame."[111] The fusion of athletic
and cosmic battle imagery reappears here.[112] Dasius binds himself to Christ
and becomes his athletic champion. His conquest is complete in his confession
of the Trinity, by which he overthrows the "devil's madness."[113] Once again, in
this account, the triumph of the martyr is expressed using a fusion of athletic
imagery and notions of triumph over Satan.

The interpretation of the martyr's death as a conquest over Satan is again
explicit in the *Martyrdom of Agape, Chione, and Irene*, a Diocletian martyrdom
set in Thessaloniki in Macedonia in 304 C.E. The deaths of the martyrs serve to
crush the unseen demons and deliver them to the flames to which they belong:
"Since the arrival and appearance of our Lord and Savior Jesus Christ . . . we
have now begun to conquer unseen enemies and the invisible substance of the
demons has been handed over to the flames by pure and respectable women
who were full of the Holy Spirit."[114] At the end of the first court hearing the

Roman magistrate sentences the three young women to death by burning. The mode of their execution is given a theological twist, as they will quite literally fight fire with fire. The editor notes that this short time in the fire enabled them to "overcome those that are devoted to fire, that is, the Devil and his heavenly armies of demons."[115] The phrase "heavenly armies of demons" appears to be an allusion to the war in heaven in Revelation 12 and the idea that the devil and his demons were rebellious angels in heaven. We should note that the martyrs' conquest of the demons is connected to the life of Christ. The author remarks that it is "since the advent and the presence on earth of our Lord and Savior" that Christians have begun to crush the demons. The turn of phrase presupposes both that Christ was preexistent prior to his appearance on earth and that his presence effected a change in the world. This change manifests itself in the newfound abilities of Christians to triumph over the demons, something that they presumably could not do before.

Latin Martyr Acts

Crossing the linguistic divide from Greek to Latin, we encounter an explosion of cosmic battle imagery in the Latin *acta*.[116] The devil's efforts to secure the death of Christians become a literary trope in Latin *acta*. They do not just reflect a stylistic preference but are representative of a particular worldview. Roman soldiers are consistently portrayed as the agents of the devil and their actions part of the devil's work.[117] In the *Acts of Julius the Veteran* the salary with which the officials tempt the retiring soldier is labeled Satan's money.[118] The cosmic battle motif is particularly strong in North African martyrological tradition, beginning with the early third-century *Perpetua and Felicitas* and continuing in the fourth-century Donatist *acta*.

The motif of trampling Satan underfoot becomes a literary and ideological commonplace among the Latin *acta* earlier than the Greek. In the conclusion to the fourth-century Greek *Martyrdom of Fructuosus and Companions*, the author notes that the martyrs are "crowned with a diadem and a crown that does not fade because they trod underfoot the Devil's head." The image of the devil's head crushed under the feet of the conquering martyr draws upon the mythology of both Genesis 3 and the war in heaven in Revelation 12. The trampling of the devil underfoot is a return to the primordial garden and a reminder of the serpent's curse (Gen 3:15). In Revelation a war breaks out in heaven between the angels of God, led by Michael, and the devil and his angels. In the ensuing battle the devil, variously described as a serpent, a dragon, and Satan, is thrown out of heaven and down to earth by the archangel. The devil falls to the earth, where he continues his efforts to destroy the children of God. Subsequent iconographic representations of Michael depict him trampling the head of the dragon underfoot. In Revelation the victory over the devil is connected to the witness of those who give their lives. The visionary hears a voice, which proclaims salvation: "Now have come the salvation and the power and the kingdom of our God and the authority of his Messiah, for the accuser of our comrades has been thrown down, who accuses them day and night before our God. But they have conquered him by the blood of the Lamb and by the word of their testimony, for they did not cling to life even in the face of death."[119] In artistic representations, it is Michael who casts the devil out of heaven. In Revelation, those who did not cling to life in the face of death conquer the devil both by the blood of the lamb and by their witness (τῆς μαρτυρίας αὐτῶν). Revelation may not have fully formed the idea of martyrdom, but it certainly promotes the idea that bold testimony and a willingness to give up one's life serve to conquer Satan. As early as the end of the first century C.E., therefore, some early church writers saw the testimony and death of Christians as playing a role in the cosmic battle between good and evil. It is easy to see how this passage of Revelation came to be reinterpreted in light of the deaths of Christians in the early church. It is likewise clear how rereadings of this passage led to the idea that martyrs conquered the devil with their deaths and contextualized the deaths of Christians within this cosmic battle.

Nowhere is the ideological dependence upon Revelation 12 more apparent than in the famous vision of the serpent in the early third-century Latin *Passion of Perpetua and Felicitas* 4.3–7. In the vision Perpetua sees a ladder stretching toward the heavens. Weapons embellish the sides of the ladder and threaten to cause harm to anyone who dares to climb it:

> At the foot of the ladder lay a dragon of enormous size, and it would attack those who tried to climb up and try to terrify them from doing so. And Saturus was the first to go up, he who was later to give himself up of his own accord. He had been the builder of our strength, although he was not present when we were arrested. And he arrived at the top of the staircase and he looked back and said to me "Perpetua, I am waiting for you. But take care; do not let the dragon bite you." . . . Slowly, as though he were afraid of me, the dragon stuck his head out from underneath the ladder. Then using it as my first step, I trod on his head and went up. [120]

The image of Perpetua treading on the head of the dragon as she ascends the ladder to heaven becomes emblematic for later martyrdoms that equate trampling the dragon's head with conquest of Satan.[121] It takes its leave from the image in Revelation, of the dragon cast out of heaven to wage war against

Christians on earth. The vanquishing of Satan from heaven in the cosmic battle is rewritten in the image of the martyrs trampling the devil's head on their path to the heavens. In a fulfillment of the serpent's curse (Gen 3:15), Perpetua becomes an actor on the cosmic stage, is propelled outside of history, and steps into the world of biblical mythology. In a reversal of the "Fall of Man," she tread's on Satan's head to reenter the paradisiacal garden. In this way, the martyr is drawn into the narrative of the cosmic battle between good and evil; as we will see, their actions become associated with those of the angelic armies, and their deaths serve to reinforce the conquest over Satan.

The portrayal of the martyr's death using the language of conquest of the devil is strongest among North African *acta*.[122] This trend appears to have been inaugurated by the famous diary of Perpetua, who litters her journal with biblically based images of triumph over Satan. In addition to her vision of the dragon, discussed earlier, Perpetua recalls a dream in which she is transformed into a man and wrestles with an Egyptian in the arena. Upon waking, she interprets her dream as an impending struggle with the forces of evil. She writes, "When I awoke I realized that it was not with wild animals that I would fight but with the Devil, but I knew that I would win the victory."[123]

The *Passion of Perpetua and Felicitas* was an extraordinarily popular account, particularly in North Africa, and as a result exerted considerable influence over the style and content of subsequent *acta*. The consistent interpretation of Perpetua's martyrdom in terms of victory over Satan becomes a trope in later North African martyrdoms that sought to recapture the magic of Carthage's favored daughter.

The *Martyrdom of Marian and James* is one of two extant North African *acta* whose authors worked in conscious imitation of the *Passion of Perpetua and Felicitas*. Throughout the account, the devil attempts to consume, capture, and destroy the Christians. Persecution, torture, and execution are a result of his efforts. The devil himself is insatiate, angry,[124] deceptive,[125] and maddened with hunger for the martyrs.[126] This animalistic portrait serves, no doubt, to juxtapose the controlled, fasting, and dispassionate Christians with their opponents. Once again, the deaths of both the martyrs and Christ are described as "victories,"[127] a description that implicitly aligns the deaths of the martyrs with that of Christ as both are described using the same language of victory over Satan.

References to the devil in the Latin martyrdoms are more than mere apocalyptic window dressing. They make carefully constructed theological statements about the cosmic drama and the martyrs' place in it. *Montanus and Lucius*, another North African martyrdom modeled on *Perpetua and Felicitas*, provides an explanation of the mechanics of the martyrs' triumph over Satan that so closely parallels Aulén's *Christus Victor* theory; it could have been written by the author himself. Like *Marian and James*, the account links the individual accomplishments of the martyrs to the death of Jesus: "The more intense the temptation, the more powerful is the one who conquers it within us: indeed, it is not a struggle, but rather a victory under the shield of the Lord. To God's servants it is nothing to be killed; and hence death is nothing when the Lord crushes its sting, conquers its struggle, and triumphs by the trophy of the cross."[128] The mention of the cross here is very significant as it links the conquest of the devil and death by the martyrs to the triumph of the cross.[129] Their conquest is tied to Christ crushing death by the cross. In the *Martyrdom of Montanus and Lucius*, the triumph is over both the devil and death. The martyrs' victory lays the Devil low in 6.4 and 10.2, but they also conquer death in 19.6. In his summary of ancient sources, Aulén struggles to find examples where conquest language is linked to the cross.[130] The *Martyrdom of Montanus and Lucius* fills this lacuna in Aulén's work; the function of the deaths of the martyrs is modeled on and follows upon the triumph of the cross. The cross is the decisive act that enables imitators of Christ to overcome the devil and death.

At the same time as *Martyrdom of Montanus and Lucius* articulates the martyrs' death as conquest of the devil and death, it utilizes the language of "ransom." The author of the related *Martyrdom of Marian and James* summarizes the efficacy of the deaths of the martyrs in the following way: "For here too he works ever with the love of a father, to the end that the very ransom we believe to be paid by our own blood is granted to us by God almighty."[131] The use of the term "ransom" is, again, a distinctive one. Biblical and patristic authors use the concept of "ransom" to describe the saving work of the death of Christ.[132] The concept proves problematic for later authors who debate to whom the ransom is paid; is it paid to the devil or to God?[133] Aulén argues that in the classical theory of atonement God pays the ransom to himself out love for humankind. In the *Martyrdom of Montanus and Lucius* the same idea is present; the ransom paid in blood is a gift from the paternal God. The fascinating part is that here, the idea is applied to the deaths of martyrs. The blood of the martyrs is the ransom paid by the love of God. The extension of the ransom idea so that it incorporates not only the death of Christ but also the deaths of martyrs is striking and has astonishing repercussions for the construction of the classical theory of atonement. Whereas in Aulén's formulation, human beings are helpless pawns in the cosmic battle, here they have agency and importance. To be sure, the victory of Christ is the event that enables them to achieve victories, but their own deaths have salvific significance. They are not only empowered to triumph over Satan; their deaths serve the same role as "ransoms" to God.

Our brief survey of cosmic battle ideology in the *acta martyrum* yields some startling conclusions for both historical theology and the study of martyrdoms.

First, popular though it was, *Christus Victor* ideology was not ubiquitous in portrayals of the martyrs' deaths. With the exception of the *Letter of the Churches of Lyons and Vienne*, it is virtually ignored in second-century Greek *acta* and was introduced by later redactors into the earliest martyrdoms. Interest in the cosmic battle gained impetus in the third and fourth centuries, particularly among Latin authors. Geographically speaking, the theme is more highly developed in North African martyr acts and finds a particular home in the work of later Donatist authors. It would be a mistake to attempt to use this evidence to draw firm conclusions about the geographic distribution of *Christus Victor* in general. Cosmic battle imagery plays an important role in the soteriologies of many prominent Greek theologians and homilists. What the geographic and linguistic evidence would suggest is that there was a shift in the literary tastes of early Christians in the period. With the dispersion of popular martyrdom accounts like the *Passion of Perpetua and Felicitas*, Christian authors in the East developed a taste for martyrdom narratives cast as cosmic battles. This observation has important ramifications for the understanding of the function of apocalyptic literature and imagery in ancient Christianity. It suggests that apocalyptic literature had aesthetic, as well as cathartic, value.

In the history of ideas, the *acta* fill a lacuna in the development of the apocalyptic cosmic myth into Aulén's *Christus Victor*. In his narration of the evolution of *Christus Victor*, Aulén moves from a discussion of Irenaeus to the patristic authors of the fourth century. The *acta* demonstrate the dissemination and gradual development of this idea in the second to fourth centuries. Additionally, their constant allusion to Revelation 12 demonstrates the vital role that the Apocalypse played in the evolution of this idea. The triumph over Satan as soteriological event is no longer the intellectual product of the ecclesiastical elite. We do not need to attribute *Christus Victor* to the genius of distinguished church fathers like Gregory of Nyssa or even Irenaeus. For while their individual contributions were important, their arguments formed part of and drew upon a traditional homiletical tradition that viewed salvation as a battle and cast Satan as the deathly sea monster vanquished by Christ.

Perhaps most important, the *acta* can redress the rather narrow purview of Aulén's work. Aulén's myopic focus on Christ renders his characterization of ancient views of the triumph over Satan one-sided and incomplete. The triumph of Christ over Satan is programmatic and instructive for other Christians who are drawn into the cosmic battle by his example. Christians do not stand helpless on the sidelines as Christ battles the devil; they are the battlefield on which Christ and the devil contest with one another, and they are soldiers in the war on Satan.

At the same time, our survey has significance for the study of the martyr acts. In the history of scholarship, references to the work of the devil have often led to the characterization of the *acta* as superstitious or *Kleinliteratur*. Our study suggests that portrayal of the deaths of the martyrs as victories over Satan can be understood as theologically instructive. References to Satan are not superstitious folklore; they reflect an emerging theological trend in the early church. They form an important part of the history of the *Christus Victor* model of salvation and enable us to trace out the history and development of this idea. Martyrdom stories may appear sensationally superstitious, but they can easily be read as earnestly theological.

Martyrdom as Model

Above all else, the deaths of the martyrs are viewed as models for the audiences of the *acta*.[134] The basic premise of imitating the moral conduct of a model was, as we saw in the first chapter of this book, a fundamental premise in Greco-Roman philosophical, political, pedagogical, and religious circles. In exhorting their congregants to imitate their behavior, founder figures like Paul were no different from their philosophical compatriots. Indeed, the literature of the Jesus movement is permeated with exhortations to imitate Christ, Paul, and the heroes of Israel.[135] These exhortations were particularly grounded in the models' experience of suffering and persecution. In martyrs the early church found champions of this *imitatio* ethic who were held up both as imitators of Christ and as models for attentive congregants. In this way, the authors of the *acta* presented martyrs both as models for emulation and as the perfect imitators of Christ.

The use of moral *exempla* hardly began with the *acta martyrum*. The author of Hebrews provides a lengthy list of examples drawn from the history of Israel to demonstrate to his audience the merit of faithfulness. By happy coincidence, a number of these heroes exhibited faithfulness despite their persecution. The technique of providing lists of *exempla* is a valuable rhetorical and pedagogical tool, but for Christians it also became a part of religious tradition. In exhorting the church in Corinth to eschew jealousy, Clement of Rome uses examples from Israel's history and the early church to offer a series of types and antitypes for his readers. In *First Clement* 5 he turns from the "ancient examples" and begins to review the "noble examples" from his own generation. He describes the persecution and death of Peter and Paul and offers them as examples of endurance. The same shift from ancient Israelite to early Christian *exempla* is found in the opening of the *Passion of Perpetua and Felicitas*. Here the author tentatively places the martyrs of Carthage into a history that memorializes religious heroes for exemplary purposes, saying:

The deeds recounted about the faith in ancient times were a proof of God's favor and achieved the spiritual strengthening of men as well; and they were set forth in writing precisely that honor might be rendered to God and comfort to men by the recollection of the past through the written word. Should not then more recent examples be set down that contribute equally to both ends? For indeed these too will one day become ancient and needful for the ages to come, even though in our own day they may enjoy less prestige because of the prior claim of antiquity.[136]

The text presents the memorialization of religious *exempla* as a facet of Christian life. They serve a distinct purpose in "strengthening" the will of the audience and providing examples of proper conduct. Whereas here in the *Passion of Perpetua and Felicitas* the author is hesitant to equate the martyrs with more ancient *exempla*, later writers go further in extolling the martyrs as equals of the ancient heroes.[137] The cautious suggestion of the author of the *Passion of Perpetua and Felicitas*, that these martyrs will one day be revered as greatly as ancient examples, is proved to be true. With the passage of time, additional layers to the mimetic economy are added so that each successive generation of martyrs models their conduct on that of their predecessors.

The chains of imitation grow ever longer with the passage of time. The mid-fourth-century Donatist *Martyrdom of Maximian and Isaac* expands the mimetic hierarchy by constructing elongated chains of imitation.[138] For not only do martyrs imitate Christ, but martyrs of later generations imitate their predecessors and serve as models for members of their congregation. The conclusion of the work exhorts Christians who have already confessed Christ to "follow their own pattern," to imitate the martyrs who went before them and to strengthen those around them:

Now brothers and sisters, all these conditions which led them to the heavenly kingdom come round to you. These exemplars compel you. This situation drove them on first to these glories for your sake. The multitude of your own confessions made you teachers through your oft repeated professions of faith. Now they advise you concerning martyrdom. Your pattern which encourages others likewise now encourages you. Now they are holding out their arms to you from heaven, waiting for the time when they will run to meet you.[139]

The construction of elaborate chains of imitation involving figures from the past is familiar to us from the opening of the *Passion of Perpetua and Felicitas*. The construction of the mimetic economy here in the *Martyrdom of Maximian and Isaac* is rhetorically forceful and sophisticated, drawing together promises of fellowship with the martyrs with exhortations to follow and become good examples.

In presenting their protagonists as examples, the authors of the *acta* both utilize the rhetorical and pedagogical technique of the *exemplar* and place their narratives within a religious history that viewed individuals as models for members of the church. In the North African examples we have looked at so far, the premise for viewing martyrs as models is based upon a tradition of viewing biblical heroes as models. For many authors of the *acta*, however, there was only one model that was of true importance, the model presented in Jesus. For the authors of these martyr acts, martyrs were models for others by virtue of the fact that they themselves were modeled on Christ. This and this alone was the decisive factor in their status as examples for the church at large.

Teaching by Example

It is clear from the acts of the martyrs that the deaths of the saints were inspirational to those who watched their execution. In the words of Tertullian, "The blood of the martyrs is the seed of the church."[140] Conversion is a literary topos of the genre; prison guards, soldiers, bystanders, and even procurators are swayed by the deaths of the martyrs.[141] This was not the only positive outcome of the martyrs's deaths; their deaths brought about not just conversion to Christianity but conversion to martyrdom. In short, martyrs bred martyrs.

The *acta* themselves are full of reflections upon the function of the martyr as a model for others. Frequently, the exemplary function of the martyr is cast in pedagogical terms. They serve as instructors and examples for other Christians about the path of martyrdom itself: "At any rate, in their departure [i.e., their martyrdom] they left Marian and James so disposed by their teaching and example that they would be ready to follow the fresh footprints of their glory."[142] Marian and James are the martyrs named in the title of the work; it is interesting, therefore, that the author goes to such great pains to show the ways in which the protagonists were themselves imitators of other martyrs.[143] The idea of following in the footsteps of the martyr, so vividly described here, resonates with Gospel accounts in which Jesus encourages his disciples to follow in his footsteps.[144] Their role is largely pedagogical; they are didactic examples that Christians could imitate. The instructive component of martyrdom is also emphasized in *Martyrdom of Montanus and Lucius*, where the martyrs are described as wondrous lessons that are to be recorded so that later generations may learn from their examples.[145] The memorialization of the martyrs was closely linked to the imitation of the martyrs. The author of the *Acts of the*

Abitinian Martyrs describes his work's purpose as twofold, as a means for preparation for martyrdom and memorialization: "I write with a specific two-fold resolve: that we might prepare our very selves for martyrdom by imitating them and that, when we have committed to writing the battles and victories of their confessions, we may entrust to everlasting memory those whom we believe to live forever and reign with Christ."[146] Even the celebration of the anniversary of the martyr was viewed as an opportunity to train and prepare those who would one day become martyrs themselves.[147] Memorialization of the martyrs, therefore, was not the innocent endeavor of the pious historian; it was a propagandistic attempt to inculcate the principles of martyrdom in the mind of the hearer.

Value of Models

Imitation to the point of death was itself viewed as soteriologically valuable. In the Greek version of the *Acts of Phileas*, the protagonist describes the sufferings and death of Jesus, which he interprets as a "model of salvation": "Phileas said: 'He [Jesus] knew that . . . he would be scourged and beaten and . . . he wear[s] a crown made of thorns and suffers death offering to us in this too a model of salvation."[148] Phileas's summary of events focuses on Jesus' experience of suffering and death as the paradigm for others. Through attachment to the death of Jesus, suffering and death become inherently "good," even becoming a form of "salvation." The view that Christ's death provides a model of salvation is a common one both in the *acta* and in patristic literature.[149] What is striking about this statement is that imitating the Jesus model entails only suffering and death, not a set of moral values. Strange and alien though this concept is to modern ears, at its core the model exemplified in Christ encouraged one thing: suffering.

While death alone qualified a martyr as a model, martyrs also served as embodiments of Christian virtues. Indeed, their status as exemplar is not secured merely by dying but is contingent upon the manner of their death. The composure of the martyrs throughout their trial, their nonchalant approach to imprisonment, and their indifference to torture was a means of eliciting conversion and setting examples of good conduct.[150] It is tempting to reduce the moral example of the martyrs to a single virtue—endurance or obedience—but in truth the picture is more complicated. Martyrs are not one-dimensional ethical characters. They embody a plethora of sometimes surprising virtues: obedience, endurance, piety, love, humility, forgiveness, and fearlessness.

The sine qua non of *imitatio* in the corpus of *acta* is the figure of Polycarp, bishop of Smyrna. As already discussed, Polycarp's death is variously portrayed as an imitative sacrifice with shades of conquest over Satan. While Polycarp himself is the perfect imitator of Christ, he also serves as a model of Christian virtue for the audience of the text. At the account's opening, Polycarp's avoidance of arrest is linked to a concern for imitation and a preoccupation with love: "Just as the Lord did, he too waited that he might be delivered up, that we might become his imitators, not thinking of ourselves alone, but of our neighbors as well. For it is a mark of true and solid love to desire not only one's own salvation but also that of all the brothers."[151] This can be read, somewhat cynically, as an *apologia* for Polycarp's cowardly efforts to avoid arrest. The author of the text, however, links Polycarp's hesitation to his desire that others might become imitators of him. Once again, we can see the twofold nature of the martyr as model. Polycarp acts "just as the Lord did" in order that others might become his imitators and act "as he did." We can infer from the end of this passage that the imitation of Polycarp will secure one's salvation. Polycarp's own desire to see others saved is, like Jesus', grounded in his "true and solid love," his agape.

The command to love one another is the famously vague foundation of New Testament ethics, but the author of Polycarp has something more specific in mind.[152] The discussion of agape in John 15 suggests that readers should love one another in the same way that Jesus loved them, namely, by laying down their lives for one another.[153] As we saw in the previous chapter, this idea was very influential in the *acta martyrum* where Johannine commands to love are incorporated into the deaths of the martyrs.[154] The same notion resonates in the discussion of Polycarp's desire to become a model for others in his death. His actions are born out of agape for his brothers. The narrator does not stop here in outlining the virtues of the martyrs. Their status as examples is grounded in their nobility, their endurance, their love, and their courage: "Who indeed would not revere the martyr's nobility, their endurance, their love of the Master. . . . Some indeed attained to such courage that they would not utter a sound or cry, showing to all of us that in the hour of their torment these noblest of Christ's witnesses were not present in the flesh, or rather that the Lord was there present holding converse with them."[155] The martyrs appear obedient, noble, and loving, and in their ability to endure tortures they reveal the extent of their courage and the support they receive from Christ. In a further refection toward the end of the letter, the author again links the virtue of the martyrs to their imitation of Christ: "We love the martyrs as the disciples and imitators of the Lord, and rightly so because of their unsurpassed loyalty toward their king and teacher. May we too share with them as fellow disciples."[156] The martyrs here are loved on account of their discipleship and imitation of Christ, imitation that is again linked to the performance of a specific virtue, here "loyalty."

Discipleship in the writings of Ignatius and Polycarp entails imitation of Christ in suffering. This understanding is grounded in the Markan characterization of "following Christ" as the acceptance of suffering and death. In the concluding summary of Polycarp as martyr, the author reinforces his status as a teacher, a role also ascribed to Christ in 17.3. Polycarp's μαρτύριον is again linked to the performance of the gospel, and once again he is lauded for his perseverance: "He was not only a great teacher but also a conspicuous martyr, whose testimony, following the gospel of Christ, everyone desires to imitate. By his perseverance he overcame the unjust governor and so won the crown of immortality."[157] The summation of Polycarp's importance again links his martyrdom with his imitation of Christ and his display of virtue. His suitability as a model for those "who desire to imitate him" is grounded both in his own imitation of Christ and in the instructiveness of his behavior.

Just as the author of *Polycarp* highlights a select group of virtues, so, also, other authors use the martyrs to promote their own set of values. The martyrs served as mouthpieces through which individual communities could inculcate specific behaviors. As the embodiment of Christian virtues the martyrs became charismatic caricatures of Christian ideals. The *Martyrdom of Saints Agape, Irene and Chione*, for instance, presents its three appropriately named protagonists as embodiments of the Pauline virtues of love, peace, and purity.[158] The author of the *Martyrdom of Montanus and Lucius* is particularly concerned to emphasize the importance of peace, harmony, and unity in the church, repeatedly exhorting the audience to follow the "good models" of the martyrs by remaining unified and peaceful.[159] In many *acta* the martyrs are presented as examples of courage or fearlessness.[160] In truth it seems self-evident that someone willing to die would be fearless, but the extent to which this quality is highlighted as exemplary is often overlooked in scholarship. As we already noted, the *Letter of the Churches of Lyon and Vienne* presents the deaths of the martyrs in terms of victory over Satan. This task is framed in light of their emulation of Christ. Not only were martyrs "intensely eager to imitate and emulate Christ," but their courageous defeat of the Adversary was exemplary:[161] "But his body bore witness to his sufferings, being all one bruise and wound, stretched and distorted out of any recognizably human shape; but Christ suffering in him achieved great glory, overwhelming the Adversary, and showing as an example to all the others that nothing is to be feared where the Father's love is, nothing painful where we find Christ's glory."[162] As with Polycarp, the ability to endure great physical suffering is linked to courageousness. The distorted body of the martyr is an example to others that where there is love, nothing should be feared. The same idea recurs in the description of the death of Marian in *Marian and James*. Marian is described as "courageous and confident," and his final words before his death serve inspire his fellow Christians: "And by this prophecy not only did the martyr's faith triumph over the pagans; it sounded a trumpet-call, as it were, to arouse his brethren to emulate his courage, so that in the midst of these temporal plagues the saints of God might grasp at the opportunity for a death that was precious and holy."[163] As is typical of ancient Greek heroes, Marian's courage is clearly linked to his death. For it is by dying precious and holy deaths as martyrs that his brethren will imitate that courage. We should note that the description of Marian's courage elicits a frenzy of activity; it sounds a trumpet call, it "arouses" his brethren and prompts them to "grasp" the opportunity for death. None of these responses are in any way passive; while they may not be violent, the author of the text portrays them as dynamic responses to Marian's example.

Many authors opt for a more subtle approach, describing their protagonists as particularly humble, brave, or faithful without resorting to explicit exhortation to imitate these characteristics. Of these implied virtues the most common are faithfulness and endurance, which reappear in Greek and Latin *acta* of all regions. Additionally, a number of *acta* present their protagonists as examples of particular virtues narratively. The *Martyrdom of Nicephori* is one such instance, in which the moral content of the account is deduced by the reader. The unusually charming story describes how Nicephori, a Christian tax collector, quarreled with the priest Sapricus. Sapricus was arrested, arraigned, and condemned to die as a martyr, and Nicephori followed him to the site of execution, begging forgiveness and apologizing for their quarrel. The obstinate priest refused to forgive Nicephori and at the last moment, when faced with death, recanted his beliefs. Nicephori tried in vain to persuade Sapricus to maintain his confession and in the end died as a martyr in his place. Implicitly, the account promotes the practice of forgiveness and repentance in the church. Through martyrdom the tax collector who forgives is elevated over the apostate obstinate priest. The moral vision of the story is never stated but is nonetheless unmistakably clear: practice forgiveness. The martyr serves as both the instructor in virtue and the model for imitation.

The presentation of martyrs as models for imitation serves two purposes. On the one hand, it trains other Christians to prepare themselves for martyrdom. The martyrs serve as trailblazers, carving out the pathway for those who will eventually give their lives for the name. In the *acta*, modeling one's death on that of another was a certain way to earn salvation. On the other hand, the manner of their deaths embodies a set of Christian virtues that the audiences of these texts could imitate whether or not they themselves were executed.

Martyrdom and the Moral Exemplar Model of Salvation

As we have seen, the exemplary function of the martyr's death is frequently cast in soteriological terms. Phileas, in the *Acts of Phileas*, offers a "model of salvation," and Polycarp resists arrest so that others will be saved through his example. In constructive theology, this idea is termed the "moral exemplar" model and is most frequently linked to the writings of Peter Abelard, who describes Jesus as providing a moral example of love, humility, and obedience. Abelard's soteriology is derived almost entirely from a brief appendix that he added to his commentary on Romans 3:19–26.[164] In this appendix, Abelard asks how it is possible that God, through the saving work of Jesus, is able to bind Christians to himself through love, and, furthermore, why Christians are motivated to love in the way that Christ did. He concludes that those whose love imitates and is motivated by Christ's love for them win freedom from sin and redemption through Jesus.[165]

In modern constructive theology, the subjective moral exemplar model is frequently criticized for proposing an ethic of obedience and submission.[166] Moral Exemplar and its accompanying theological theory that suffering is redemptive have had damaging and oppressive effects in the lives of many groups.[167] While the present work is not an attempt at constructive theology, it nonetheless has something to say about the Moral Exemplar model. The presumption in that model is that the example is one of obedience and submission. It is interesting to note that in the *acta martyrum* a group of texts built upon the premise that martyrs imitate Christ, obedience is only one of a slew of Christly virtues. To obedience are added love,[168] fearlessness,[169] endurance,[170] and even purity.[171] These virtues do not necessarily imply submission. In the *acta* the martyrs actively, vibrantly, and sometimes violently oppose the persecutions they face. They are engaged in intense physical combat with demonic forces, and they brazenly and boldly reprimand the Roman consuls who far outstrip them in social status and authority.[172] While martyrs may accept the will of God submissively, they speak out against the injustice of their surroundings. Passive obedience, the quality that so greatly troubles critics of the moral exemplar model, is not the hallmark of a martyr.

Conclusion

Throughout this chapter we have explored some of the main ways in which the authors of the *acta* evaluated the function and significance of the martyr's death. It is at this juncture that we turn, in accordance with tradition, to conclusions.

Given the diversity of our evidence, these observations should be read more as a commentary on the unexpectedness of our results than as a triumphant statement on the matter. We have seen that, while the deaths of some martyrs were cast as sacrifices, language of expiation and sacrifice is remarkably rare in the martyrdom accounts themselves. Moreover, the discursive function of the presentation of the martyr's death as sacrifice varies from text to text. Rhetorically, sacrificial imagery could serve to amplify the barbarity of the martyr's opponents and to contrast Roman imperialism with the kingdom of Christ. On an ecclesiastical level it had the potential to draw the audience into the world of the martyr and domesticated martyrdom by embedding it in the liturgical fabric of the church. On a narrative level it occasionally served to further the martyr's progress through to the heavens. The meaning of martyrdom as sacrifice was unfixed.

In our examination of the martyr's death as a victory over Satan, we saw that this idea was particularly strong in Gallic and North African Latin martyrdoms. Framing the martyr's role in the cosmic conflict in Christly terms elevated the role of the individual in the early church. The martyrs were generals, not foot soldiers, in God's army, their bodies serving as the battlefields upon which God and Satan contested. The tendency of redactors to amplify elements of cosmic conflict in the post-Constantinan period demonstrates the aesthetic appeal of cosmic conflict. This observation may run counter to scholarly intuition, but it is well worth noting the dramatic allure of the apocalypse.

At the same time, while the basic principle that martyrs are models was a feature of the majority of the *acta*, there was considerable disagreement about the core values that the martyrs embody. If a single and coherent message emerges from this survey, it is that there was no single coherent interpretation of the martyr's death. Ancient Christians employed a variety of linguistic and conceptual images to describe the significance of martyrdom. We have considered the function of the death of the martyr as a sacrifice, as a victory over Satan, and as a moral exemplar. Though we have examined them discretely, these elements often appear in nuanced and integrated forms in the same texts. These concepts were frequently interwoven in a manner so that while one particular soteriological model may dominate our interpretation of that individual account, other models nevertheless resonate in the background of the narrative. The *Letter of the Churches of Lyons and Vienne* presents the deaths of its protagonists as both victories over Satan and moral exemplar, and the *Martyrdom of Polycarp* combines elements of all three models. One of the more consistent features of all three perspectives, however, is that whatever the function of the martyr's death, it functions in the same way as the death of Jesus. Thus, whether or not a martyr is explicitly named as a model of virtue for others, the function of his or her own death mirrors that of Christ. Even here, though, we should be hesitant to generalize and reach broad conclusions. If we attempt to harmonize the *passiones* into a single interpretation of the martyr's death, then we do a disservice to the richness and complexity of the texts themselves.

Even if ancient Christians interpreted the death of the martyr in individual and diverse ways, they agreed that it was a special salvifically valuable death. The death of the martyr—as sacrifice, example, or victory—meant that the martyr enjoyed an unusual and highly privileged experience of the afterlife. The elevation of the martyrs, accomplished through death, raised them above and apart from the ordinary Christian dead. With our survey of the significance of the martyr's death complete, we will now leave the executioner's block and ascend with the martyr to the heavens and the afterlife.

4

The Martyr's Heaven

In the writings and sermons of modern Christians it is often proclaimed that all are equal before God. Such statements are not
without biblical support; the apothegms of the canonical Jesus
frequently describe the leveling or reversal of social and financial
status in the hereafter. The trappings of material existence will be
stripped away, and Christians will be judged on spiritual merit alone.
Irrespective of the criterion for this judgment—whether it is faith or
works is not for me to say—all meet this same uniform fate.

Such egalitarian hopes, however, are in tension with ancient
descriptions of the heavenly realm and its inhabitants. The cosmic
realm is characterized by hierarchical divisions and ontological
differences, marked by degrees of proximity to the supreme deity.
In ancient literature focusing on cosmogony, the relative status of
supernatural beings was of the utmost importance. While some
visionaries may have been somewhat reluctant to describe the form
or appearance of God, angelic attendants in the heavenly realm
receive sustained attention.[1]

From the apocalyptic visions of Enoch to the philosophical
treatises of the Gnostics, one thing is certain: heaven is hierarchical.[2]
The poles of the hierarchy remain intact: at the top of the ladder
stands the transcendent God, a being of such majesty that it often
cannot bear description, and at the bottom sits lowly humankind. In
between these two a plethora of divine beings—angels, archangels,
powers, dominions, seraphim, cherubim, the one like a son of

man, Metatron, among others—jostle for position around the heavenly throne. This preoccupying concern with angelic stratification may be the byproduct of philosophical or religious concerns to distance the transcendent God from corrupt mortality. Even so, it produces a heavenly realm at odds with notions of postmortem equality. Whatever we might want to believe, we are not all equal before God.[3]

Traditionally, martyrs have been inserted into the heavenly hierarchy alongside angels.[4] They outrank the ordinary dead yet trail behind the superior presences of God, Christ, and perhaps Mary. Their status is determined by two factors: the separation of the persons of the Trinity from other supernatural beings, and the roles they play in the afterlife. In modern Christian heavenly hierarchies the division between beings is essentially tripartite: the untouchable and unattainable Trinitarian beings; special heavenly characters such as angels, saints, and Mary; and the ordinary dead. The assumption that the members of the Trinity were essentially different from other heavenly entities led to the conclusion that martyrs shared the same status as angels. Furthermore, their roles as intercessors, visionary mentors, miracle workers, heavenly attendants, and end-time witnesses overlap with the functions ascribed to angels in apocalypses. Historically, these two factors—functional similarity and Christological separatism—have led to the conviction that angels and martyrs are functionally, and perhaps essentially, the same.

If the assumption of Christological difference is removed, it is possible to introduce another comparative model for the status and function of martyrs in the heavenly realm, that of Christ exalted. According to canonical and extracanonical traditions, Jesus describes a number of functions that he is able to perform during his earthly tenure and expects to perform after his death. The role of the exalted Christ has much in common with both biblical and apocalyptic traditions about angels and early Christian traditions about the roles of the saints.[5]

In the first four centuries of the Christian era, the identity, status, and function of all the heavenly beings—Christ, angels, archangels, martyrs, special dead, and so on—were constantly being reproduced in dialogue with one another.[6] This is to say that the status of the martyrs in the heavenly hierarchy was in flux precisely because the heavenly hierarchy itself was continuously being reshaped. In the following two chapters we will be examining the relative status and position of the martyrs through two lenses, through a comparative analysis of postmortem function and a comparative analysis of their postmortem status. In this chapter we will focus on the function of the martyrs. Traditionally, martyrs are viewed as a kind of angel, but in keeping with the theme of this work, we will examine the roles of the martyrs in light of those of the exalted Christ. In what ways do the martyrs seem more like angels, and in what ways do martyrs seem more like Christ? In what ways do they seem similar to both, and in what ways dissimilar? It is true that martyrs perform many similar functions to angels, and the similarity between them is not contested. The intent is not to disprove the usual theory that martyrs serve the same roles as angels but, rather, to assess whether the martyrs are, in some respects, *more* like angels than Christ, or vice versa.[7] Given our results so far, it is expected that there were a variety of opinions about the functions of Christ, angels, and martyrs.

Angelomorphic Christology

In *The Open Heaven*, Christopher Rowland discusses the relative status and authority of the exalted angel in ancient Jewish religious texts.[8] He argues that the emergence of this figure is a development of the throne theophany of Ezekiel, an idea that gained momentum in the more elaborate apocalyptic visions of Daniel, Enoch, et al. Against Alan Segal, Rowland argues that—in Jewish literature—the exalted angel should not be understood as a rival power to God.[9] For Rowland, the origin of the angel's power is firmly rooted in God. This does not mean, however, that this kind of angelic doctrine did not lead to interpretations in which the power of God is rivaled by other beings. For Rowland, the muddied use of angelic doctrine is apparent in the development of early Christian Christology. As he rightly notes, early Christians drew upon a slew of contemporary Jewish ideas to articulate their views about Jesus. The exalted angelic figure of apocalyptic literature was a prime candidate for ideological assimilation and accommodation; as Rowland puts it, "The developments in angelology ... would have made it difficult for early Christians to differentiate precisely between Jesus and other prominent members of the heavenly hierarchy."[10] Rowland points to two examples where he sees angelic Christology at play, Revelation 1:13–17 and Hebrews 1:4–14.[11] In the Apocalypse, the depiction of the exalted Christ uses the images and terminology of visions of the exalted angelic figure, the "one like a son of man," from Daniel 7:9–14.[12] In Revelation, argues Rowland, the author may be reluctant to describe explicitly Christ as an angel, but the *function* of Christ is very similar to that of angelic intermediaries. Like the angelic attendants of the Jewish apocalyptic tradition, Christ serves as a heavenly tour guide for the apocalyptist and the source of revelation about the secrets of God (cf. Rev 1:1 and 22:16).[13]

Rowland's argument that ideas about the exalted Christ were in part framed by ancient angelology is further supported by the comparison of Christ and the angels in Hebrews 1:4–14. Here the relationship between Christ and the angels is decidedly complex as the author of Hebrews seeks both to utilize angelic Christology to explain the identity of Christ and also to amend it in order to place Christ above the angels. Hebrews differentiates between Christ and other divine beings by accenting the distinctive filial relationship between Christ and God (Heb 1:1f.), his exaltation as a consequence of his sacrificial death (Heb 1:3), and his inheritance of a superior divine name (Heb 1:4; cf. Phil 2:11). The exaltation to the right hand of God and the possession of the divine name are themselves characteristics of other exalted heavenly beings.[14] The author of Hebrews, therefore, utilizes angelic christology in his description of the activities of the exalted Christ. Simultaneously, however, the author works to demonstrate the superiority of Jesus over and against these angels and to correct an actual or potential belief that the exalted Jesus was a kind of angel.[15] He does this by highlighting the role of the angels as servants of Christ (Heb 1:6-7, 14), the filial relationship of Christ to God (Heb 1:3, 5), his exaltation on account of his death (1:3), the superiority of his name (Heb 1:4), and his seat at the right hand of God (Heb 1:3, 13).

The complex use of angelic Christology in the early church is important to our study in two respects. First, it draws our attention to the inherent instability of these figures in the early church. The relative status and functions of the exalted Christ and the angels were by no means clear. Second, Hebrews' exaltation of Christ above the angels is grounded in the particular death he suffered, the acclamation of sonship, and the possession of a superior name. In the *acta* these concepts will likewise be applied to the martyrs, and, according to the thought of Hebrews, these achievements would vault the martyrs above the angels and into the realm of Christly divine sonship.[16]

Remnants of this angelic Christology persisted into the second century. The popular *Shepherd of Hermas* exhibits a certain ambiguity about the identity of its highest authority, the most distinguished angel.[17] In some instances this figure seems to be identical with the Son of God (Herm., *Vis.* 5.2; Herm., *Sim.* 7.1-3; 9.1.3). In a single instance the highest angel appears to be Michael (Herm., *Sim.* 8.3.3), but this example is viewed as an anomaly in which the equation of the Son of God with Michael is the product of oral performance or allegorical necessity. In the majority of instances, therefore, the supreme angelic figure is the Son of God. The identification of Christ with biblical angelic figures continues in the writings of Justin Martyr,[18] the Gospel of Thomas,[19] and—according to Hippolytus—the visions of Elchasai.[20] A variation on this theme is found in the *Ascension of Isaiah*, where at every stage in the descent through the heavenly spheres the Lord takes on the form of an angel (10.17-31).[21] The idea that Christ merely assumes the form of an angel is an augmented form of angelic Christology. Rather than viewing Christ as identical with a (great) angel, it is possible that in the *Ascension of Isaiah*, writings of Justin, and the *Shepherd of Hermas* a certain degree of angelomorphism is at work.[22]

Christ is described as having taken the form of an angel rather than as having actually been an angel.

While the different statuses of Christ and the angels will become important in our next chapter, for our discussions of the relative *functions* of these beings, it does not matter whether the angelic characterization of Christ is angelomorphic or not. Even if we are reluctant to accept the suggestion that borrowing from Jewish apocalypticism led to a kind of angelic or angelomorphic Christology, the example of the "one like a son of man" from Daniel 7:13 offers solid evidence for the influence of angelology on Christology. For if the figure in Daniel 7:13 is, as most scholars would agree, an angelic being, we must acknowledge the widespread adoption of this character as an explanatory device used to illuminate the person of Jesus.[23] The application of this title to Jesus does not necessarily mean that early Christians thought Jesus *was* an angel, but it logically entails that the symbolic characteristics and functions of the "one like a son of man" were applied to Jesus just as they previously and contemporaneously fed into Jewish angelology. As a result and regardless of whether or not anyone believed Jesus *to be* an angel, similar symbolic referents, terms, and functions were ascribed to both the exalted Jesus and members of the angelic hosts. For our purposes, the salient point is that the functions ascribed to the exalted Christ developed in dialogue with contemporary angelology.

The possibility that the characterization of the exalted Christ was influenced by a kind of angelic theology complicates the nature of this endeavor. The task of comparison is not merely a matter of assessing in what respects the martyrs are more or less similar to Christ in opposition to angels. For, according to this model, we would expect to find a number of functions shared by all three groups, in which case it is impossible to assert that the martyrs are assimilated to either group. The situation demands that we refine the method further, paying particular attention to those respects in which martyrs share commonalities with Christ but not with angels, and vice versa. We should also attempt, insofar as is possible, to use as the basis of our comparison literary texts that include two or more of these groups. The function and characteristics of angels, Christ, and martyrs vary from text to text. Given that angels can serve different functions in different accounts, it is hardly fair to arbitrarily select the portrait of angelic beings in any one given text in order to artificially highlight its difference from or similarity to the portraits of martyrs. Accordingly, texts that are in some way linked to one another or include descriptions of two or more groups are to be preferred over isolated examples. In the event that we discover shared functions among all three groups, we must not assume with previous generations of scholars that the martyrs are being assimilated to the angels unless there is some other indication in the text that unambiguously leads us to this conclusion.

The Ascent to Heaven

It is an uncomfortable and willfully overlooked thread in Christian tradition that the dead will not enter heaven until the final judgment.[24] Until that time they lie dormant in the earth, awaiting a final trumpet call and summons to judgment at the heavenly court. The roots for this idea can be traced back to the dawn of the Jesus movement, to the references to the temporary slumber of the dead and the final eschatological judgment of the world.[25] Like any theological concept of importance, ideas about resurrection and afterlife varied from writer to writer and were influenced by a slew of contemporary Jewish, biblical, and pagan ideas about the afterlife.[26] From among such variety, a single tradition consistently appears in all of the Jesus movement and early Christian church: Jesus was resurrected from the dead. The nature and details of this resurrection were open to debate, but this, the crux of Christian confession, was true for almost all.[27]

Like Jesus, Christian martyrs were believed to ascend directly to heaven at the moment of their death, their martyrdom serving as their passport to the throne of God. The extent to which the rapidity of the ascension of martyrs to heaven is part of an *imitatio Christi* hinges upon contemporary notions about resurrection as it was more generally construed. After all, if everyone ascends to heaven at death, the exaltation of the martyrs is decidedly less remarkable. With this in mind, we shall move to the ideas about the afterlife found in the literature of the Jesus movement and early church.

When we turn to more general notions of the afterlife in ancient Judaism and Christianity, it becomes clear that there was no single view on the postmortem expectations of the ordinary dead. If the place of Jesus at the right hand of God was relatively secure, the future hopes of ordinary Christians were rather less stable. Early Christian writers worried about the nature of afterlife, the timetable for resurrection, and the role of eschatological judgment. For our purposes, we will focus primarily on the issue of the timing of the resurrection, particularly with reference to eschatological judgment.

Eschatological Resurrection

By far the most prevalent conception of the resurrection of the dead in early Christian circles was the idea that the dead would be resurrected at the end of time before the eschatological judgment.[28] This point was eloquently made by Stuiber, who argued that the idea of an interim period preceding resurrection was a consistent thread throughout early Christian communities.[29] The general resurrection of Christians was intimately connected to the resurrection of Christ himself and would come at the end of time when the archangel sounded his call. For Paul, the resurrection of Christ was discussed in purely relational terms (cf. 1 Thess 4:14; Phil 3:10–11; Rom 6:5). His focus is not on the abstract significance of the resurrection in general but more precisely on its ramifications for his followers. In 1 Thessalonians, Paul describes the eschatological resurrection of the dead in the following way:

> For since we believe that Jesus died and rose again, even so, through Jesus, God will bring with him those who have died. For this we declare to you by the word of the Lord, that we who are alive, who are left until the coming of the Lord, will by no means precede those who have died. For the Lord himself, with a cry of command, with the archangel's call and with the sound of God's trumpet, will descend from heaven, and the dead in Christ will rise first. Then we who are alive, who are left, will be caught up in the clouds together with them to meet the Lord in the air; and so we will be with the Lord forever. Therefore encourage one another with these words.[30]

Here Paul literally and figuratively lays the groundwork for the idea that deceased Christians slumber in the earth until the eschatological awakening. This notion proved to be foundational in the writings of second-century Christian thinks like Clement, Justin, and Irenaeus. As for Paul, Clement writes that the resurrection of Christ is programmatic for the future, eschatological resurrection of all Christians, serving as a constant reminder of the future resurrection.[31] When the kingdom of God appears, the resurrection will be disclosed and the dead will be raised up from their tombs.[32]

A number of early Christian writers argued against those who believed in the immediate ascent of the soul at the moment of bodily death. Using an exegetical tactic, Irenaeus, the second-century heresiologist bishop of Lyons, took Jesus as the model. He pointed out that even Jesus had to wait three days before being resurrected and that, accordingly, so Christians would have to wait in an interim state before their resurrection.[33] In the same way, writing in the middle of the second century in Rome, Justin argued that Christians had to wait until the final Day of Judgment, when there would be a resurrection on earth.[34] Justin's argument presupposes his belief in a thousand-year reign in the heavenly Jerusalem during which prophets and good Christians would mingle in bodily form on earth. He places general resurrection in the future at

the eschaton, but his argument also presumes a thousand-year reign on earth
to which many in the ancient world did not subscribe.

The picture of resurrection described in Justin appears to have been
gleaned from the partial resurrection of the just in the book of Revelation.[35]
John the Divine describes a preliminary resurrection of a thousand years limited to those special few who had given their lives as a testimony:

> Then I saw thrones, and those seated on them were given authority
> to judge. I also saw the souls of those who had been beheaded for
> their testimony to Jesus and for the word of God. They had not
> worshiped the beast or its image and had not received its mark on
> their foreheads or their hands. They came to life and reigned with
> Christ a thousand years. (The rest of the dead did not come to life
> until the thousand years were ended.) This is the first resurrection.
> Blessed and holy are those who share in the first resurrection. Over
> these the second death has no power, but they will be priests of God
> and of Christ, and they will reign with him a thousand years. (Rev
> 20:4–6)

We will return to the significance of enthronement and judgment in the subsequent sections of this chapter. For the moment, we will focus on the timing of
this resurrection. Those who were executed on behalf of their testimony are
resurrected and reign with Christ for a special period. This first resurrection
indicates a particular status and special privilege enjoyed by those executed for
their refusal to worship the beast. This passage of Revelation seems to have
fostered the idea, prevalent in the *acta martyrum*, that martyrs were raised
before ordinary people.[36]

In the controversial ending to the *Didache*, resurrection is intimately connected with the Second Coming, so much so that it is marked as a sign of the
return of Christ and the eschaton. The conclusion to the work describes the
signs of the eschaton using a conflation of biblical references taken largely
from the apocalyptic signs following the death of Jesus in Matthew 24: "Then
the signs of truth will be manifest: first a sign of a rip in the sky, then a sign of
a trumpet, and third a resurrection of the dead. But not of all the dead. For as it
has been said, 'The Lord will come and all of his holy ones with him.' Then the
world will see the Lord coming on clouds of the sky . . ."[37] The tantalizingly
fragmentary nature of the ending leaves us hanging at exactly the point at
which (we must imagine) the *Didache* takes its leave from the text of Matthew.[38]
We can only assume that things get more interesting from here on. The enig-
matic partial resurrection envisioned in the phrase "not of all the dead" is open
to a number of interpretations. It could be that, like some other ancient writers,

the author of the *Didache* imagines that only those who have lived good lives will be resurrected.[39] If this were the case, we would expect to find other passages in the *Didache* explicitly warning that only the righteous would be raised in the last days.

Another possibility presents itself in the idea of the "first resurrection" noted in Revelation 20:4–6, where those who had died for their faith are resurrected early, before everyone else. The fragmentary nature of *Didache* 16 makes it impossible to know what follows it; perhaps as in Revelation there is another more general resurrection to come. Again, though, if these holy ones are resurrected on the basis of their testimony, we would expect independent confirmation of the importance of this in the rest of the *Didache*. While scholars are in agreement that the ending of the *Didache* refers to an apocalyptic judgment, there is some confusion about the precise timing of this resurrection. The majority of scholars assume that the final judgment takes place in the presumed lost ending that follows verse 8.[40] Against this Aaron Milavec has argued that "the burning process of testing" (*Did.* 16.5) is the process of judgment and that the *Didache* thus argues for a partial resurrection of only the saints.[41]

The concept that only the faithful few will be resurrected in the last days is found elsewhere in early Christian literature. In his *Epistle to the Trallians*, Ignatius follows Paul's lead in 1 Corinthians 15 by associating general resurrection with that of Christ. Just as Christ was truly raised from the dead, so also those who have faith will be raised. Without this belief in Christ Jesus, however, Igantius and his readers do not "have true life."[42]

While the majority of Christian authors agree that there will be a general resurrection immediately preceding the eschatological judgment, there are some who stratify or limit this resurrection in order to privilege those who had led faithful lives. The idea that only a particular group of people would be resurrected manifested itself in different ways among early Christians. For the author of Revelation, and possibly also the *Didache*, there was a preliminary resurrection of righteous individuals with strong "testimonies." For Ignatius, only the just would be resurrected.

Immediate Resurrection and Ascension

While belief in final eschatological resurrection may have been widespread in the writings of the early church, there were some notable exceptions. Paul, for example, adheres to the principle of eschatological resurrection in general but appears willing to allow himself the privilege of a speedy ascent to heaven. In Philippians 1:23 he describes his desire to "depart and be with Christ," assuming, it would seem, that for himself ordinary rules do not apply.[43]

A particularly curious tradition regarding the resurrection of the dead comes down to us in Matthew 27:51–53. Immediately following the death of Jesus, at the moment of the tearing of the temple veil, the graves of the dead are opened: "At that moment the curtain of the temple was torn in two, from top to bottom. The earth shook, and the rocks were split. The tombs also were opened, and many bodies of the saints who had fallen asleep were raised. After his resurrection they came out of the tombs and entered the holy city and appeared to many."[44] The account describes a scene much like that of a modern horror movie. The graves of the dead are opened, and the resurrected saints travel to Jerusalem as a testimony of Jesus. That this passage occurs only in Matthew but uses unfamiliar language of "saints" rather than the more usual Matthean terminology of "the just" indicates that this may come from a pre-Matthean source.[45] The scene combines a number of eschatological elements, ripping veil, earthquake, and resurrection perhaps as an indication that the eschaton had arrived and a general resurrection had begun.

Even if Matthew believed that the end had drawn near and intended his readers to understand these events as apocalyptic signs of the coming kingdom, in the early church these passages were read otherwise. That the eschatological night of the living dead (general resurrection) had yet to occur meant that the passage was reread in terms of the special identity of those who were resurrected. Whereas for members of the Jesus movement all Christians were viewed as "saints," in branches of later Christianity the non-Matthean term ἅγιος comes to have a special and particular meaning. It denotes those who were marked out from among the ordinary Christian populace as especially close to God.

In the second and third centuries this designation was applied initially to martyrs and, later, to ascetics. This particular application meant that for readers of Matthew in the early church, 27:51–53 was interpreted as a reference to martyrs, not to Christians more generally. Thus, while for Matthew the term ἅγιος may have implied angelic beings or biblical heroes, for later church readers the use of this term marked this verse out as a reference to a special group of Christians.[46] In the context of an early church sanctifying certain heroes as "special," this event was probably reread as a special and limited resurrection offered to the chosen few.

Another example of exceptional assumption to heaven appears in the Gospel of Luke. One of the condemned criminals beseeches Jesus to remember him when Jesus comes into his kingdom. Jesus' response promises that he will also receive some kind of paradisiacal postmortem existence: "Then he [the criminal] said, 'Jesus, remember me when you come into your kingdom.' He [Jesus] replied, 'Truly I tell you, today you will be with me in Paradise.'"[47] Jesus' response here, while dramatic, certainly calls into question the logic of a delayed resurrection of the ordinary dead. It also casts doubts on the general death and resurrection schema employed by all the evangelists. After all, Jesus dies on the cross and *three days later* rises from the dead. Whether he ascends to heaven that day or forty days later is up for debate, but it runs against the grain of the entire Jesus story to suggest that he ascends to paradise on the day of his death.[48] Luke may well assume that Jesus' ψύχη or πνεῦμα goes to paradise immediately after his death and that his bodily resurrection takes place on the third day. Regardless of the schematics of Jesus' ascent to heaven, this incident demonstrates the principle that certain just individuals received special treatment in the afterlife. The criminal mentioned in Luke becomes, in martyrological literature, the prototype for the immediate resurrection of the martyr (Cyprian, *Ep.* 72.22.2).[49]

While Matthew and Luke offer examples of exceptional circumstances in which individuals were resurrected before the day of judgment, there may have been whole groups of Christians who believed that the resurrection had begun. Alan Segal argues that Gnostic ideas about the afterlife differed from and were established in antithesis to orthodox ideas.[50] For the Gnostics, Segal writes, pneumatic rather than fleshly resurrection was the focal point of postmortem hopes. The ascent of the soul rather than the resurrection of the body was the critical point of salvation, and this was achieved regardless of the mode of death. Though not itself a Gnostic text, the Gospel of Thomas illustrates this sentiment: "His disciples said to him: 'When will the repose of the dead occur? And when will the new cosmos come?' He said to them: 'This thing which you expect has come, but you do not recognize it.'"[51] Segal may be correct in pointing out that Gnostic resurrection was an ongoing spiritual exercise, not an eschatological event. In following the work of Elaine Pagels, however, he may push the idea that Gnostic pneumatic salvation was constructed in opposition to "orthodox" ideas of bodily resurrection too far.[52] He mistakenly frames martyrdom within this orthodox tradition about bodily resurrection. To be sure, there are Gnostic texts, such as the *Testimony of Truth*, that critique the idea that martyrdom ensured salvation, but this should not lead to the conclusion that martyrdom, bodily resurrection, and orthodoxy were intrinsically tied to one another.[53] There is a plethora of approaches to the nature of resurrection exhibited in the *acta*. Even as Polycarp is particularly concerned with fleshly resurrection, the *Acts of Justin* and *Acts of Apollonius* write about the judgment of the soul. In the *Acts of Apollonius*, the protagonist sums up his views of the afterlife, saying, "to believe that the soul is immortal, to be convinced that there will be a judgment after death and that there will be a reward given by God after the resurrection, to those who have lived a just life, for their labors on behalf of virtue."[54] Nowhere in this description is there mention of fleshly resurrection. On the contrary, the philosopher Apollonius is more concerned with the immortality of the soul. The *Acts of Apollonius* falls squarely within the parameters of "orthodoxy" and does not conform to the polarization of "orthodox" (i.e., martyrological) and "Gnostic" ideas regarding bodily resurrection outlined by Segal.

Segal's observations about Gnosticism draw our attention to the fact that there was no single unified perspective regarding the timing of resurrection. His argument about the difference between "Gnostic" and "orthodox" views of the afterlife exposes the importance of the resurrection in intra-Christian disputes. A particular view of the afterlife often served as a prerequisite for membership in certain Christian groups. As we have noted, his findings are oversimplified and as a result inaccurate. Consequently, we should not immediately discount "Gnosticism" and Gnostic views on the afterlife from the worldview that surrounded the literature and practice of martyrdom.

Repose of the Just Souls

A final and important theme commonly found in pseudepigraphic literature is the idea of the repose of the just. This idea augments the established notion of the final eschatological resurrection and judgment with the idea that those righteous individuals who die in the interim will be held in a kind of heavenly waiting room until the final judgment of the world. In the Book of the Watchers in *1 Enoch*, the eschatological judgment of transgressors, both angelic and human, is a lingering threat behind the work. The place of punishment in an accursed valley is already being prepared in *1 Enoch* 27 for those who "utter with their mouth an improper word against the Lord."[55] At the same time, however, provision is made for the souls of the righteous. In Enoch's second journey in *1 Enoch* 22, he comes to a holding area at the western point of a great mountain. His angelic guide informs him that,

> these hollow places (are intended) that the spirits of the souls of the dead might be gathered into them. For this very (purpose) they were created, (that) here the souls of all the sons of men should be gathered. And behold, these are the pits for the place of their confinement. Thus they were made until the day (on) which they will be judged, and until the time of the day of the end of the great judgment, which will be extracted from them.[56]

According to 22.2, this area is divided into four compartments, three dark—for the evil—and one illuminated by a spring of water.[57] The angel goes on to say that in the interim period until the final judgment, the souls of those interred in the pits will experience treatment justified by their conduct during life. Final judgment is anticipated in chapters 24–25, but a preliminary retribution will be administered until that time. In *1 Enoch* the focus of this passage is on the idea that the wicked receive punishment even before the great day of punishment. In fact, it is this idea that prompts the seer to proclaim the righteous judgment of the Lord in 22.14. The souls of the righteous are the recipients of a kind of blessing, but they are still located at the ends of the earth, not in the celestial realm.

A more promising future is found in the *Ascension of Isaiah.* In the heavenly ascent of Isaiah described in the second portion of the work, the seer recounts how he saw the souls of the just from the time of Adam in the seventh heaven:

> And there I saw all the righteous from the time of Adam onwards. And there I saw the holy Abel and all the righteous. And there I saw Enoch and all who were with him, stripped of (their) robes of the flesh; and I saw them in their robes of above, and they were like the angels who stand there in great glory. But they were not sitting on their thrones, nor were their crowns of glory on them. And I asked the angel who (was) with me, "How is it that they have received these robes, but are not on (their) thrones nor in (their) crowns?" And he said to me, "They do not receive the crowns and thrones of glory . . . until the Beloved descends in the form in which you will see him descend . . . he will rise on the third day. . . . And then many of the righteous will ascend with him, whose spirits do not receive (their) robes until the Lord Christ ascends and they ascend with him. Then indeed they will receive their robes and their thrones and their crowns, when he has ascended into the seventh heaven."[58]

In the *Ascension of Isaiah*, the idea of the spiritual afterlife of the just is decidedly complex. In this passage we read a description of the postmortem existence of those righteous individuals whose life span predated that of Jesus (the Beloved). Apparently, they ascend to the highest, seventh heaven and enjoy a glorification like that of angels but do not receive their thrones or crowns. For these, they must wait until the descent and ascent of the Beloved, at whose ascension they will receive the remainder of their heavenly rewards. The same idea appears in the first section of the *Ascension of Isaiah*, in a discussion of the Second Coming of the Lord. Following the ascension of the Beloved and a precise interlude of 1,332 days, the Lord will return from the heavens with his angels and saints (4.13–14). At this time of eschatological judgment, the heavenly saints wear their robes, the righteous on earth will ascend to heaven, and "there will be a resurrection and a judgment in their midst" (4.18). While the text is unclear on this point, it appears that the saints from above and the pious from the earth ascend to heaven before the general resurrection and judgment scene (4.17; cf. 9.24–25). They relax and anticipate the eschaton.

The Martyr's Experience of Heaven

Turning now to the deaths and spiritual afterlives of the martyrs, we find a very different picture. In contrast to ordinary pious individuals, martyrs did not have to wait for a final judgment to catch their first glimpse of eternal life. They neither slept beneath the ground nor twiddled their thumbs in a pneumatic storage facility. On the contrary, the *acta* display a consistent belief in the translocation of the souls of the martyrs to the heavenly throne at the very moment of death. In the words of Robin Lane Fox, "The martyrs bypassed the long delays, the intervals of cooling and refreshment, the minor corrections and discipline, the years of waiting in Abraham's bosom. They sped straight to Christ and his Father."[59]

As we might expect, the fate of the martyr after death is a frequent topos in the *acta* themselves, where statements about the fate of the martyrs are found both on the lips of the martyrs themselves and in narrative conclusions offered by the unseen authors of these texts. A plethora of images drawn from biblical texts and ancient culture is variously employed to describe the passage of the martyr from earth to heaven.

Immediate Ascent to Heaven

At the moment of their deaths the martyrs pass immediately into the heavenly realm, where they receive the rewards of their martyrdom. The immediacy of this transition is exemplified in the proclamation of the Scillitan martyr Nartazalus that "today we are martyrs in heaven."[60] This notion is not unique to Latin martyrdoms; on the contrary, it is a commonplace in martyrological literature.[61] The moment of martyrdom is consistently described as the moment of "departure to God": "Life was what they asked for and he gave it to them, and this they shared with their neighbor when they departed victorious to God. . . . In peace they departed to God."[62] Death as the moment of departure to God becomes a topos in martyrological literature. It is in heaven that the status of martyr is truly enjoyed. As the Scillitan martyrs proclaim, they are martyrs *in* heaven (*in caelis*), and it is in heaven that they reside following their deaths.[63]

The notion of immediate ascension to heaven is further illustrated in a famous speech in the *Martyrdom of Polycarp*, in which the protagonist asks that he be given a share in the cup of Christ and be received that day in heaven. He prays:

> to have a share among the number of the martyrs in the cup of
> Christ, for the resurrection unto eternal life of both the soul and the
> body in the immortality of the holy spirit. May I be received this day
> among them before your face as a rich and acceptable sacrifice, as
> you, the God of truth who cannot deceive, have prepared, revealed
> and fulfilled beforehand. Hence I praise you, I bless you and I glorify
> you above all things, through that eternal and celestial high priest
> Jesus Christ.[64]

As is frequently noted, Polycarp's request draws upon the biblical image of the cup of wrath imbibed by Christ in the Gospels.[65] This image associates the death of Polycarp and other martyrs with that of Christ. But he further asks to be received into God's presence that very day. The mechanics of this reception suggest that he will be received into God's presence as a sacrifice, presuming that, just as the scent of the burnt offering rose to God, so also Polycarp would ascend to be received by God. The use of sacrificial language, rather than that of heavenly ascent, to describe Polycarp's reception in heaven is highly unusual in martyrdom accounts, but it nonetheless demonstrates a belief that a martyr proceeded to the presence of God at the very moment of death.[66]

A slew of biblically based images are employed by the authors of martyrdoms to cast the act of dying as the fulfillment of a biblical ethical command. The *Martyrdom of Pionius*, for example, draws upon the image of the narrow gate in order to present the martyr's death as the highly selective ethical pathway to God: "After his victory in the great combat he passed through the narrow gate into the broad, great light."[67] The motif of the narrow gate recalls a saying of Jesus in Matt 7:13–14//Luke 13:24 in which passage through ἡ στενὴ πύλη is part of the arduous path to salvation. The allusion to this image serves a number of purposes. It underscores the ethical fidelity of the martyr and his adherence to the commands of the Savior. It also recasts the arduous and difficult nature of salvation in terms of martyrdom. While Matthew and Luke doubtless saw the narrow gate as something less demanding than martyrdom, for the author of *Pionius*, it was the martyr's death.

For Pionius, passing through the narrow gate leads to immediate resurrection. The immediacy and assured nature of the reward explain his impatience to die.[68] The martyr declares: "I am hurrying that I may awake all the more quickly, manifesting the resurrection from the dead."[69] The hurried approach to martyrdom is not unique to Pionius, but his answer implies a curious state of affairs as regards the afterlife.[70] The idea that martyrdom will permit him to "awake all the more quickly" implies a temporal distinction in attaining a place in heaven. We can infer from his statement that his speedy "resurrection" is a direct result of his martyrdom.[71]

Pionius is not alone in hastening toward resurrection and eternal life. Bishop Fructuosus, martyred under Decius, is similarly eager to arrive in heaven. When Christians bring him drugged wine to drink, Fructuosus refuses on the grounds that it was a fast day. He declines to break his fast, confident in the belief that he would eat at the heavenly banquet that awaited him.[72]

Fructuosus's confidence in his imminent resurrection lasts to the end. After the flames burn through the restraints that bind him to the stake, Fructuosus and his companions remain unmoved, they kneel in prayer and joy, "assured of the resurrection."[73] Fructuosus's confidence is apparently well-founded; at the moment of his death two members of the governor's household behold a vision of the bishops' ascent to heaven:

> After this the usual miracles of the Lord were not lacking. Babylas
> and Mygdonius, two of our brethren in the household of the gover-
> nor Aemilianus, saw the heavens open, and this they also revealed to
> Aemilianus' daughter, their mistress according to the flesh: there was
> the saintly bishop Fructuosus together with his deacons rising
> crowned up to heaven, with the stakes to which they had been bound
> still intact.[74]

The vision of the heavenly ascent of the bishop, flanked by two deacons, recalls the crucifixion of Jesus.[75] That they wear crowns indicates that their martyrdom is complete and they have been received into heaven. The immediacy of their ascent is again confirmed by the language used by the martyrdom's chief actors. The two visionaries, emboldened by what they had seen, berate Aemilianus the Roman prefect for his actions and invite him to behold the vision, saying, "Come and see how those whom you have condemned to death today have been restored to heaven and to their hopes" (*Mart. Fruct.* 5.2). The invitation is likely an allusion to bodily transfiguration and resurrection, but the point remains the same. As with the other martyrs we have examined, Fructuosus and his companions ascend to heaven on the day of their martyrdom.

The immediacy of the ascent of the martyrs to heaven can be juxtapositioned with the postmortem expectations of ordinary Christians. Discussion of the fate of ordinary Christians can be gleaned from the writings of contemporary Christians.[76] Even within the acts of the martyrs themselves, there is an awareness of the difference between the resurrection of those who were martyred and those were not. The *Testament of the Forty Martyrs of Sebaste* deals with the situation of a confessor who is released. For those who are executed the expectation is clear that they will receive the appropriate rewards and promises and pass into heaven, here described in prayer as the "kingdom": "To the divine soul and spirit we pray that all of us may obtain God's eternal blessings and his kingdom, now and for ever."[77] In the case of a boy named Eunoicus, a confessor imprisoned with the martyrs, the situation is markedly different: "If he [the young boy Eunoicus] . . . be preserved unharmed by the grace of Christ and should still be counted among the living, we urge that he devote himself with all freedom to our tomb, and we exhort him to keep the commands of Christ that on that great day of resurrection he may share with us in our rewards."[78] The martyrs pray that Eunoicus will be preserved from harm, that he will tend to their tomb, and that he will keep the commands of God so that following the resurrection he will be able to share in their refreshment. The rewards described here may well be an allusion to the heavenly banquet enjoyed by the martyrs. If this is the case, this passage implies that the martyrs will enjoy the heavenly banquet prior to the "great day of resurrection." It is only after this presumably eschatological resurrection that Eunoicus as a pious Christian will be able to partake in this banquet.[79] The situation envisioned is that martyrs will proceed directly to the heavenly buffet table, but pious confessors must await the end of time.

Mode of Ascent

In recounting the martyr's admission into heaven, a number of images are employed. In the *Martyrdom of Polycarp*, the martyr is drawn into God's presence in the manner of a burnt offering. Sacrificial imagery is rarely used to describe the mechanics of ascent, although it is also alluded to in the *Martyrdom of Conon*, where the translocation of the martyr to heaven is described using sacrificial language: "The blessed Conon was brought as an offering to God the king of the ages" (*Mart. Conon* 6.7).

More often, the language of resurrection and sometimes heavenly ascent is used. In the case of famed North African martyrs Perpetua and Saturus, the language of heavenly ascent is employed. In her well-known vision, Perpetua scales a precarious and dangerous version of Jacob's ladder as she ascends toward heaven:

> I saw a ladder of tremendous height made of bronze, reaching all the
> way to the heavens, but it was so narrow that only one person could
> climb at a time. To the sides of the ladder were attached all sorts of
> metal weapons: there were swords, spears, hooks, daggers and
> spikes; so that if anyone tried to climb up carelessly or without

paying attention, he would be mangled and his flesh would adhere to
the weapons. At the foot of the ladder lay a dragon of enormous size
and it would attack those who tried to go up.[80]

Perpetua's ascent is fraught with danger and difficulty. The ladder is at once
narrow, guarded by a dragon, and adorned with hazardous materials. As is
frequently noted, the mode of her transition to heaven and its portrayal as
ascent reflect the arduous nature of martyrdom and the influence of apocalyptic traditions of heavenly ascent.

Given the close literary ties between the *Passion of Perpetua and Felicitas*
and other Carthaginian martyrdoms, it is not surprising that the same imagery
of climbing up to heaven reappears. In the vision of the eschatological judgment scene contained in the *Martyrdom of Marian and James*, Marian climbs
the scaffold upon which Christ and Cyprian are seated in order that he might
join them at the judgment seat.[81] Similarly, in the diary that constitutes the first
portion of the *Martyrdom of Montanus and Lucius*, the martyrs describe their
tortures in the following way: "We climbed this high tower of torment as though
we were climbing up to heaven."[82]

While North African martyrs scale their way up to heaven, the move to
heaven is less arduous for others. For some, the transition comes at the behest
of angelic transporters who snatch away the soul of the martyr and carry it to
the heavens. An example of this is found in the martyrdom of Irenaeus, bishop
of Sirmium, whose final prayer expresses this desire: "Lord Jesus Christ, who
deigned to suffer for the world's salvation, let your heavens open that your
angels may take up the soul of your servant Irenaeus, who suffers all this for
your name and for the community that has been formed from your Catholic
Church at Sirmium. I beg and implore your mercy that you will deign to receive
me and to confirm them in your faith."[83] For other martyrs, angelic transport
seems wholly unnecessary. The transferal to heaven appears to be a natural,
almost automatic, flight of the soul to the heavens in which the soul or spirit of
the martyr "departs" to heaven at the moment of death.[84] The flight of the soul
to heaven is sometimes cast in almost naturalistic terms. In a vision in the
Martyrdom of Montanus and Lucius, the Lord from heaven instructs the presby-
ter Victor: "'The spirit hastens to its God and the soul, now near her sufferings,
has sought her proper place.'"[85]

The Heavenly Welcoming Committee

Upon arrival in the heavenly realm the martyrs could expect to be warmly greeted
as conquering heroes. They ascended to join the ranks of those distinguished

enough to become heavenly tenants. As we might expect, most martyrdom accounts assume the presence of God, Christ, and angels in heaven, and more often than not, it is Christ who "receives" them after their deaths.[86] The martyr Maximillian, for example, expects that if he is martyred he will live with Christ.[87] Both *Polycarp* and *Fructuosus* indicate that the martyr can expect to join the ranks of those martyrs who had come before him.[88] To the ranks of the martyrs Fructuosus, like the author of the *Ascension of Isaiah*, adds the prophets.[89] The North African martyrdom *Marian and James* includes the patriarchs in the heavenly court, writing that the martyrs were restored to them in glory when they were delivered from the world.[90]

Several martyrdoms add more ambiguous groups to the heavenly court. A number of accounts refer to the presence of "saints" in heaven. The soldier-martyr Dasius expects that "after death I shall inherit eternal life together with all the saints (τῶν ἁγίων)."[91] The precise referent of the term "saints" is unclear and of critical importance. A possible allusion is being made to LXX Psalm 88:8, where God sits in the council of his "holy ones" or "saints."[92] Critical interpretations of this and other references to the holy ones in the Hebrew Bible maintain that the "holy ones" are angelic beings.[93] Although this interpretation is by no means assured, it is supported by later biblical and extracanonical material that refers to angels in this way.[94] While the association of the holy ones with angels persists into the early Christian period, it also assumes a new meaning in Paul as a way of referring to members of the Christian community. In his epistles Paul frequently uses the term to refer to devoted members of his community.[95] The exclusivity of this category for Paul becomes even more acute in 1 Cor 6:2–3, where Paul writes that the saints will judge the whole world, even the angels.[96] In the first three centuries of the early church, then, the term "saint" had a broad meaning and denoted catechumens as well as members of the churches in much the same way that the term "faithful" is applied today.[97]

It is certainly possible that Dasius here refers to the pious Christian dead, but given the historical context of fourth-century Christianity and an emerging cult of the saints, it seems probable that he refers to other martyrs or Christians of special note rather than ordinary members of the church. After all, the martyrdom uses the adjective ἅγιός to describe the martyred Dasius himself. This reading is confirmed by a more specific discussion of the saints in yet another soldier martyrdom, the *Acts of Julius the Veteran*. In this narrative Julius accepts death and eternal life in preference to earthly life, saying, " 'I have chosen death for now, that I might live with the saints forever.' "[98] This notion of habitation "with the saints" is confirmed and explicated by a fellow Christian soldier bystander, Isichius, who asks Julian to convey a message to another martyr, Valentio, who has already proceeded "to the Lord" (4.2); Julius completes his martyrdom requesting the Lord "to receive my spirit together with your holy martyrs" (4.5). It would seem, then, that in *Julius the Veteran* at least, the terms "saint" and "martyr" are used interchangeably, as indeed they were in many later Christian circles.

A similar ambiguity appears in the *Martyrdom of Conon*. Just before his death, the martyr Conon prays he will be received into heaven by Christ and dwell among "the just" after his death: "Lord Jesus Christ receive my soul; rescue me from these bloodthirsty hounds, and give me rest in the company of all your just ones (τῶν δικαίων) who have fulfilled your will."[99] As with τῶν ἁγίων the precise referent of τῶν δικαίων is uncertain as it has a variety of meanings in scriptural texts and literature contemporary with the *Martyrdom of Conon*. In biblical texts it was used in reference to those who do God's will, particularly the patriarchs,[100] prophets,[101] and those who died innocently.[102] The term implies a particular relationship with God[103] and is even used of the Messiah in the Septuagint.[104] It would seem, then, that like the *Ascension of Isaiah*, the author of the *Martyrdom of Conon* expects that heaven will contain righteous individuals who may or may not have also been martyrs.

Before proceeding to the activities of the martyrs in heaven, we should briefly note an instance in which the martyrs' earthly life and their ascension into heaven overlap. In the *Martyrdom of Agape, Irene and Chione*, the martyrs begin to take up residence in heaven even before their death. Before their deaths the three women martyrs flee to a mountain, where they take refuge and pray. The narrator adds that through their prayer their souls already lived in heaven.[105] This passage seems to suggest that a martyr's status and place in heaven could be attained even before death itself by means of prayer and confession.[106] Given that the bodies of the three female martyrs are specifically mentioned as remaining on the earth, however, we should not assume that this passage proposes a permanent premortem ascension to heaven. The belief that prayer or other liturgical activities could translocate the community of believers into the heavenly worship has some precedent in the literature of Qumran.[107] It may very well be that the same idea of participating in heavenly worship was prevalent in Christian circles and is at work in the *Martyrdom of Agape, Irene and Chione*. Alternatively, the reference to the mountain may evoke images of the ascent of the righteous individual or seer, an idea common to Judeo-Christian apocalyptic literature. In neither case should we view these as examples of permanent assumption into heaven, but they nonetheless challenge the otherwise strict notion that only martyrs ascend to heaven at the moment of their deaths.

While the landscape of ideas about resurrection is dense and cluttered, certain general themes can be noted. With respect to the *timing* of resurrection from the dead, members of the Jesus movement maintained that Jesus had been resurrected on the third day and that the faithful dead would be resurrected just before the final judgment. With respect to the timing of resurrection, therefore, it is safe to say that martyrs are more similar to Christ than they are to other dead Christians. There are some notable exceptions to the idea of an eschatological resurrection, most interestingly the status of the "saints" in *Ascension of Isaiah* and the idea of the ascension of "special dead."

While the acts of the martyrs may utilize the general conception of the immediate resurrection of the "special dead" prevalent in antiquity, their application of the idea is strategic and selective. Amid the diverse representations of heaven, there are a number of trends that can be remarked upon. The idea of resurrection in these accounts centers on the privileged position of the martyrs over and against the ordinary dead and other members of the "special dead." Apostles, patriarchs, and prophets make rare appearances in the martyrdom narratives, and the immediate resurrection of the martyr contrasts with the delayed resurrection of ordinary Christians. Within the world created by the martyrdom narratives, only martyrs can rest assured of immediate ascension to heaven. The reinterpretation of the idea of the "special dead" in these accounts is strategic. It reconstructs heaven as martyr territory.

Heavenly Banquet

Once they arrived in heaven, martyrs could expect to attend the ongoing heavenly banquet. Martyrdom, after all, is physically draining, and we can imagine they had worked up quite the appetite. James, one of the headlined characters in the *Martyrdom of Marian and James*, beholds a vision of the martyr Agapius and exclaims, "I am on my way to the banquet of Agapius and the other blessed martyrs!"[108] The allure of the banquet is such that bishop Fructuosus puts off eating in prison in anticipation of his imminent attendance of the heavenly feast.[109] The *Testament of the Forty Martyrs* contains the same idea of postmortem heavenly refreshment.[110] The idea that heaven is a gastronomical affair is once again biblically based. Lawrence Schiffman has argued that belief in an eschatological messianic banquet played a significant role in the day-to-day life of the sectarian Qumran community.[111] He goes so far as to suggest that the Qumran community looked forward to a regular series of banquets in the future.[112] On more than one occasion, Jesus refers to the "eating and drinking" that will take place in the heavenly kingdom.[113] This idea is furthered by Matthew's repeated use of the wedding feast in his parables of the kingdom.[114] In

Jewish expectation and the Gospel of Matthew, the heavenly banquet is an eschatological event and a symbol of a new age. For the martyrs, however, the banquet had already begun.

Further support for this idea may be found in Roman catacomb paintings that depict individuals feasting around a table with bread, wine, and fishes.[115] Scholars have debated the precise reference of these paintings, seeking to locate their origins in either eucharistic or pagan *refrigeria*.[116] In pagan ritual practices the *refrigeria* were occasions when people would visit the tomb of a deceased relative to hold a commemorative meal in their honor. These practices, it is argued, were easily adapted to the cult of the martyrs, and inscriptional evidence from Rome and North Africa suggests *refrigeria* were a common feature in the veneration of saints. While there is no doubt as to the existence of these practices, and their derivation from pagan rituals seems relatively secure, this does not mean that the ideological significance of the *refrigerium* has been exhausted or explained.

In pagan practice, the *refrigerium* had a very clear underlying significance. The dead, for whom the meals were offered, were often believed to be thirsty.[117] The ritualistic pouring out of libations and consumption of food therefore had a vicarious benefit.[118] In return, the dead could offer little by way of assistance to the living, certainly nothing approaching the support of a martyr. The dead were being fed and watered as they wandered thirsty and helpless in the shades of Hades. With respect to the martyrs, the situation was notably different. As already noted, the martyrs had ascended to heaven. While they were able to and certainly did leave heaven to appear in visions or attend feasts held in their honor, their postmortem existence was certainly a step up from any kind of earthly one. As we have seen, they already enjoyed a heavenly banquet. Given that the martyrs were satiated banqueters with no ostensible need for *refrigeria*, we must ask, what was the logic of the performance of *refrigeria* in Christian contexts? How did notions of a heavenly banquet overlap and intersect with funerary practices of offering libations to martyrs?

One piece of this puzzle is supplied by the heretofore unnoted importance of the heavenly banquet in the ideology of martyrdom and its associated funerary practices.[119] If we return to the previous example of the *Testament of the Forty Martyrs*, we can see a significant link between the practice of the *refrigerium* and eschatological feasting: the boy Eunoicus is exhorted to tend to the tomb of the forty martyrs, a responsibility that presumably involved cultic activities. If he does this, he is promised a share in the refreshment (*refrigeria*) of the martyrs on the great day of resurrection. The text states that the martyrs are already refreshed and that these rewards can be shared by pious Christians after the resurrection.

This passage could imply that the "refreshment" was the same as that received through cultic practice, but this seems somewhat illogical. After all, on the day of resurrection, when the good are sorted from the bad, who will be left to perform these cultic activities on behalf of the martyrs? No one, presumably. The eschatological refreshment, therefore, seems more likely to be that of the heavenly banquet. In this case the cultic practice of the *refrigerium* and the traditional idea of a heavenly banquet are drawn together in the context of the cult of the saints. The overlap between the *refrigerium* and the heavenly banquet motif augments their significance. I wish to tentatively suggest that the practice of offering *refrigerium* to the martyrs was not only a ritual offering on behalf of the dead drawn from pagan tradition but also a means of ritualistically sharing in the heavenly banquet in which the martyrs already partook. The basic notion of participating in heavenly practices via ritualistic or liturgical practice was well established.[120] Even if this suggestion is discarded, the subject of artistic depictions of meals on catacomb walls is still open for debate. Just as they may depict *refrigeria* offered in the tombs, they might equally represent either the feasting of the martyrs in heaven or the eschatological banquet to come.[121]

At the same time as the heavenly banquet illuminates catacomb art and associated practices, it contributes to our understanding of Christian asceticism or *askesis*. In a series of publications, Andrew McGowan has discussed the significance of diet, ritual meals, and asceticism in North Africa.[122] McGowan uses the martyrdom accounts to parse attitudes toward the martyr's diet. He identifies both a strategy of abundance, in which martyrs were fed by members of the Christian community, and a strategy of asceticism, in which martyrs were encouraged to abstain from food and drink. Within the context of incarceration and bodily privation, McGowan sees these strategies as a way of modeling a distinctive Christian identity over and against Roman attempts to control the Christian body.

McGowan's thesis offers an insightful look into the strategies that shaped attitudes toward diet in Carthage, but he does not note the contrast between earthly *askesis* and heavenly feasting. Many of the martyrdom accounts that McGowan identifies as positive examples of the ascetic impulse contrast this asceticism with an opulent vision of heavenly abundance and feasting. The disparity between the abbreviated present privation and eternal future reward is an elementary feature of martyrdom accounts. Like other privations, sufferings, and torments, the *askesis* of the martyr is short-lived and temporary. This is not to say that ascetic practices are insincere, but rather that their value both for the practitioner and for potential mimics is tied to the epicurean delights that they anticipate. Asceticism remains an act of resistance, but it functions somewhat differently. Bishop Fructuosus's refusal of drugged wine resists Roman attempts to control him inasmuch as he dismisses bodily discomfort as an attempt to "save his appetite." The reinterpretation of fasting in this way belittles the effects and intended aims of imprisonment and bodily deprivation.

Heavenly Choir

A primary function of the angels in heaven is as heavenly attendants. The epistle to the Hebrews describes them as "ministering spirits" (Heb 1:14) and relegates them to subordinate roles. As servants, they shuffle back and forth between heaven and earth directing tours,[123] fetching and carrying,[124] and guarding entryways and gates.[125] To say that they are glorified bouncers would not be an understatement. Martyrs do not appear to share in these menial tasks and rarely appear as servants in heaven. Even though they are courageous warriors of God who vanquish the devil, they do not take on the role of heavenly law enforcement. There is, however, one critical celebratory task in which they do participate: the eternal praises of the heavenly choir.

In Christian tradition, the notion of a heavenly chorus of angels developed out of the scene of the heavenly throne room in Isaiah 6. Here Isaiah beholds three seraphim, guarding the throne of God and singing "Holy, holy, holy is the Lord of hosts; the whole earth is full of his glory!" (Isa 6:3). The idea that the angels were engaged in constant praise was popular in later Jewish and Christian texts that frequently referred to the musical activities of the heavenly choirs.[126] The popularity of this idea was such that certain communities conceptualized their own worship as participation in the heavenly liturgy.[127]

The same concept reappears in the *acta* where the martyrs aspire to sing with the choirs of angels. The theme is far from omnipresent. It does not appear until the *Passion of Perpetua and Felicitas*, and in this case the martyrs themselves do not sing. In a vision of heaven, the martyr Saturus describes hearing voices chanting "holy, holy, holy" (cf. Isa 6:3 and Rev 4:8),[128] but he does not participate in the heavenly refrain. The sound of the unseen choir connects Saturus's vision with those of Isaiah and John the Divine, implicitly identifying him as a prophetic visionary and reconstructing his vision within a biblical metatext.

The idea appears in full for the first time in the Diocletianic account of the *Martyrdom of Agape, Irene and Chione*. Here the narrator notes that by overcoming the devil they will "endlessly praise along with the angels the God who had showered this grace upon them."[129] The connection between triumph over the devil and heavenly liturgy is instructive for our understanding of liturgy in Thessaloniki. The association suggests that liturgy functions as a thanksgiving for cosmic victory and, moreover, that participants in the Thessalonian liturgy are drawn into the cosmic contest through song. Their own performances of praise give thanks for and anticipate eschatological victory. In both the *Passion of Perpetua and Felicitas* and the *Martyrdom of Agape, Irene and Chione*, the heavenly choir serves to legitimize the earthly liturgy. It is noteworthy, however, that references to the martyrs singing with the angels *in the early acta themselves* are extraordinarily rare.[130]

Paradisiacal Heaven

The majority of martyr acts imply that heaven is a heavenly court or throne room.[131] In a number of North African texts, however, heaven is a paradisiacal garden comparable to that of Eden. In the *Passion of Perpetua and Felicitas*, Perpetua has a vision of heaven in which she encounters a shepherdlike figure: "Then I saw an immense garden, and in it a grey-haired man sat in shepherd's garb; tall he was, and milking sheep. And standing around him were many thousands of people clad in white garments. He raised his head, looked at me, and said 'I am glad you have come my child.'"[132] Perpetua's literary offspring, *Marian and James*, describes how God grants the martyrs a more extensive tour of the heavenly garden: "Our road lay through a country with lovely meadows, clad with the joyous foliage of bourgeoning woods, shaded by tall cypress and pine trees that beat against the heavens, so that you would think that the entire spot all round was crowned with fertile groves. In the center was a hollow that abounded in pure water and in the fertilizing watercourses of a crystal spring."[133] The detailed descriptions of the spacious gardens in these two texts certainly recall the paradisiacal state of Eden and draw upon the idea expressed in the Book of the Watchers that Eden continued to exist.[134] The *Martyrdom of Marian and James* combines this idea with the familiar language of the Good Shepherd used in both the Psalms and Gospels as a metaphor for God's provision. The image of God as the Good Shepherd resonates with the opening of the ever-popular Psalm 23, in which God tends to the needs of his "flock." This idea serves as inspiration for gospel portraits of Jesus, who repeatedly uses shepherd imagery to refer to himself (Matt 18:12; John 10:2, 11–12). The vision of Perpetua is a fusion of language regarding God's shepherd like provision with the idea of a heavenly Eden wrapped up in a tidy apocalyptic visionary bundle.

Intercession

Given their reputation for virtue in life, it is unsurprising that martyrs would continue to exhibit a little *philanthropia* in death. Following their deaths, martyrs stayed involved in the activities and lives of ordinary Christians. In the cult

of the saints they served as intercessors for humankind with God. Recent scholarship, most notably the work of Peter Brown, has demonstrated the social and
economic importance of intercession and saintly patronage in late antique
Christianity.[135] Using a sociological model of patron-client relations, Brown
and others have argued that the intercession of the saints served a societal function, with distinct economic and spiritual benefits for all. The application of the
patron-client model to all aspects of the cult of the saints has been universally
accepted. At the same time, however, there are references to saintly intercession in third-century *acta* that predate formal cultic practices. Even if these texts
should be dated later than is normally argued, we should still consider the possibility that the intercession of the martyrs has ideological or interpretative significance.

A prime example of the intercession of the martyr on behalf of others is
found in Potamiaena, the Alexandrian maiden described by both Eusebius and
Sozomen.[136] The narrative is replete with allusions to Christly traditions. Her
death serves the same inspirational purpose as that of the Markan Jesus, whose
crucifixion is the catalyst for the proclamatory statement of the centurion.[137] Even
more than her death, however, her postmortem visionary appearance serves to
assimilate her to the risen Christ of Luke-Acts, who appears to Paul on the road
to Damascus (Acts 9:1–17). In Acts, the sudden appearance of Christ to a perse-
cutor elicits his conversion; so too Potamiaena appears not only to Basilides but
to many others, even calling them by name as Jesus had done (Acts 9:4),
prompting their conversion. Potamiaena's postmortem activity of recruiting
martyrs for the church has much in common with the postmortem activities of
Jesus in Acts.

Potamiaena's role in the conversion and recruitment of additional martyrs,
however, goes further than mere name-calling. A notable feature of the *acta*'s
description of Potamiaena's behavior is her role as an intercessor and conduit
for grace: "He [Basilides] is said to have replied that three days after her martyrdom Potamiaena appeared to him at night and put a crown on his head; she
said that she had requested his grace from the Lord and had obtained her
prayer, and that she would welcome him before long."[138] Here it is Potamiaena's prayerful intercession that has obtained salvation for Basilides. She
becomes the conduit through which grace is brokered and channeled. She
prays on his behalf to the Lord and secures his status as martyr and the confer-
ral of heavenly reward symbolized in the bestowal of the crown. While it is
unclear if Basilides himself desires such a status, it is clear that it is Potamiaena
who obtains it for him.

Moreover, that it is Potamiaena herself who crowns Basilides and Potamiaena who secures the gift of grace indicates the instrumental role that she plays.

The reception of the "crown of martyrdom" is a common image used to describe the rewards bestowed upon the martyrs.[139] Ordinarily, however, it is Christ himself who crowns his victorious martyrs (cf. Rev 2:10 and *Acts of Maximilian* 3.2; *Acts of Julius the Veteran* 4.2). That Potamiaena bestows the crown indicates that she has stepped into the Christly role. The theologically laden language of grace here is striking. By her actions, Potamiaena secures a portion of the grace of the Lord for Basilides. In Pauline discussions of the mechanics of grace bestowing, Jesus serves as the means by which Christians have access to the grace of God (cf. Rom 5:2; 1 Cor 1:3). It is through Jesus and, more precisely, through Jesus' death that grace becomes available to Christians. The same idea of obtaining grace through another person is at work here in the *Martyrdom of Potamiaena and Basilides*. Only now it is Potamiaena who acts as the conduit for grace (albeit the grace of Jesus). Presumably, her credentials for this position are likewise grounded in her special death. In the economy of grace there has been a shift in roles. The Lord Jesus has become the exalted source of grace, and the martyr has slipped into the intercessory role he has vacated.

In the third and fourth centuries, the practice of intercession seems particularly prominent in a group of martyrdoms from Carthage. The trend begins with the oft-cited example from the *Passion of Perpetua and Felicitas* in which Perpetua has a series of visions of her dead brother, Dinocrates. In her initial vision, the deceased Dinocrates suffers:

> I saw Dinocrates coming out of a dark hole, where there were many others with him, very hot and thirsty, pale and dirty. On his face was the wound he had when he died. Now Dinocrates had been my brother according to the flesh; but he had died horribly of cancer of the face when he was seven years old, and his death was a source of loathing to everyone. Thus it was for him that I made my prayer. There was a great abyss between us: neither could approach the other. Where Dinocrates stood there was a pool full of water; and its rim was higher than the child's height, so that Dinocrates had to stretch himself up to drink. I was sorry that, though the pool had water in it, Dinocrates could not drink because of the height of the rim. Then I woke up realizing that my brother was suffering.[140]

In this, the first vision, Dinocrates manifests the usual features of the helpless dead. As was traditional in Greco-Roman thought, he is thirsty. He occupies a cave, perhaps an allusion either to the shades of Hades or to a kind of interim well of the souls such as that in *1 Enoch*. Either way, his situation is dire. He struggles in vain to reach the pool of water, here surely a symbol not of martyrdom but of baptism.[141] Upon awakening from her vision, Perpetua is confident that she can help him. She prays for him "day and night" with tears and sighs. On the day she is transferred to prison, Perpetua sees another vision:

> I saw the same spot that I had seen before, but there was Dinocrates
> all clean, well dressed and refreshed. I saw a scar where the wound
> had been; and the pool that I had seen before now had its rim
> lowered to the level of the child's waist. And Dinocrates kept drinking
> water from it, and there above the rim was a golden bowl full of
> water. And Dinocrates drew close and began to drink from it, and yet
> the bowl remained full. And when he had drunk enough of the water,
> he began to play as children do. Then I awoke, and I realized that he
> had been delivered from his suffering.[142]

Perpetua's prayers liberate her dead brother from his suffering. The symbolic transformation of the child picks up on traditional language of baptism and salvation. He was dirty but now is clean; he has new clothes and is now refreshed (*referigerantem*). The language of refreshment again draws upon the matrix of cultic practices associated with the *referigium*, an allusion reinforced by the mention of the golden bowl of water. The difference here is that what would in pagan practices have been secured by a commemorative meal is here accomplished by the prayers and supplications of the saintly confessor. The symbolic nature of the child's condition, and in particular his dirtiness, would lead us to believe that Perpetua's intercession achieves more than quenching the thirst of a deceased soul. As a result of her intercession he is cleaned, receives new clothes, and drinks from a pool of water. All three of these images have baptismal undertones that, we must assume, would not have been lost on the hearer.[143]

The intercessory role of the martyr reappears in another Latin Carthaginian martyrdom associated with the *Passion of Perpetua and Felicitas*: the *Martyrdom of Marian and James*. Here a deceased martyr prays that two virtuous young women of his earthly acquaintance might also become martyrs:

> Agapius had long before perfected the mysteries of his faith by
> martyrdom. There were two young women, Tertulla and Antonia,
> whom he loved most dearly as though they were his own daughters.
> When after often repeated prayers he begged God that they too might
> become martyrs with him by divine favor, he won the confidence of
> his merits by the following revelation. For he heard the words, "Why
> do you continue to beg for something you have obtained by a single
> prayer?"[144]

It is clear that the prayers of the martyr have a special efficacy. Unlike Perpetua, Agapius secures his request by a single prayer. The situation is also markedly different. Like Potamiaena, Agapius intercedes in order to secure the favor of martyrdom for those who were still living. This curious situation underscores the positive view of martyrs and martyrdom in the eyes of Carthaginian martyrs. It further indicates that martyrdom was not the achievement of the martyr but a blessing from God. This idea runs contrary to modern definitions of martyrdom in which martyrdom is constructed as a choice on the part of the individual. In both *Potamiaena and Basilides* and *Marian and James*, martyrdom involves the blessing and favor of God. These texts highlight the belief in the role of God in orchestrating martyrdom, not merely in the sense that God allows events to transpire that would lead someone to martyrdom but that God in fact chooses to grant martyrdom as a gift.[145]

Archaeological evidence indicates that, from the end of the third century, the intercession of the martyrs became big business. Appeals could be made for healings, for economic profit, for the forgiveness of sins, and so forth.[146] The proximity of the martyrs to the throne of God meant that they had more opportunity to secure a positive result. In these earlier literary accounts, however, we see martyrs interceding to secure very specific kinds of reward. In the case of Perpetua, she prays on behalf of her deceased brother and secures a transformation in his postmortem experience. We might logically infer that she has secured some kind of salvation or postmortem baptism. At the very least his situation is greatly improved. In the case of Potamiaena and Agapius, they pray to God that their earthly friends might become martyrs and secure this special status for them. Interestingly enough, in both cases the actions and details of the deaths of the secondary martyrs Basilides, Tertulla, and Antonia are strikingly brief. There is little detail about the trial of Basilides, and the martyrs Tertulla and Antonia receive no attention at all, save the concluding point that they also died. It would seem, in this early period, that martyrs interceded on behalf of Christians in their communities in order that others might attain the status of martyr and the benefits that entailed.

The description of the martyrs as intercessors and as mediators between humans and the divine has analogues both in the actions of angels and in the person of Christ. As is widely acknowledged, angels served as messengers of God, as mediators and go-betweens. They served auxiliary roles as heavenly guides and military commanders, but their roles were essentially mediatory.[147] Angels do not generally intercede on behalf of the fate of individuals or humanity.[148] On the contrary, they are the messengers *of God*, and they mediate his desires and wishes to humans, rather than vice versa.

This is in contrast to Christ, whose intercessory roles place him on the side of humankind. In biblical accounts Christ intercedes for humankind in two ways: his death serves a soteriological function that atones for the sins of humanity,[149] and he serves as an advocate in the heavenly court. Because the soteriological dimensions of Jesus' death and its similarities with martyrdom were discussed in the previous chapter, we will focus here on Christ's role as an advocate. In his epistle to the Romans, Paul describes how the exalted Christ, seated at the right hand of the father, intercedes for humanity in the heavenly realm: "Who is to condemn? It is Christ Jesus, who died, yes, who was raised, who is at the right hand of God, who indeed intercedes for us."[150] In heaven, we can suppose, Christ appears at moments of judgment to intercede on behalf of Christians. Intercession here is tied to judgment, but more generalized proclamations of Jesus' intercessory role abound. First Timothy declares that "there is one God and one mediator between God and men, the Man Christ Jesus."[151] These passages illustrate the idea that Jesus could intercede on behalf of humankind to secure their salvation and freedom from condemnation. A similar idea undergirds the earlier examples of saintly intercession that we examined earlier; the martyr secures salvation on behalf of someone else. In this respect, therefore, the intercession of the martyrs is more similar to the intercessory work of Christ than it is to that of the angels, as both the martyrs and Christ intercede to secure the salvation of others. To be sure, the martyrs secure a very specific kind of favor on behalf of their beneficiaries, but it is still a profound and soteriologically significant event.

Judgment

As every ancient writer with a linear sense of time knows, all good things must come to an end, and this end is most properly marked by an eschatological judgment scene of cosmic proportions. In the words of Paul, "We must all appear before the judgment seat of Christ, so that each one may receive good or evil, according to what he has done in the body" (2 Cor 5:10). The belief in eschatological judgment permeates the fabric of early Christian life in its literary, artistic, and liturgical products. Eschatological judgment serves as the setting for the delivery of punishment; earthly injustices will be overturned, and the wicked will be brought low.

In the literature of the Jesus movement, the dominant idea was that the world would be judged by God and Christ. Sinners would be resurrected, only to meet final and everlasting punishment. That this judgment would be exacted on the basis of earthly existence is everywhere assumed. Both the Markan and

Johannine Jesuses describe the ramifications of denying Christ in the here and now:

> Mark 8:38: "Those who are ashamed of me and of my words in this adulterous and sinful generation, of them the Son of Man will also be ashamed when he comes in the glory of his Father with the holy angels."[152]

And again:

> John 12:48: "The one who rejects me and does not receive my word has a judge; on the last day the word that I have spoken will serve as judge."[153]

In the writings of the early church, as in Mark and John, the relationship between present action and future judgment is frequently connected to belief in Christ. Indeed, Ignatius writes in his letter *To the Smyrneans* that judgment is prepared even for the heavenly beings if they do not believe.[154]

For the martyr, however, the ordinary rules do not apply. By their deaths they escape judgment altogether. The knowledge that they escape judgment serves as a focal point for the martyrs' attentions and a motivating factor behind their deaths.[155] Two motifs of judgment are utilized in the acts of the martyrs. The first image is an eschatological purge, a judgment by fire by God. This notion was particularly popular in second-century Rome, where both the *Acts of Ptolemaeus and Lucius* and the *Acts of Justin* refer to the destruction of the world by fire.[156] The very brief *Acts of Ptolemaeus and Lucius*, contained within Justin's *2 Apology*, has very few references to Christian beliefs at all. Nonetheless, the unnamed Christian wife warns her husband that those who do not live just, virtuous lives are destined to be consumed by the eternal fire (*2 Apology* 2.2). Unsurprisingly, given his authorship of *Ptolemaeus and Lucius* and participation in the *Acts of Justin*, Justin Martyr makes a similar declaration that the world will be consumed by fiery judgment (*Acts of Justin* B 5.2).

The idea is not unique to Rome or to texts associated with Justin Martyr. Pionius also bears witness to "the judgment by fire that is to come."[157] Nor is the notion of fire as a form of punishment independent of other ideas about the eschaton. The martyr Conon warns his accusers to be wary of the judge that could sentence them to Hades: "Beware lest the Judge sentence you to a Hades that is unsurpassed, a fire unquenchable forever, where the worm does not die and the fire is not quenched" (*Mart. Conon* 5.7; cf. Mark 9:48). In this last example, the idea of judgment by fire is linked to that of a heavenly tribunal or court scene in which a person is condemned to fire. The martyrs circumvent the all-consuming eschatological fire, the fires of Hades, and even the heavenly tribunal itself. Their exceptional status when it comes to judgment means that they face neither the fires of Hades nor the judgment by God.

We should note that the judgment by fire envisioned in the *Martyrdom of Pionius* and the *Martyrdom of Conon* are qualitatively different from the idea of the eventual consumption of the world by fire in the Roman *acta*. In the former, the fiery judgment draws upon the traditional biblical notions that Gehenna and Hades are actual locations to which a person can be sent. In the case of Justin, Apollonius, and Ptolemaeus, the destruction of the world by fire is linked to Stoic philosophical ideas about the future conflagration of the entire world by flames (*ekpyrosis*).[158] While the image of judgment by fire is superficially similar in both types, we should note their ideological distinctiveness.

While for the most part eschatological judgment is considered to be a proprietary right of Christ, there are some hints that others could aspire to share in the judiciary role of the Lord. For Paul, the eschatological fate of the angels was rather more uncertain. In Paul's heavenly supercourt the faithful Christians will serve as judges over the whole world, from the angels down: "Do you not know that the saints will judge the world? And if the world is to be judged by you, are you incompetent to try trivial cases? Do you not know that we are to judge angels—to say nothing of ordinary matters?"[159] In its original context, Paul almost certainly meant that Christians would serve as judges at the eschaton. Elsewhere in the Pauline corpus the term ἅγιος denotes members of the Christian community, and we have no reason to suppose that he means anything else here.[160] For members of the early church, particularly those interested in martyrs, the term gleamed with special and particular significance.[161] Read within the context of the ideology of martyrdom, phrases such as this suggested that, in the future, martyrs would serve as co-judges with Christ.

The most prolonged discussion of this theme in a martyrdom account itself is found in the *Martyrdom of Marian and James*, a third-century North African text with close literary ties to the *Passion of Perpetua and Felicitas*. In this account the martyr Marian has a dream of the heavenly tribunal, in which he avoids judgment and is lifted, quite literally, to the position of judge:

> "My brothers," he said, "I was shown the towering front of a shining high tribunal; in which, instead of the prefect, sat a judge of a very handsome countenance. There was a scaffold there, whose lofty platform was reached not merely by one but by many steps and was a great height to climb. Up to it were brought ranks of confessors, group by group, whom the judge ordered to be executed by the sword. It came to my turn. And then I heard a loud clear voice saying 'Bring up Marian!' So I started to climb the scaffold when all of a

sudden Cyprian appeared at the judge's right hand. He stretched out
his hand and lifted me up to a higher spot on the scaffold; then he
smiled at me and said 'Come sit with me.' So it happened that I too
sat nearby while the other groups were being tried."[162]

In this account, the famed martyred bishop Cyprian is the one who invites Marian to ascend higher on the heavenly scaffold. Because Cyprian is seated in the
familiar place of honor at the right hand of the judge, we can assume that Marian too ascends to this place of privilege.[163] Marian does not receive judgment
at all and is set apart and above the series of condemnations taking place below
him. While the text does not explicitly describe him as participating in judgment, his placement with Cyprian at the right hand of the "judge" indicates
that he is one who metes out judgment rather than receives it. In either case,
we should note that angels are never described as co-judges with Christ. Indeed,
it seems that, for angels, judgment and reign with Christ constitute the glass
ceiling through which they cannot hope to pass.

In some instances, collegiality with Christ in heaven extended further than
judgment alone. Some martyrs expect that they not only will dwell with Christ
in heaven but will reign with him.[164] The portrayal of Christ in a royal role was
a well-established theme in biblical and extracanonical literature. Likewise, the
extension of Christ's royal inheritance to other Christians on the grounds that
they also were children of God also has a biblical basis. We will discuss the
status that the martyrs acquire as a result of reigning with Christ in the next
chapter. For the time being it is sufficient to note that the martyrs, like Christ,
serve a royal administrative role in heaven. For our purposes, one example will
suffice. In the epistle that precedes the account of their martyrdom, the martyrs
of *Montanus and Lucius* anticipate ruling with Christ in heaven:

There is no other way that we may receive eternal life and reign
with Christ, unless we do what he commanded us to do, he who
promised us life and the kingdom. Finally the Lord himself in his
teaching promised that those would obtain God's inheritance who
had lived in peace with their brothers, saying: Blessed are the
peacemakers for they shall be called children of God. The Apostle
explains this by saying, we are the children of God, and if children,
then heirs, heirs of God and co-heirs with Christ, provided that we
suffer with him so that we may be glorified with him. If only a son
can be an heir, and only a peacemaker can be a son, then only one
who destroys the peace of God cannot attain to his inheritance. And
we assert this because of the admonition and the vision we have
from God.[165]

The same phrase is repeated later in the martyrdom when the narrator describes the atmosphere accompanying the martyrs' death: "The entire solemn atmosphere of the march proclaimed a martyr about to reign with God, and already reigning in mind and heart."[166] Here the narrator describes the martyr as about to reign "with God," a distinction usually reserved for Christ alone. The theological and Christological ramifications of these sayings will be discussed in the next chapter. What should be made clear here is that martyrs are not merely servants and choirboys in heaven; they are royalty as well.

Conclusion

In this chapter we have seen how diverse ancient views of heaven were in the acts of the martyrs. The structure of heaven itself varies from account to account, with the most vivid descriptions originating in the more apocalyptically-styled North African accounts. In addition to the traditional scholarly view of martyrological heaven as a paradisiacal garden, we find throne rooms, tribunals, banqueting halls, and palaces. We should resist the temptation to separate these out as discrete models of heaven. They coexist so that in *Marian and James* the banqueting hall in the heavenly palace sits surrounded by a paradisiacal garden carefully landscaped with streams, green pastures, and sheep, as a narrative description of the Psalm 21.

Noticeably absent from these topographies of heaven in the *acta* are descriptions of multiple heavens. The multiple hierarchically stratified heavens familiar to the readers of Jewish and Christian apocalyptic literature are nowhere to be found.[167] Heaven remains hierarchically ordered, but these divisions are more subtly articulated along a horizontal axis, through the identification of heavenly rooms and seating plans, not through stratified heavens and gateways.

Even if ideas about heaven itself vary, there is greater consistency in the presentation of the martyr's afterlife. The martyr's assimilation to Christ did not end with his or her death. Following the execution, a welcoming committee greeted the martyr in heaven, and he or she began a new career as heavenly attendant, chorister, intercessor, judge, or ruler. Traditionally, the martyr is viewed as a peer of the angels, performing similar, somewhat monotonous tasks. Upon a close reading of the *acta*, however, a more diverse curriculum emerges. While some texts, such as the *Martyrdom of Agape, Irene, and Chione*, portray their protagonists as functioning as angels, in other cases, the martyrs performed the same tasks as the exalted Christ. As eschatological judges of the dead, dispensers of grace, and intercessors between God and human beings, the martyrs fulfill roles that far outstrip those of their angelic counterparts. As choristers in the heavenly choir and attendants at the heavenly throne, the martyrs act as angelic beings. We should not conclude, therefore, either that the martyrs act unequivocally as angels or that they act unequivocally as Christ. Nor should we assume that there was a consensus on the matter. The martyrs share a number of functions with both, even as the angels and Christ shared similarities with one another.

The similarities between the ways that ancient Christian communities conceptualized the functions of Christ and the functions of the martyrs in the martyr acts are intriguing; however, because they suggest that the importance and status of Christ and the martyrs were similarly imagined. The martyrs' role as eschatological judge in heaven goes further than mere workplace familiarity. The distinctiveness of these roles suggests that, for some communities, the martyrs enjoyed an elevated status in heaven, a status above that of the ordinary dead and the angels. It is to an examination of this elevated status, and its burgeoning possibilities for Christian anthropology, that we will now proceed.

5

The Martyr as Divine Heir

In the previous chapters, we have followed the martyrs as they retraced the footsteps of Jesus. They gladly assume his sufferings and punishments, mouth his words, and mime his execution. They ascend the heavenly scaffold in pursuit of him, undertaking Christlike services of intercession and judgment. And, at the end of their work, they recline alongside their savior, savor the aromas of the heavenly banquet, and rest upon heavenly thrones. How, we might ask, was the exalted martyr understood by the audiences of the acts of the martyrs? How were they regarded in terms of heavenly status? Were they seen as angels or superangels? As heavenly heroes or paradisiacal prophets? Or perhaps, in keeping with their mimesis, as new Christs and saviors?

Within the martyr acts there are numerous allusions to the status and function of the martyr after death. The enthronement of the martyrs, their participation in judgment, and their filial relationship to God all suggest a particularly elevated and Christly role in the heavens. As a genre, however, the acts of the martyrs are not systematic theology, and drawing conclusions about the status of the martyr in these texts involves considerable inference and interpretative play. The presentation of the status of the martyr is ambiguous; they are described using language and imagery traditionally used of Christ, but the relationship between the two is never fully parsed. This ambiguity has proved frustrating for scholars who have made recourse to the writings of the church fathers to construct a picture of the martyr's status in heaven.[1]

The theological richness of the writings of patristic authors makes them an alluring source for scholars of martyrdom. The slew of homilies on the lives and deaths of the saints prove particularly attractive given that they were read alongside the acts of the martyrs. It is easy to view them as the interpretative key to the martyrdom accounts themselves. The writings of the church fathers, however, are influenced by and represent more than just early Christian ideologies of martyrdom. They intersect with contemporary theological, ecclesial, and pastoral disputes. In the case of the status of the martyrs, the particular author's understanding of Christology, soteriology, angelology, and cosmology influences the way that the martyr is presented. Statements about the martyrs in the homilies and exhortations of the church fathers need to be contextualized within the thought, character, and life of that particular author. They should not be naively and unproblematically imported into study of the martyr acts as if they offer the solution to the ambiguity therein. Nor should we assume that the extant sermons or homilies of grand theologians like Augustine or John Chrysostom are representative of the sermons of anonymous priests in small churches throughout the Roman Empire. In focusing on the *passiones* separately from the writings of the church fathers, I do not mean to imply that they are somehow superior to or separate from other church writings. It is merely an attempt to explore the various ways that the martyrs may have appeared to ancient audiences of the *passiones*, to allow the language and the terminology of the martyrdom narratives to come to the fore, and to sit reflectively (if somewhat uncomfortably) with the ambiguities that this kind of reading yields.

Rather than retreating to the writings of the church fathers, therefore, our discussion of the status of the martyrs in heaven will begin with the language and imagery of the *passiones* themselves. We will attempt to put aside our preconceptions about the ordering of the heavenly spheres and ask ourselves, what hierarchical structure is being constructed in these texts? How is the martyr being ranked alongside other heavenly identities? In the absence of explicit taxonomies of the heavenly hierarchy, we will be attentive to imagery and language that refer to status or hierarchical structures. Such language includes regal imagery, descriptions of hierarchically ordered heavenly space, familial imagery that utilizes language of inheritance, and comparisons with other heavenly beings.

Enthronement, Reign, and Judgment

Within the writings of both the acts of the martyrs and the church fathers, a number of postmartyrdom rewards are taken for granted. The martyrs will be immediately transported to heaven. They will receive immortality, variously referred to as the "divine gift," "divine glory," and "eternal life," and they will be "crowned" with glory, the victor's crown, and the crown of immortality. Such statements are truisms in the ancient churches. The specifics of the martyrs' rewards, however, are more interesting and varied.

A central motif in iconographic and literary depictions of martyrs in the afterlife is their enthronement in heaven. In religious imagery enthronement is a powerful motif that evokes ideas of sovereignty, authority, and divinity. In Judeo-Christian traditions enthronement is closely associated with monarchy, messianism, and divine kingship.[2] Christ's assumption of the monarchic throne of Psalm 110, for instance, plays a critical role in establishing him as king and divine son. The close association of sovereignty and enthronement in biblical traditions suggests that the enthronement of the martyrs is no accident of heavenly *placement*. Given the preponderance of texts using enthronement imagery to characterize the exaltation of Jesus, it would seem that in their enthronement the experiences of the martyrs parallel that of Jesus. We should be wary, however, of assuming that the enthronement of a martyr *necessarily* implies his or her divinity and sovereignty. We should ask instead how the thrones of the martyrs and their places of honor in the heavens relate to the throne of God or the enthronement of Christ. Are the thrones identical, similar, or arranged hierarchically?

The literature of the Jesus movement and early church provides manifold prophecies of the enthronement of Jesus and others associated with him. Such texts certainly form analogues to the enthronement of the martyrs in heaven, but not all envision situations of postmortem enthronement and exaltation. In parsing out the significance of the martyrs' enthronement, we must be careful to demarcate between passages that describe enthronement generally and passages in which enthronement follows as a consequence and "reward" for suffering and death.

In the Gospel of Mark, the request of the sons of Zebedee to sit at the right and left hands of Jesus "in glory" presupposes that Jesus will be enthroned as king in a messianic era. As already noted, Jesus' response to the sons of Zebedee indicates that enthronement with him follows as a consequence of martyrdom.[3] It is only by drinking the cup of wrath, like Jesus, that they can hope to achieve this kind of exaltation. For the Markan Jesus, then, enthronement is a postmortem activity stemming from suffering and death.[4] While we should not assume that Mark intends to present Jesus' own enthronement solely as a consequence of his death, it seems probable that this is the case, and it is clear that for Jesus' followers enthronement is the result of martyrdom.

The notion of messianic enthronement reappears in Mark in the account of Jesus' trial before the Judean Council (14:53–72). At a critical moment, Jesus is asked if he is the Messiah and responds affirmatively, "I am, and you will see the Son of Man sitting on the right of the Power and coming with the clouds of heaven."[5] Jesus' prediction evokes Psalm 110:1 and forms part of the complex Markan reinterpretation of messianic expectation in which the Messiah must suffer and will be exalted after his death.[6] This reinterpretation of messianic expectation certainly accords with Jesus' response to the sons of Zebedee that if they wish to be exalted, they must suffer. Even if the suffering and death of the disciples in Mark do not hold the same significance as the death of Jesus himself, the pattern of death and postmortem enthronement and exaltation is certainly the same.

The author of Hebrews is especially interested in the enthronement of Christ after death. The seat of Christ at the right hand of the Father appears in the beautifully constructed chiastic opening sentence of the work:

> A In many and various ways God spoke of old to our
>   fathers by the prophets;
>   B but in these last days he has spoken to us by
>   a Son,
>   C whom he appointed the heir of all things,
>   D through whom also he created the world.
>   C[1] He reflects the glory of God and bears the very
>   stamp of his nature, upholding the universe
>   by his word of power.
>   B[1] When he had made purification for sins,
>   he sat down at the right hand of the Majesty on
>   high,
> A[1] having become as much superior to angels as the
>   name he has obtained is more excellent than theirs.[7]

The link between death and exaltation is explicit; "having made a purification for sins,"[8] he "took a seat at the right hand of the Majesty on high" (Heb 1:3). The reference to Christ's exaltation is made through allusion to the much-cited Psalm 110.[9] The adverbial phrase "on high" is added to underscore the point that the exaltation takes place in the transcendent heavenly realm.[10] There is no mention of resurrection as the author focuses on exaltation, perhaps considering resurrection and exaltation as synonyms.

As in Mark, saving death (the purification for sins) and exaltation (resurrection and installation on a heavenly throne) are chronologically and ideologically linked. Death precedes exaltation. In the chiasm the reference to exaltation is immediately followed by a comparison between Christ and the angels. This section of the chiasm anticipates the ensuing discussion of the relative importance of heavenly occupants that takes up the rest of chapter 1. Here, as later, the superiority of Christ is grounded in his receipt of a superior name and in his enthronement at the right hand of power. It is his possession of a special name (Son) and his subsequent enthronement and exaltation as a consequence of his salvific death that place Christ above the angels.[11] In the ensuing verse, the assertion of this superiority will be expanded upon. The distinction between the Son and the angels is predicated upon God's instructions to him: "But to what angel has he ever said, 'Sit at my right hand until I make your enemies a footstool for your feet?'" (Heb 1:13). The exaltation of Christ, his enthronement, and his filial relationship to God are the factors that elevate Christ above the angels.[12]

In Revelation we come across, for the first time, an unequivocal example of enthronement and exaltation as a reward for martyrdom. In the sequence of letters to the churches of Asia Minor, certain promises are extended to the addressees as a reward for endurance and fidelity. In 3:21a, the Philadelphians are offered exaltation as their heavenly reward: "To the one who conquers, I will grant him to sit with me on my throne, as I myself conquered and sat down with my Father on his throne."[13] Conquest, in Revelation, is modeled upon the activity of Christ, whose victory over Satan is achieved through his death. The promise extended here to the reader is an offer to reign with Christ and share his throne. Within Revelation, the promise of reigning with Christ appears with marked frequency, but it is only here that "the one who conquers," the martyr, is promised a seat on the throne of Christ.[14] Here, as in the other examples we have considered, a connection is made between exaltation and death. It is death and conquest that lead to exaltation and enthronement. This is true both in the exaltation of Christ and in the exaltation of his martyrs. In exaltation, as in death, the fate of the martyr mirrors the pattern of Christ.

Enthronement and reign are frequently linked to the ability to pass judgment over others. Even before great persecutions and martyrdom became de rigueur, the idea of ascending to heaven and becoming rulers and judges with Christ was already present in the writings of the New Testament. Reigning with Christ as a reward for a particularly outstanding showing while on earth is mentioned in four separate instances—in the Gospels of Luke and Matthew, 2 Timothy 2:11–12, and Revelation 3:21. A comparison of the four statements is revealing:

Luke 22:28–30: "But you [the disciples] are they that have continued with me in my trials; and I appoint unto you a kingdom, even as my Father appointed unto me, that you may eat and drink at my table in my kingdom; and you shall sit on thrones judging the twelve tribes of Israel."[15]

Matt. 12:28: "Truly I tell you at the renewal of all things, when the son of man is seated on his throne of glory, you who have followed me will also sit on twelve thrones, judging the twelve tribes of Israel."[16]

2 Tim. 2:12: "If we endure we will also reign with him."[17]

Rev 3:21: "To the one who conquers I will give a place on my throne, just as myself conquered and sat down with my father on his throne."[18]

In all four passages the promise of shared authority and corule with Christ is dependent upon a particular action. In Matthew and Luke the promises are being given in the immediate context to the apostles—those who "continue" with Jesus (Luke 22:28) and "follow" (Matt 19:28) him. Perhaps the evangelists intended these promises to extend more broadly to all their readers who "followed" Jesus. In Revelation, however, the promise is directed to those who "overcome," to the martyrs. The connection between enthronement, reign, and judgment was established within the period of the Jesus movement. These texts laid the groundwork for the idea that the martyrs would share in the reign and judgment of God.[19]

Turning to the acts of the martyrs, we see that a number of the *acta* refer to the martyrs' enthronement and reign over the world. The martyrs of the *Passion of Perpetua and Felicitas* approach closer to the divine throne than the angels, and they arbitrate in the decision making of church. Where the angels fall back in fear, the martyrs approach with boldness. Their intervention in the management of the church and their arbitration in ecclesiastical and episcopal affairs served a social function for the audiences of the account. The narrative both institutionalizes and authorizes a particular group. At the same time, it also served to place the martyrs within a Christian hierarchy that breached the celestial divide. Positioned above the angels, they served to mediate disputes between bishops and priests. As newly appointed "heads" of the church, the martyrs serve a role analogous to that of Christ.

In a similar manner, the martyrs of the *Martyrdom of Montanus and Lucius* expect that they will "receive eternal life and reign with Christ,"[20] and the martyr Flavian, as he approaches the place of execution, is described as a "martyr about to reign with God."[21] Although these statements are merely passing references, they are further supported by comments in patristic literature and iconographic depictions of the saints. Both Cyprian and Origen agree that enthronement, reign, and judgment with God in the heavenly tribunal are the rewards of the faithful martyred dead.[22] In the iconography of the church, the martyrs—like Jesus—are depicted enthroned in majesty, an iconographic imitation of the enthronement of Christ.[23]

As we saw in the previous chapter, in the *acta* the authority to judge is not restricted solely to God or even to Christ but is—upon occasion—extended to the martyrs. The *Martyrdom of Marian and James* describes how Cyprian invites Marian to ascend higher on the heavenly scaffold. As Cyprian is seated in the familiar place of honor at the right hand of the judge, we can assume that Marian too ascends to this place of privilege. Marian does not receive judgment at all and is set above the series of condemnations taking place below him. Marian's placement with Cyprian at the right hand of the "judge" indicates that they are the ones delivering judgment. The scene is reminiscent of Christ's promise of a seat on his throne (Rev 3:21) and conveys the special power and status of the martyr. Heavenly space (and with it heavenly hierarchy) is reordered so that the martyr is aligned with Christ in the scene of eschatological judgment. In both early *acta* and other early Christian texts, the idea of enthronement is connected to superior status and the authority to pass judgment. The enthroned martyr participates in the judgment of the ordinary dead.[24]

The elevation of Marian serves to connect him both to Christ and to the famed martyred bishop Cyprian, arguably the most famous of the North African martyrs. The association of a martyr with a more established figure in the church is a rhetorical trope in martyrdom literature that serves to elevate the lesser-known martyr in the eyes of the audience. Ordinarily the connection is forged in the swan songs of life; the martyr Basilides is a soldier at the execution of Potamiaena, for instance. The elevation of Marian to the right hand of Cyprian reproduces the biblical and regal imagery of Psalm 110 so that Marian is both assimilated to Christ and connected to Cyprian. Within the context of Marian's cult the enthronement of the martyr served to bolster the position of his cult in relation to competing local martyr cults. Enthronement served to acquire status both for the martyr in the posited heavenly hierarchy and for those responsible for his memorialization.

There appears to have been a general consensus that the martyrs would reign with Christ.[25] Yet the rhetorical function of enthronement varies from account to account. In the *Martyrdom of Marian and James*, it negotiates the authority and position of a particular cult. In the writings of Cyprian and Origen, it is a reward for obedience and compliance with the teachings and ideals of the church embodied in the martyr and symbolized by their death. In a similar manner, the martyrs of the *Passion of Perpetua and Felicitas* are empowered to adjudicate in ecclesiastical disputes. Enthronement elevated the martyr in the heavenly hierarchy and the martyr's cult above local competition.

Inheritance, Sonship, and the Family of God

In the *acta* the martyrs and, occasionally, all members of the Christian community are presented as "children of God." Language of family and exclusivity permeate these texts, reinforcing the connection between Christ and the martyrs and underscoring the elevated position of the saints themselves. For modern audiences well versed in the rhetoric of spiritual siblinghood in Christ this imagery is mundane. The familiarity of the familial overshadows the rhetorical and ideological function of the martyrs' special relationship to God. The description of the martyrs as children of God is more sophisticated and developed in the martyr acts than it is in the writings of the Jesus movement or modern professions of spiritual family. The martyrs's relationship to Christ involves extended discussion of their inheritance and a play upon Roman understandings of the family and inheritance. In exhorting his or her readers to unity and peace, the author of the *Martyrdom of Montanus and Lucius* provides an elaborate and nuanced description of the reign and inheritance of the martyrs in heaven. The author weaves together the traditional idea of the kingdom of God with Pauline interest in shared sonship with Christ:

> There is no way that we may receive eternal life and reign with
> Christ, unless we do what he commanded us to do, he who promised
> us life and the kingdom. Finally the Lord himself in his teaching
> promised that those would obtain God's inheritance who had lived in
> peace with their brothers, saying: Blessed are the peacemakers for
> they shall be called children of God. The Apostle explains this by
> saying, we are the children of God, and if children, then heirs, heirs
> of God and co-heirs with Christ, provided that we suffer with him so
> that we may be glorified with him. If only a son can be an heir, and
> only a peacemaker can be a son, then only one who destroys the
> peace of God cannot attain to his inheritance. And we assert this
> because of the admonition and the vision we have from God.[26]

The passage is particularly interesting because it is not directly concerned with the status of the martyr but rather with ecclesiastical harmony. Here the idea of suffering as the path to inheritance with Christ is present in a dulled and subdued manner. The reference to coinheritance is linked to shared suffering. It is a provision that modifies the otherwise automatic shared inheritance of Christians. In order to be a son or daughter of God and share in the inheritance of Christ, one must first be a peacemaker, but in order to share in the glorification of Christ, one must be a cosufferer with him.

The discussion of the sonship of North African Christians focuses on shared inheritance, not on the nature of sonship. The *Martyrdom of Marian and James* describes the martyrs as "Christi coheredes," coheirs with Christ.[27] Even if we assume, for it is not stated, that Christ is the "only-begotten" child of God, Christians are also "children of God" and, consequently, share in the inheritance of Christ. In apportioning out the inheritance, no apparent distinction is made between those who participate or share in the suffering of Christ and Christ himself. The Latin term for "coheirs," *coheredes*, seems to imply that the inheritance is shared equally, but this cannot be stated unequivocally. No distinction—biological, ontological, or hierarchical—is made between the sonship of Christ and the sonship of his fellow sufferers. Tempting though it may be to understand the sonship of Christ ontologically and the sonship of the suffering Christians as adoption, no such language is employed. Furthermore, just as the sufferers are glorified on account of their suffering, so Christ's exaltation is assumed to follow as a consequence of his own afflictions. We cannot contrast, therefore, the effortless and automatic inheritance of the "biological" child, Christ, with the earned adopted sonship of the sufferers. It is precisely the dearth of such specifics that makes the relative status of the martyrs and Christ so problematic.

In the Latin version of the *Acts of Phileas*, the protagonist twice remarks upon his expectation that at death he will become a coheir of Christ. In his interrogation by the prefect Culcianus, the prefect refers to the presence of Phileas's wife, perhaps as an attempt to appeal to Phileas's emotions. The martyr responds in the nonchalant manner typical of martyrs, stating his affinity for Christ in preference to his earthly ties. In doing so, he suggests that his wife too might be called to martyrdom: "The Lord Jesus Christ is the redeemer of the souls of us all. It is he whom I serve in chains. And he who has called me to the inheritance of his glory can also call her."[28] Two possible readings present themselves: either Phileas's wife is a non-Christian, and Phileas here refers to her potential conversion as an induction into the glory of Christ; alternatively, she is Christian and—like Phileas—could become a martyr and inherit the glory of Christ. The latter possibility is supported by a second use of inheritance language in the *Acts of Phileas*. As Phileas goes out to the place of execution, one of his brothers requests a stay of execution on his behalf. Upon learning of the delay, Phileas retorts that he made no such request but that instead he "owes a great thanks to the emperors and prefect that [he] has been made a coheir of Christ Jesus."[29] Here the acquisition of inheritance is synonymous with his death. Death for Christ is the means by which Phileas shares in the inheritance of Christ. We can conclude, therefore, that when Phileas suggests that his wife could be called to share in the inheritance of Christ, he means that Christ can call her to martyrdom.

In the *Acts of Phileas* and other martyr acts, inheritance is frequently tied to a particular early Christian understanding of family. This in turn evolves out of a particular way of reading scriptural instructions about family. The Gospels contain a number of statements praising those who abandon family in order to follow Jesus. In the parable of the rich man in Mark 10:29–30, Jesus commends those who leave their worldly and familial responsibilities in order to follow him: "Jesus said, 'Truly I tell you, there is no one who has left house or brothers or sisters or mother or father or children or fields, for my sake and for the sake of the good news, who will not receive a hundredfold now in this age— houses, brothers and sisters, mothers and children, and fields with persecutions—and in the age to come eternal life.'"[30] Mark may not have intended that all members of the Christian community abandon their families. The promise of rewards, the expectation of persecution, and the abandonment of family may be directed solely toward the disciples. Additionally, he may be alluding to and addressing the estrangement that individuals would feel if they alone joined a new religious group.[31] Irrespective of Mark's own position, for readers of Mark's Gospel, particularly those experiencing martyrdom, the abandonment of family was more of a reality. The pattern of sacrificing in the here and now for an abundant reward of the same kind in the afterlife is familiar to readers of the martyrdom accounts, who were accustomed to abandoning nation, ethnicity, and family for heavenly replacements.

Whether or not the evangelists themselves intended to advocate the abandonment of family, a number of early Christians understood them in this way. In the *Martyrdom of Irenaeus*, the bishop of Sirmium, the martyr repeatedly rejects his family on the basis of scriptural passages. In an attempt to appeal to his emotions and sense of familial duty, the Roman prefect Probus questions Irenaeus. He asks Irenaeus if he has a wife or children, to which Irenaeus replies in the negative. Probus then asks Irenaeus who—if he has no family— the people weeping at Irenaeus's trial are. Irenaeus offers the following response by way of explanation: "'We have a commandment from our Lord Jesus Christ,' replied Irenaeus who said, 'He who loves his father or his mother or his wife or his siblings or his parents more than me, is not worthy with me' For this reason, looking to God in the heavens and bearing in mind his promises and despising all else, Irenaeus insisted that he neither had nor knew any other kin."[32] The commandment that Irenaeus cites is Matt 10:37//Luke 14:25. The martyr here interprets the sayings of Jesus regarding family as legally binding laws or precepts. Irenaeus ignores the pleas of his family to sacrifice and instead physically and metaphorically focuses his gaze on heaven.[33]

The replacement of the biological family with the adopted spiritual family is prevalent in the *acta*. The *Testament of the Forty Martyrs* interprets the Lord's Prayer as a reconfiguration of familial relations in the Christian community: "For the invisible God is revered in our brothers whom we see;[34] and though this saying refers to our biological siblings, the meaning is extended to all those who love Christ. For our God and holy Saviour declared to be brothers not those who shared a common nature, but rather those who were bound together in the faith by good deeds and who fulfill the will of our Father who is in heaven."[35] This passage in the *Testament of the Forty Martyrs* reinterprets notions of Christian family through the lens of the biblical and liturgical concept of God as paterfamilias. The declaration of the Savior has reshaped Christian notions of family so that Christians are bound not to their biological family but rather to their spiritual siblings. The family bond is maintained and strengthened through the perpetuation of good deeds and the desire to follow the will of the heavenly father. As elsewhere in the *Testament*, "good works" creep to the forefront of God's demands; it is through good works that salvation and Christian identity are secured.[36] The concluding allusion to the Lord's Prayer refers the audience of the *Testament* to their identity as part of the Christian family, an identity constantly reinforced through liturgical practice and proclamation.

While the *Testament of the Forty Martyrs* seems happy to construct the Christian family as a "brotherhood of all believers,"[37] other martyrdoms restrict membership even further. In the *Acts of Phileas*, mentioned earlier, Phileas abandons his presumably Christian family for a new family of apostles and martyrs: "The lawyers, the clerks, together with the *curator* and all of Phileas' relatives, embraced his feet and begged him to have regard for his wife and concern for his children. But it was like water wearing away at a rock. He rejected what they said, claiming that the apostles and martyrs were his kin."[38] Phileas's family's attempt to prevent his martyrdom may suggest that they are not Christian. Yet even if Phileas's family is not Christian, it is noteworthy that he identifies only the apostles and martyrs as his kin. He does not, as we might expect, align himself with the Christian family more broadly conceived; he identifies solely with those of special rank and distinguished accomplishments. The rejection of the general idea of a Christian family is also found in the *Martyrdom of Irenaeus*, where Irenaeus rebuffs his wife and children, declaring that he has no family. In the case of Irenaeus we can reasonably assume that his family is Christian even if they try to dissuade him from martyrdom.[39] It may well be the case that it is the unseemly behavior of his family that causes Irenaeus to reject them, but whatever his motivation, he does so decisively. In both these cases a privileged family of martyrs and a special brotherly relationship to Christ are established over and against the legal constructions of family.

Although it is from a little later than our period, the *Apostolic Constitutions* offers further evidence of the special filial relationship of the martyr to God. At the beginning of book 5 the martyrs are called "brothers of the Lord" and "children of the Most High": "For he that is condemned for the name of the Lord God is an holy martyr; a brother of the Lord, the son of the Most High, a receptacle of the Holy Spirit, by whom every one of the faithful has received the glory of the holy Gospel, by being vouchsafed the incorruptible crown, and the testimony of his sufferings, the fellowship of Christ's blood, and the conformity to his death for adoption."[40] Once again we see the martyrs taking the position of favored children of God in the Christian family. Their relationship with both Christ and the "Highest" (God) is predicated on their testimony and martyrdom. The fraternal comingling of blood is here not Eucharistic but martyrological; the martyrs are blood brothers with Christ.

Our understanding of the nature of the relationship between the martyrs and God is affected by the theological character of the *Apostolic Constitutions* as a whole. Composed between 375 and 380, the *Apostolic Constitutions* is a composite work that blends a number of earlier documents: the third-century *Didascalia Apostolorum*, the *Didache*, and the *Apostolic Tradition*. The theological views of the compiler of the work are considerably debated. Some, such as Funk, the editor of a definitive 1905 edition of the work, viewed the work as "orthodox," arguing that any suspicious doctrinal statements came from the compiler's source.[41] Others, most notably Cuthbert H. Turner, argue strongly in favor of an Arian compiler.[42] If the compiler of the *Constitutions* is an Arian, this would necessarily affect his or her presentation of the sonship of Christ and his relationship to his adopted siblings, the martyrs. The subordination of Christ to God eroded the division between the divine Son and the rest of humanity. Accordingly, it strengthened the ties between Christ and his brothers and sisters, the martyrs.

Origen tentatively suggests an alternative familial model involving martyrs in his *Exhortation to Martyrdom* 14. In his interpretation of the Matthean redaction of Mark 10:29–30, Origen offers a new understanding of family in which martyrs, like Abraham, become heads of their own families of believers:

And if there are fathers about whom it was said to Abraham, "You
shall go to your fathers in peace when you have been buried in a good
old age," someone might say (though I do not know whether he
would be speaking the truth) that perhaps those fathers are those
who were once martyrs and left children behind, in return for whom
they have become fathers of the fathers, the patriarch Abraham and
the other patriarchs. For in all likelihood those who have left children
behind and become martyrs are fathers not of infants but of fathers.[43]

Origen's vision of the martyrs' family offers yet another conceptualization of the spiritual Christian family. Once again we see the creation of a better kind of family, this time of patriarchs and martyrs, in which the martyrs head up the superfamily in the heavens.[44] Origen's construction of the martyr's family is interesting in the way that it plays with and adapts ancient constructions of the family. Given the patriarchal structure of the Roman household, the idea of serving as patriarch to a family of patriarchs underscores the elevated position of the martyr in the Christian hierarchy. Whereas ordinarily God would serve as the father of the Christian family, here the martyr is positioned above Abraham—the quintessential patriarch—as "father of fathers."

The special familial relationship of the martyrs and Christ continues the elitist theme in the acts of the martyrs. Some of the accounts constantly reinforce the distinctive and privileged position of the martyrs vis-à-vis ordinary Christians. In the case of the family of martyrs and their relationship to Christ, their privileged position either as favored sons of God or as part of their own special family cordons them off from the ordinary Christian audience of the accounts. The family of martyrs is offset against the more general family of Christians.

There are, we have seen, a variety of ways in which family is reconstructed in the martyr acts. The early Christian idea that participation in the Christian family replaced the legal and biological family is further refined in the martyr acts. The saying of Jesus regarding the abandoning of one's family is cited to support a reading of Matthew 10 in which family abandonment functions as a call to martyrdom.[45] The exchange of the biological family for the martyrological spiritual family becomes a literary topos. It is an exchange predicated on heavenly reward and divine inheritance. The precise dynamics and structure of this family of martyrs vary. For some, the martyrs are heads of the family of Christ, favored brethren among the faithful. In other accounts the martyrs constitute their own special family, which was cordoned off from the rest of the Christian congregation. In a number of instances, this sense of family is expressed using specifically Pauline language of inheritance, sonship, and a filial relationship with God. In all these cases, the special position of the martyrs in their relationship with Christ and the Father is predicated upon their suffering, their abandonment of earthly family, and their imitative deaths. Through their deaths they assume the same position as Christ in the divine family; they become coheirs with Christ worthy of the same rewards, promises, and status.

Angelic Imagery

One of the more popular views of the martyrs' status in heaven is that they share the functions and place of the angels.[46] In the words of Derrett, "martyrs are angels."[47] In the previous chapter, we saw the ways in which the functions of the martyrs sometimes differ from those of angels, but there still remain the related question of status. As important as the martyrs' angelic nature has been for scholarly narratives, the *acta* themselves have little to say on their relative status. Instead we find a number of accounts that implicitly or explicitly compare martyrs to angels before their deaths. The example par excellence is the martyrdom of Stephen in Acts, which describes the face of Stephen shining like that of an angel. In a similar manner the imprisoned Christians in the *Martyrdom of Polycarp* are described as "being no longer men but angels."[48] Such references provide clear indications that there were some who viewed martyrs as a kind of angel, but we should be sensitive to the timing of such comparisons. In both these instances, it is the premortem martyr-confessor who is compared to the angels. The comparison can be read, as it seems to have been by the author of Acts, as anticipating the exaltation of the martyr *as an angel* after death. At the same time, however, it would be rash to conclude from a handful of premortem comparisons that the exalted martyr is a kind of angel.

Turning from the *passiones* to the writings of the church fathers, it is evident that, prior to the fourth century, explicit comparisons between the martyrs and angels are rare; there are a few references in Tertullian, for instance.[49] When it comes to pre-Constantinian church writings on the nature of the exalted martyrs, Origen is the most frequently cited source. His *Exhortation to Martyrdom* provides a nuanced and sophisticated description of the martyrs as angels in heaven.[50] Origen's identification of the martyrs in heaven as angels appears straightforward. Read in light of Nicean Christology and modern Christian understandings of the heavenly hierarchy, it seems that martyrs and angels share the same rank and nature. We might be tempted to conclude from this that Origen exemplifies the unproblematic early church views on the status of the martyr in heaven. His statements about martyrs and angels, however, are not made in an intellectual vacuum. In order to treat Origen and his writings about martyrs judiciously, we must view his statements about martyrs within the wider context of his cosmology, angelology, and Christology.

In the field of historical theology, Origen's Christology and angelology are viewed as among the most problematic areas of his work. There are a number of places where Origen describes Christ as part of the hierarchy of angels, the most famous example of which is Origen's reading of the Seraphim of Isaiah 6 in *De Principis* 1.iii.4:

The [or a] Hebrew teacher would say that the two Seraphim, which are described in Isaiah as having six wings and crying to one another saying "Holy, holy, holy is the Lord God of Sabaoth," are to be understood as the only-begotten Son of God and the Holy Spirit. We, indeed, also think that what is said in the song of Habbukuk, "in the midst of two living beings" (or "two lives") "thou shalt be known," is to be understood of Christ and the Holy Spirit.[51]

The designation of Christ and the Holy Spirit here as angels implicitly subordinates the Son to the Father. As a result of this Origen was labeled, perhaps unfairly, as the source for the Arian heresy.[52] In the history of Christianity the designation of Christ as an angel was one of the main reasons for Origen's condemnation.[53] What is fascinating for our purposes, however, is the overlap of the identities of Christ and the angels.[54] Origen's description of the martyrs as angels, therefore, does not exclude a comparison with Christ or clearly demarcate between the status of these heavenly beings. According to Origen, both Christ and the martyrs found a place in the enlarged spectrum of the angelic hierarchy. The description of the martyrs as angels means neither that martyrs are angels in the modern sense nor that martyrs, Christ, and the angels are clearly separated from one another in terms of rank or status.

The Status of the Martyr and *Theosis*

Our brief survey of the imagery and language of the *passiones* would appear to suggest that there was a range of ways in which the martyr's status in the heavens was interpreted. In the constantly shifting winds of heavenly identities, the martyr was variously viewed as coheir and coruler with Christ, part of an elect family of martyrs, and an angelic being. The application of regal imagery and the terminology of inheritance suggest that the martyrs shared the rank and status of the exalted Christ. The resulting picture is both ambiguous and complex. The status of the martyr was by no means established and involved considerable overlap with that of Christ. In constructing heavenly hierarchies, ancient authors were careful to delineate the martyrs from the ordinary dead and the ordinary audience. This demarcation served an important societal function by preserving the martyrs as separate and distinct exemplars even as the audience was invited inside the martyrdom itself.

Despite the ambiguous presentation of the exalted martyr, many would reject the possibility that martyrs shared the status of Christ outright on ontological grounds. According to the proclamations of Nicea and Chalcedon, Christ was unique and ontologically distinct from human beings. Given the early church preoccupation with establishing Christ's divinity *in essence*, some might argue that a comparison between Christ and other non-Trinitarian heavenly beings is woefully inappropriate. After all, how can we speak of the martyrs and Christ as equal in heaven if Christ is part of the transcendent Trinity?

My task here is not to say (much less prove) that martyrs were considered to be ontologically divine or that anyone confessed them as Gods.[55] Instead, I am interested in the *statio* of the martyr and the ways that this status approximated that of Christ as a result of their Christological mimesis. Given that our interest lies in status and not ontology, even mentioning the term may be something of a red herring that leads us into the territory of Christological debate and complex doctrinal issues. Even though our interests lie elsewhere, it is nonetheless important that we engage the extent to which issues of ontology preclude the possibility of equal or shared status.

First, we should begin by noting the lack of interest that the acts of the martyrs exhibit in ontology. The martyrs are not described using language of essence, human or divine. The category of *ousia* is apparently not one that was relevant to the communities producing these texts. The absence of terminology should not, as some have understood it, be read as de facto evidence that the martyrs were of lower status.[56] It is precisely the lack of controversial theological terms such as *ousia* that makes the presentation of the martyrs so suggestive and ambiguous. In the absence of clear demarcation, the presentation of the martyrs as "sons and daughters of God," as "coheirs" with Christ, and as exalted and enthroned beings reigning over creation tilts ambiguously toward the conclusion that martyrs were viewed as equal to Christ. We should not understand this equality in terms of essence but in terms of status. In their postmortem exaltation, the martyrs share the status of Christ as enthroned children of God.

The interpretation of the status of the martyr hinges on the identity and education of the audiences of the martyrs. For those in the fourth century and beyond, schooled in and sensitive to Christological debate and Trinitarian theology, language of the martyr's exaltation is significant but does not suggest shared status. For those unaware of or uninterested in ontological categories, or invested in adoptionist Christology, the exaltation of the martyr may have been understood as indicative of shared status.[57]

Concern about the Status and Mimesis of the Martyr

For historians, ascertaining precisely how ancient audiences understood the status of the martyr is extremely difficult. One way for us to gauge the way that the status of the martyr was understood by early Christians is to examine how the martyr's status-elevating *imitatio* was treated by patristic authors. In principle, the mimesis of the martyr should have been unproblematic. *Imitatio Christi* was a principle that extended into all aspects of early Christian life. Liturgical acts, the performance of the Eucharist, baptismal rites, even reading aloud from scripture came to be viewed as ways of imitating and embodying Christ.[58] In many cases, these were practices that—like martyrdom—enabled the individual to transform him- or herself into an image of the divine. *Theosis* through the imitation of Christ, therefore, is not an idea exclusive to the ideology of martyrdom.

Given the proliferation of practices oriented around *theosis*, it is strange that the martyrological mimesis raised so many heckles. Yet as we will see, for a number of patristic authors, the martyr's imitation was a cause for concern. Unlike other forms of *imitatio Christi*, martyrdom caused considerable anxiety and debate among patristic authors who were concerned about the relative status and popularity of the martyrs and Christ. In fact the idea that martyrdom should function just like any other kind of *imitatio* is an argument put forward by Augustine as part of a rhetorical strategy to dull the impact of the martyrs.[59]

Concern about the martyrs overflows into the *acta* themselves, where the relative position and importance of the martyrs and Christ is also an issue. A number of later *acta* make great efforts to emphasize the status of Christ over the martyrs in a self-conscious effort to avoid confusion. Such concerns indicate that for some ancient Christians the superiority of the death of Christ over and against those of the martyrs was not readily apparent. That patristic authors went to such great efforts to clarify "orthodox" teaching on such matters suggests that this was a concern for church leaders. That this type of *imitatio* anxiety is particular to the martyrs is itself a testimony to the distinctiveness of the martyr's mimesis. This controversy did not surround other less dramatic forms of mimesis; it is an issue particular to the *imitatio* of the martyr.

Concerns about the *imitatio* of the martyrs tend to focus on the idea that martyrs could share the status of Christ. For a number of later authors, the possibility that some viewed the martyrs as ontologically deified was a potential problem. While for the church fathers themselves, this was a philosophical impossibility, they remained concerned that members of their communities failed to appreciate the clear-cut distinction between Christ and his mimics. The authors who will be discussed here fall outside our period of study. They do not serve here as evidence for how earlier Christian audiences understood the status of the martyrs. Instead, they demonstrate that even in a later period, when Christological issues were even more sensitive, there were some who treated and regarded the martyrs as equal with Christ. That Augustine was worried about members of his communities worshiping martyrs demonstrates that not every ancient Christian or Christian practice held the ontological distinctiveness of Christ as paramount.

Augustine

Of the stalwarts of the patristic age, few church writers enjoy the illustrious status of Augustine. Yet in his approach to martyrdom Augustine appears inconsistent and capricious, changing his position on the martyrs at least twice during his career.[60] The majority of studies on Augustine identify three periods in the development of his ideas about the cults of the martyrs. Between 390 and 401, Augustine appears disinterested in martyrdom. References to martyrdom appear only within the context of *refrigeria* practices and Manichaean critique of the cult of the saints as repackaged paganism. Augustine's response, in his *Contra Faustus*, centers on Christians' desire to imitate the example of the martyrs, connect themselves to the martyrs' merits, and benefit from their intercession. In the course of his entanglement with the Donatists (410–15), Augustine is forced to address martyrdom more directly. The Donatist focus on martyrdom and their ability to harness the charisma of martyrs force Augustine to react strongly against the martyr-centered practices. He attempts to contextualize martyrs within orthodoxy arguing that martyrdom cannot exist outside the love of the church. From 415 onward, Augustine switches positions largely due to his acquisition of the relics of Stephen. The possession of a portion of the relics of the illustrious protomartyr brought relic power to Augustine's episcopacy and enabled him to benefit from the authority and power of Saint Stephen.

In analyzing Augustine's many works dealing with saints and martyrs, scholars have detected a number of prominent themes.[61] Augustine presents the saints both as imitators of Christ and as models for his congregation. Time and again, Augustine is extremely careful to distinguish between the worship of God and the worship of the saints. In his sermon on the birthday of Fructuosus, for example, Augustine cites the *Martyrdom of Fructuosus* as evidence that martyrs ought not to be worshiped as Gods: "And he answered, 'I do not worship Fructuosus, but I worship God whom Fructuosus also worships.' In this way he admonished us to honor the martyrs, and with the martyrs to worship God. . . . But only the true God ought to have a temple, only to the true God should sacrifice be offered."[62] In the conclusion of the sermon on Fructuosus, Augustine is prepared to veer close to subordinationism, to couch his argument for the inferiority of the saints to God in the language of the cult of the saints:

Even Christ himself, though he is God, though he is one God with
the Father, though he is the Word of the Father only-begotten, equal
and coeternal with the Father; yet insofar as he was prepared to be a
man . . . he preferred to be a sacrifice rather than to demand sacrifice,
insofar as he is a man. Because insofar as he is a God, everything that
is owed to the Father is also owed to the only-begotten Son. For that
reason, dearly beloved, venerate the martyrs, praise, love, proclaim,
honor them. But worship the God of the martyrs.[63]

Here Augustine toys with the theme of *imitatio Christi* and the martyrs' mimetic
relationship to Christ. In a stroke of genius, Augustine turns the mimetic relationship on its head, arguing that Christ qua man did not demand worship or
sacrifice and that martyrs, therefore, should not be worshiped. In using the
humanity of Christ in this way, Augustine sails into dangerous waters, but he
does so once again to distinguish between the worship of Christ and the veneration of the martyrs.

Augustine's overriding concern with the proper worship of the saints is not
limited to his sermons on the birthdays of martyrs. In his *Tractates on the Gospel
of John*, Augustine again returns to the difference between Christ and martyrs,
this time focusing on their ontological difference and varying redemptive
capacities:

Although brethren die for brethren, yet no martyr's blood is ever
shed for the remission of the sins of brethren, as was the case in
what he did for us; and in this respect he bestowed not on us aught
for imitation, but something for congratulation. In as far, then, as the
martyrs have shed their blood for the brethren, so far have they
exhibited such tokens of love as they themselves perceived at the
table of the Lord. In all else, then, that I have said, although it is out
of my power to mention everything, the martyr of Christ is far
inferior to Christ himself.[64]

His concern here is to demonstrate the inferiority of the martyr to Christ, not
in the trappings of their worship but in the undergirding assumptions about
their natures, status, and relative importance: "But let us not be supposed to
have so spoken as if on such grounds [imitation of Christ] we might possibly
arrive at an equality with Christ the Lord, if for his sake we have undergone
witness bearing even unto blood."[65] Once more, we see in Augustine a theo-
retical concern with the status and nature of the martyr. He is anxious to demonstrate the differences between the martyr and Christ, a difference grounded
in the sinlessness of Christ and his redemptive function.

Since the work of Campenhausen, Augustine's preoccupation with the worship of the saints has been interpreted as a desire to avoid the cult of the martyrs replacing the cult of Christ.[66] This aim "is affirmed in every study about Augustine's martyrology."[67] Additionally, we should note Augustine's dislike of the rowdy drunken behavior involved in the cult of the saints.[68] Yet our brief examination of these passages has shown that Augustine's concern is more with the *kind* of worship and veneration offered to the martyrs and the perception of the martyrs' status vis-à-vis Christ.

In his sermons, Augustine objects to the *worship* of the martyrs, not their veneration. Augustine is concerned that the kinds of worship offered to God are being offered to the martyrs. He objects to the equality that identical ritual practices confer. There seems no doubt that the popularity of the cult of the saints made Augustine uneasy, but his discomfort with the martyrs' imitation of Christ is grounded in its theological implications. He is concerned to demonstrate that they are not equal to Christ.[69] His theologically minded discussion of the inferiority of the martyrs makes no mention of the cult of the saints, but rather the possibility that the martyrs' imitation of Christ leads some to believe the martyrs are equal and equivalent to Christ. Campenhausen may be right in deducing that Augustine disapproves of the popularity of the cult of the saints, but he seems even more anxious about the status and beliefs about the martyrs that it encourages.[70]

By constantly centering the veneration of the martyrs on Christ, Augustine attempts to reposition Christ at the head of the mimetic chain. Appeals to the martyrs' imitation of Christ serve to subordinate the martyrs to Christ. The reordering of the mimetic hierarchy certainly preserves Augustine's own place in the ecclesiastical hierarchy, but it is possible that Augustine has bona fide theological concerns as well. His aim is not to encourage worship of Christ but to discourage *worship* of the martyrs. By linguistically dividing the *worship* of Christ from the *veneration* of the martyrs, Augustine sets up a ritual hierarchy that elevates Christ above the martyrs.

Given his preoccupation with the relative status and kinds of worship offered to martyrs and Christ, it seems likely that Augustine was combating practices and beliefs that did not distinguish between the two. It is all too tempting to conclude that popular belief in North Africa maintained that Christ and the martyrs were ontologically identical and hierarchically equal. There is, however, no concrete evidence for this. While it is a possibility, it is just as likely that Augustine's audience simply did not distinguish—ritually or theologically—between the martyrs and Christ. In this situation, the problem for Augustine would have been a set of practices and beliefs that implied that the martyrs and Christ were equal. Even if we cannot speak concretely about the situation in

Carthage, it is clear that the relative status of the martyrs and Christ was an issue for Augustine. There were groups whose practices—if not their confessional statements—treated the martyrs as though they were Christs.

Victricius of Rouen

We do not have to look far for examples of Christian writers proposing the martyrs' participation in the divine identity of Christ. In *De laude sanctorum*, Victricius, the early sixth-century bishop of Rouen, offers a justification for the veneration of relics that casts the martyrs not only as enthroned monarchs but as participants in the divine nature through adoption.[71] Like many before him, Victricius praises the martyr as an "imitator of Christ" but goes further, employing explicitly regal and apostolic imagery to the saints:

> And the apostles and saints ascended to the throne of the Redeemer, both by the ordinance of the spiritual mystery and by the sacrifice of the body as victim and by the payment of the blood and sacrifice of the passion, as Christ himself says in the Gospel: "When the Son of Man is seated on his throne of glory, you too shall sit on twelve seats of judgment, judging the twelve tribes of the sons of Israel."[72]

The martyrs' accession to the throne of God is grounded in the promises made to the apostles in Matthew 19:28. Here Victricius extends to the martyrs the promises that Jesus makes to the apostles, allowing them a share in eschatological judgment. Like others, the martyrs are cast as sons of God and as such as participants in the eternality and divinity of God.[73] In a controversial move, Victricius posits that the martyrs share not only in divine attributes like divinity and eternity but even in the substance of the godhead: "Perhaps, at this point, someone will cry out in protest " 'Is the martyr, then, the same as the highest power and the absolute and ineffable substance of godhead?' I say he is the same by gift not by property, by adoption not by nature; and that this happens so that, when the great day comes, he who received imperial power will not seem to have acquired it, nor he who gave to have suffered loss."[74] Victricius's view is by no means representative of the majority of the church in the sixth century. His argument that the martyrs have the same properties as God through adoption offers a kind of sophisticated adoptionist perspective that would have offended many. The martyrs and even their relics are divinized, not through nature but via adoption. Victricius himself seems aware of the controversial nature of his argument. After all, it is no small thing to proclaim the *relics* of the saints of the same substance as the Trinity. For our purposes, he offers an example of potential understandings of the relative status of the martyrs and Christ. For Victricius, the martyrs are unambiguously and unequivocally a part of the Trinity, forming part of God in their exaltation. Victricius offers unassailable evidence that some believed the exalted martyrs to share in the divine exalted status of God.[75]

John of Damascus

In his *Exposition of the Orthodox Faith*, the seventh-century hero of the Greek East, John of Damascus, boldly declares that "surely also the saints are Gods, Lords, and Kings." The application of language of divinity and sovereignty to saints endows them with a status that far outstrips that of the ordinary dead or the angels. This is the language usually reserved for Christ. Out of context, this statement appears to confer ontological equality between God and the saints. But John of Damascus does not intend to imply this kind of divinity. He goes on to qualify his statement, writing:

> Now I mean gods and kings and lords not in nature, but as rulers
> and masters of their passions, and as preserving a truthful likeness to
> the divine image according to which they were made (for the image
> of a king is also called king), and as being united to God of their own
> free-will and receiving him as an indweller and becoming by grace
> through participation with him what he is himself by nature.[76]

The qualification certainly clarifies the ontological issue; saints are Gods, but not Gods in essence. This passage illustrates the tension between the assimilation of the beloved martyr to Christ and polytheism. Throughout his writings on martyrs, John of Damascus uses highly exalted Christological language to describe the status of the saints. The martyrs are called coheirs with Christ, sons of God, and Gods. He uses incarnational language to describe how God dwells in the body of the martyr; elsewhere, he describes their worship as identical to that paid to God. Yet even as he utilizes such elevated imagery for the saints, he takes great care to avoid ontological deification, dulling the impact of his words with prosaic explanations of their virtues.

John of Damascus treads a fine line; the martyrs are not Gods by nature, but through the indwelling of God and *participatio* they become what God is by nature. In describing the saints, John of Damascus navigates the difficult course between the exaltation of the saints and the heresy of polytheism. In his explanation of the veneration of the saints, he is attentive to the potential misunderstandings that his defense of the saints can cause, presumably because such beliefs were commonplace among those who participated in the cult of the saints.[77] His caution in identifying martyrs as Gods and in counteracting the belief that they were Gods *in nature* indicates that this interpretation was a very real one in antiquity. That the confusion could arise and that it needed correction tells us both that some identified the martyrs as Gods absolutely and that this interpretation caused concern on the part of the church leaders.

The treatments of the status of the martyrs in the writings of Augustine, Victricius of Rouen, and John of Damascus do not serve as evidence of the views of the communities that produced the *passiones*. They provide evidence for the variety of ways that Christians continue to discuss the status of the martyrs in a period when the ontological nature of Christ had come to the forefront of theological debate. They illustrate that it *was possible* for early Christians to view the martyrs as sharing the status of the exalted Christ.

Conclusion

As in all things, the *passiones* themselves can be frustratingly ambiguous when it comes to the status of the martyrs. In terms of their position in the mimetic and heavenly hierarchy, the martyrs appear to share a more elevated place in the heavens than is traditionally accorded to them. Imagery of enthronement, judgment, and divine sonship suggest that the martyrs share in the lineage of a heavenly royal family. Where martyrs and angels appear together, as in the *Passion of Perpetua and Felicitas*, the expectant angels of Saturus's vision "pay homage" to the arriving martyrs.[78] The behavior of the angels and the application of Christological language of divine sonship to the martyrs suggest a certain superiority to the angels. We should not conclude, however, that the elevation of the martyrs above the angels was in any way a widespread belief. References to the angelic splendor of the martyrs, and comparisons between the martyrs and angels in the writings of Tertullian and Origen illustrate the complexity of this issue and indicate that—for many—martyrs were a kind of angel.

What emerges from these observations is that nothing is clear; the characterization of the martyrs is ambiguous and open-ended. There was a variety of ideas about the status of the martyrs; for some the martyrs were like angels, for others they appear as second Christs, for others still they were discretely identified as martyrs, exalted in a manner that does not parallel our own ideas. It is precisely this ambiguity that is able to yield differing opinions about the martyrs in the writings of Augustine, Origen, John of Damascus, and others. The ambiguous relationship of the martyrs and Christ is shaped by the liturgical practices and the Christological assumptions of the audience and readers.

In the second and third centuries, when Christological and anthropological doctrines remained unfixed and varied, the position of the martyrs in the heavenly hierarchy was variable. The martyrs were exalted in their status, but questions about their nature went unaddressed and unregulated. The undefined nature of the martyrs' status is nevertheless a productive ambiguity for scholarship. The lack of clear definition illustrates the overzealous manner in which some have labeled martyrs "angels." We cannot unproblematically state that exalted martyrs were anything. We need to pay attention to the ways in which the identity of the martyrs was shaped in particular communities and texts. There was no universally maintained understanding of the heavenly hierarchy into which the martyrs were neatly slotted. The identities and relative status of spiritual beings—like the deceased martyrs—were constantly being produced and reproduced in light of social, theological, and political concerns.

The ambiguity surrounding the identity of martyrs in heaven calls into question scholarly preoccupations with divine essence and indicates the extent to which issues of anthropology and Christology remained unresolved. Even though the martyrdom accounts are preoccupied with status and hierarchy, this status was not constructed in terms of divine essence. The elevation of the martyrs opens the door for their own imitators and gleams with possibility for others.

Conclusion

Suffering in imitation of Christ was not the invention of the authors of the acts of the martyrs. As we saw in the first chapter, imitation of Christ by suffering was a critical part of the ideology of discipleship in the Jesus movement and a foundational element of membership in the Christian community. For those interested in the deaths of their Christian peers and in preparing others for martyrdom, recourse to the Christly paradigm was a traditional interpretative move. It is a rhetorical stance that can be traced from Paul, to the authors of stories about Jesus and the apostles, to Clement and Ignatius. In its most basic form, connecting personal and communal suffering to that of Jesus is neither original nor surprising. It serves to inculcate a particular set of ethical norms, to model good behavior, and to combat perceived enemies. Encasing the deaths of the martyrs in scripture was a powerful rhetorical move.

Narratives about the death of Jesus were used to frame descriptions of the deaths of early Christians. The martyrs speak the words of the dying Christ and physically embody his self-control. The imitation of Christ in the martyr acts is about more than simple repetition. In their presentation of martyrs as Christly imitators, the martyr acts construct their own portraits of Christ and martyrological ideals. The image of Christ, glimpsed through the cloudy window of the martyrs, is controlled, stoic, and apathetic. The emotional appeals of the agony of Gethsemane are nowhere to be found. Read in the context of persecuted communities that valued both suffering and self-control, the stoic Jesus was the most appealing.

The person of Christ read through the stories of the martyrs is no less important than scriptural portraits. Just as in modern society ideas of Jesus' personality float independently from the scriptural narratives that might validate them, so too in the context of ancient martyrdom the Christ presumed by and alluded to in the martyr's imitation wielded influence on ancient audiences. The broad audience for and popularity of the martyrdom narratives meant that the Christ of the martyr acts was as forceful a personality as any scriptural, iconographic, or homiletical portrait. As we have seen, Augustine's anxiety over the relative status of church worship and the cult of the saints indicates that Eucharistic worship in churches was less popular than attending *martyria* on festival days. Given the comparative popularity of the cult of the saints, it is plausible that more Christians attended feasts in honor of the saints than Eucharistic rituals in honor of Christ.[1]

If this is the case, then the celebration of the saints was an important way in which Christians encountered Christ. The reading of the death of Jesus in dialogue with the deaths of the martyrs was *at least* one of the primary ways that Christians encountered the person and character of Christ. If the "average" Christian's experience of Jesus was shaped by the saints' feasts days, then their understanding of Christ was likewise viewed through the lens of martyrdom. The Christ reflected in the martyr's gaze is the Christ known to Christians out of the churches and in the *martyria*. The importance of the martyrs' Christ should not be minimized as yet another example of reception history, but as one of the primary ways that Christ lived in the memory of the early church.

The popularity of the cult of the saints and martyrs as Christly imitators meant that they threatened scriptural portrayals of Jesus. With their spectacular displays of endurance, witty closing remarks, and composed self-presentation, the martyrs threatened to usurp the passion of the Christ. The modification of the Lukan passion narrative under pressure from Stephen's more "Christly" martyrdom illustrates the extent to which *imitatio Christi* shaped not only notions of martyrdom but also ideas about Jesus. The dialogical relationship between the acts of the martyrs, the passion narratives of Christ, and the Christ presented in the martyrdom accounts served to shore up the ideal of suffering like Christ.

The imitation of Christ in the characterization of the martyrs was about more than the ideals of suffering and Christly imitation. The performance of Christ in the body of the martyr serves the social, theological, liturgical, rhetorical, and political needs of the communities using these texts. *Imitatio* as ritual and literary performance was a strategic practice. It amplified the authority of the already powerful martyr. It endowed those who shaped the martyr's memory with the authority to adjudicate in ecclesiastical matters, to promote particular values, ethics, and doctrines, and to elevate the standing of particular churches against their competitors. Rhetorically, then, resurrecting Christ in the martyrs was a powerful move that invoked the unassailable character of the Savior to promote a particular agenda.

The martyr's death was read theologically, both in imitation of the function of the death of Christ and as part of the redemptive program of God. A variety of models of redemption were at work in the *acta*, and these models were often connected to geographically located theological and exegetical traditions. The dominant scholarly view of the martyr's death as sacrifice represents only part of the picture. The apocalyptic myth of cosmic battle with Satan was more prevalent in the acts of the martyrs. The value of the martyrdom accounts, and other "popular" literature, for historical theology is often overlooked in preference for the overt systematic treatises of patristic authors. Yet the *acta* present early evidence of the development of different theories of salvation, not merely as a means of filling in the lacunae in reconstructions of the history of ideas, but as forces that generated and shaped theological traditions. The martyr acts subvert both the idea of theology as an intellectual exercise and the assumed importance of individual thinkers and personalities. They demonstrate that theology is not exclusively the territory of a cadre of intellectual bishops; rather, it was available as part of the unregulated and uncontrollable cult of the saints.

Even as we have seen the broadening of theological discourse in the *acta*, the martyrdom accounts raise questions about the idea of an elite and privileged access to God. On the one hand, the public performance of the *acta* serves both to inculcate an ethic of *imitatio Christi* and to allow the audience to participate in the martyr's activity. Listening to the accounts of martyrdom read in liturgical settings creates an avenue into the world and identity of the martyr. On the other hand, as we have seen, the martyrdom accounts establish hierarchies of difference that distance the martyrs from other Christians. The discussion of heavenly affairs in chapter 4 demonstrates the way in which constructions of the afterlife privilege the martyr over and against the postmortem expectations of ordinary Christians. Martyrs alone go directly to heaven, and martyrs alone avoid judgment. Their place in heaven—enthroned and reigning with God—elevates the martyr above the rank and file of the Christian congregation.

In some cases, the cordoning off of the martyr goes even further. The martyrs make up their own familial cadre of martyrs and apostles and are distanced from their Christian relatives. The construction of a hierarchy that removes martyrs from their audience is in tension with the idea that the performance of the martyrdom is a way of inviting Christians to participate in the act of martyrdom itself. The performance of the accounts serves both to draw audience and martyr together in liturgical union and to force them apart through hierarchical divisions. In practice, this tension may have served a pedagogical function; it reinforced the martyr's authority and paradigmatic role while enabling the audiences to participate in the martyr's position through acts of liturgical and ethical obedience.

The elevated position of the martyr, in liturgical practice as well as literary presentation, did not go unnoted. As we have seen, the presentation of the martyr as *alter Christus* contributed to a number of sticky theological problems for the church. Within the context of discussions about the cults of the saints, ancient authors such as Augustine and John of Damascus attempted to correct the potential view that martyrs were equal to Christ.

While the mere act of writing this book appears to bind them together, the martyr acts are not a homogeneous group. What emerges out of this study is the considerable diversity of opinions, scriptural interpretations, and views of martyrdom that they represent. Even though many of these accounts clothe their protagonists in the robes of Jesus, their aims, theological interpretations, and rhetorical strategies vary greatly. *Imitatio Christi* is a persistent theme in these accounts, but the ambitions of this imitation, its literary resonances, and its theological underpinnings should not be seen as a single phenomenon.

More than anything else, then, imitation of Christ in the *acta* reveals the diverse ideologies of martyrdom at work in the second and third centuries. The tendency to speak of martyrdom as though it were a homogeneous ideology and practice is undermined by the richness of ideas present in writings about martyrs. Contrasting views about salvation, heaven, and the martyr's death and status demonstrate the way in which ideas about martyrdom were shaped differently by their particular communities. The heterogeneity should be a boon to the scholar rather than something to gloss over. These differences enable us to trace the contours of Christianity in particular socioeconomic groups and geographic locations. Just as there was no singular view of Christ, there was no homogeneous view of the other Christs—the martyrs.

Appendix

Composition and Setting of the Acts of the Martyrs
Referenced in This Work

As with any historical source, the dating and composition of the acts of the
martyrs play a critical part in their interpretation. While this book is concerned with the history of ideas and development of certain theologies, it is
greatly indebted to the work of early church historians. This appendix is a
summary of the historical judgments made by the present author regarding
the provenance of these accounts. It serves both as a resource for readers
interested in pursuing study of a particular martyrdom and as a means to
facilitate greater transparency in my work. It is not a comprehensive history
of martyrdom accounts purporting to be from this period or a complete list
of secondary literature pertaining to the texts described. While this list
includes the major Greek and Latin works composed before the end of the
Diocletian persecution, it does not include discussions of accounts composed
outside this period. The legends associated with the death of Saint Lawrence,
for example, are not included. For this reason a number of later Greek and
Latin works together with the majority of Coptic and Syriac martyrdoms are
not included. In addition, martyrs known to have died but for whom there
are no martyr acts composed during this period are not included.

Evaluating the credibility of sources for this period is enormously
difficult. The majority of martyrdom accounts are extracted from the
writings of later collectors or historians. Eusebius, a primary source for
accounts of the deaths of martyrs, for instance, wrote his *Historiae Ecclessiae*
sometime after the end of the Diocletian period. We should not pretend that
Eusebius's treatment of his sources meets our own high expectations for
historiography. At the same time, the very nature of ancient history requires
that we make some compromises. If we discount every martyrdom account
potentially tainted by the hands of later editors, we will be left with no
sources, for all ancient literature is potentially corrupted by the compilers of

the manuscripts in which they are found. The historian is therefore forced to engage in a slippery negotiation with ancient authors and sources. In our case, as for other studies of this kind, the assessment of an account's reliability is the result of an individual appraisal.

Methodologically, I follow my predecessors in using legal information to ascertain the earliest date at which a text could have been composed. A reference to forcible handing over of scriptures to the authorities, for instance, is a clear indication that a text could not have been composed before the reign of Diocletian. I do not maintain, however, that this information can be reliably used to ascertain the date at which the martyrs died. It seems plausible to me that some martyrdom stories circulated orally before they were written down, or that the martyrdom accounts are heavily redacted versions of earlier accounts. In my treatment of martyrdom accounts my interest is in the way the martyr's death is presented and received by the communities using these texts. I remain convinced that these stories, compelling and inspiring as they are, cannot be used to retrieve the words of the historical martyrs.

This appendix is extremely cursory and is meant more as a means of disclosure than a thorough treatment of these accounts. For more detailed assessments I refer the reader to the writings of A. A. R. Bastiaensen, Gerd Buschmann, Gary Bisbee, Jan den Boeft, Jan Bremmer, Hans Freiherr von Campenhausen, Pio Franchi de' Cavalieri, Boudewijn Dehandschutter, Michael Holmes, Giuliana Lanata, Giuseppe Lazzati, Victor Saxer, David Woods, and the other luminaries of martyrological scholarship whose works are merely mentioned in passing here. For recent notes on the editions used here, the reader is directed to Jan den Boeft and Jan Bremmers' series "Notiunculae Martyrologicae," published in *Vigiliae Christianae*.

List of Martyrdoms Arranged Alphabetically by Martyr's Name

Acts of the Abitinian Martyrs (= *Acts of Saturninus, Dativus, and Their Companions*)
Martyrdom of Agape, Irene, Chione, and Companions
Acts of Apollonius
Acts of Carpus, Papylus, and Agathonice
Acts of Cassian
Acts of Claudius, Asterius, and Their Companions
Martyrdom of Conon
Martyrdom of Crispina
Acts of Cyprian (= *Acta Proconsularii*)
Martyrdom of Dasius
Acts of Eupl(i)us
Acts of Felix the Bishop
Martyrdom of Fructuosus and Companions
Martyrdom of Irenaeus Bishop of Sirmium
Martyrdom of Julius the Veteran
Acts of Justin and His Companions

Martyrdom of Lucian and Marcian
Letter of the Churches of Lyons and Vienne
Acts of Marcellus
Martyrdom of Marian and James
Passion of Maxima, Donatilla, and Secunda
Acts of Maximilian
Martyrdom of Maximus
Martyrdom of Montanus and Lucius and Their Companions
Passion of Perpetua and Felicitas
Acts of Phileas
Letter of Phileas
Martyrdom of Philip of Heraclee
Martyrdom of Pionius
Martyrdom of Polycarp
Martyrdom of Potamiaena and Basilides
Martyrdom of Ptolemaeus and Lucius
Acts of Saturninus, Dativus, and Their Companions (= *Acts of the Abitinian Martyrs*)
Acts of the Scillitan Martyrs
Testament of the Forty Martyrs of Sebaste

Abbreviations

Anal. Boll.	*Analecta Bollandiana.* Brussels: Société des Bollandistes, 1882–.
AS	Bollandus, Jean et socii. *Acta Sanctorum.* 71 vols. Brussels: Societé de Bollandistses, 1642–1906.
Bastiaensen	Bastiaensen, A. A. R., et al. *Atti e Passioni dei Martiri.* Milan: Mondadori, 1987.
Bedjan	Bedjan, Paul. *Acta Martyrum et Sanctorum.* 7 vols. Paris: Via dicta de Sèvres, 1890–97.
BHL	*Biblioteca hagiographica latina antiquae et mediae aetatis.* 2 vols. Brussels, 1898–1901.
BHO	*Biblioteca hagiographica orientalis.* Brussels, 1910.
BISBEE	Bisbee, Gary. *Pre-Decian Acts of the Martyrs and Commentarii.* Edited by Margaret R. Miles and Bernadette J. Brooten. Harvard Dissertations in Religion 22. Philadelphia: Fortress Press, 1988.
DACL	*Dictionnaire d'archéologie et chrétienne et de Liturgia.*
DHGE	*Dictionnaire d'histoire et de géographie ecclésiastiques.*
Frend	Frend, W. H. C. *Martyrdom and Persecution in the Early Church.* Oxford: Blackwell, 1965.
JECS	*Journal of Early Christian Studies*
KKR	Knopf, R. *Ausgewählte Märtyrerakten.* Tübingen: Mohr, 1901. 3rd ed. by G. Krüger, 1929. 4th ed. by G. Ruhbach, 1965.
Lanata	Lanata, G. *Gli atti dei martiri come documenti processuali.* Milan: Giuffre, 1973.

Lazzati   Lazzati, Giuseppe. *Gli sviluppi della letteraturs sui martiri nei primi
                  quattro secoli.* Turin, Società Editrice Internazionale, 1956.
Musurillo   Musurillo, Herbert. *Acts of the Christian Martyrs.* Oxford:
                  Clarendon Press, 1972.
RE   Pauly, A., G. Wissowa, and W. Kroll. *Real-Encyclopädie der
                  classischen Altertumswissenschaft.* Stuttgart: Metzger, 1893–.
Reitzenstein   Reitzenstein, R. *Die Nachrichten über den Tod Cyprians.* Heidelberg:
                  Winter, 1913.
Reymond   Reymond, E. A. E., and J. W. B. Barns. *Four Martyrdoms from the
                  Pierpont Morgan Coptic Codices.* Oxford: Clarendon Press, 1973.
Ruinart   Ruinart, Thierry. *Acta primorum martyrum sincera et selecta.* 1689
                  ed. Ratisbon, 1859.
Saxer, *Bible* Saxer, Victor. *Bible et hagiography: Textes et thèmes bibliques dans les
                  actes des martyrs autentiques des premiers siècles.* Bern: Peter Lang,
                  1986.
Saxer, *Saints* Saxer, Victor. *Saints anciens d'Afrique du Nord.* Rome: Tipografia
                  Poliglotta Vaticana, 1979.
Tilley   Tilley, Maureen. *Donatist Martyr Stories: The Church in Conflict in
                  North Africa.* Liverpool: Liverpool University Press, 1996.

Martyrdom of Agape, Irene, Chione, and Companions

Greek: codex Vaticanus graecus 1660; Latin: Gugliemo Sirleto in Ruinart, 424–27.
Musurillo, 280–93; KKR, 95–100; Pio Franchi de' Cavalieri, *Studi e Testi* 9 (1902):
1–19. For a discussion of biblical imagery, see Saxer, *Bible*, 129–32.

This account contains the martyrdom of a group of women from Saloniki in Macedonia—Agape, Irene, Chione, and four companions (Agatho, Cassia, Philippa, and Eutychia). The narrative dates the events to March/April of 304 and refers to Diocletian's
edict demanding the surrender of holy books. The presence of a specific reference to the
legal basis for the arrest of the women, together with the absence of miracles and visions,
would seem to indicate that the martyrdom was composed soon after the executions.
This should not lead us to believe, however, that the *acta* are historically reliable accounts
of the historical martyrs' words. The disproportionate length of the trials of some of the
martyrs would seem to indicate that the events are subject to interpolation by hagiographic editors.

Initially the women flee to the mountains, where they form a holy group (perhaps
a proto-ascetic group), but they are later captured by soldiers and brought to trial. The
trial takes place in three hearings. At first Agape and Chione are sentenced to death, the
others being spared on account of their youth and/or pregnancy (Eutychia in 4.3, 5). In
the second hearing Irene is questioned and sentenced to stand naked and exposed in a
brothel used by soldiers. God protects Irene, and she is sentenced to burn. There is no
further note about her companions. The account includes frequent references to
Thessalonians, which may suggest that the account had a liturgical use in Thessaloniki.

Nasrallah, Laura. "Empire and Apocalypse in Thessaloniki: Interpreting the Early Christian Rotunda." *JECS* 13 (2005): 465–508.

Palmeri, A. "Agape." *DHGE* 1 (1912): 876.

Acts of Apollonius

Greek: Codex Parisinus graecus 1219. Armenian: *Armenian Lives of the Fathers* (Venice, 1874), 138–43.

Musurillo, 90–105; KKR, 30–34; Klette, *Der Process und die Acta S. Apollinii* (Leipzig, 1897), 92–131. For a discussion of biblical imagery, see Saxer, *Bible*, 75–86.

The *Acts of Apollonius* is extant in both Greek and Armenian. Eusebius informs us that Apollonius was a wealthy, educated Roman executed under Commodus in 185. The Paris manuscript calls Apollonius "the man in sackcloth," which may have led to the designation of Apollonius as an "ascetic" in the Armenian version. Otherwise the Greek account presents Apollonius as a philosopher offering an *apologia*. There are notable discrepancies between Eusebius's version and the Greek *acta*. It seems likely that the martyrdom was originally set in Rome (as per Eusebius's account) but that there were at least two separate literary traditions. Saxer hypothesizes that the earliest tradition was composed in the third century.

The text seems to suggest two hearings and two speeches (2–9; 14–44) in which Apollonius decries the beliefs of the Athenians, Cretans, Egyptians, and Syrians. There is considerable overlap between the content of Apollonius's speeches and other Christian "apologetic" literature. The bibliography on the account is enormous, much of which can be located in Saxer's article debating the underlying second-century *acta*.

Freudenberger, R. "Die Überlieferung von Martyrium des römischen Christen Apollonius." *Zeitschrift für die Neutestamentliche Wissenschaft* 60 (1969): 111–30.

Griffe, E. "Les Actes du martyr Apollonius et les problèmes de la base juridique des persecutions." *Bulletin de Literature Ecclésiastique* 53 (1952): 65–76.

Klette, E. Theodor. *Der Process und die Acta S. Apolloni.* Texte und Untersuchungen zur Geschichte der altchristlichen Literatur 15.2. Leipzig: J. C. Henrichs, 1897. 92–13.

Saxer, Victor. "L'apologie au Sénat du martyr romain Apollonius." *Mélanges de l'École française de Rome. Antiquité* 96 (1984): 1017–38.

———. "*Martyrium Apollonii Romani:* Analyse structurells et problème d'authenticité." *Rendiconti della Pontifica Accademia Romana di Archeologia* 46 (1983–84): 269–98.

Acts of Carpus, Papylus, and Agathonice

Codex Parisinus graecus 1468; codex Latinus 4 of the library of Bergamo.

Bastiaensen, 33–46 and 384–390; Musurillo, 22–37; Pio Franchi de' Cavalieri, *Studi e Testi* 33 (1920): 3–45; KKR, 8–13; Lazzati, 131–37. For a discussion of biblical imagery, see Saxer, *Bible*, 99–110.

The deaths of these Italian martyrs are placed by Eusebius (*Hist. eccl.* 5.15.48) during the reign of Marcus Aurelius. The command to sacrifice, on the other hand, suggests to Guilbert that the account is Decian. Guilbert's hypothesis can certainly account for the legal grounds on which the martyrs are executed and would indicate that even if the martyrs died in the period of Marcus Aurelius, the exhortatory focus of the account is the mid-third-century Decian audience.

The account is extant in two versions, Greek and Latin. The Greek and Latin recensions are very different from one another. In the Latin recension Carpus is identified as a bishop, and an almost apologetic explanation of Agathonice's "voluntary" martyrdom is offered. Given the unlikelihood of an editor removing either element from the narrative, it is more plausible that the Latin is a later, perhaps fourth-century abridgment from the earlier Greek with editorial explanations for Agathonice's actions (so, Musurillo).

Guilbert, Joseph de. "La date du martyre des SS. Carpos, Papylos et Agathionicé." *Revue des Questions Historiques* 83 (1908): 5–23.

Harnack, Adolf von. "Die Akten des Karpus, des Papylus, und der Agathonike. Eine Urkunde aus der Zeit Mark Aurels." *Texte und Untersuchung der zur Geschichte der altchristlichen Litteratur* 3 (1888): 440–54.

Lietzmann, Hans. "Die älteste Gestalt der Passio SS. Carpi, Papylae et Agathonices." Pages 46–57 in *Festgabe von Fachgenossen und Freunden Karl Müller zum siebzigsten Geburtstag dargebrach.* Edited by Otto Scheel. Tübingen: J. C. B. Mohr, 1922.

Schneider, A. M. "Das Martyrium der heiligen Karpos und Papylos zu Konstantinopel." *Jahrbuch des Deutschen Archaologischen Instituts* 49 (1934): 416–418.

Acts of Cassian

E. C. Owen, *Some Authentic Acts of the Early Martyrs* (Oxford: Clarendon Press, 1927), 125–26; Ruinart 342–45.

This account relays the martyrdom of the notary who recorded the proceedings against Marcellus. The text is inspired by and is a conscious imitation of the *Acts of Marcellus*, connecting Cassian to Marcellus in a manner similar to the *Martyrdom of Pionius* and the *Martyrdom of Polycarp*. It is, as Ruinart notes, a pendant to the earlier martyr act (Ruinart, 345). The death of Cassian is interwoven with that of Marcellus and is rendered almost incomprehensible without it. The theme of the notary revolting against his civil duty and declaring himself a Christian is found also in the *Acts of Genesius* and may be tied more broadly to the notion of imperial servants (soldiers, civil servants, etc.) rejecting their traditional roles in favor of Christianity. Given the literary ties to the *Acts of Marcellus* (the execution is dated to around 298 C.E.), it is impossible that the account can be dated prior to the turn of the fourth century. As the text functions as an expansion of the earlier tradition, it would be reasonable to suppose that some time had passed before the composition of the *Acts of Cassian*. The *Acts of Cassian* forms part of the hagiographic development of the legends associated with Marcellus.

Acts of Claudius, Asterius, and Their Companions

KKR, 106–9; Ruinart, 309–11. For the redaction of the *acta,* see Pio Franchi de' Cavalieri, *Studi e Testi* 5 (1932): 107–18.

Asterius, Claudius, and their brother Neon were martyred under Diocletian together with two Christian women—Domnina and Theonilla. According to the narrative, the brothers were denounced by their stepmother–who was looking to take control of their assets—to Lysias, the proconsul of Cilicia. The three men and Domnina were scourged to death while Theonilla, a Christian widow, was beaten and burned to death with live coals. The account was set during the period of Diocletian persecution, but the sensational aspects of the account suggest it is later still.

Martyrdom of Conon

Athanasios Papadopoulos-Kerameos, *Analecta Hierosolumitkés Stachuologías.* 5 vols. (St. Petersburg: Kirshbaum, 1898), 348–49.
Musurillo, 186–93; KKR, 64–66.

This is an almost novelistic, exquisitely well-written narrative of a Greek who claims to be from Nazareth and who in old age has settled in Carmena (most likely Carma in Phrygia or Pisidia), where he had been employed on the irrigation canals. The details of the account (the arrival of the prefect, the empty city, the seizure of Conon to answer for all Christians) are historically improbable. The entire account has the tone and feel of a moral tale, which may suggest a pedagogical or catechetical setting for the story. Like Sanctus in the *Letter of the Churches of Lyons and Vienne* and the protagonists of the *Martyrdom of Irenaeus,* and the *Martyrdom of Pionius,* Conon refuses to answer the questions of his accusers. He claims to be from Nazareth and the "family of Christ" (4.2), a self-description that a number of scholars have read literally as evidence that Conon was a biological descendent of Jesus. It seems to me more likely to be metaphorical. Delehaye agrees with the Roman martyrology that Conon was martyred under Decian (*Propylaeum Decembris,* 87), but the reliability of the account is in question.

Delehaye, Hippolyte. *Propylaeum ad Acta Sanctorum Decembris.* Brussels: Société des
    Bollandistes, 1940.

Martyrdom of Crispina

Codex Augustodunensis 34; codex Remens S. Theodor. Musurillo, 302–9; KKR, 109–11; Pio Franchi de' Cavalieri, *Studi e Testi* 9 (1902): 32–35; Ruinart, 447–49; Saxer, *Saints,* 133–42.

According to the narrative, Crispina was a prominent woman in Thacora (Numidia) arrested by the proconsul Annius Anullinus and executed December 304. Monceaux argues that the first part of the *acta* is authentic enough, but the second part of the narrative (especially where the proconsul orders Crispina's head to be shaved) seems—to him—a little suspicious because it is unparalleled in other martyrdom accounts. We should note that Augustine's sermons mention Crispina and add a number of details not mentioned in the martyrdom (cf. *Serm.* 286, 354). Assuming the tripartite form critical distinction is correct, the third part of the text (2.1–3) may be historically reliable.

Monceaux, P. "Les Actes de Sainte Crisipine, martyre à Theveste." Pages 383–89 in
    Mélanges Boissier: Recueil de mémoires concernant la littérature et les antiquités romaines dédié à Gaston Boissier à l'occasion de son 80e anniversaire. Paris: Fontemoing, 1903.

Acts of Cyprian

Catholic version: See Reitzenstein, below. Donatist version: Theological Manuscript 33 f 38th of Würzburg Library (in Maier, *Le dossier du donatisme*, 123–26).
Bastiaensen, 193–232 and 478–490; Musurillo, 168–75; KKR, 62–64; Lazzati, 153–59; Ruinart, 261–64; Saxer, *Saints*, 82–86; Tilley, 3–5. For a discussion of biblical imagery, see Saxer, *Bible*, 127–28.

One of the most influential martyrdom stories among ancients Christians, the *Acts of Cyprian* record the trial and execution of the North African Bishop Cyprian of Carthage. In addition to the *acta*, there are multiple references to his death in Jerome and Augustine. Cyprian had escaped the Decian persecutions by going into hiding (cf. Cyprian, *Epistle* 20), after which he was engaged in heated discussions over the status of "heretical baptisms" and the lapsed. Cyprian was eventually executed under the emperor Valerian. In the Diocletian persecution, the figure of Cyprian became a rallying point for Carthiginian Christians.

It is likely that a version of Cyprian's martyrdom was composed shortly after his death. Cyprian's responses in the account both follow his line of reasoning in *Epistle* 20 and also underscore his bravery and seek to prove that he did not run from the Decian persecutions out of cowardice. Delehaye argued that the account of his death was composed in three stages, reflected in the three different scenes of the text (interrogations on August 30, 257, a second interrogation September 13–14, 258, and a final trial and execution scene), but this argument has not garnered much support.

The *acta* are preserved in two distinct versions—a Donatist version called the *Life and Passion of Cyprian* by Pontius, and the Catholic *acta*. The Donatist version differs in detail in three main points—the disguise of Cyprian, his response *Deo laudes*, and the presence of other martyrs from the beginning of the text. Otherwise, the Donatist version interpolates little into the account. This could indicate either that the division of the manuscripts into two competing versions is overstated or that there was a certain reverence for the integrity of the text itself.

Maier, Jean-Louis. *Le dossier du donatisme*. Berlin: Akademie-Verlag, 1987–89.
Reitzenstein, R. "Bemerkungen zur Märtyrerliteratur: II. Nächträge zu den Akten
    Cyprians." *Nachrichten von der königlichen Gesellschaft der Wissenchaften zu Göttingen* (1919): 177–219.

———. "Ein donatistisches Corpus cyprianischer Schriften." *Nachrichten von der königlichen Gesellschaft der Wissenchaften zu Göttingen* (1914): 85–92.

———. "Die Nachrichten über den Tod Cyprians. Ein philologischer Beitrag zur Geschichte der Märtyrerliteratur," *Sitzungsberichte der Heidelberger Akademie der Wissenschaften* 1 (1913): 12–17.

Martyrdom of Dasius

Codex Parisinus graecus 1539.
Musurillo, 272–79; KKR, 91–95.

The only source for this text was published by Franz Cumont in 1897 and describes the trial of a Christian soldier, Dasius, who was stationed at Durostorum. Dasius refuses to play the part of "king" in a licentious feast held at Saturnalia. Despite considerable scholarly fascination with the feast of Saturnalia, there is no historical evidence for the ritual self-immolation mentioned at the beginning of the text. It is possible that this incident has been confused with the Sacian feast of the Persians or the *pharmakoi* legends during which criminals wandered around in the guise of kings before being put to death. In my opinion, the association of this practice with Christian martyrs would have a certain irony in light of the influence of the *pharmakos* legends on the execution of Jesus (for a discussion of the *pharmakoi*, see Adela Yarbro Collins, "Finding Meaning in the Death of Jesus," *Journal of Religion* 78 [1998]: 175–96). At any rate, Dasius refuses to participate in the festival, and when he feels he is being tricked into performing the pagan role, he overturns the images and disrupts the incense in the festival. Delehaye considers the text to be inauthentic. The inclusion of language of Christological and Trinitarian debates in Dasius's confession suggests that the account was composed later than the Diocletian period.

Cumont, F. "Les Actes de S. Dasius." *Anal. Boll.* 16 (1897): 11–15.
Delehaye, H. "Les Acts de S.Dasius." *Anal. Boll.* 27 (1908): 217–18.
Doren, R. von. "Dasius." *DHGE* 14 (1960): 92.
Lang, A. "The Martyrdom of St. Dasius." *Man* 1 (1901): 83–84.

Acts of Eupl(i)us

Recension A: codex Parisinus graecus 1173; Pio Franchi de' Cavalieri, *Studi e Testi* 49 (1928): 1–54. Recension B: Ruinart, 437–38.
Musurillo, 310–19; KKR, 100–102 For a discussion of biblical imagery, see Saxer, *Bible* 133–38.

The text is set in Catania (Sicily), but Eupl(i)us's origins and ecclesiastical status are unknown. In the Greek he is known as Euplus, in the Latin as Euplius. He appears outside a chamber, where the *corrector Siciliae* Calvisianus is conducting a hearing, and somewhat brashly enters the council room. Euplus comes bearing scriptures, but his actions are not those of a *traditor;* he seems to be flaunting his illegal Christianity against Diocletian's first edict. Euplus refuses to recant under torture and is executed with the Gospels hung around his neck, perhaps as an ironic play on Pauline notions of slavery in Christ. The Roman martyrology celebrates Euplus on April 12, but the authenticity of the *acta* is questioned by Musurillo on account of the fact that the proceedings do not follow the prescriptions of Diocletian's edicts. Euplus and Agathonice are together viewed as "voluntary martyrs." Like many other martyrdoms, the *acta* includes a some-what incongruous Trinitarian reference, which may suggest that it was redacted later than the early fourth century.

Corsaro, F. "Studi sui documenti agiografici intorno al martirio di S. Euplo." *Orpheus* 4 (1957): 33–62.
Martin, Victor. *Apologie de Philéas.* Geneva: Bibliotheca Bodmeriana 1964.

Acts of Felix the Bishop

Musurillo, 266–71; KKR, 90–91; Ruinart, 390–91.

The *Acts of Felix the Bishop* is yet another textually difficult account engaged by Hippolyte Delehaye. Felix was bishop of Tibiuca the location of which is largely unknown. Duncan-Jones uses Magnilianus, the curator, to locate Tibiuca in Henchir Bou Cha. Diocletian's first edict was not put into effect in this region until June 5, 303 C.E suggesting that the account must have been composed after this date. The *curator* Magnilianus interrogates the priest Aper and the lectors Cyril and Vitalis, and the trail leads to Felix, who is arrested following his return from Carthage. The *curator* orders a postponement of three days before returning Felix to Carthage to await trial before the *proconsul Africae.* The *legatus* imprisons Felix before his sentencing to death on July 15 by Annius Anullinus. In Ruinart's text an interpolator has inserted an account of Felix's voyage to Venusium, where he is finally beheaded by the prefect. It seems likely that Felix was confused with a local Italian saint of the same name, or the interpolation could be part of a general hagiographic trend of expanding and complicating the trial process with the inclusion of pilgrimage establish-ing voyages. The account is included in both Maier and Tilley as part of the Donatist *acta.*

Delehaye, Hippolyte. "La Passion de S. Felix de Thibuica." *Anal. Boll.* 39 (1921): 241–76.
Duncan-Jones, R. "An African Saint and His Interrogator." *Journal of Theological Studies* 25 (1974): 106–10.
Maier, Jean-Louis. *Le dossier du donatisme.* Berlin: Akademie-Verlag, 1987–89.
Monceaux, P. *La Passio Felicis: etude critique sur les documents relatifs au martyre de Félix, évêque de Thibiuca.* (Paris: Burdin, 1905).

Martyrdom of Fructuosus and Companions

Codex Colbert 1–3; Codex RR. PP Fuliensium Parisiensium; S. German 2; Compendiens; Floriac. S. Bened.; PP Caelestin Paris; Boheri 2; S. Mariani Autissiodorensis (= Ruinart).

Musurillo, 176–85; KKR, 83–84; Pio Franchi de' Cavalieri, "Gli Atti di S. Fructuoso di Tarragona," *Studi e Testi* 65 (1935): 182–94.
NB: there is a paraphrase of this text in Prudentius, *Peristephanon* 6. Cf. Augustine, *Serm.* 273.

The *Martyrdom of Fructuosus* relays the arrest of Fructuosus, bishop of Tarragona, Spain, and two of his deacons, Augurius and Eulogius, on Sunday, January 16, 259, and their execution the following Friday. The conclusion of the work, with its description of the appearance of Fructuosus after his death and a somewhat eulogistic passage, is likely to be a later addition to the account. Multiple biblical allusions—the removal of sandals, the drugged cup of wine, the postmortem appearances, and so forth—hint at a greater complexity and purpose. The account has much in common with the *Martyrdom of Polycarp*—both Polycarp and Fructuosus comment upon the "single hour" of their martyrdom in drawing out the antithesis with the eternality of judgment, both "bear in mind" the entire Catholic Church (a suspiciously late-sounding turn of phrase comparable to statements of Augustine), and neither is nailed to the stake, being bound instead. In both accounts their ability to withstand the flames without nails seems to indicate a certain intensification of the *imitatio* motif. Both bishops draw their lives to a close with prayer. The connection between the two accounts provides information about the literary dissemination of the *Martyrdom of Polycarp* and indicates that *Fructuosus* was composed later than the fourth-century redaction of the *Martyrdom of Polycarp*.

Martyrdom of Irenaeus Bishop of Sirmium

Musurillo, 294–301; KKR, 103–5; Ruinart, 432–34.

Irenaeus was bishop of Sirmium, a city perched on the river Save in Pannonia (now in Serbia) around the turn of the fourth century. The account is a relatively simple trial-torture-execution conducted under the auspices of the *praeses* Probus. The date of the martyrdom seems to be 304 and—given the absence of supernatural hagiographic elements—it is likely that it was composed shortly afterward. According to the *Martyrdom of Pollion*, Probus enforced Diocletian's fourth edict against the clergy and arrested Irenaeus, Pollion, and Montanus. Irenaeus is tortured in front of his wife and children (whom he denies knowing), placed in jail, and brought to a second hearing. He is beheaded, and his body is thrown into the river.

Mócsy, A. "Pannonia." *RE*, suppl. 9 (1962): 587–88.

Martyrdom of Julius the Veteran

Codex bibliothecae publicae Cenomannensis 217 (in the Public Library, Le Mans, France).
Musurillo, 260–65; KKR, 105–6.

Julius was an aged soldier who had served twenty-seven years in the army and was stationed at Durostorum in Moesia Inferior. His martyrdom took place under the notorious fourth edict of Diocletian. Julius was tried before the judge Maximus, who is named *praeses* and seems to be the *legatus Augustalis*. On account of its simplicity, the account has been accepted by scholars as historically reliable. An interesting feature in the text is the attempt to bribe the aging soldier to sacrifice to the gods with the promise of "eternal glory," which is a deliberate parody of the Christian afterlife.

Acts of Justin and His Companions

Recension A: codex Parisinus graecus 1470; Musurillo, 42–47; Pio Franchi de' Cavalieri, *Studi e Testi* 33 (1920): 5–17. Recension B: codex Cantabrigiensis add. 4489; codex Hierosolymitanus sancti Sepulchri 6; codex Vaticanus graecus 1667. Musurillo, 47–53; Pio Franchi de' Cavalieri, *Studi e Testi* 8 (1902): 33–36; KKR, 15–18. Recension C: codex Hierosolymitanus sancti Sepulchri 17; codex Vaticanus graecus 1991. Musurillo, 54–61; Lazzati, *Gli Sviluppi*, 124–27; Bastiaensen, 47–58 and 391–96. For a discussion of biblical imagery, see Saxer, *Bible*, 19–26.

The *Acts of Justin* records the trial of Justin and six (or seven) of his companions before Rusticus, the famed Stoic adviser of Marcus Aurelius. Justin's death may have been engineered by his Cynic competitor Crescens (2 *Apology* 3). It is unclear from the *acta* precisely what the legal situation was: Rusticus asks Justin what sort of life he leads and what kind of meetings they hold. In all the recensions, however, the sentence appears to hinge upon the refusal to sacrifice. The *acta* survive in three distinct recensions that appear to have been redacted over a long period of time (see Bisbee for specifics). The redactions show an increased interest in relic collection, the ideology of martyrdom, heresiology, and liturgy. Nevertheless, modern scholars have negatively evaluated the *Acts of Justin* like Justin's own works; Musurillo calls it "[a] dull, prosaic document" (xix).

Bisbee, Gary A. "The Acts of Justin Martyr: A Form-Critical Study." *Second Century* 3
    (1983): 129–57.
Burkitt, F. C. "The Oldest Manuscript of St. Justin's Martyrdom." *JTS* 11 (1909):
    61–66.
den Boeft, Jan and Jan Bremmer. "Noctiunculae Martyologicae." *Vigiliae Christianae* 35
    (1981): 43–56.
Freudenberger, Rudolph. "Die Acta Justini als historisches Dokument." Pages 24–31 in
    Humanitas-Christianitas: Walter v. Loewenich zum 65 Geburstag. Edited by
    Karlmann Beyschlag. Wittern: Luther, 1968.

Martyrdom of Lucian and Marcian

Ruinart, 212–14.

Ruinart divides the text into two parts: the first a legend (omitted in most translations and dating from the fifth century), and the second a more mundane trial and execution that can be traced back to an original text. The trial takes place before the proconsul Sabinus. Lucian identifies his profession as the "condition of freedom and the adoration of the mysteries of God." En route to their funeral pyres, the martyrs utter a prayer and end with a biblically styled "into your hands we commend our spirits."

Letter of the Churches of Lyons and Vienne

Eusebius, *Hist. eccl.* 5.1.3–2.8.

Bastiaensen, 59–96 and 397–404; Musurillo, 62–85; KKR, 18–27. For a discussion of biblical imagery, see Saxer, *Bible*, 37–72.

Eusebius is the sole source for this text, which purports to be an encyclical letter written by the communities of Lyons and Vienne (Gaul) to the churches of Asia and Phrygia. The letter records an anti-Christian uprising in the summer of 177 (although some, like. Meinhold, have doubted the date). The sequence of events is very convoluted, and the legal basis of the events seems muddled. As a result, Thompson doubted the authenticity of all parts of the letter, arguing that it was, at best, a late third-century composition. His theory, ingenious as it is, fails to account for the similarities between *Lyons* and the writings of Irenaeus. In an attempt to ground the martyrdom in historical events, J. H. Oliver, Frend, and others suggested that the Christians were substituted in the arena for *trinqui* (a kind of cost-efficient gladiator) at the Festival of Three Gauls. There is, however, no corroborating evidence for this theory. Even if the letter is historically reliable, it may have been reworked by a third-century redactor or Eusebius himself (cf. the cruelty of the soldiers and the mention of the beast in 1.5, 42, 47; 2.6; the term "virgin mother" used of the church in 1.45 parallels the late third-century Methodius of Olympius, *Symposium* 3.8). The text is very detailed and provides vivid descriptions of the multiple punishments and tortures of the martyrs, a hallmark of the later martyrdom accounts. Since Othmar Perler's work, the majority of scholars have viewed *Lyons* as literarily and ideologically dependent on 4 Maccabees.

Oliver, J. H., and R. E. A. Palmer. "Minutes of an Act of the Roman Senate." *Heperia* 24 (1955): 320–49.

Perler, Othmar. "Das vierte Makkabaeerbuch, Ignatius von Antiochien und der ältesten Martyrerberichte." *Rivista di archeologia cristiana* 25 (1949) 47–72.

Quentin, H. "La liste des martyres de Lyon." *Anal. Boll.* 39 (1921): 113–38.

Rougé, Jean, and Robert Turcan. *Les martyrs de Lyons (177)*. Paris: Éditions du CNRS, 1978.

Saxer, Victor. "Les 'Actes des Martyrs anciens' chez Eusèbe de Césarée et dans les Martyrologies syriaque et hiéronymien." *Anal. Boll.* 102 (1984): 85–95.

Thompson, J. A. "The Alleged Persecution of the Christians at Lyons in 177." *American Journal of Theology* 16 (1912): 359–84; 17 (1913): 249–58.

Acts of Marcellus

Musurillo, 250–59; KKR, 87–89; Lazzati, 143–45. For the process of redaction, see, particularly, Hippolyte Delehaye, "Les actes de S. Marcel, le centurion," *Anal. Boll.* 41 (1923): 257–87; Saxer, *Saints*, 125–30.

The *Acts of Marcellus* is one of a slew of *acta* concerned with the portrayal of soldier martyrs. In the account, Marcellus, a centurion of *legio II Traiana*, throws down his *balteus* (sword belt), to the scandal of his compatriots. He is arrested and imprisoned and receives hearings before both Anastasius Fortunatus (*praefectus legionis* at Tingis) and Aurelius Agricolanus (deputy praetorian prefect). When Agricolanus realizes the treacherous nature of Marcellus's actions, he condemns him to die by decapitation. At this point the textual evidence becomes problematic. Delehaye has divided the manuscripts into two recensions, M and N, of which M is widely viewed as the more reliable. N places the events at Léon in Galicia and makes Marcellus a centurion of *legio VII Gemina*. De Gaiffier pointed out further complications in the N recension and cast doubt on Delehaye's dual-recension theory. The texts that make up recension N differ widely from one another. The account seems to have inspired the *Acts of Cassian of Tingis* (see above), which presents the martyrdom of Cassian, the *notarius* at the trial of Marcellus (see Ruinart, 345).

Gaiffier, B. de. "A propos de S. Marcel le centurion" *Archivos Leonenses* 45–6 (1969) 13–23.

———. "L' 'Elogium' dans la passion de S. Marcel le Centurion." *Archivium latinitatis medii aevi*. Bulletin du Cange 16 (1942): 127–36.

———. "S. Marcel de Tanger ou de Léon? Évolution d'une légende." *Anal. Boll.* 61 (1943): 116–39. This adds the variants of codex Matritensis A.76.

Seston, W. "A propos de la 'Passio Marcelli centurionis.'" Pages 239–46 in *Aux sources de la tradition Chrétienne: Mélanges offerts à M. Maurice Goguel*. Edited by J. J. von Allmen. Neuchâtel: Delachaux and Niestlé, 1950.

Martyrdom of Marian and James

There are ten extant manuscripts; the primary one is codex Augustodunensis 34. Musurillo, 194–213; KKR, 67–73; Pio Franchi de' Cavalieri, *Studi e Testi* 3 (1900): 47–61; Ruinart, 268–74; Lazzati, 190–200; Saxer, *Saints*, 88–103.

This account is very similar in terms of form and content to the *Passion of Perpetua and Felicitas*. It is composed in an elegant rhetorical style (*elocutio novella*) in imitation of the earlier account. The strong similarities between The *Martyrdom of Marian and James*, the *Martyrdom of Montanus and Lucius*, and the *Passion of Perpetua and Felicitas* have raised doubts about the authenticity of the two later accounts. Even though the styles of *Mart. Mar* and *Mart. Mont.* are very different from one another, their similarity to the *Passion of Perpetua and Felicitas* might lead us to suppose that they originated in the same social context. Alternatively, we might posit that there was a distinctive style of martyrdom found specifically in North Africa.

The narrative itself is very complex. James (a deacon), Marian (a lector), and the anonymous author are traveling through Numidia when they stop at Muguae, a suburb of Cirta. Simultaneously, the governor of the province sent soldiers to arrest the bishops Agapius and Secundius. The soldiers pass through Muguae and arrest the three Christians, who are brought to trial in Cirta. There then follows a series of prophetic visions and tortures before their execution by drowning in a river. The text was known to Augustine (*Serm.* 284) and likely reached its final form before 310 C.E.

Passion of Maxima, Donatilla, and Secunda

The only surviving manuscript was edited by Charles De Smedt in *Anal. Boll.* 9 (1890): 107–16. Pio Franchi de' Cavalieri, *Studi e Testi* 65 (1935): 76–97; Tilley, 13–24.

The execution of these martyrs is also attested in the *Martyrdom of Crispina*. The dating of the account is notoriously difficult. The internal evidence of the text and the Carthiginian calendar suggest that the martyrs were executed on July 30 and *Crispina* was executed in December 304 C.E., thus suggesting a *terminus a quo* of July 30, 304. The text notes that the women were interred in a place for those thrown to the beasts and mentions the inability of the Christians to obtain their remains. Monceaux and Delehaye have argued that the story about Secunda is a secondary interpolation. She appears late in the narrative and is not linked to the condemnation of the other two women. The young women are modeled both on the young men of Daniel and on the person of Jesus. The discussion of magic is exceptional for Christian martyrdom and may be tied to the martyrs' steadfastness and apparent immunity to torture (so, Tilley).

Delehaye, H. "Contributions récentes à l'hagiographie de Rome et d'Afrique." *Anal. Boll.* 54 (1936): 298–300.
Monceaux, P. *Histoires littéraire de l'Afrique chrétienne depuis les origins jusqu' a l'invasion arabe.* Paris: Leroux, 1901–23. 3.150–151.

Acts of Maximilian

Codex Sarensis (from Salisbury)
Jean Mabillon, ed., *Vetera Analecta* (Paris: Apus Montalant, 1675–85), 4.566. Musurillo, 244–49; KKR, 86–87; Ruinart, 340–42; Lazzati, 138–40; Bastiaensen, 238–45 and 491–97; Saxer, *Saints,* 117–24.

According to the account, the proconsul Dion had traveled to Tebessa in Numidia for the purpose of recruiting soldiers for the *legio III Augusta*. Fabius Victor presents his son for service, but Maximilian refuses to accept the seal and office. He is condemned to die. The mention of the precise age of the young man (twenty-one years, three months, and eighteen days) is almost like an epitaph. The body of Maximilian is taken by Pompeiana and buried at Carthage near the remains of Cyprian. This feature both associates Maximilian with the more famous martyr and legitimizes his relics.

Bremmer, J., and J. den Boeft. "Notiunculae Martyrologicae II." *Vigiliae Christianae* 36 (1982): 383–402 at 393–95.

Brock, P. "Why Did St. Maximilian Refuse to Serve in the Roman Army?" *Journal of Ecclesiastical History* 45 (1994): 195–209.

Cacitti, R. "Massimiliano—un obiettore di coscienza del tardo impero." *Humanitas* 36 (1980): 828–41.

Leclercq, H. "Militarisme (XIII): Le martyre du conscript Maximilien." *DACL* 11 (1933): 1133–37.

Siniscalco, P. "Bibbia e letteratura cristiana d'Africa nella 'Passio S. Maximiliani.'" Pages 595–613 in *Forma Futuri: Studi in onore del Cardinale Michele Pellegrino*. Turin: Bottega D'Erasmo, 1975.

Woods, David. "St. Maximilian and the *Jizya*." Pages 266–76 in *Hommages à Carl Deroux. V. Christianisme et Moyen Âge, Néo-latin et survivance de la latinité*. Edited by P. Defosse. Collection Latomus 279. Brussels: Latomus, 2003.

Zuckerman, C. "Two Reforms of the 370s: Recruiting Soldiers and Senators in the Divided Empire." *Revue des Études Byzantines* 56 (1998): 79–139, at 136–39.

Martyrdom of Maximus

M. Simonetti, *Studi Agiografici* (Rome: Signorelli, 1955), 85–87.

The *Martyrdom of Maximus* contains a very brief account of the trial of the merchant Maximus before Optimus, the proconsul of Asia, in Ephesus. Maximus is one of the so-called "voluntary martyrs" (see Euplus, above). When the edict condemning Christians was announced by Decius, Maximus, a local merchant, presented himself to Optimus. He was ordered to sacrifice to the goddess Diana, but refused and was tortured and stoned to death. The brevity of the work and the absence of narrative flourishes have led many scholars to view this account as historically reliable.

Martyrdom of Montanus and Lucius and Their Companions

Codex Augiensis XXXII; codex Bruxellensis 207–8; codex Parisinus latinus 5289; codex Trevirensis Bibl. Civ. 1151; codex Remigianus [missing].
Musurillo, 214–39; KKR, 74–82; Pio Franchi de' Cavalieri, *Studi e Testi* 22 (1909): 3–31; Ruinart, 275–82; Lazzati, 201–13 (see notes on the *Martyrdom of Marian and James*, above)

The document describes the martyrdom of Carthaginian clergy purportedly under Valerian. The style is simpler than the *Martyrdom of Marian and James*, but its authenticity is doubted due to its imitation of the literary style of the *Passion of Perpetua and Felicitas*. On account of the vision of Cyprian, Cavalieri argues that the document is based on an account written by a disciple of Cyprian. D'Alès has gone so far as to suggest that this disciple was Pontius the deacon.

Others scholars have reacted more strongly, condemning the work as a "deliberate forgery" (Rendel Harris and Gifford). Schulze proposes that the piece is a propagandistic work from the Diocletian era, which seems, at least, to recognize the importance of these kinds of martyr genealogies. Given the popularity of Cyprian, it is not necessary to attribute the work to a specific disciple. We can assume that many were eager to harness the charismatic power of the martyred Cyprian to validate their own accounts.

The text can be divided into two sections—an epistolary-visionary section (1–11) and the account of the martyrs' death (12–23). Lazzati sees a liturgical style in the rhetorical flourishes of the account, which may suggest that the martyrdom was composed for use as part of the veneration of the saints in North Africa.

D'Alès, A. *Recherches de Sciences Religieuse* 9 (1918): 319–78. Disputed by Delehaye in *Anal. Boll.* 39 (1921): 171.

Dolbeau, F. "La passion de saints Lucien et Montan." *Revue des Etudes Augustiniennes* 29 (1983): 89–82.

Monceaux, P. *Histoire littéraire de l'Afrique chrétienne depuis les origins jusqu' à l'invasion arabe*. Paris: Leroux, 1901–22. 2.156, especially.

Rendel Harris, J., and S. K. Gifford. *The Acts of the Martyrdom of Perpetua and Felicitas*. London: C. J. Clay and Sons, 1890, 26ff.

Passion of Perpetua and Felicitas

Greek: codex Hierosolymitanus sancti S. Sepulchri 1 Latin: codex Salisburg; codex Compendiens.
Bastiaensen, 107–48 and 412–52; Musurillo, 106–31; KKR, 35–43; Lazzati, "Note critiche al testo della Passio SS. Perpetuae et Felicitas," *Aevum* 30 (1956): 177–189; C. J. M. J. van Beek, *Passio Sanctarum Perpetuae et Felicitatis, latine et graece*, FP 43 (Bonn: Hanstein, 1938). For a discussion of biblical imagery, see Saxer, *Bible*, 87–96.

A conflation of literary genres, this work includes trial, sufferings, diary, and apocalyptic visions. It focuses on the martyrdom of the well-educated Perpetua and is full of images of motherhood and military battle. The visions and images evoke comparisons with the *Shepherd of Hermas* and Revelation 12. The date of the martyrdom is debated; the women fought the beasts *in natali Getae Caesaris*, which has been variously read as Geta's actual birthday, his acclamation as Caesar, or the date of his accession. Cf. Augustine, *Serm.* 280; Tertullian, *De anima* 55.4. The preservation of a version of the account in Tertullian indicates that the *passio* itself can be dated early. See Lazzati for the early history of reception.

Beek, C. J. M. J. van. *Passio Sanctarum Perpetuae et Felicitatis*. Nijmegen: Dekker and van de Vegt, 1936.

Braun, René. "Nouvelles observations linguistiques sur le rédacteur de la 'Passio Perpetuae.'" *Vigiliae Christianae* 33 (1979): 105–17.

Bremmer, Jan N. "Perpetua and Her Diary: Authenticity, Family, and Visions." Pages 77–120 in *Märtyrer und Märtyrerakten*. Edited by W. Ameling. Stuttgart: Steiner, 2002.

Cobb, L. Stephanie. *Dying to Be Men: Gender and Language in Early Christian Martyr Texts*. Gender, Theory and Religion. New York: Columbia University Press, 2008. 94–113.

Fridh, Åke. *Le problème de la Passion des saintes Perpétue et Félicité*. Studia Graeca et Latina Gothoburgensia 26. Stockholm: Almquist and Wiksell, 1968.

Habermehl, Peter. *Perpetua und der Ägypter oder Bilder des Bösen im frühen afrikanischen Christentum: Ein Versuch zur Passio sanctarum Perpetuae et Felicitatis*. Berlin: Akademie Verlag, 1992.

Halporn, James W. "Literary History and Generic Expectations in the Passio and Acta Perpetuae." *Vigiliae Christianae* 45 (1991): 223–41.

Lefkowitz, Mary R. "The Motivations for St. Perpetua's Martyrdom." *Journal of the American Academy of Religion* 44 (1976): 417–21.

Osiek, Carolyn. "Perpetua's Husband." *JECS* 20 (2002): 287–90.

Perkins, Judith. "The *Passion of Perpetua:* A Narrative of Empowerment." *Latormus* 53 (1994): 837–47.

———. "The Rhetoric of the Maternal Body in the *Passion of Perpetua*." Pages 313–32 in *Mapping Gender in Ancient Religious Discourses*. Edited by Todd Penner and Caroline Vander Stichele. Leiden: Brill, 1967.

Pettersen, A. "Perpetua: Prisoner of Conscience." *Vigiliae Christianae* 41 (1987): 139–53.

Robert, Louis. "Une vision de Perpétue martyre à Carthage en 203." *Comptes Rendus de l'Académie des Inscriptions et des Belles-Lettres* 126 (1982): 228–76.

Ronsse, Erin. "Rhetoric of Martyrs: Listening to Saints Perpetua and Felicitas." *JECS* 14 (2006): 283–327.

Rossi, Mary-Ann. "The Passion of Perpetua, Everywoman of Late Antiquity." Pages 53–56 in *Pagan and Christian Anxiety: A Response to E. R. Dodds*. Edited by R. Smith and J. Lounibos. Lanham, Md.: University Press of America, 1984.

Salisbury, Joyce. *Perpetua's Passion: The Death and Memory of a Young Roman Woman*. New York: Routledge, 1997.

Shaw, Brent D. "The Passion of Perpetua." *Past and Present* 56 (1993): 3–45.

Letter of Phileas

Eusebius, *Hist. eccl.* 8.10.
Musurillo, 320–27; KKR, 111–13.

Phileas was bishop of Thmuis in the Thebaid at the beginning of the fourth century. It seems he was arrested shortly after his consecration at Alexandria. Phileas took a stand against Melitius, bishop of Lycopolis, who had accused bishops of leniency toward the lapsed. After opposing Melitius and while imprisoned at Alexandria, Phileas composed the letter describing the sufferings of the martyrs of his diocese. The *Letter* seems to describe martyrdoms taking place under Diocletian's fourth edict. See the article by W. Ensslin, *RE* 19 (1938): 2132–33; and H. Leclercq, *DACL* 14 (1939): 703–9. The *Martyrdom of Phileas* is extant in both Greek and Latin (see below).

Acts of Phileas (= Acts of Phileas and Philerome)

Recension A: Victor Martin, *Papyrus Bodmer XX: Apologie de Philéas évêque de Thmouis* (Geneva: Bibliotheca Bodmeriana, 1964) 24–52; P Bodmer XX.
Recension B: F. Halkin, *Anal. Boll.* 81 (1963): 1927. New Latin text codex Bruxellensis 7984.
Bastiaensen, 247–338 and 498–581; Musurillo, 328–53; KKR, 113–16; Ruinart, 519–21 (older latin text); Saxer, *Bible*, 133–38.

The *Acts of Phileas* records the martyrdom of Phileas of Thmuis, the apparent author of the *Letter of Phileas*. The account survives in two recensions, Greek and Latin, the latter of which includes the execution of Philoromus, one of Phileas's companions. The Greek edition was published in 1964 as part of the Bodmer Papyrus and, for paleographic reasons, can be dated 310–50 C.E. For the Greek edition, therefore, we have a terminus ad quem of 350 C.E. The Greek edition is fragmentary; as a result, the Latin edition has formed the basis for most modern editions. The relationship between the two traditions is complex. Although there are points of contact between them, they are noticeably different from one another. It seems likely, as Saxer notes, that evolving oral traditions can account for differences between the two. This position may well be modified as Pietersma has presented some additional Phileas material not included in earlier scholarly discussions.

Pietersma, A. *The Acts of Phileas, Bishop of Thmuis.* (Geneva: Cramer, 1984).

Martyrdom of Philip of Heraclee

Ruinart, 440–48; Pio Franchi de' Cavalieri, *Studi e Testi* 27 (1905): 97–103.

The text describes bishop Philip as pure in heart and elevated above his peers. According to the narrative, he was not at all troubled by the great persecution and experienced the process of being martyred as an "epiphany." Philip and his companions (Severeus, Hermes, and some others who are unnamed) were brought before Aristemachus at Heraclee. Philip, perhaps drawing upon biblical language, refers to himself as the church's physician (cf. *Martyrdom of Coluthus*). Throughout the account the martyrs repeatedly cite Isaiah, Jonah, Susannah, and Daniel. The bodies of the martyrs are unscathed by their execution and instead are filled with youth and beauty.

Martyrdom of Pionius

Codex Marcianus graecus 359.
Bastiaensen, 149–92 and 453–76; Musurillo, 136–67; KKR, 45–57; Ruinart, 188–98.
For a discussion of biblical imagery, see Saxer, *Bible*, 11–26.

The *Martyrdom of Pionius* is a lengthy martyrdom written in the style of the *Letter of the Churches of Lyons and Vienne* and connected to the *Martyrdom of Polycarp*. The dating is uncertain. The prominence of Polemon, the reference to the emperor's edict (3.2), and the explicit dating (23) would normally secure a Decian dating, but the questioning, the imprisonment, the strong anti-Semitism, and elaborate discussion of satanic involvement seem to be out of place with the time of the Decian persecution. Recent studies by the late Louis Robert (continued and assembled by Robin Lane Fox) have compared the *Martyrdom of Pionius* to material evidence for Christian life in ancient Smyrna. Both have argued, forcefully, that this is an authentic account dating to the Decian period. E. Leigh Gibson's deft handling of the speeches demonstrates that the lengthy homiletical speeches, replete with anti-Semitic remarks, are still open to interpretation. She locates these within the context of intra-Christian polemic against Christians who visited synagogues.

Gebhardt, Otto von. "Das Martyrium des heiligen Pionius." *Archiv für slavische Philologie* 18 (1896): 156–71.
Gibson, E. Leigh. "Jewish Antagonism of Christian Polemic: The Case of the *Martyrdom of Pionius*." *JECS* 9 (2001): 339–58.
Robert, Louis. *Le martyre de Pionios, prêtre de Smyrne*. Ed. G. W. Bowersock and C. P. Jones. Washington, D.C.: Dumbarton Oaks, 1994.
Rordorf, W. "Zum Problem des »grossen Sabbats« im Polykarp- und Pioniusmartyrium." Pages 246–51 in *Pietas: Festschrift für Bernhard Kötting*. Edited by Ernst Dassmann and K. Suso Frank. JbAC. Ergänzungsband 8. Münster: Aschendorf, 1980.
Wohleb, L. "Die Uberlieferung des Pionios-Martyriums." *Römische Quartalschrift* 37 (1929): 173–77.

Martyrdom of Polycarp

Codex Parisinius graecus 1452; codex Hierosolymitanus sancti Sepulchri I; codex Baroccianus 238; codex Chalcensis Mon 95 [missing]; codex Vindobonensis graecus eccles iii; codex Mosquensis 150.
Bastiaensen, 3–32 and 371–383; Musurillo, 2–22; KKR, 1–8; Ruinart, 77–82 (Latin), 82–91 (Greek). For a discussion of biblical imagery, see Saxer, *Bible*, 27–36.

Of all the martyrdom accounts, the dating of the *Martyrdom of Polycarp* is the most contested and important. Its place as the "first Christian martyrdom" and the presumed connection between Polycarp and the Apostolic age has led to a scholarly commitment to an early dating unparalleled by discussions of other accounts. At least three different questions are at play here: When did Polycarp die? When was the account composed? And, has the account been interpolated?

For our purposes the date of Polycarp's actual death is somewhat irrelevant. Unless he died, as some have suggested, in the late 170s, this is still a remarkably early account. The date of Polycarp's death does not mean, however, either that the martyrdom was composed immediately afterward or that it is in any way an "authentic" account of the words and deeds of the martyr. Scholars, such as B. Dehandschutter, Gerd Buschmann, and Sara Parvis, who attempt to demonstrate the authenticity of the account, are forced to construct elaborate hypotheses to explain the miraculous elements of the narrative. For instance, Parvis suggests that the biblically styled dove that flies out of the body of the martyr is a bird that happened to be passing by at that moment. Attempts to position Polycarp as the earliest martyrdom account are frequently bound up in labors to prove its authenticity.

There are a number of indications in the text itself that the martyrdom should be dated later than the second century. To begin with, there are two distinct literary traditions. Eusebius's account is much briefer and omits a great deal of the early portion of the martyrdom. The martyrdom account contains quotations from nearly every book in the canonical New Testament, including Revelation, Hebrews, and the late dated Pastoral Epistles. Were the *Martyrdom of Polycarp* composed in the second century, we would hardly expect such comprehensive familiarity with the as yet nonexistent canon to the exclusion of noncanonical texts.

Furthermore, the text exhibits an extremely sophisticated and nuanced view on martyrdom. The author is conscious of potential misunderstandings of the martyr's imitation of Christ and goes to some lengths to distinguish between the status of Christ and that of the martyr (17–19). Were this, as is claimed, the first text to use the term *martys* in a technical sense, we would hardly expect to find such caution and nuance. To believe that the *Martyrdom of Polycarp* is the first martyrdom account is to believe not only that it inaugurates a paradigm shift in the understanding of the term *martys* but that with this new development in thought the authors became instantly aware of potential pitfalls of the veneration of martyrs, even though the category had only just come into existence!

Perhaps most telling is the lack of evidence that the martyrdom had any *literary* impact before the second part of the third century. To be sure there was a historical Polycarp who died in Smyrna in the middle of the second century. The literary account of his death, however, is considerably less reliable. It purports to be a letter to all the churches in the world, but there is no evidence of literary influence until the Decian *Martyrdom of Pionius* and *Martyrdom of Fructuosus*. Scholars treat the *Martyrdom of Polycarp* as a genre-creating text, but if it was dispatched as a letter in 166, there is no evidence of its impact on Christian literature for nearly a hundred years after its composition.

For these reasons it seems more likely to me that the *Martyrdom of Polycarp* in its extant form can be dated no earlier than the middle part of the third century and the persecution of Decius. It was then edited in the fourth century, when references to the cult of the saints (13, 18) and the "catholic church" (1.1) were added. The colophons to the account and the references to the worn pages of the text are consistent with the literary conventions of textual *inventio*. There may well have been an earlier version of the martyrdom that circulated in the late second and early third centuries, but access to this—let alone the words of the historical Polycarp—is impossible.

This brief statement of my own opinion does nothing to undermine the monumental contributions of Dehandschutter and Buschmann, but I think it raises some problems for the way that the *Martyrdom of Polycarp* is treated by scholars. The impact that it has had in scholarship does not accurately represent the impact that the text—as we have received it—had in the ancient world.

Barnes, T. D. "A Note on Polycarp." *JTS* 18 (1967): 433–37.

Boeft, Jan den, and Jan Bremmer. "Notiunculae Martyrologicae V." *Vigiliae Christianae* 49 (1995): 146–64.

Brightman, E. E. "The Prayer of St. Polycarp and Its Concluding Doxology." *JTS* 23 (1922): 391–92.

Buschmann, G. *Martyrium Polycarpi—Eine forMarkritische Studie: Ein Beitrag zur Frage nach der Enstehung der Gattung Märtureakte.* BZNW 70. Berlin: Walter de Gruyter, 1994.

Dehandschutter, Boudewijn. *Martyrium Polycarpi: Ein literair-krittisch studie.* BETL 52. Leuven: Leuven University Press, 1979.

———. "The New Testament and the *Martyrdom of Polycarp*." Pages 395–406 in *Trajectories through the New Testament and the Apostolic Fathers.* Edited by Andrew F. Gregory and Christopher M. Tuckett. Oxford: Oxford University Press, 2005.

———. *Polycarpiana: Studies on Martyrdom and Persecution in Early Christianity: Collected Essays.* Leuven: Leuven University Press, 2007.

Grégoire, H., and P. Orgels. "La veritable date du martyre de Polycarpe (23 févr. 177) et le *Corpus Polycarpianum*." *Anal. Boll.* 69 (1951): 1–38.

Marrou, H. I. "La date du martyre de saint Polycarpe." *Anal. Boll.* 71 (1953): 5–20.

Meinhold, Peter "Polycarpos." *RE* 21 (1952): 1661–93.

Parvis, Sara. "The Martyrdom of Polycarp." *Expository Times* 118 (206): 105–12.

Ronchey, S. *Indagine sul martirio di san Policarpo.* Rome: Istituto storico per il medio evo, 1990.

Martyrdom of Potamiaena and Basilides

Eusebius, *Hist. eccl.* 6.5; Palladius, *Lausiac History* 3 (a slightly different account in which Isiodore of Alexandria tells the story as he heard it from the lips of Antony).
Musurillo, 132–35; KKR, 44–45.

Palladius dates the martyrdom to the reign of Maximian (286–305), but Eusebius's turn-of-the-third-century dating is generally more accepted. Eusebius mentions the judge Aquila, who is assumed to be Subsatianus Aquila, prefect of Egypt, 205–10. Eusebius notes that the martyrs are numbered among the followers of Origen. The form of Potamiaena's martyrdom is unusual—burning pitch is dripped over her body (cf. Palladius *Lausiac History* 3.2.18–19). The story of Basilides is one of the first mentions of a rebellious soldier showing compassion to the Christians and for that reason is viewed by Musurillo to be somewhat suspect. There are earlier references to the "conversion" of a soldier (cf. the martyrdom of James in a fragment of Clement's *Hypostases* preserved in Eusebius, *Hist. eccl.* 9.2), so there is no reason to be especially suspicious of this incident. The additional material found in Palladius, however, is secondary. The mention of postmortem visions at the conclusion of the work is likely to be a later addition. Both martyrs are mentioned in the Martyrologium Hieronymianum on June 28.

Bakker, Henk. "Potamiaena: Some Observations about Martyrdom and Gender in Ancient Alexandria." Pages 331–50 in *The Wisdom of Egypt: Jewish, Early Christian, and Gnostic Essays in Honour of Gerard P Luttikhuize*. Edited by Anthony Hillhorst and Geurt Hendrick van Kooten. Leiden: Brill, 2005.

Bardy, Gustave. "Basilide (3)." *DHGE* 6 (1932): 1175–76.

Martyrdom of Ptolemaeus and Lucius

Justin Martyr, *2 Apol.* 2; Musurillo, 38–41; KKR, 14–15; Miroslav Marcovich, ed., *Iustini Martyris Apologia pro Christianis* Patristische Texte und Studien 38 (Berlin: Walter de Gruyter, 1994), 138–40.

The martyrdom of Ptolemaeus is preserved in the second *Apology* of Justin Martyr. Ptolemaeus, a Christian teacher living in Rome under Marcus Aurelius, was a friend of Justin whose arrest and trial were engineered by the disgruntled ex-husband of an instructee. Lucius is known only through his connection with Ptolemaeus and is described as a bystander who complains at the injustice of the charges against the Christian teacher and is subsequently executed with him. The description of the incident by Justin would seem to indicate that the martyrdom must have occurred 150–60. The recent study by Paul Parvis argues that *2 Apology* is a pseudepigraphal creation that was composed in light of Justin's own martyrdom. This would place the dating of the account later.

Parvis, Paul. "Justin, Philosopher and Martyr: The Posthumous Creation of the Second Apology." Pages 23–37, 172–77 in *Justin Martyr and His Worlds*. Edited by Paul Parvis. Minneapolis, Minn.: Fortress Press, 2007.

Acts of Saturninus, Dativus, and Their Companions (= Acts of the Abitinian Martyrs)

Bibliothèque Nationale Latin Manuscripts 5297, 5318, 9714, 17625; Trier 1152; Montepessulanus (Montpelier) 1.
Ruinart, 414–22; Pio Franchi de' Cavalieri, *Studi e Testi* 8 (1935): 3–71; Tilley, 25–50.

There is both a Catholic (see Pio Franchi de' Cavalieri, *Studi e Testi* 65 [1935]: 1–71) and a Donatist version (BHL 5297) of the *acta*. French commentary on the account has engaged only with the Catholic version. Ruinart, likewise, reproduces the Catholic version in his collection. The account is concerned with events surrounding the Carthaginian bishop Mensurius (d. 311/2), who was later charged as a *traditor*, and his deacon Caecilian, who succeeded him as bishop. A group of Christians arrested in Abitina (a village outside of Carthage) were brought to trial under Anulinus (cf. *The Martyrdom of Felix*). Strangely, Bishop Mensurius posted his own guard outside of the prison. In the Donatist *acta* this interference is viewed as a hostile attack on the Abitinian Christians. The references to specific political events indicate that the account was composed by

Donatists shortly after the events described, for local use, most likely during the episcopacy of Mensurius or Caecilian.

Maier, Jean-Louis. *Le dossier du donatisme.* Berlin: Akademie-Verlag, 1987–89.

Acts of the Scillitan Martyrs

Greek: codex Parisinus graecus 1470; Latin: codex Musei Britannici 11.880; codex Vindobonensis latinus 377; codex Ebroicensis 37.
Bastiaensen, 97–106 and 405–11; Musurillo, 86–89; KKR, 28–29; Lazzati, 128–30; Ruinart, 131–32; Saxer, *Saints,* 31–34. For a discussion of biblical imagery, see Saxer, *Bible,* 72–74.

Widely considered to represent one of the earliest, most "historically accurate," and "authentic" traditions in the martyrological tradition (see Bisbee, Musurillo, Frend), there is still the difficulty of the varying lists of the martyrs' names and the fact that only some of the martyrs are interrogated and mentioned at the first sentencing. This has led Corsaro and Karpp to propose models of redaction in which additional martyrs were added to the text. Alternatively, it is possible that the full list is not mentioned early in the account because not all of the martyrs are interrogated. This is the earliest dated document from Latin Christianity and the first to note the existence of a Latin Bible (12). The notes provided by Bastiaensen et al. are exceptional.

Bonner, Gerald. "The Scillitan Saints and the Pauline Epistles." *Journal of Ecclesiastical History* 7 (1956): 141–46.
Corsaro, F. "Note sugli 'Acta Martyrum Scillitanorum.'" *Nuovo Didaskaleion* (Catanis, 1956), 5–51. Summarizes the somewhat large amount of literature on the Scillitan martyrs. Follows the theory of de Labriolle that to the original six martyrs from Scillium six others were added from the martyrology of Carthage.
Hanslik, R. "Secretarium und Tribunal in den Acta Martyrum Scillitanorum," 163–67. In *Mélanges Christine Mohrmann: Nouveau recueil offert par ses anciens élèves.* Edited by L. J. Engels, H. W. F. M. Hoppenbrouwers, and A. J. Vermuelen. Utrecht: Spectrum, 1963.
Karpp, H. "Die Zahl der Scilitanischen Märtyrer." *Vigiliae Christianae* 15 (1961): 165–72.

Testament of the Forty Martyrs of Sebaste

Codex Vindobonensis theol 10; codex Parisinus graecus 1500; paleoslavonic version from codex 180 of library of Troitsko-Sergievskaya Monastery, Zagorsk (Russia).
Bastiaensen, 339–52 and 582–83; Musurillo, 354–62; KKR, 116–19; G. N. Bonwetsch, "Das Testament der vierzig Märtyrer," *Studien zur Geschichte der Theologie und Kirche,* ed. G. N. Bonwetsch and R. Seeberg, i.1 (Leipzig, 1897), 75–80.

Composed in encyclical form (like other early martyr acts *Mart. Pol.* and *Lyons*) by Meletius, the *Testament of the Forty Martyrs of Sebaste* recounts the story of forty soldiers who were put to death under Licinus (308–24) in Armenia at Sebaste. Both Basil and Gregory of Nyssa composed a number of eulogies for the martyrs. There is also an *Acts of the Forty Martyrs of Sebatse* extant in Greek (Gebhardt, 171–81), Syriac, and Slavonic that is considered by most scholars to be a later, inauthentic composition. Cavalieri is convinced that the martyrs were soldiers and that they were executed by exposure. Against Cavalieri, Reitzenstein expressed strong reservations that any part of the *acta* is reliable. The simplicity of the document and the obscurity of the geographic locations mentioned might lead us to believe that the text is a genuine letter. The focal point of the account seems to be the proper interment of the martyrs' bones (1.3). Meletius's concern that the relics would be divided up is a practical one paralleled in a number of Syriac texts and hagiography discussing the remains of ascetic monks. The remainder of the letter is filled with standard exhortation and greetings.

Bonwetsch, N. "Das Testament der vierzig Märtyrer zu Sebaste." *Neue kirchliche* 3 (1892): 705–26.

Haussleiter, J. "Zu dem Testament der vierzig Märtyrer zu Sebaste." *Neue kirchliche* 3 (1892): 978–88.

Notes

INTRODUCTION

1. Citations in Greek from the New Testament are taken from the twenty-seventh edition of the *Novum Testamentum Graecae*, Barbara Aland, et al., eds. (Stuttgart: Deutsche Bibelgesellschaft, 1993) and translations from the NRSV. Unless otherwise noted, citations from the acts of the martyrs follow the critical editions and translations in Herbert Musurillo, *Acts of the Christian Martyrs* (Oxford: Clarendon Press, 1972). Greek editions and translations of martyrdom accounts not appearing in Musurillo are individually noted. For further details on the manuscripts, text-critical editions, and translations of the individual martyrdom accounts, consult the appendix.

2. Ign., *Rom.* 6.3 (trans. Michael W. Holmes, *Apostolic Fathers: Greek Texts and English Translations*, 2d ed.; Grand Rapids, Mich.: Baker Books, 2007).

3. Daniel Boyarin notes that martyrdom "was a central aspect of the experience of the Imitation of Christ"; *Dying for God: Martyrdom and the Making of Christianity and Judaism* (Stanford, Calif.: Stanford University Press, 1999), 95. See also Elizabeth A. Castelli, *Martyrdom and Memory: Early Christian Culture Making*, Gender, Theory, and Religion Series (New York: Columbia University Press, 2004), 51. While all agree that there is a connection between imitation of Jesus and martyrdom, not everyone is of the opinion that this represents an important theme in early Christian martyr acts. Judith Lieu regards the theme as underexplored and ultimately ambiguous. See Judith M. Lieu, *Neither Jew Nor Greek? Constructing Early Christianity*, Studies of the New Testament and Its World (London: T & T Clark, 2002), 221–22.

4. Judith Perkins, *The Suffering Self: Pain and Narrative Representation in the Early Christian Era* (New York: Routledge, 1995), 13.

5. In her important book, *The Suffering Self*, Judith Perkins answers the question *why* Christians focused on the exemplary suffering of the Savior. Perkins views martyrdom and the willingness to suffer as a sociological phenomenon. Christian culture in the early church, according to Perkins, was one in which suffering (whether or not in imitation of Christ) was a good. The details of this mimesis and the way that it can inform our understanding of biblical interpretation, historical theology, and social interactions have yet to be discussed. For a discussion of the theme of imitation more generally, see Henri Crouzel, "L'imitation et la 'suite' de Dieu et du Christ dans les premiers siècles chrétiens: sources gréco-romaines et hébraïques," *Jahbuch für Antike und Christentum* 21 (1978): 7–41.

6. For a discussion of Christ dwelling in the martyr, see the excellent article of Jan den Boeft, "Martyres sunt hominess fuerunt," in *Fructus Centesimus: Mélanges Gerard J. M. Bartelink*, Instrumenta Patristica 19, ed. A. A. R. Bastiaensen, A. Hilhorst, and C. H. Kneepkens (Steenbrugge and Dordrecht: Kluwer, 1989), 115–24.

Jan den Boeft and Jan N. Bremmer have argued (presumably on the basis of this view) that *imitatio* fails to "bring out the fundamental personal relationship of the martyrs with Christ" (Jan den Boeft and Jan N. Bremmer, "Notiunculae Martyrologicae IV," *Vigiliae Christianae* 45 [1991]: 106).

7. Contra Jan N. Bremmer, who sees this as a categorical distinction between the apocryphal acts and the *acta martyrum* (Jan N. Bremmer, *The Rise and Fall of the Afterlife* [London: Routledge, 2002], 103). There are, as we will see in chapter 2, many examples in which the martyr acts mirror the death of Jesus narratively. Bremmer's language of invisibility and his insistence that we are attentive to the "mode of discourse" are extremely apt.

8. Contra Judith Lieu, who sees this as "ambiguous" and "ambivalent" (*Neither Jew nor Greek?*, 221–22). This seems to me a measured and guarded presentation of the kinds of martyrdom that should be emulated. The rhetorical delineation of martyrdom along biblical lines is an interesting way to perform the division between "good" and "bad" martyrdom.

9. See, for example, on Origen, R. P. C. Hanson, *Allegory and Event: A Study of the Sources and Significance of Origen's Interpretation of Scripture* (Louisville, Ky.: Westminster John Knox Press, 2002); J. Christopher King, *Origen on the Song of Songs as the Spirit of Scripture: The Bridegroom's Perfect Marriage-Song*, Oxford Theological Monographs (Oxford: Oxford University Press, 2005); David Dawson, *Allegorical Readers and Cultural Revision in Ancient Alexandria* (Berkeley: University of California Press, 1992). Origen is one of the few examples of a third-century author who has received this attention. More frequently, studies focus on Jerome, Augustine, or John Chrysostom.

10. A prime example of this is found in the Ancient Christian Commentary on Scripture series, which provides a reference guide for the interpretation of biblical works in early church authors. See, for example, Thomas C. Oden and Christopher A. Hall, *Mark*, Ancient Christian Commentary on Scripture, New Testament 2 (Downers Grove, Ill.: InterVarsity Press, 1998). See also Robert Louis Wilken, Angela Russell Christman, and Michael J. Hollerich, *Isaiah: Interpreted by Early Christian and Medieval Commentators*, Church's Bible (Grand Rapids, Mich.: Eerdmans, 2007).

11. Methodologically, any study of interpretation must address the problem of interpretative allusions and references. In seeking to understand how traditions about Jesus are being reread in this study, we must first establish a criterion for determining *if* a Jesus tradition is being reread. In cases where a text is explicitly cited or a comparison with Jesus is explicitly stated, this task is relatively easy. In instances where actions of words of Jesus are *alluded* to, the task is decidedly more complex. For the purposes of this work, we will assume that if an allusion is discernible in the minds of readers—be they ancient or modern—then this interpretation bears explanation and interpretation. For a history of literary allusion and theory, see Joseph Pucci, *The Full-Knowing Reader: Allusion and the Power of the Reader in the Western Literary Tradition* (New Haven, Conn.: Yale University Press, 1998); and William Irwin, "What Is an Allusion?" *Journal of Aesthetics and Art Criticism* 59 (2001): 287–97. For a structualist discussion of how allusion functions, see Ziva Ben-Porat, "The Poetics of Literary Allusion," *PTL: A Journal for Descriptive Poetics and Theory of Literature* 1 (1979): 105–28.

12. For a more nuanced study of the interpretation of the New Testament, see Andrew F. Gregory and Christopher M. Tuckett, *The Reception of the New Testament in the Apostolic Fathers* (Oxford: Oxford University Press, 2005); *Trajectories through the New Testament and the Apostolic Fathers* (Oxford: Oxford University Press, 2005).

13. See, for example, Musurillo, *Acts of the Christian Martyrs*, as a prime example of the tendency to note only the use of prolonged citations and to leave their significance unexplored in his introduction to the works. More elaborate notes on the significance of the use of biblical citations are provided in the anthology of texts in J. W. van Henten and Friedrich Avemarie, eds., *Martyrdom and Noble Death: Selected Texts from Graeco-Roman, Jewish and Christian Antiquity* (London: Routledge, 2002).

In the study of the martyr acts themselves, narrative allusion allows us to fully appreciate the importance of the biblical canvas upon which the martyr's death was painted. For some scholars, such as Judith Lieu, the paucity of explicit citations connecting the death of the martyrs to the death of Jesus renders their imitation ambiguous (Lieu, *Neither Jew nor Greek?*, 220–22). Allusion expands the purview of martyrly mimesis in ancient literature.

14. Victor Saxer, *Bible et hagiographie: Textes et thèmes bibliques dans les actes des martyrs authentiques des premiers siècles* (Bern: Peter Lang, 1986); "The Influence of the Bible in Early Christian Martyrology," in *The Bible in Greek Christian Antiquity*, ed. Paul M. Blowers (Notre Dame, Ind.: University of Notre Dame Press, 1997), 342–74. Saxer's study analyzes both biblical quotations and allusions in the early Christian martyrdom accounts that he considers to be authentic, that is to say, historically reliable and accurate. His analysis of the accounts focuses initially on the individual accounts and then on certain themes (the content of the confession, the etymology of martyrdom, martyrdom as liturgy, mysticism, marriage, and conquest) that he discerns in the hagiographic literature. While Saxer remains committed to the scholarly discussion of the term "martyr" and treats only authentic accounts, his work is an exceptional study of the use of biblical traditions in martyrdom accounts.

Remarkably, Saxer shies away from the theme of *imitatio Christi* in hagiographic literature, focusing instead on the influence of the Bible on the development of martyrdom as a practice (see pp. 221–23, where he views imitation of Christ as part of martyrdom as mysticism). The lacuna in Saxer's work is one that this present study seeks to fill.

15. See further discussion on the social setting of the martyrdom accounts below. Martyr acts and associated practices have frequently been treated as examples of "popular religion" in the early church. The category of "popular religion" is highly problematic because it presupposes a simplistic divide between "elite" and "popular" religious practices in the ancient world. Historically, scholars have emphasized the "vulgar" quality of "popular religion," thereby reinforcing the divide (see Peter Brown, *The Cult of the Saints: Its Rise and Function in Latin Christianity* [Chicago: University of Chicago Press, 1981], 16, 32). For a classical treatment of the cult of the martyrs as "popular religion," see R. van den Broeck, "Popular Religious Practices and Ecclesiastical Policies in the Early Church," in *Official and Popular Religion: Analysis of a Theme for Religious Studies*, ed. P. H. Vrijoh and Jean Jacques Waardenburg (Berlin: Mouton de Gruyter, 1979), 11–54.

16. I am adapting Michael Holmes's view of the use of scripture in the *Martyrdom of Polycarp*, which he correctly characterizes as a purposeful interpretation. See Michael W. Holmes, "The *Martyrdom of Polycarp* and the New Testament Passion Narratives," in *Trajectories through the New Testament and the Apostolic Fathers*, ed. Andrew F. Gregory and Christopher M. Tuckett (Oxford: Oxford University Press, 2005), 407–32. See further discussion of the mechanics of literary mimesis in the section "Narrative Mirroring of the Passion Narrative" in chapter 2.

17. Concluding the study at this point is not intended to imply that the conversion of Constantine brought the age of martyrdom to a close. The end of the fourth century brought with it a boom in hagiography. For the purposes of limiting the scope of this book, we will take the conversion of Constantine as an artificial ending point to our study.

18. In rhetorical exhortations to imitate a particular group or person, imitation functions to create and reinforce this power dynamic. It reproduces the hierarchical relationship between the thing that is imitated and the imitator. As Elizabeth Castelli notes, "The copy cannot aspire to the privileged status of 'the model'" (Elizabeth A. Castelli, *Imitating Paul: A Discourse of Power*, Literary Currents in Biblical Interpretation [Louisville, Ky.: Westminster John Knox Press, 1991], 16). Imitation, according to this usage, establishes a particular set of societal relationships.

There are other settings, however, in which imitation serves to destabilize this initial hierarchy. In Freudian views of psychological development, children learn through identification (imitation) of the parent. Freud writes, "In the first case one's father is what one would like to *be* and in the second he is what one would like to *have*" (Sigmund Freud, *The Standard Edition of the Complete Psychological Works of Sigmund Freud, vol.* 18, ed. James Strachey, et al. [London: Hogart Press, 1953], 106). The relationship with the parent is paradoxical in the sense that the child yearns both to be like the parent and to *be* the parent. The copy seeks, in this context, to appropriate the power, status, and position of the model. In still other settings the copy may subvert the position of the model through imitation. Parody, such as Lucian's *Peregrinnus*, works in exactly this way. For a classic discussion of the subversive potential of mimicry in a postcolonial setting, see Homi Bhabha, *The Location of Culture* (London: Blackburn, 1994). While imitation is grounded in and establishes a hierarchy of differentiated status, mimesis can also be used to destabilize this hierarchy, to acquire power, and to usurp status.

It is clear that not all of these models apply to the martyr acts, in which the martyr's imitation is constructed. The acquisition of power here is more complicated. Those producing the accounts acquire power for themselves by presenting their martyrs as better imitators as Christ. They seek to usurp the power and position of other Christly representatives (bishops, other martyrs, apostles, priests) in the Christian hierarchy. There is, however, the unintentional effect of producing figures whose charisma and Christliness inadvertently usurp the status of Christ. This thin line between Christ and the martyrs will be examined in chapter 5.

19. For a discussion and critique of this division, see Richard Bauckham, *God Crucified: Monotheism and Christology in the New Testament* (Grand Rapids, Mich.: Eerdmans, 1998). It would, to my mind, be fascinating to see Bauckham's interest in divine identity applied to the early martyrs.

20. A comparison of the essence of martyrs and Christ is not undertaken because it is assumed that both before and after the fact such a comparison is futile—before the fact in that the study is not undertaken, and after the fact in that the assumption of futility is grounded in later Christological assertions.

21. For a discussion of the history of the work of the Bollandists, see Hippolyte Delehaye, *L'œuvre des bollandistes à travers trois siècles, 1615–1915*, Subsidia hagiographica 13A (Brussels: Société des Bollandistes, 1959).

22. Jean Bollandus et socii, *Acta Sanctorum*. 71 vols. (Brussels: Société des Bollandistes, 1642–1906).

23. Theodoricus Ruinart, *Acta primorum martyrum sincera et selecta* (Ratisbonae: G. Josephi Manz, 1859).

24. Adolf von Harnack, *Studien zur Geschichte des Neuen Testaments und der Alten Kirche* (Berlin: Walter de Gruyter, 1931).

25. Otto von Gebhardt, *Acta Martyrum Selecta. Ausgewählte Martyreracten und andere Urkunden aus der Verfolgungszeit der christlichen Kirche* (Berlin: A. Dunker, 1902).

26. In this study we will use a broader corpus of texts—not only those texts deemed historically reliable but also martyrdoms likely to have been composed before 320 C.E. For further discussion see appendix.

27. Hans Freiherr von Campenhausen, *Die Idee des Martyriums in der alten Kirche* (Göttingen: Vandenhoeck & Ruprecht, 1936).

28. Norbert Brox, *Zeuge und Märtyrer: Untersuchungen zur frühchristlichen Zeugnis-Terminologie*, Studien zum Alten und Neuen Testament 5 (Munich: Kösel-Verlag, 1961) See also H. Strathmann, "Martus, etc.," *Theological Dictionary of the New Testament*, ed. Gerhard Kittel (Stuttgart: W. Kohlhammer, 1939), vol 4. 477–520; Th. Baumeister, *Die Anfänge der Theologie des Martyriums* (Münster: Aschendorff, 1980), 239–45; Gerd Buschmann, *Das Martyrium des Polycarp* (Göttingen: Vandenhoeck und

Ruprecht, 1998), 98–107. All these scholars maintain the scholarly consensus that the notion of "martyr" emerges in the mid-second century.

29. G. W. Bowersock, *Martyrdom and Rome* (Cambridge: Cambridge University Press, 1995).

30. W. H. C. Frend, *Martyrdom and Persecution in the Early Church* (Oxford: Blackwell, 1965).

31. J. W. van Henten, *The Maccabean Martyrs as Saviours of the Jewish People: A Study of 2 and 4 Maccabees*, Supplements to the Journal for the Study of Judaism 57 (Leiden: Brill, 1997), 6–9.

32. Nicole Kelley has argued that philosophical training even served as a model for preparation for martyrdom. See Nicole Kelley, "Philosophy as Training for Death: Reading the Ancient Christian Martyr Acts as Spiritual Exercises," *Church History* 75 (2006): 723–47.

33. For a discussion of this phenomenon, see the introduction in Musurillo, *Acts of the Christian Martyrs*, xi–lxxiii; Lieu, *Neither Jew Nor Greek?*, 211–31.

34. See, for example, the mid-second-century *Acts of Justin*, a text in which the witness of the martyrs is self-identified as Christian. Given that the notion of a martyr is etymologically derived from the act of bearing testimony, it stands to reason that the content of that confession is similarly important for understanding the notion of Christian identity. At the same time, we should note that it is the martyrdoms that begin to stress Christian identity over and against other forms of societal affiliation.

35. For the Roman rite, see the Catholic Church and the International Committee on English in the Liturgy, *General Instruction of the Roman Missal*, Liturgy Documentary Series, 2 (Washington, D.C.: United States Conference of Catholic Bishops, 2003). For the origins of the Roman rite, see Josef A. Jungmann, *The Mass of the Roman Rite: Its Origins and Development (Missarum sollemnia)* (New York: Benziger, 1951). For a discussion of the ritual elements in the Roman rite, see Catherine M. Bell, *Ritual Theory, Ritual Practice* (New York: Oxford University Press, 1992).

36. Augustine, *Serm. Dom.* 315.

37. As part of the Acts of the Apostles, the martyrdom of Stephen was performed as "scripture" during the liturgy.

38. A number of subsequent councils, however, condemned the practice. The Roman Council of 494 actually condemned the public reading of the *acta* (PL LIX, 171–72). The Sixth Council of Carthage, in 401, protested against the cult of martyrs whose martyrdom was not certain. Subsequently, the Trullan Council at Constantinople in 692 excommunicated those who were responsible for the reading of spurious *acta*. We should note that, in these latter two instances, the problem is not the reading of the *acta* per se but the reading of potentially unreliable *acta*. These decrees may well have been a reaction to "heretical" or at least "doctrinally different" martyrdom accounts, and banning the reading of such accounts only reveals the degree of influence and power that these texts exerted.

39. Demetrios's position in Thessaloniki was secured by the erection of a vast basilica, the Hagios Demetrios, in the fifth century. For a discussion of the cult of

Demetrios, see James Constantine Skedros, *Saint Demetrios of Thessaloniki: Civic Patron and Divine Protector* (Harrisburg, Pa.: Trinity Press International, 1999).

40. See *Acta Sanctorum Oct. III*, 863–69; Brian Borchardt, *Two Saints: The Martyrdom of St. Sergius & St. Bacchus* (Fond du Lac, Wis.: Seven Hills Press, 2004).

41. While the preservation of some homilies, like Gregory of Nyssa's encomium on Theodore the General, reflects the prominence of the actual saints among ancient Christians, we should not assume that the extant homilies of the church fathers reflect the relative importance of ancient martyrs. Ancient homilists like Gregory were as prone to geographic partisanship as anyone else, and we should not assume that his selection of saints represents more than his personal preferences and geographic location. As with all ancient documents, the homilies on the martyrs are preserved in a piecemeal and sporadic fashion. As fortunate as we are to be in possession of the homilies of John Chrysostom and Gregory of Nyssa, we lack transcriptions of less illustrious bishops and priests.

42. Augustine, *Conf.*, 6.2.2. Later in his career Augustine attempts to outlaw this practice.

43. For a discussion of the practice of offering commemorative meals for the dead, see the section "Heavenly Banquet" in chapter 4.

44. See Robin Darling Young, *In Procession before the World: Martyrdom as Public Liturgy in Early Christianity* (Milwaukee, Wis.: Marquette University Press, 2001).

45. See Ibid.

46. See, for example, the work of Andrew McGowan, who has highlighted the various forms of Eucharistic practice at play in the early church. Andrew Brian McGowan, *Ascetic Eucharists: Food and Drink in Early Christian Ritual Meals*, Oxford Early Christian Studies (Oxford: Clarendon Press, 1999).

47. *Pass. Perp.* 21.7.

48. Tertullian, *Apol.* 1.

49. Baptismal liturgies do, in the case of *The Apostolic Tradition*, precede and lead into the Eucharist. But the focus of the liturgy in this case is not so much sacrificial metaphors but ritual cleanliness and porosity of the body. Catechumens are not permitted to eat with the faithful (27), nor do they receive the kiss of peace until after their baptism (21). See Paul F. Bradshaw, Maxwell E. Johnson, and L. Edward Philips, *The Apostolic Tradition: A Commentary*, Hermeneia: A Critical and Historical Commentary on the Bible (Minneapolis, Minn.: Fortress Press, 2002).

50. Given the controversy over baptisms in the Carthaginian church after the Decian persecution, it is likely that *Pass. Perp.* served the additional purpose of redefining baptism within this debate.

51. Tertullian, *Bapt.* 16.2; Origen, *Comm. Matt.* 16.6; Cyril of Jerusalem, *On the Words Crucified and Buried*, lecture 13.21.

52. References to and instructions regarding the martyrdom of catechumen are given in *The Apostolic Tradition*, 19.

53. In the case of early martyrdom accounts such as *Lyons*, it is precisely this epistolary form that ensured the letter's preservation in the writings of Eusebius of Caesarea. We might compare this to the messages to Smyrna and Philadelphia in Revelation.

54. The exhortatory function of the *acta* is highlighted in Young, *In Procession before the World*, 14–15, who draws a fascinating comparison with the idea of Christ himself as a letter in the *Odes of Solomon*.

55. Traditionally, apologetic has been conceived of as the self-representation of a minority group toward a majority other. This view is epitomized in the work of R. M. Grant, who argues that Christian apologetics are a response to external critique or persecution. The defensive nature of apologetic as advocated by Grant and others seems particularly persuasive when we consider the numerous self-proclaimed apologies that address themselves to emperors (Justin Martyr, *1 Apol.*; Athenagoras, *Legatio*). See Robert McQueen Grant, *Greek Apologists of the Second Century* (Philadelphia: Westminster Press, 1988). More recent studies have begun to suggest that the texts of the apologists are composed for Christian communities struggling to develop an identity against the backdrop of a hostile Roman government and disinterested parent religion. See Frances Young, "Greek Apologists of the Second Century," in *Apologetics in the Roman Empire: Pagans, Jews and Christians*, ed. Mark Edwards, Martin Goodman, and Simon Price (Oxford: Oxford University Press, 1999).

56. Tessa Rajak, "Talking at Trypho: Christian Apologetics as Anti-Judaism in Justin's Dialogue with Trypho the Jew," in *Apologetics in the Roman Empire: Pagans, Jews and Christians*, ed. Mark Edwards, Martin Goodman, and Simon Price (Oxford: Oxford University Press, 1999), 25.

57. Unspoken in the sense that Christian converts themselves may not have ventured such criticisms. Certainly critics like Celsus were not shy in voicing their objections to Christianity, and Christians like Origen felt the need to respond to these criticisms.

58. For the fascinating way in which female martyrs were gendered and Christians masculinized, see L. Stephanie Cobb, *Dying to Be Men: Gender and Language in Early Christian Martyr Texts* (New York: Columbia University Press, 2008).

59. Brown, *Cult of the Saints*.

60. Codex Mosquensis 150 (s. XIII) in the Synodal Library, Moscow; cf. Secundus of Barka in Athanasius, *History of the Arians* 65.

61. Even as we have parsed them out here, there is overlap between liturgical and heresiological settings. A martyrdom account can serve a heresiological function in a liturgical setting even if it is not composed using a heresiological genre. Carving up the function of martyrdom in this way raises the age-old problem of genre, form, and function. The form of the martyrdom genre may be set (or at least limited to a number of subforms such as the *passio* or the *acta*), but the text may function in a number of ways, only some of which directly correlate to the social location in which the text is functioning. In other words, there can be multiple social settings for a text and multiple functions within each setting.

CHAPTER 1

1. This chapter does not attempt to trace out the development of martyrdom in the Jesus movement. Those passages of the New Testament that came to influence

emerging ideologies of martyrdom will be addressed, where relevant, in the subsequent chapters of this work. The goal of this chapter is to focus our attention upon passages that particularly reinforce the idea that suffering and death were a way of imitating Jesus. For a discussion of martyrological texts in the New Testament, see Th. Baumeister, *Die Anfänge der Theologie des Martyriums* (Münster: Aschendorff, 1980).

2. Abraham J. Malherbe, *Moral Exhortation: A Greco-Roman Sourcebook*, Library of Early Christianity 4 (Philadelphia: Westminster Press, 1986), 135–36.

3. Hermann Koller, *Die Mimesis in Der Antike: Nachahmung, Darstellung, Ausdruck* (Bernae: A. Francke, 1954). This view has been challenged by Gerald Else, who claims a Doric origin for the word group. See Gerald Else, "'Imitation' in the Fifth Century," *CP* 73 (1958): 78–79.

4. Plato, *Republic* 10, is the classical starting point for scholarly discussion of aesthetic mimesis. The expulsion of the poets from his ideal city has elicited a slew of scholarly works attempting to determine whether mimesis is, for Plato, a positive or negative thing and whether or not Plato is consistent in his use of the term. W. C. Greene, "Plato's View of Poetry," *Harvard Studies in Classical Philology* 29 (1918): 1–75, J. Tate, "'Imitation' in Plato's Republic," *Classical Quarterly* 22 (1928): 16–23; Tate, "Plato and Imitation," *Classical Quarterly* 26 (1932): 161–69. Against these McKeon argues that Plato utilizes the term in a number of ways. See Richard McKeon, "Literary Criticism and the Concept of Imitation in Antiquity," *Modern Philology* 34 (1936): 1–35. In her address of the subject, Elizabeth Castelli observes that what is at stake in Plato's discussions is the relationship between mimesis and truth. Castelli writes that this constant tension between mimesis and real knowledge forms a consistent theme in the Platonic dialogues. See Elizabeth A. Castelli, *Imitating Paul: A Discourse of Power*, Literary Currents in Biblical Interpretation (Louiseville, Ky.: Westminster John Knox Press, 1991), 62–64.

Aesthetic mimesis is also addressed by Aristotle. In contrast to his former teacher, Aristotle does not view aesthetic mimesis negatively or with reservation. Instead, he views it as intrinsically linked to and grounded in human nature (*Poet.* 1448b).

5. The explanation of the creation of the world in terms of universal models and earthly copies most likely began with Democritus in the fifth century (Diels Kranz 68 B 34). Cf. Aristotle, *Metaph.* 987 B, and Plato, *Tim.* 41BC; 42 E; 48E; Plato, *Symp.* 190B; and (in later Jewish Hellenism) Philo, *Opif.* 16.

6. In Greco-Roman antiquity, the idea of following, imitating, and assimilating to God was a pervasive theme in many philosophical schools. See Plato, "the philosopher can take God as his model because he knows God" (*Leg.* 732A-B; cf. *Leg.* 716C-D and *Theaet.* 176A-B). Epictetus, the true Stoic, is "a man who has set his heart upon changing from a man into a god" (*Diatr.* 3.19.27).

7. On the superiority of living exemplars, see, on teachers, Quintillian, *Inst.* 2.2.8. Cf. also Dio Chrysostom, *Discourses* 55.4–5; Isocrates, *Evagoras* 73–77; Plutarch, *Aem.* 1–2; Demetrius, *Style* 1.4–6; Lucian, *Demon.* 1–2.

8. Philo, *Mos.* 1158; Wis 4:2; *T. Benj.* 3.1–2, 4.1–3. The pedagogical function of imitating God is a feature of the second-century Christian text the *Epistle of Diognetus*, which exhorts its reader to imitate God (10.4). For an excellent discussion of *mimetes*

theou in this work see Michael Heintz, *"Mimetes Theou* in the *Epistle to Diognetus,"
Journal of Early Christian Studies* 12 (2004): 107–19.

9. A chief proponent of this view is Ernst Käsemann, who in his writings on
Philippians rejects absolutely the presence of the *imitatio Christi* in the writings of
Paul. Ernst Käsemann, "Critical Analysis of Philippians 2:5–11," *Journal for Theology
and the Church* 5 (1968): 45–88. *Imitatio* anxiety persists in the writings of scholars
who will seek to avoid the term entirely even when it seems appropriate. Larry W.
Hurtado, "Following Jesus in the Gospel of Mark—and Beyond," in *Patterns of
Discipleship in the New Testament*, ed. Richard Longenecker (Grand Rapids, Mich.:
Eerdmans, 1996), 9–29.

10. See Thomas à Kempis, *Opera omnia* (Freiburi: Herder, 1902). The best
English translation is, to my mind, still that of William Benham, *The Imitation of
Christ: Four Books* (London: J. C. Nimmo & Bain, 1882).

11. Even the great early church scholar Hans Freiherr von Campenhausen
distinguishes between what he sees as the New Testament theme of following after
Christ (*Nachfolge*) and nonbiblical terms as a matter of replicating Christlike qualities
(*Nachahmung*). See Hans Freiherr von Campenhausen, *Die Idee der Martyriums in der
Alten Kirche* (Göttingen: Vandenhoeck & Ruprecht, 1964), 156.

12. See, particularly, the instructions given to the disciples in Mark 8:34–38;
10:37–40; and Ign., *Rom.* 4.1–2; 6.2–3; and discussion of these passages, below.

13. See, for example, *Mart. Pol.*, where the narrator remarks that the martyrs are
loved "as disciples and imitators of the Lord" (18.3), a phrase that implies that ideas of
discipleship and *imitatio* find their nexus in the practice of martyrdom.

14. See, for example, Käsemann, "Critical Analysis of Philippians 2:5–11," 45–88.

15. See the discussion of Phil 2:5–11, below.

16. Gerald Hawthorne, "The Imitation of Christ: Discipleship in Philippians," in
Patterns of Discipleship in the New Testament, ed. Richard Longenecker (Grand Rapids,
Mich.: Eerdmans, 1996), 168–78. See also Larry Hurtado, "Jesus as Lordly Example in
Philippians 2:5–11," in *From Jesus to Paul: Studies in Honour of Francis Wright Beare*, ed.
J. C. Hurd and G. P. Richardson (Waterloo, Ontario: Wilfred Laurier University Press,
1984), 113–26.

17. The presumed threat posed by Ignatian imitation to Christology is articulated
in Theodor Preiss, "La mystique de l'imitation du Christ et de l'unité chez Ignace
d'Antioche," *Revue d' histoire et de philosophie religieuses* 17 (1938): 197–241. A number
of scholars have attempted to rehabilitate Ignatius. See, particularly, the work of
Tinsley, who labors to demysticize Ignatius and remove the stain of Alexandrian
docetic Christology from his work. E. J. Tinsley, "The *Imitatio Christi* in the Mysticism
of St. Ignatius of Antioch," *Studia Patristica* 64 (1957): 553–60. Others take a more
critical approach, arguing that Ignatian *imitatio* is essentially a misreading of Paul by
Ignatius! See Thomas Forsyth Torrance, *The Doctrine of Grace in the Apostolic Fathers*
(Edinburgh: Oliver and Boyd, 1948), 66–68. Underlying these theories is a desire to
render imitation safe for theological consumption.

18. Again, the lines of this dispute are drawn along canonical boundaries. Placing
the expectations of suffering and death outside the canon gives it the appearance of

being optional. The early Christian martyrs are commendable figures of the past, but they are figures derived from an era of gladiators and cruelty of mythical proportions.

19. Castelli, *Imitating Paul*, 21–34.

20. As is the case with all of the Pauline epistles, the precise dating of the letter hinges upon the particular scholarly reconstruction of the life of Paul inasmuch as this can be determined from the epistles themselves and the Acts of the Apostles. The letter itself appears to have been written to a young church, probably from Corinth, shortly after Paul's departure from Thessaloniki. A number of scholars, most notably Michaelis and Schmittals, have argued for a later dating. They propose that the epistle was composed during Paul's third missionary journey from Ephesus or Athens. They argue that certain statements in the letter presuppose that a significant period of time had passed since Paul had visited Thessaloniki. For example, the Pauline mission had greatly expanded (1:7–9), the church had experienced persecution (2:14), congregation members had died (4:13–18), and opponents of Paul appear to have acquired a degree of influence (4:3, 11–12). These arguments seem unpersuasive because they discount entirely the evidence of Acts and discount the tone of the letter, which seems addressed to a young church soon after Paul's visit to Thessaloniki. For summaries of these arguments, see Werner Georg Kümmel, *Introduction to the New Testament* (Nashville, Tenn. Abingdon Press, 1975), 257–59; Brown, *Introduction*, 456–66.

21. For an eloquent discussion of the occasion of the letter, see Abraham J. Malherbe, *The Letters to the Thessalonians: A New Translation with Introduction and Commentary*, Anchor Bible Commentary 32B (New York: Doubleday, 2000), 77–78.

22. Castelli, *Imitating Paul*, 94.

23. Th 2:14: "ὑμεῖς γὰρ μιμηταὶ ἐγενήθητε, ἀδελφοί, τῶν ἐκκλησιῶν τοῦ θεοῦ τῶν οὐσῶν ἐν τῇ Ἰουδαίᾳ ἐν Χριστῷ Ἰησοῦ, ὅτι τὰ αὐτὰ ἐπάθετε καὶ ὑμεῖς ὑπὸ τῶν ἰδίων συμφυλετῶν καθὼς καὶ αὐτοὶ ὑπὸ τῶν Ἰουδαίων."

24. Phil 3:17–21: "Συμμιμηταί μου γίνεσθε, ἀδελφοί, καὶ σκοπεῖτε τοὺς οὕτω περιπατοῦντας καθὼς ἔχετε τύπον ἡμᾶς. πολλοὶ γὰρ περιπατοῦσιν οὓς πολλάκις ἔλεγον ὑμῖν, νῦν δὲ καὶ κλαίων λέγω, τοὺς ἐχθροὺς τοῦ σταυροῦ τοῦ Χριστοῦ, ὧν τὸ τέλος ἀπώλεια, ὧν ὁ θεὸς ἡ κοιλία καὶ ἡ δόξα ἐν τῇ αἰσχύνῃ αὐτῶν, οἱ τὰ ἐπίγεια φρονοῦντες. ἡμῶν γὰρ τὸ πολίτευμα ἐν οὐρανοῖς ὑπάρχει, ἐξ οὗ καὶ σωτῆρα ἀπεκδεχόμεθα κύριον Ἰησοῦν Χριστόν, ὃς μετασχηματίσει τὸ σῶμα τῆς ταπεινώσεως ἡμῶν σύμμορφον τῷ σώματι τῆς δόξης αὐτοῦ κατὰ τὴν ἐνέργειαν τοῦ δύνασθαι αὐτὸν καὶ ὑποτάξαι αὐτῷ τὰ πάντα."

25. Willis Peter De Boer, *The Imitation of Paul: An Exegetical Study* (Kampen, Netherlands: J. H. Kok, 1962), 179.

26. Ernst Lohmeyer, *Kyrios Jesus: Eine Untersuchung zu Phil 2, 5–11*, Sitzungsberichte der Heidelberger Akademie der Wissenschaften. Philosophisch-Historische Klasse. Behandlung 18 Bericht 4 (Heidelberg: Carl Winter, 1928); Ernst Lohmeyer, *Die Briefe an die Philipper, an die Kolosser und an Philemon* (Göttingen: Vandenhoeck & Ruprecht, 1930). Since Lohmeyer's work, scholars have sought to identify Christological hymns in the remainder of the New Testament. The precise content of such lists varies; R. P. Martin cites John 1:1–14; Col 1:15–20; Phil 2:6–11; 1 Pet 1:18–21; 2:21–25; 3:18–22; and 1 Tim 3:16 as "putative hymns" in Ralph P. Martin, *A Hymn of Christ: Philippians 2:5–11*

in Recent Interpretation and in the Setting of Early Christian Worship (Downers Grove, Ill.: InterVarsity Press, 1997), 19. Cf. Jack T. Sanders, who adds Eph 2:14–16 but rejects the use of 1 Pet 1:18–21 and 2:21–25. See Jack T. Sanders, *The New Testament Christological Hymns: Their Historical Religious Background* (Cambridge: University Press, 1971), 10–11, 16. A number of scholars question the presence of such a hymn here in Philippians, regarding the evidence as inconclusive. See C. F. D. Moule, *The Birth of the New Testament*, Harper New Testament Commentaries (New York: Harper & Row, 1962), 25ff.

27. Phil 2:5–11: "τοῦτο φρονεῖτε ἐν ὑμῖν ὃ καὶ ἐν Χριστῷ Ἰησοῦ, ὃς ἐν μορφῇ θεοῦ ὑπάρχων οὐχ ἁρπαγμὸν ἡγήσατο τὸ εἶναι ἴσα θεῷ, ἀλλὰ ἑαυτὸν ἐκένωσεν μορφὴν δούλου λαβών, ἐν ὁμοιώματι ἀνθρώπων γενόμενος· καὶ σχήματι εὑρεθεὶς ὡς ἄνθρωπος ἐταπείνωσεν ἑαυτὸν γενόμενος ὑπήκοος μέχρι θανάτου, θανάτου δὲ σταυροῦ. διὸ καὶ ὁ θεὸς αὐτὸν ὑπερύψωσεν καὶ ἐχαρίσατο αὐτῷ τὸ ὄνομα τὸ ὑπὲρ πᾶν ὄνομα, ἵνα ἐν τῷ ὀνόματι Ἰησοῦ πᾶν γόνυ κάμψῃ ἐπουρανίων καὶ ἐπιγείων καὶ καταχθονίων καὶ πᾶσα γλῶσσα ἐξομολογήσηται ὅτι κύριος Ἰησοῦς Χριστὸς εἰς δόξαν θεοῦ πατρός."

28. Lohmeyer, *Die Briefe an die Philipper, an die Kolosser und an Philemon*, 98.

29. The notion that Christ's death should be taken as a model for martyrdom has been forcefully rejected by Käsemann and a host of Protestant scholars who follow him. See Käsemann, "Critical Analysis of Philippians 2:5–11," 55–59.

30. Martin, *Hymn of Christ*, 290–91. There is, of course, a strong tradition of preexistence both in Western thought and in certain strains of modern theological thought. See Terryl L. Givens, *When Souls Had Wings: Pre-Mortal Existence in Western Thought* (New York: Oxford University Press, 2009).

31. Despite the fact that the Corinthian correspondence preserves more information about Paul's dealings with the community there than any other letter, reconstructing the sequence of events is notoriously difficult. The chronology of events, sequence of letters, and, in particular, number of letters found in 2 Corinthians have been the subject of extended debate. In the case of 1 Corinthians, the unity is largely agreed upon. While some, like Johannes Weiss, have sought to identify breaks in the flow of the letter (10:1–22; 13) and posited a division into three letters, Letter A (1 Cor 10:1–23; 6:12–20; 11:2–34), Letter B (1 Cor 7:1–9:23; 10:24–11:1; 12–15; 16), and Letter C (1 Cor 1:1–6:11), there is no absolute proof of differing situations within the letter. See Johannes Weiss, et al., *The History of Primitive Christianity* (New York: Wilson-Erikson, 1937). In the case of 2 Corinthians, the situation grows increasingly complicated. The composite nature of the letter has been widely acknowledged since the work of Johann Semler. See Johann Salomo Semler, *Abhandlung von freier Untersuchung des Canon* (Halle, 1771–1775). For a summary of partition theories since Semler, see Hans Dieter Betz, *2 Corinthians 8 and 9: A Commentary on Two Administrative Letters of the Apostle Paul*, ed. George W. MacRae, Hermeneia: A Critical and Historical Commentary on the Bible (Philadelphia: Fortress, 1985), 10–27. For our purposes in examining the Corinthian correspondence as texts that shaped later Christian thought, it is not especially important to trace the precise chronology of the events.

32. 1 Cor 4:15–17:"ἐὰν γὰρ μυρίους παιδαγωγοὺς ἔχητε ἐν Χριστῷ ἀλλ' οὐ πολλοὺς πατέρας· ἐν γὰρ Χριστῷ Ἰησοῦ διὰ τοῦ εὐαγγελίου ἐγὼ ὑμᾶς ἐγέννησα. παρακαλῶ οὖν ὑμᾶς, μιμηταί μου γίνεσθε. διὰ τοῦτο ἔπεμψα ὑμῖν Τιμόθεον, ὅς ἐστίν μου τέκνον ἀγαπητὸν καὶ πιστὸν ἐν κυρίῳ, ὃς ὑμᾶς ἀναμνήσει τὰς ὁδούς μου τὰς ἐν Χριστῷ [Ἰησοῦ], καθὼς πανταχοῦ ἐν πάσῃ ἐκκλησίᾳ διδάσκω."

33. William F. Orr and James Arthur Walther, *I Corinthians: A New Translation* (Garden City, N.Y.: Doubleday, 1976). Pace Hans Lietzmann and Werner Georg Kümmel, *An Die Korinther I–II*, Handbuch zum Neuen Testament 9 (Tübingen: Mohr Siebeck, 1949).

34. Archibald Robertson and Alfred Plummer, *A Critical and Exegetical Commentary on the First Epistle of St. Paul to the Corinthians*, 2d ed., International Critical Commentary (Edinburgh: T & T Clark, 1971), 90; De Boer, *The Imitation of Paul*, 146; and E. J. Tinsley, *The Imitation of God in Christ: An Essay on the Biblical Basis of Christian Spirituality*, The Library of History and Doctrine (Philadelphia: Westminster Press, 1960), 139.

35. B. Sanders, "Imitating Paul: 1 Cor 4:16," *Harvard Theological Review* 74 (1981): 361–63; Castelli, *Imitating Paul*, 110–11.

36. Gordon D. Fee, *The First Epistle to the Corinthians* (Grand Rapids, Mich.: Eerdmans, 1987), 186.

37. Exhortations to harmony and greater unity cohere with the broader exhortatory aim of 1 Cor 1–4 and the letter as a whole, which responds to tensions and discord within the community. Finally, the verses immediately preceding (vv. 9–13) have in view Paul's own conformity to a life of suffering and difficulty. Given the agenda of the letter as a whole, the immediate context of the passage, and the preponderance of these themes elsewhere in Paul, there seems no reason that he does not have in mind all these interpretations.

38. This not only serves as an effective means of garnering rhetorical power for Paul but also sets a precedent for later generations of Christians. Paul lays the groundwork for the idea that congregations should look to intermediary figures as models of Christian behavior. This will become particularly important in the cult of the saints where the saints take on this intermediary role as imitators of Christ and models for Christian worshipers.

39. The meaning of imitation here has been variously interpreted. Some see it as a call to imitate Jesus' servitude (Lietzmann and Kümmel, *An Die Korinther*, 53); his obedient sacrifice even unto death in Hans Conzelmann, *1 Corinthians: A Commentary on the First Epistle to the Corinthians*, trans. James W. Leitch; ed. George W. MacRae; Hermeneia: A Critical and Historical Commentary on the Bible (Philadelphia: Fortress Press, 1975), 180, and Fee, *The First Epistle to the Corinthians*, 490; his humility in William S. Kurz, "Kenotic Imitation of Paul and of Christ in Philippians 2 and 3," in *Discipleship in the New Testament*, ed. Fernando F. Segovia (Philadelphia: Fortress Press, 1985), 106; his mission to those who were lost in Orr and Walther, *I Corinthians*, 251; his self-sacrifice more generally in De Boer, *Imitation of Paul*, 158; or the setting aside of personal rights and privileges in Linda L. Belleville,"Imitate Me, Just as I Imitate Christ: Discipleship in the Corinthian Correspondence," in *Patterns of*

Discipleship in the New Testament, ed. Richard N. Longenecker (Grand Rapids, Mich.: Eerdmans, 1996), 120–41.

40. Jesus' gentle and forbearing nature (2 Cor 10:1), his poverty (2 Cor 8:9), the extreme hardships that characterized his life (2 Cor 4:10), and his frail human nature (2 Cor 13:4).

41. C. K. Barrett, *Commentary on the Second Epistle to the Corinthians* (New York: Harper and Row, 1973), 300.

42. The historical situation that prompted Paul to write the letter cannot be firmly pinned down. Clearly, Paul had caught wind of anti-Pauline sentiment at Galatia. Pauline opponents had persuaded his converts into acceptance of the Torah and circumcision (Gal 4:21–31; 5:2; 6:12–13). Paul refers to his opponents as "the circumcised" (οἱ περιτεμνόμενοι), but it is difficult to ascertain whether these are Jews or Gentiles who were circumcising themselves. For a history of research into the Pauline opponents, see Robert Jewett, "The Agitators and the Galatian Congregation," *New Testament Studies* 17 (1971): 198–212. The precise dating of the letter rests upon complex reconstructions of the chronology of Paul's letters and his missionary journeys. The absence of information in Galatians itself further complicates this problem. Because Romans was Paul's final letter (Rom 15:25; cf. Acts 20:2–3), Galatians must have been composed prior to Romans. Consequently, the dating of Galatians between 50 and 55 CE can only be proposed tentatively. See Kümmel, *Introduction to the New Testament*, 304; Hans Dieter Betz, "Spirit, Freedom and the Law," *Svensk exegetisk årsbok* 39 (1974): 145–60; Brown, *Introduction*, 474–77.

43. Gal 6:17: "τοῦ λοιποῦ κόπους μοι μηδεὶς παρεχέτω· ἐγὼ γὰρ τὰ στίγματα τοῦ Ἰησοῦ ἐν τῷ σώματί μου βαστάζω."

44. Deissmann argues that they are amuletic marks similar to those mentioned in Egyptian papyri. This explanation falters due to a lack of evidence and the improbability that Paul would compare his experience to Egyptian amulets. See Adolf Deissmann and A. J. Grieve, *Bible Studies: Contributions, Chiefly from Papyri and Inscriptions, to the History of the Language, the Literature, and the Religion of Hellenistic Judaism and Primitive Christianity* (Edinburgh: T & T Clark, 1901), 358–60.

45. So Traugott Schmidt, *Der Leib Christi eine Untersuchung zum urchristlichen Gemeindegedanken* (Leipzig: A. Deichert, 1919), 212; Otto Schmitz, *Die Christus-Gemeinschaft des Paulus im Lichte seines Genetivgebrauchs*, Neutestamentliche Forschungen: Reihe 1, Paulusstudien, Heft 2 (Gütersloh: C. Bertelsmann, 1924), 185ff.; and Erich Dinkler, "Jesu Wort vom Kreuztragen," in *Neutestamentliche Studien für Rudolf Bultmann zu seinem 70. Geburtstag am 20. August 1954*, ed. Walther Eltester, (Berlin: A. Töpelmann, 1954), 110–29.

46. Hans Dieter Betz, *Nachfolge und Nachahmung Jesu Christi im Neuen Testament*, Beiträge zur Historischen Theologie 37 (Tübingen: Mohr Siebeck, 1967), 183.

47. Castelli, *Imitating Paul*. I am grateful to my friend James A. Kelhoffer for sharing with me his Bourdieusian idea of suffering as cultural capital and making available to me prepublication versions of his forthcoming work on the subject.

48. This is not the agenda of *all* gospels; cf. *Gos. Thom.* or *Gos. Truth.*

49. The theory that the gospels conform to the Greco-Romans genre of *bioi* (life) is widely, although not universally, accepted. For a discussion of the debate surrounding the genre of the gospels, see Richard A. Burridge, *What Are the Gospels? A Comparison with Graeco-Roman Biography*, 2d ed. (Grand Rapids, Mich.: Eerdmans, 2004).

50. See, for example, Käsemann, "Critical Analysis of Philippians 2:5–11," 45–88. The unnecessary division between discipleship and *imitatio* is, in my mind, linked to a certain strain of anti-Catholicism in Protestant scholarship that wants to avoid introducing a vulgar Catholic theology to the New Testament. See above.

51. For example, see *Mart. Mar.* 7.4, in which Christ appears in a vision to a would-be martyr and exhorts him to "follow me quickly." The idea of following Jesus here clearly involves martyrdom.

52. Prior to the nineteenth century, priority was accorded to the gospel of Matthew on the basis of Augustine's statement that Mark was the epitomist of Matthew (*De Consensu Evangelistarum* 1.2.4). This argument was effectively challenged in the nineteenth century by a cadre of German scholars. For the classic defense of Marcan priority, see G. M. Styler, "The Priority of Mark," in *The Birth of the New Testament*, ed. C. F. D. Moule (London: Black's, 1981). For a critical evaluation of the recent revival of interest in the Griesbach hypothesis, see Christopher M. Tuckett, *The Revival of the Griesbach Hypothesis: An Analysis and Appraisal* (Cambridge: Cambridge University Press, 1983).

53. A variety of alternative theories for the precise location of the Gospel have been proposed. Following the testimony of Papias preserved in Eusebius, *Hist. eccl.* 2.25.7, a number of scholars have proposed that the Gospel was written in Rome during the Neronian persecution. See, for example, Martin Hengel, *Studies in the Gospel of Mark* (Philadelphia: Fortress Press, 1985). Other theories place the location of the Gospel closer to the setting of the Gospel events themselves. The frequent redactional references have led some to argue that the Gospel was originally composed there. So, Ernst Lohmeyer, *Galiläa und Jerusalem* (Göttingen: Vandenhoeck & Ruprecht, 1936). Others, like Joel Marcus, argue more broadly for the region of Syria-Palestine; see Joel Marcus, *Mark 1–8: A New Translation with Introduction and Commentary*, Anchor Bible Commentary Series 27 (New York: Doubleday, 1999), 25–36.

54. This possibility is suggested by Bauckham, who challenged the traditional consensus that Mark was composed for a particular community and argued instead that the gospel was written for a broader readership. Bauckham's arguments are based largely on the cosmopolitan nature of the ancient church. The Jesus movement was characterized by early wandering leaders (Peter, Paul, Ignatius, and others) who traveled spreading the message. Given this state of affairs and ecumenical slant of the gospel, does it not seem probable that the gospels were composed as encyclicals? To Bauckham's general observations on the church can be added specific textual examples in which Mark explains Jewish traditions and Aramaic linguistic terms for a non-Jewish audience (see Mark 5:41; 7:11; 15:34) and specifically addresses the audience (Mark 13:14). See Richard Bauckham, "For Whom Were the Gospels Written?" in *The Gospels for All Christians: Rethinking the Gospel Audiences*, ed. Richard Bauckham

(Grand Rapids, Mich.: Eerdmans, 1997), 9–48. A detailed critique of Bauckham's hypothesis is provided in Marcus, *Mark 1–8*, 25–28.

55. Philip Davis, "Christology, Discipleship and Self-Understanding in the Gospel of Mark," in *Self-Definition in Early Christianity: A Case of Shifting Horizons: Essays in Appreciation of Ben F. Meyer from His Former Students*, ed. David Hawkin and Tom Robinson (Lewiston, Maine: Mellen, 1990), 109. Cf. David A. Capes, "*Imitatio Christi* and the Early Worship of Jesus," in *The Jewish Roots of Christological Monotheism: Papers from the St. Andrews Conference on the Historical Origins of the Worship of Jesus*, ed. Carey C. Newman, James R. Davila, and Galdys S. Lewis, SJST 63 (Leiden: Brill, 1999), 295.

56. Davis, "Christology, Discipleship and Self-Understanding in the Gospel of Mark," 109.

57. Hurtado, "Following Jesus in the Gospel of Mark," 26–27.

58. So, Ibid., 27. Hurtado will call Jesus the "true model of Christian discipleship," yet he shies away from the term "imitation." What is imitation if not modeling one's behavior and action on something else? Hurtado's description of discipleship is one of imitation, but he is loath to employ the term explicitly.

59. Mark 8:34–38: "Καὶ προσκαλεσάμενος τὸν ὄχλον σὺν τοῖς μαθηταῖς αὐτοῦ εἶπεν αὐτοῖς, Εἴ τις θέλει ὀπίσω μου ἀκολουθεῖν, ἀπαρνησάσθω ἑαυτὸν καὶ ἀράτω τὸν σταυρὸν αὐτοῦ καὶ ἀκολουθείτω μοι. ὃς γὰρ ἐὰν θέλῃ τὴν ψυχὴν αὐτοῦ σῶσαι ἀπολέσει αὐτήν· ὃς δ' ἂν ἀπολέσει τὴν ψυχὴν αὐτοῦ ἕνεκεν ἐμοῦ καὶ τοῦ εὐαγγελίου σώσει αὐτήν. τί γὰρ ὠφελεῖ ἄνθρωπον κερδῆσαι τὸν κόσμον ὅλον καὶ ζημιωθῆναι τὴν ψυχὴν αὐτοῦ; τί γὰρ δοῖ ἄνθρωπος ἀντάλλαγμα τῆς ψυχῆς αὐτοῦ; ὃς γὰρ ἐὰν ἐπαισχυνθῇ με καὶ τοὺς ἐμοὺς λόγους ἐν τῇ γενεᾷ ταύτῃ τῇ μοιχαλίδι καὶ ἁμαρτωλῷ, καὶ ὁ υἱὸς τοῦ ἀνθρώπου ἐπαισχυνθήσεται αὐτόν, ὅταν ἔλθῃ ἐν τῇ δόξῃ τοῦ πατρὸς αὐτοῦ μετὰ τῶν ἀγγέλων τῶν ἁγίων."

60. See C. E. B. Cranfield, *The Gospel According to Saint Mark: An Introduction and Commentary*, Cambridge Greek Testament Commentary (Cambridge: University Press, 1959), 397–98.

61. Robert Horton Gundry, *Mark: A Commentary on His Apology for the Cross* (Grand Rapids, Mich.: Eerdmans, 1993), 433–40.

62. I follow Menzies and Branscomb in seeing the reference to the cross as the product of the evangelist. See Allan Menzies, *The Earliest Gospel: A Historical Study of the Gospel According to Mark* (London: Macmillan, 1901); Bennett Harvie Branscomb, *The Gospel of Mark*, The Moffatt New Testament Commentary Series 2 (New York: Harper & Bros., 1937).

63. That the mode of Jesus' execution was part of the core teaching of the Jesus movement is apparent in our earliest sources, the Pauline epistles. Apart from the resurrection, Paul preserves few references to the teachings or life of Jesus. It is noteworthy, therefore, that he mentions the cross on a number of occasions in his letters (1 Cor 1:17–18; Gal 5:11; 6:12, 14; Phil 2:8; 3:18).

64. This cannot be stated with any certainty. The connection between Peter and Mark is based upon the tradition of Papias preserved within Eusebius. The earliest references to the martyrdom of Peter date to the end of the first century, after Mark's

gospel was written (John 21:18–19; *1 Clem.* 4; 1 Pet 5:13). Thus, if we are even slightly suspicious of the testimony of Papias, we cannot assume that Mark was aware of the details of Peter's death. Nevertheless, the possibility exists that Mark was aware of this tradition and subtly prefigures it here. If this is the case, Peter would be implicitly presented as the first imitator of the exempla exhibited in Christ and thus a model in his own right. This is precisely the argument that is more fully developed in the passage from *1 Clem.*, see below.

65. The basis for Gundry's argument is that this saying can be traced back to the historical Jesus. If this is the case, then he assumes that the historical Jesus shares his knowledge of the workings of the Roman legal system, realizes the inability of the disciples to select the means of their execution, and therefore intends the cross to be understood figuratively. It seems unlikely to me that the historical Jesus would have been privy to this kind of legal knowledge. Then again, it seems unlikely to me that this phrase originates with the historical Jesus himself. Whether it is Jesus or Mark, I assume that the source of this phrase would have been willing to sacrifice legal verisimilitude for the dramatic impact of the command to "take up one's cross."

66. Luke 9:23: "Ἔλεγεν δὲ πρὸς πάντας, Εἴ τις θέλει ὀπίσω μου ἔρχεσθαι, ἀρνησάσθω ἑαυτὸν καὶ ἀράτω τὸν σταυρὸν αὐτοῦ καθ' ἡμέραν καὶ ἀκολουθείτω μοι."

67. Origen, *Mart.*, 36.

68. Cf. Tertullian, *Fug.*, 7.

69. In her otherwise excellent work *Neither Jew nor Greek?* Judith Lieu writes that "it is remarkable how little is made" of the command to take up one's cross (222). While she notes the spiritualized interpretation of Tertullian (*Idol.* 12.2) and the passage from Origen's *Mart.* 12, she does not mention this explicit interpretation in the *Ac. Euplus*, which would seem to undercut the force of her argument somewhat.

70. *Ac. Euplus*, Recension B 1.5: "Euplius aperiens legit: Beati qui persecutionem patiuntur propter iustitiam, quoniam ipsorum est regnum caelorum. et alio loco: Qui uult uenire post me, tollat crucem suam, et sequatur me." Text Theodoricus Ruinart, *Acta primorum martyrum sincera et selecta* (Ratisbonae: G. Josephi Manz, 1859), 437; translation emended from Herbert Musurillo, *Acts of the Christian Martyrs* (Oxford: Clarendon Press, 1972), 314.

71. Mark 10:37–40: "οἱ δὲ εἶπαν αὐτῷ, Δὸς ἡμῖν ἵνα εἷς σου ἐκ δεξιῶν καὶ εἷς ἐξ ἀριστερῶν καθίσωμεν ἐν τῇ δόξῃ σου. ὁ δὲ Ἰησοῦς εἶπεν αὐτοῖς, Οὐκ οἴδατε τί αἰτεῖσθε. δύνασθε πιεῖν τὸ ποτήριον ὃ ἐγὼ πίνω ἢ τὸ βάπτισμα ὃ ἐγὼ βαπτίζομαι βαπτισθῆναι; οἱ δὲ εἶπαν αὐτῷ, Δυνάμεθα. ὁ δὲ Ἰησοῦς εἶπεν αὐτοῖς, Τὸ ποτήριον ὃ ἐγὼ πίνω πίεσθε καὶ τὸ βάπτισμα ὃ ἐγὼ βαπτίζομαι βαπτισθήσεσθε, τὸ δὲ καθίσαι ἐκ δεξιῶν μου ἢ ἐξ εὐωνύμων οὐκ ἔστιν ἐμὸν δοῦναι, ἀλλ' οἷς ἡτοίμασται."

The passage itself presents a number of text and form-critical problems, and a number of scholars have attempted to divide Mark 10:35–45 into smaller units. A two-part division is proposed by Schweizer, who separates the narrative into 10:35–41 and 10:42–45. See Eduard Schweizer, *The Good News According to Mark*, trans. Donald Harold Madvig (Richmond, Va.: John Knox Press, 1970), 217. The great form critic Bultmann identifies four seams in the text. See Rudolf Karl Bultmann, *The History of the Synoptic Tradition*, 2d ed. (Oxford: Blackwell, 1963), 66–69. For our purposes, the form-critical issues are of lesser importance both because the present flow of the narrative was logical to the author of Mark and because it was received by early Christians in its present form.

72. A number of scholars have argued that James and John anticipate eschatological exaltation. Jack Dean Kingsbury proposes that James and John have in mind the "glory of God's end-time kingdom." Jack Dean Kingsbury, *Conflict in Mark: Jesus, Authorities, Disciples* (Minneapolis, Minn.: Fortress Press, 1989), 109. Similarly, Donahue and Harrington have read Mark 10:37 as a reference to the heavenly throne room and banquet. See John R. Donahue and Daniel J. Harrington, *The Gospel of Mark* (Collegeville, Minn.: Liturgical Press, 2002), 311–12. The situation envisaged is more probably a run-of-the-mill military ruler. See Craig A. Evans, *Mark 8:27–16:20*, Word Biblical Commentary 34B (Nashville, Tenn.: T. Nelson, 2001), 114–19.

73. This is another embarrassing incident that reveals the disciples' lack of understanding. Matthew softens the narrative by emending the story so that it is the mother of the sons of Zebedee who makes the audacious request (cf. Matt 20:20–21).

74. Patrick Henry Reardon, "The Cross, Sacraments and Martyrdom: An Investigation of Mark 10:35–45," *St. Vladimir's Theological Quarterly* 36 (1992): 107.

75. Gundry, *Mark*, 584.

76. David Seeley, "Was Jesus Like a Philosopher? The Evidence of Martyrological and Wisdom Motifs in Q, Pre-Pauline Traditions and Mark," in *Society of Biblical Literature Seminar Papers*, ed. D. J. Lull, (Atlanta, Ga.: Scholars Press, 1989), 540–49.

77. Cf. Mark 7:11; 13:14.

78. Donahue and Harrington, *The Gospel of Mark*, 311; Jer 25:15–29; Ps 75:8; Isa 51:17, 22.

79. The same image of the cup in connection with the passion is picked up in Augustine's commentaries on the Psalms where he writes: "But what is it to receive the cup of salvation, but to imitate the Passion of our Lord? . . . I will receive the cup of Christ, I will drink of our Lord's Passion." Eucharistic imagery resonates strongly here, but the participation in Christ's passion through drinking of his cup recalls the cup of wrath in Mark.

80. Gerd Theissen, *The Gospels in Context: Social and Political History in the Synoptic Tradition* (Minneapolis, Minn.: Fortress Press, 1991), 197–98. The use of the metaphoric image of the cup in the context of martyrdom occurs in *Mart. Isa.* 5:13, *Mart. Pol.* 14:2, and *Mart. Mar.* 6. 14, and the vision of the bishop Marculus who sees a silver cup, golden crown, and palm branch in a vision *Mart. Marculus*, 8.

81. The Hebrew Bible refers to suffering inflicted by humans as a kind of submersion (Ps 69:1–3, 14–15; Job 9:31; 2 Sam 22:5; Ps 18:4, 42:7). In addition, Josephus uses βαπτίζω to refer to suffering at the hands of humans in *J.W.* 4.33 §137. See Reardon, "The Cross, Sacraments and Martyrdom," 584.

The interpretation of martyrdom as a kind of baptism is found in *Acts of Paul and Thekla* 2.34, where Thecla baptizes herself by diving into a pool of ravenous seals. The same motif appears in the *Passion of Perpetua and Felicitas* where Saturus is covered by so much blood that he experiences a "second baptism" and declares himself "well washed." The notion that martyrdom served as a substitute for baptism is found in early liturgical texts such as Hippolytus's *Apostolic Tradition* 19.2, where a catechumen can be baptized by his or her own blood. The provenance of *The Apostolic Tradition* may be decidedly late, and it may only reflect the practice in Rome, but it nevertheless indicates that there was an association between martyrdom and baptism in the early church.

82. A significant difficulty with this theory is the lack of ancient sources describing the martyrdom of John. The death of James is recounted in Acts 12:2, but sources suggesting that John suffered a similar fate are late. For a discussion of the evidence pertaining to the fate of John, see H. Latimer Jackson, *The Problem of the Fourth Gospel* (Cambridge: Cambridge University Press, 1918), 142–49. Most of Jackson's sources are fourth-century and from Asia Minor.

83. In patristic readings, this passage will be consistently interpreted as an exhortation to suffer like Christ. See, for example, Augustine, *Tract. Ev. Jo.* 28.5.2.

84. Hurtado, "Following Jesus in the Gospel of Mark," 25.

85. C. K. Barrett, "Imitatio Christi in Acts," in *Jesus of Nazareth: Lord and Christ: Essays on the Historical Jesus and New Testament Cristology*, ed. Joel B. Green and Max Turner (Grand Rapids, Mich.: Eerdmans, 1994), 252.

86. That the Acts of the Apostles was composed by Luke is suggested by the opening title, where the author looks back to the gospel dedicated to Theophilus (Acts 1:1). Some, however, have denied the common authorship of the works, largely on the grounds that it was hardly necessary for Luke to recount the ascension on two separate occasions. Nevertheless, the vocabulary, similarity of expression, style, thematic interest, and theology suggest that they stem from the hand of the same author. Moreover, the narrative unity underscored by Lukan parallelism binds the two works together. For arguments against Lukan authorship of Acts, see A. W. Argyle, "The Greek of Luke and Acts," *New Testament Studies* 20 (1973–74): 441–45. For those in favor, see Robert C. Tannehill, *The Narrative Unity of Luke-Acts: A Literary Interpretation*, Foundations and Facets (Philadelphia: Fortress Press, 1986).

87. Hanz Conzelmann, *Acts of the Apostles: A Commenatry on the Acts of the Apostles*, trans. James Limburg; ed. Eldon Jay Epp; Hermeneia: A Critical and Historical Commentary on the Bible (Philadelphia: Fortress, 1987), 61.

88. With respects to this last point, the request for forgiveness, there is a textual difficulty in the text of Luke. A number of early witnesses do not include the crucial phrase "Father forgive them for they know not what they do." The inclusion of the phrase here, therefore, would be an attempt by members of the early church to draw the Lukan Jesus and the protomartyr Stephen even closer. See the discussion in Bruce Metzger, *A Textual Commentary on the Greek New Testament*, corrected edition (London: United Bible Societies, 1975), 201. The acts of the martyrs are themselves a heretofore-unnoted early witness to this tradition. A large number of martyrdoms include this phrase and explicitly interpret it as a quotation of the words of Jesus. This makes them some of the earliest witnesses to the tradition. For further discussion, see the section "Narrative Mirroring of the Passion Narrative" in chapter 2.

89. Those who continue to argue in favor of Petrine authorship point to the use of the first-person singular (1:3, 7, 8, 9, 10–12; 2:20–25; 3:15; 5:1, 2), the apparent

reflection of the personality of Peter in the text and the historic association of the letter with the apostle himself. See, for example, Peter Ketter, *Hebräerbrief, Jakobusbrief, Petrusbrief, Judasbrief*, Die Heilige Schrift für das Leben erklärt, Bd. 16/1 (Freiburg: Herder, 1950). Neither the use of the first person nor the ability to imitate the apparent "personality" of Peter is, to my mind, beyond the capabilities of the skilled pseudonymist.

90. For a classic statement against Petrine authorship, see Francis Wright Beare, *The First Epistle of Peter* (Oxford: Blackwell, 1947), 44.

91. This conclusion is based on the implied point of origin in "Babylon" (5:13). Babylon was frequently associated with Rome (cf. Rev 14:8; 16:19; 17–18) on the basis of its status as the dominating power in the Mediterranean in the first century C.E. This is supported by the traditional association with Simon Peter and similarities in language between 1 Pet and *1 Clem.*

92. See Norbert Brox, *Der erste Petrusbrief*, Evangelisch-katholischer Kommentar zum Neuen Testament (Zürich: Benziger Verlag, 1979), 39.

93. Beare, *The First Epistle of Peter*, 34. That Ignatius would not cite 1 Pet if he knew it seems particularly strange in light of his frequent use of the Pauline epistles and the considerable thematic agreement between 1 Peter and Ignatius on the subject of suffering.

94. The assumption that 1 Peter envisions official persecution is based on two elements: the reference to universal suffering in 5:9 and the admonition to be prepared to give an apologia for being Christian in 3:15. In the case of the latter, we should compare similar statements in the gospels (e.g., Mark 13:11) which do not seem to envision official persecution. Dating 1 Peter to a specific period of persecution is further complicated by the absence of evidence for official widespread persecutions during the reigns of these emperors. For a summary of the evidence for official persecution during this period, see Paul J. Achtemeier, *1 Peter: A Commentary on First Peter*, ed. Eldon J. Epp, Hermeneia: A Critical and Historical Commentary on the Bible (Minneapolis, Minn.: Fortress, 1996), 29–33.

95. So, Achtemeier, *1 Peter*, 34–36; John Hall Elliott, *1 Peter: A New Translation with Introduction and Commentary*, Anchor Bible Commentary 37B (New York: Doubleday, 2000), 100.

96. So, Achtemeier, *1 Peter*, 48–50.

97. For the geographic location of the addresses, see Elliott, *1 Peter*, 84–94.

98. 1 Pet 2:20–22: "ποῖον γὰρ κλέος εἰ ἁμαρτάνοντες καὶ κολαφιζόμενοι ὑπομενεῖτε; ἀλλ' εἰ ἀγαθοποιοῦντες καὶ πάσχοντες ὑπομενεῖτε, τοῦτο χάρις παρὰ θεῷ. εἰς τοῦτο γὰρ ἐκλήθητε, ὅτι καὶ Χριστὸς ἔπαθεν ὑπὲρ ὑμῶν ὑμῖν ὑπολιμπάνων ὑπογραμμὸν ἵνα ἐπακολουθήσητε τοῖς ἴχνεσιν αὐτοῦ."

99. 1 Pet 4:12–14: "Ἀγαπητοί, μὴ ξενίζεσθε τῇ ἐν ὑμῖν πυρώσει πρὸς πειρασμὸν ὑμῖν γινομένῃ ὡς ξένου ὑμῖν συμβαίνοντος, ἀλλὰ καθὸ κοινωνεῖτε τοῖς τοῦ Χριστοῦ παθήμασιν χαίρετε, ἵνα καὶ ἐν τῇ ἀποκαλύψει τῆς δόξης αὐτοῦ χαρῆτε ἀγαλλιώμενοι. εἰ ὀνειδίζεσθε ἐν ὀνόματι Χριστοῦ, μακάριοι, ὅτι τὸ τῆς δόξης καὶ τὸ τοῦ θεοῦ πνεῦμα ἐφ' ὑμᾶς ἀναπαύεται."

100. As has been frequently noted, the epistle to the Hebrews is not an epistle, was not written by Paul, and not directed to the Hebrews. It is more frequently classified as

an exhortatory word or homily composed sometime toward the end of the first century. The linguistic and thematic parallels with 1 *Clem.* suggest that the two works emerged out of a similar ecclesiastical setting. This suggests a dating between 60–100 C.E., but there are no compelling reasons to support a more precise dating. Hebrews addresses a particular situation (10:32–34), but the location of the addressees is more difficult to ascertain. For a discussion of the issues of dating, authorship, and genre of Hebrews, see Harold W. Attridge, *The Epistle to the Hebrews: A Commentary on the Epistle to the Hewbrews*, ed. Helmut Koester, Hermeneia: A Critical and Historical Commentary on the Bible (Philadelphia: Fortress, 1989), 1–13.

101. Heb 12:1–4: "Τοιγαροῦν καὶ ἡμεῖς τοσοῦτον ἔχοντες περικείμενον ἡμῖν νέφος μαρτύρων, ὄγκον ἀποθέμενοι πάντα καὶ τὴν εὐπερίστατον ἁμαρτίαν, δι' ὑπομονῆς τρέχωμεν τὸν προκείμενον ἡμῖν ἀγῶνα ἀφορῶντες εἰς τὸν τῆς πίστεως ἀρχηγὸν καὶ τελειωτὴν Ἰησοῦν, ὃς ἀντὶ τῆς προκειμένης αὐτῷ χαρᾶς ὑπέμεινεν σταυρὸν αἰσχύνης καταφρονήσας ἐν δεξιᾷ τε τοῦ θρόνου τοῦ θεοῦ κεκάθικεν. ἀναλογίσασθε γὰρ τὸν τοιαύτην ὑπομεμενηκότα ὑπὸ τῶν ἁμαρτωλῶν εἰς ἑαυτὸν ἀντιλογίαν, ἵνα μὴ κάμητε ταῖς ψυχαῖς ὑμῶν ἐκλυόμενοι.Οὔπω μέχρις αἵματος ἀντικατέστητε πρὸς τὴν ἁμαρτίαν ἀνταγωνιζόμενοι."

102. For a detailed exposition on this chapter, see Attridge, *Hebrews*, 253–59.

103. Ibid., 27.

104. This view followed that of Eusebius of Caesarea (*Hist. eccl.* 3.17; 4.26.5–11). Despite a brief period in the nineteenth century when Revelation was dated to the reign of Nero, Domitian has remained the firm favorite among scholars of the Apocalypse. See J. C. Wilson, "The Problem with the Domitianic Date of Revelation," *New Testament Studies* 39 (1993): 587–605; Adela Yarbro Collins, "Dating the Apocalypse of John," *Biblical Research* 26 (1981): 33–45; Collins, "Myth and History in the Book of Revelation: The Problem of Its Date," in *Traditions in Transformation: Turning Points in the Biblical Faith*, ed. Baruch Halpern and Jon D. Levenson (Winona Lake, Ind.: Eisenbraums, 1981), 377–403.

105. G. E. M. De Ste. Croix, "Why Were the Early Christians Persecuted?" in *Christian Persecution, Martyrdom, and Orthodoxy*, ed. G. E. M. De Ste. Croix, Michael Whitby, and Joseph Street (Oxford: Oxford University Press, 2006), 105–52.

106. Boudewijn Dehandschutter, "The Meaning of Witness in the Apocalypse," in *L'apocalypse johannique et l'apocalyptique dans le nouveau testament*, ed. Jan Lambrecht (Leuven: Leuven University Press, 1980), 283–88.

107. Ignatius also uses the term to describe Jesus (Ign., *Phld.* 7.2).

108. Rev 2:13: "Οἶδα ποῦ κατοικεῖς, ὅπου ὁ θρόνος τοῦ Σατανᾶ, καὶ κρατεῖς τὸ ὄνομά μου καὶ οὐκ ἠρνήσω τὴν πίστιν μου καὶ ἐν ταῖς ἡμέραις Ἀντιπᾶς ὁ μάρτυς μου ὁ πιστός μου, ὃς ἀπεκτάνθη παρ' ὑμῖν, ὅπου ὁ Σατανᾶς κατοικεῖ."

109. Lucy Grig, *Making Martyrs in Late Antiquity* (London: Duckworth, 2004), 16.

110. Rev. 3:21: "ὁ νικῶν δώσω αὐτῷ καθίσαι μετ' ἐμοῦ ἐν τῷ θρόνῳ μου, ὡς κἀγὼ ἐνίκησα καὶ ἐκάθισα μετὰ τοῦ πατρός μου ἐν τῷ θρόνῳ αὐτοῦ." (cf. Rev 1:6; 5:10; 20:4, 6; 22:5). The promise that Christians will reign with Christ may be related to Dan 7:18, 27. What is striking about this passage is that it is presumably through suffering and death that the members of the churches will achieve this.

111. In Revelation, discipleship is eschatologically orientated. See David E. Aune, "Following the Lamb: Discipleship in the Apocalypse," in *Patterns of Discipleship in the New Testament*, ed. Richard N. Longnecker, McMaster New Testament Studies 1 (Grand Rapids, Mich.: Eerdmans, 1996), 269–84. The rewards granted to those who follow the Lamb in Revelation form the basis for later Christian speculation on the rewards attained by the martyrs in heaven. See the section "Enthronement, Reign, and Judgment" in chapter 5.

112. With the linchpin of Domitianic persecution removed, dating of *1 Clem.* ranges from 70 to 140 C.E. For a survey of the evidence, see John A. T. Robinson, *Redating the New Testament* (London: SCM Press, 1976), 327–34. For a detailed discussion of the later dating, see Lawrence L. Welborn, "On the Date of 1 Clement," *Biblical Research* 29 (1984): 35–54.

113. See chapter 2, throughout.

114. Unless otherwise noted, translations of Ignatius are taken from William R. Schoedel, *Ignatius of Antioch: A Commentary on the Letters of Ignatius of Antioch*, ed. Helmut Koester, Hermeneia: A Critical and Historical Commentary on the Bible (Philadelphia: Fortress, 1985).

115. The earliest quotation of Ignatius in Irenaeus *Haer.* 5.28.4 concerns his famous statement longing to become bread for the wild beasts (Ign., *Rom.* 4.1).

116. Theodor Zahn, *Ignatius von Antiochien* (Gotha: Friedrich Andreas Perthes, 1873); Joseph Barber Lightfoot, *The Apostolic Fathers* (London: Macmillan, 1885). Lightfoot's exhaustive three-volume text-critical study in part 2 of his *Apostolic Fathers* has become the cornerstone for modern scholarship on Ignatius.

117. Schoedel, *Ignatius of Anitoch*, 7. For challenges to the scholarly consensus, see, particularly, the work of Reinoud Weijenborg, *Les lettres d'Ignace d'Antioche, étude de critique littéraire et de théologie: Mis en français par Barthélemy Héroux* (Leiden: Brill, 1969); Josep Rius-Camps, *The Four Authentic Letters of Ignatius, the Martyr*, Orientalia Christiana Analecta 213 (Rome: Pontificium Institutum Orientalium Studiorum, 1980); and Robert Joly, *Le dossier d'Ignace d'Antioche* (Brussels: Éditions de l'Université de Bruxelles, 1979). Of these, Joly's reconstruction is the most compelling but fails to displace the work of Lightfoot. A detailed discussion of Joly's work is found in C. P. Bammel, "Ignatian Problems," *Journal of Theological Studies*, n.s., 33 (1982): 62–97. Clear summaries of their positions are provided by Schoedel, *Ignatius of Antioch*, 5–7.

118. Ign., *Eph.*, 10.1–3: "Καὶ ὑπὲρ τῶν ἄλλων δὲ ἀνθρώπων ἀδιαλείπτως προσεύχεσθε· ἔστιν γὰρ ἐν αὐτοῖς ἐλπὶς μετανοίας, ἵνα θεοῦ τύχωσιν. ἐπιτρέψατε οὖν αὐτοῖς κἂν ἐκ τῶν ἔργον ὑμῖν μαθητευθῆναι. πρὸς τὰς ὀργὰς αὐτῶν ὑμεῖς πραεῖς, πρὸς τὰς μεγαλορημοσύνας αὐτῶν ὑμεῖς ταπεινόφρονες. πρὸς τὰς βλασφημίας αὐτῶν ὑμεῖς τὰς προσευχάς, πρὸς τὴν πλάνην αὐτῶν ὑμεῖς ἑδραῖοι τῇ πίστει, πρὸς τὸ ἄγριον αὐτῶν ὑμεῖς ἥμεροι, μὴ σπουδάζοντες ἀντιμιμήσασθαι αὐτούς. ἀδελφοὶ αὐτῶν εὑρεθῶμεν τῇ ἐπιεικείᾳ· μιμηταὶ δὲ τοῦ κυρίου σπουδάζωμεν εἶναι." The text of this and all following citations of Ignatius are taken from Bart D. Ehrman, *The Apostolic Fathers*, Loeb Classical Library 24–25 (Cambridge, Mass.: Harvard University Press, 2003).

119. See the section "Martyrdom as Model" in chapter 3, and chapter 2, throughout.

120. As Schoedel says, discipleship is a "martyrological theme" for Ignatius. Schoedel, *Ignatius of Antioch*, 45.

121. "For though I am in bonds and can know heavenly things such as angelic locations and the archontic conjunctions, visible and invisible, for all that I am not already a disciple. For many things are lacking to us so that we may not lack God" (Ign., *Trall.* 5.2). Schoedel views the play on words in "lacking" God to the obverse of the more familiar Ignatian expression "to attain to God." Attaining to God means in a metaphorical sense to acquire God (cf. Augustine, *Serm. Dom.* 331.6.5). See Schoedel, *Ignatius of Antioch*, 145. Discipleship is also tied to martyrdom in Ign., *Rom.* 2.1–3.3.

122. Ign., *Eph.* 3.1: "Οὐ διατάσσομαι ὑμῖν ὡς ὤν τις. εἰ γὰρ καὶ δέδεμαι ἐν τῷ ὀνόματι, οὔπω ἀπήρτισμαι ἐν Ἰησοῦ Χριστῷ. νῦν γὰρ ἀρχὴν ἔχω τοῦ μαθητεύεσθαι καὶ προσλαλῶ ὑμῖν ὡς συνδιδασκαλίτας μου. ἐμὲ γὰρ ἔδει ὑφ' ὑμῶν ὑπαλειφθῆναι πίστει, νουθεσίᾳ ὑπομονῇ, μακροθυμίᾳ."

123. Ign., *Rom.* 4:1–2: " ἄφετέ με θηρίων εἶναι βοράν, δι' ὧν ἔνεστιν θεοῦ ἐπιτυχεῖν. σῖτός εἰμι θεοῦ καὶ δι' ὀδόντων θηρίων ἀλήθομαι, ἵνα καθαρὸς ἄρτος εὑρεθῶ τοῦ Χριστοῦ. μᾶλλον κολακεύσατε τὰ θηρία, ἵνα μοι τάφος γένωνται καὶ μηθὲν καταλίπωσι τῶν τοῦ σώματος μου, ἵνα μὴ κοιμηθεὶς βαρύς τινι γένωμαι. τότε ἔσομαι μαθητὴς ἀληθῶς Ἰησοῦ Χριστοῦ."

124. *Ac. Phileas:* "nondum passi sumus. Nunc incipimus pati. Nunc coepimus esse discipuli Christi."

125. Ign., *Rom.* 6.2–3: "σύγγνωτέ μοι, ἀδελφοί· μὴ ἐμποδίσητέ μοι ζῆσαι, μὴ θελήσητέ με ἀποθανεῖν, τὸν τοῦ θεοῦ θέλοντα εἶναι κόσμῳ μὴ χαρίσησθε μηδὲ ὕλῃ ἐξαπατήσητε· ἄφετέ με καθαρὸν φῶς λαβεῖν· ἐκεῖ παραγενόμενος ἄνθρωπος ἔσομαι. ἐπιτρέψατέ μοι μιμητὴν εἶναι τοῦ πάθους τοῦ θεοῦ μου."

126. Schoedel, *Ignatius of Antioch*, 183.

127. Martyrdom may have in turn shaped the way in which the New Testament itself was formed. For the impact of ideologies of martyrdom on the formation of the Christian canon, see M. Farkasfalvy and William R. Farmer, *The Formation of the New Testament Canon: An Ecumenical Approach* (Mahwah, N.J.: Paulist Press, 1983).

CHAPTER 2

1. The sharp divide between *Hochliteratur* (literature written for and produced by the Greco-Roman cultural elite) and *Kleinliteratur* (literature written by and for the plebians) as posited by Franz Overbeck and Adolf Deissmann has been challenged by the opening chapter of Harry Gamble's analysis of literacy in the ancient world. See Harry Y. Gamble, *Books and Readers in the Early Church: A History of Early Christian Texts* (New Haven, Conn.: Yale University Press, 1995). Nevertheless, there remains a pervasive feeling among scholars that the *scriptores ad martyrum* represent the tawdry underbelly of Christian literature.

2. Richard B. Hays, *Echoes of Scripture in the Letters of Paul* (New Haven, Conn.: Yale University Press, 1989), 16. Hays himself realizes the importance of understanding the context in which traditions were read, but I would venture to push this idea

further. The relationship between the determinative subtext, the text, and the context is highly complex and dialogical. Even scriptural texts, authoritative though they may be for imagined authors or communities, continue to be shaped by the contexts of their reading. In short, the patterns of influence in such echoing are multidirectional.

3. *Mart. Pol.* 1.2: "περιέμενεν γὰρ ἵνα παραδοθῇ, ὡς καὶ ὁ κύριος, ἵνα μιμηταὶ καὶ ἡμεῖς αὐτου γενώμεθα."

4. See also *Mart. Pol.* 17.3.

5. *Lyons* 2.2: "ζηλωταὶ καὶ μιμηταὶ Χριστοῦ ἐγένοντο."

6. *Mart. Mont.* 14.9.

7. "Even though we should not lay the subject of Christ before thee, yet the sufferings of Christ are portrayed indelibly in the worshippers of Christ." *Mart. Barsamya* (*ANF* 8.687).

8. For further discussion, see the section "Mark" in chapter 1.

9. Musurillo translates this phrase as a "witness in accordance with the gospel." See Herbert Musurillo, *Acts of the Christian Martyrs* (Oxford: Clarendon Press, 1972), 3. His translation is largely based on the assumption that *Mart. Pol.* is early and represents a point at which *martyrion* meant "witness" rather than "martyrdom." I prefer "martyrdom" here because it more concretely brings out the narrative contrast between Quintus and Polycarp. This contrast reflects an ongoing church debate about whether or not one should offer oneself for death. In this debate the key idea is offering oneself for martyrdom, not verbal witness.

10. *Mart. Pol.* 1.1–2:"σχεδὸν γὰρ πάντα τὰ προάγοντα ἐγένετο,ἵνα ἡμῖν ὁ κύριος ἄνωθεν ἐπιδείξῃ τὸ κατὰ τὸ εὐαγγέλιον μαρτύριον. περιέμενεν γὰρ ἵνα παραδοθῇ, ὡς καὶ ὁ κύριος, ἵνα μιμηταὶ καὶ ἡμεῖς αὐτοῦ γενώμεθα, μὴ μόνον σκοποῦντες τὸ καθ' ἑαυτούς, ἀλλὰ καὶ τὸ κατὰ τοὺς πέλας. ἀγάπης γὰρ ἀληθοῦς καὶ βεβαίας, ἐστιν μὴ μόνον ἑαυτὸν θέλειν σώζεσθαι ἀλλὰ καὶ πάντας τοὺς ἀδελγούς."

11. Ibid., 4: "διὰ τοῦτο οὖν, ἀδελφοί,οὐκ ἐπαινοῦμεν τοὺς προσιόντς ἑαυτοῖς ἐπειδὴ οὐχ οὕτως διδάσκει τὸ εὐαγγέλιον." This more measured approach to martyrdom, particularly with respect to "voluntary martyrdom," is not exclusive to *Mart. Pol.* A similar view is found on the lips of the distinguished martyr-bishop Cyprian in the *Ac. Cyprian* 1.5 ("ne quis se ultro offerat"). It is more common, however, outside of the *acta* and particularly in the writing of Clement of Alexandria, *Strom.* 10.

12. Germanicus, a bit player in *Mart. Pol.* pulls the beast on top of himself, an act interpreted by the narrator as courageous and pious (3.1–2). Michael Holmes has emphasized the importance of reacting to rather than initiating martyrdom in *Mart. Pol.*'s theology of martyrdom. He writes that it "is a matter of divine calling rather than human accomplishment." See Michael W. Holmes, "New Testament Passion Narratives," 421.

13. *Mart. Pol.* 19.1: "οὐ μόνον διδάσκαλος γενόμενος ἐπίσημος ἀλλὰ καὶ μάρτυς ἔξοχος οὖ τὸ μαρτύριον πάντες ἐπιθυμοῦσιν μιμεῖσθαι κατὰ τὸ εὐαγγέλιον Χριστοῦ γενόμενον."

14. *Mart. Agape* 1.2: "καὶ τοῖς εὐαγγελικοῖς νόμοις πειθόμεναι."

15. Ibid.: "καὶ φεύγουσι μὲν τοὺς διώκοντας κατὰ τὴν ἐντολήν."

16. For a discussion of the cult of Dionysos at Thessaloniki, see Karl P. Donfried, "The Cults of Thessalonica and the Thessalonian Correspondence," *New Testament Studies* 31 (1985): 336–56.

17. This symbolic reading is further supported by other symbolic elements in the account, for example, the symbolic interpretations of the three girls' names in 2.2–3.

18. Having left their families and city, the women gain a new "parent," Abraham. This is in contrast to the gospel of Mark, where members gain new families "brothers, sisters, mothers" and (some would argue) a new father—God in heaven (See Mark 10:29–30).

19. I have followed the NRSV translation here. The *hina* clause could be rendered more forcefully, however, so that this sentence reads, "Just as I have loved you so you too must love." This rendering would make the command to love, and its martyrologi-cal implications, all the more powerful.

20. John 13:34–35: "ἐντολὴν καινὴν δίδωμι ὑμῖν, ἵνα ἀγαπᾶτε ἀλλήλους, καθὼς ἠγάπησα ὑμᾶς ἵνα καὶ ὑμεῖς ἀγαπᾶτε ἀλλήλους. ἐν τούτῳ γνώσονται πάντες ὅτι ἐμοὶ μαθηταί ἐστε, ἐὰν ἀγάπην ἔχητε ἐν ἀλλήλοις."

21. John 15:9–13: "καθὼς ἠγάπησέν με ὁ πατήρ, κἀγὼ ὑμᾶς ἠγάπησα· μείνατε ἐν τῇ ἀγάπῃ τῇ ἐμῇ. ἐὰν τὰς ἐντολάς μου τηρήσητε, μενεῖτε ἐν τῇ ἀγάπῃ μου, καθὼς ἐγὼ τὰς ἐντολὰς τοῦ πατρός μου τετήρηκα καὶ μένω αὐτοῦ ἐν τῇ ἀγάπῃ. Ταῦτα λελάληκα ὑμῖν ἵνα ἡ χαρὰ ἡ ἐμὴ ἐν ὑμῖν ᾖ καὶ ἡ χαρὰ ὑμῶν πληρωθῇ. αὕτη ἐστὶν ἡ ἐντολὴ ἡ ἐμή, ἵνα ἀγαπᾶτε ἀλλήλους καθὼς ἠγάπησα ὑμᾶς. μείζονα ταύτης ἀγάπην οὐδεὶς ἔχει, ἵνα τις τὴν ψυχὴν αὐτοῦ θῇ ὑπὲρ τῶν φίλων αὐτοῦ."

22. The Johannine interest in becoming a friend of Jesus rather than his disciple seems to be in dialogue with the Markan idea of discipleship. John one-ups the offer of discipleship by proffering friendship as the result of laying down one's life. If friendship really was preferable to discipleship, this notion was certainly lost on the authors of the *acta*, who consistently prefer discipleship in their readings of the command to love.

23. Plato, *Symp.* 179 B: "καὶ μὴν ὑπεραποθνῄσκειν γε μόνοι ἐθέλουσιν οἱ ἐρῶντες." We should note that the term for "love" here is not the same as that used in John.

24. This is implied although not substantiated in Raymond Edward Brown, *The Gospel According to John*, Anchor Bible Commentary 29B (Garden City, N.Y.: Doubleday, 1966), 682.

25. See Clement of Alexandra, *Strom.* 8.1–3, where Clement fuses the idea of dying for one's neighbor with the notion of dying for Christ on the grounds that Christ is our neighbor. Elsewhere Clement calls martyrdom the "perfect act of love" (4.4). Cf. Ignatius of Antioch, who, in describing his longing for death, refers to "incorruptible love" in relation to the Eucharist (Ign., *Rom.* 8.1). See discussion in Walther Völker, *Der wahre Gnostiker nach Clemens Alexandrinus* (Berlin: Akademie-Verlag, 1952), 566. Compare Origen, *Exhortation to Martyrdom* 2 and 20–26, in which he rereads the Maccabees as examples of love.

26. *Lyons* 1.10: "ἔχων δὲ τὸν παράκλητον ἐν ἑαυτῷ, τὸ πνεῦμα πλέον τοῦ Ζαχαρίου,ὃ διὰ τοῦ πληρώματος τῆς ἀγάπης ἐνεδείξατο, εὐδοκήσας ὑπὲρ τῆς τῶν

ἀδελφῶν ἀπολογίας καὶ τὴν ἑαυτοῦ θεῖναι ψυχήν· ἦν γὰρ καὶ ἔστι γνήσιος Χριστοῦ μαθητής, ἀκολουθῶν τῷ ἀρνίῳ ὅπου ἂν ὑπάγῃ." To this example we can add Blandina's love for Christ (1.17), the reputation of Alexandros for loving God (1.49), and the love of the martyrs in a general sense (2.6–7).

27. See the section "Ignatius of Antioch" in chapter 1.

28. *Mart. Agape* 5.3: "Δουλκήτιος ἡγεμὼν εἶπεν· Τίς σοι συνεβούλευσεν τὰς διφθέρας ταύτας καὶ τὰς γραφὰς μέχρι τῆς σήμερον ἡμέρας φυλάξαιφ Εἰρήνη εἶπεν· Ὁ θεὸς ὁ παντοκράτωρ ὁ εἰπὼν ἕως θανάτου ἀγαπῆσαι αὐτόν."

29. Laura S. Nasrallah, "Empire and Apocalypse in Thessaloniki: Interpreting the Early Christian Rotunda," *Journal of Early Christian Studies* 13 (2005): 465–508.

30. Ibid., especially 504–5. We should note, however, that the use of imperial language and imagery is a common theme throughout the *acta* and one not exclusively tied to Thessaloniki. We might compare the Roman martyrdom the *Acts of Apollonius* for the apposition of Christ *pantokrator* to the emperor. Whether this kind of co-option of imperial language for the purpose of resistance is the product of similar circumstance or literary tradition is hard to say, but we should note its wide dispersion.

31. *Mart. Mont.* 23.3: "Habetis, inquit, fraters dilectissimi, nobiscum pacem, si noueritis ecclesiae pacem et dilectionis unitatem seruaueritis. nec putetis pauca esse quae dixi, cum et domins noster Iesus Christus passioni proximus haec nouissime dixerit: Hoc est, inquit, mandatum meum, ut diligatis inuicem, sicut dilexi uos."

32. For anti-*unitas* rhetoric in the Donatist *acta*, see Maureen A. Tilley, *Donatist Martyr Stories: The Church in Conflict in North Africa* (Liverpool: Liverpool University Press, 1996).

33. Cyprian, *Test.* 3.3; Cyprian, *Unit. eccl.* 14; Cyprian, *Zel. liv.* 12; Augustine, *Unit. eccl.*

34. We should be wary, however, of connecting this theme too firmly with schism in Carthage. The invocation of the command to love one another in the context of an injunction to peace and unity is also found in the Ethiopic version of the apocryphal *Ep. Apos.* Here, the apostles enjoin their readers to love and obey one another, that peace may rule among them (*Ep. Apos.* 18). Division had been an ongoing threat to the Christian church since Paul wrote to the Corinthians; we should not assume, therefore, that this interpretation of the Johannine command to love is exclusively Carthaginian.

35. Clement of Alexandria, *Strom.* 4.9, in which he cites Luke 12:8, 11–12 and Matt 10:32 as proof-texts for martyrdom. See also Cyprian, *To the Martyrs* 8.

36. *Lyons* 1.15: "ἐπληροῦτο δὲ τὸ ὑπὸ τοῦ κυρίου ἡμῶν εἰρημένον ὅτι ἐλεύσεται καιρὸς ἐν ᾧ πᾶς ὁ ἀποκτείνας ὑμᾶς δόξει λατρείαν προσφέρειν τῷ θεῷ."

37. Some scholars such as Saxer have argued that mimetic practices in the martyrdom accounts are examples of Christian mysticism. See Victor Saxer, *Bible et hagiographie: Textes et thèmes bibliques dans les Actes des martyrs authentiques des premiers siècles* (Bern: Peter Lang, 1986), 221–23. While there are passages that can be understood in terms of mystical practices inviting communion with Christ, this is not necessary. Imitating Christ through suffering was a fundamental part of early Christian identity.

38. For a discussion of the citation of biblical texts in the early martyrdom accounts, see Saxer, *Bible et hagiographie*.

39. The advantages that I have identified here are to an extent illusiory. Even though the relationship between Jesus traditions and narrative reworkings of these traditions may be more stable than patristic interpretations of scripture, they are just as amorphous. We cannot be sure of the precise nature of the Jesus traditions used by the authors of the *acta*, and we should expect that many sources are mingled together in the background to these texts. These sources probably include oral traditions, homiletical tropes, written accounts that are no longer extant, as well as written sources known to scholars today. While the relationship between narrative reworking and Jesus traditions may be stable, the Jesus tradition itself is not. We should further note that the martyr acts *remake* scriptural texts even as they reproduce them. Gospel "parallels" are, in the words of Michael Holmes, "the fruit of an act of interpretation." See Holmes, "New Testament Passion Narratives," 422.

40. *Mart. Fruct.* 3.2.

41. This designation is made by John Chrysostom, *Homily* 2 (PG 59.701).

42. The phrase is lacking in P^{75} x^1 B D* W θ 070. 579. 597 1241 it^{a,d} syr^s cop$^{sa, bo}$.

43. x* A D^2 L Δ Ψ 0250 33 28 f^1 f^{13}180 205 it$^{aur, b,c,e,f,l}$ vg syr^{c,p,h,pal} cop^{bo} arm eth geo slav Diatessaron Jocabus Justus$^{acc. to Hegesipp}$ Irenaeus^{lat} Origen^{lat} Hippolytus Eusebius Eusebian Canons Ps-Ignatius Apostolic Constitutions Gregory-Nyssa Amphilochius Didymus^{dub} Ps-Clementines Ps-Justin Chrysostom Cyril. This abbreviated list is taken from UBS[4].

44. Thomas M. Bolin, "A Reassessment of the Textual Problem of Luke 23.34a," *Proceedings of the Eastern Great Lakes and Midwestern Biblical Society* 12 (1992): 131–44.

45. Jason A. Whitlark and Mikeal C. Parsons, "The 'Seven' Last Words: A Numerical Motivation for the Insertion of Luke 23.34a," *New Testament Studies* 52 (2006): 191 n. 13.

46. Ibid., 193.

47. Joël Delobel, "Luke 23:34a: A Perpetual Test-Critical Crux?" in *Sayings of Jesus Canonical and Non-Canonical: Essays in Honor of Tjitze Baarda*, ed. William L. Petersen, Johan S. Vos, and Henk J. de Jonge (New York: Brill, 1997), 25–36.

48. Delobel's assumption here, although seemingly intuitive, is predicated upon the pious belief that the interplay between the person of Jesus and the persons of the martyrs was one-directional. Ironically, it is exactly this kind of assumption among early church readers that may have led to the insertion of the logion into Luke see below.

49. Like Delobel, Raymond Brown considers the influence of the relationship between Jesus and Stephen on the textual history of Luke 23:4a. He entertains the possibility that the prayer of Stephen could have influenced the Lukan account but dismisses this possibility on the grounds that the Lukan passion narrative is already martyrological. Much depends on exactly what Brown expects us to understand by martyrological, but it is unclear why an already established understanding of Jesus' death as martyrological would preclude the amplification of this understanding by later redaction. With the development of the genre, numerous literary elements of

martyrdom accounts such as the forgiveness of executioners would emerge, mutate, and metamorphose. It was not uncommon for literary elements that developed later in the evolution of the genre to find themselves retrojected into earlier *acta*. We need only look to the amplification of language of torture for evidence of this (see the textual history of the *Ac. Just.*). Given that *imitatio Christi* was present in the Jesus movement from the Pauline epistles onward, we should expect that prior to the establishment of the canon and where textual evidence suggests it, there was interplay between traditions regarding Jesus and traditions regarding martyrs. Raymond E. Brown, *The Death of the Messiah: From Gethsemane to the Grave, a Commentary on the Passion Narratives in the Four Gospels*, Anchor Bible Reference Library, 2 vols. (New York: Doubleday, 1994), 2.978.

50. These are summarized in Ibid., 979.

51. If Jesus' prayers for forgiveness are directed at the Romans, rather than the Jews, this problem is eliminated. See G. R. Cardas, "A Pentateuchal Echo in Jesus' Prayer on the Cross: Intertextuality between Numbers 15.22–31 and Luke 23:34a," in *The Scriptures in the Gospels*, ed. C. M. Tuckett (Leuven: Leuven University Press, 1997), 605–16. Cardas ultimately argues that the prayer is directed toward the Jews.

52. The question of ignorance here again rests upon the addressees. If directed at the Romans, the prayer merely indicates their lack of information.

53. This—the most traditional argument—is enthusiastically defended by J. Rendel Harris and Adolf von Harnack, who both assume that αὐτοῖς here refers to the Jews and not the Romans. For the substance of the argument, see Adolf von Harnack, *Studien zur Geschichte des Neuen Testaments und der Alten Kirche* (Berlin: Walter de Gruyter, 1931). The argument that the logion was removed on account of anti-Jewish sentiment falls flat when we consider its preservation in the Western text. Eldon Epp has carefully argued that the Western text contains many anti-Judaic tendencies. See Eldon Jay Epp, "The 'Ignorance Motif' in Acts and Anti-Judaic Tendencies in Codex Bezae," *Harvard Theological Review* 55 (1962): 51–62. On the application of Epp's theory to Luke 23:34a, see Jacobus H. Petzer, "Anti-Judaism and the Textual Problem of Luke 23.34," *Filologia Neotestamentaria* 5 (1993): 199–203.

54. See, for example, the observation of the Alands regarding D, the prototypical Western text, that additions and omissions "betray the touch of a significant theologian" in Kurt Aland, Barbara Aland, and Erroll F. Rhodes, *The Text of the New Testament: An Introduction to the Critical Editions and to the Theory and Practice of Modern Textual Criticisms* (Grand Rapids, Mich.: Eerdmans, 1987), 109. For a discussion of the Western text, see J. Neville Birdsall, "The Western Text in the Second Century," in *Gospel Traditions in the Second Century: Origins, Recensions, Text, and Transmission*, ed. William L. Petersen, Christianity and Judaism in Antiquity 3 (Notre Dame, Ind.: University of Notre Dame Press, 1989), 3–17.

55. Whitlark and Parsons, "The 'Seven' Last Words: A Numerical Motivation for the Insertion of Luke 23.34a," 203–4.

56. The suggestion that incorporating the logion into Luke brought numerical harmony to the sayings (three from John, three from Luke, one each from Matthew and Mark) does not seem, to me, to be particularly convincing. See Ibid., 204. That the

theme of forgiveness is already prevalent in Luke is more persuasive but does not appear more relevant than the parallelism with the death of Stephen.

57. David Flusser, "Sie wissen nicht, was sie tun," in *Kontinuitaet und Einheit: fuer Franz Mussner*, ed. Paul Mueller and Werner Stenger (Freiburg: Herder, 1981), 179–96.

58. Cf. Eusebius, *Hist. eccl.* 2.23.16. The saying is virtually identical to Luke 23.34a: "κύριε θεὲ Πάτερ ἀφες αὐτοῖς οὐ γάρ οἴδασιν τί ποιοῦσιν."

59. See discussion below.

60. The dating of *Mart. Pol.* as "third century" may appear surprising. For a discussion of the dating of *Mart. Pol.*, see the appendix.

61. In addition to the explicit framing of the martyrdom in terms of imitation, the parallels between the passion narrative and the *Martyrdom of Polycarp* include: the delay in being handed over (1.2), the distance from the city at the point of arrest (5.1), the protagonist's prophesying of his own death (5.2; 12.3), the betrayal of the protagonist by "someone close" to him (6.2), the participation of a character named Herod in the events that lead to the death of the protagonist (6.2), the invocation of robbery as a motivating factor in the arrest and trial (7.1), the apprehending of the protagonist at night (7.1–2), the obedience to the will of God (7.1), entering the city on an ass (8.1), the Roman authorities equivocating over the sentence of death (9.3–11.2), the intervention of the bloodthirsty, Jewish crowd (12.2–13.1), stabbing (16.1), and the timing of the protagonist's death around passover (21). For a discussion of the use of the New Testament in *Mart. Pol.*, see Boudewijn Dehandschutter, "The New Testament and the *Martyrdom of Polycarp*," in *Trajectories through the New Testament and the Apostolic Fathers*, ed. Andrew F. Gregory and Christopher M. Tuckett (Oxford: Oxford University Press, 2005), 395–406. For a discussion of the relationship between *Mart. Pol.* and the passion narratives, see M.-L. Guillaumin, "En marge du 'Martyre de Polycarpe': Le discernment des allusions scripturaires," in *Forma Futuri: Studi in onore del Cardinale Michele Pellegrino* (Turin: Bottega d'Erasmo, 1975), 462–69; B. Dehandschutter, *Martyrium Polycarpi: Ein literair-krittisch studie*, Bibliotheca ephemeridum theologicarum lovaniensium 52 (Leuven: Leuven University Press, 1979), 241–54; Gerd Buschmann, *Das Martyrium des Polykarp*, Kommentar zu den Apostolischen Vätern 6 (Göttingen: Vandenhoeck & Ruprecht, 1998); Judith M. Lieu, *Image and Reality: The Jews in the World of the Christians in the Second Century* (Edinburgh: T & T Clark, 1996), 59–63; and Michael W. Holmes, "New Testament Passion Narratives," 407–32.

62. See Leslie W. Barnard, "In Defense of Pseudo-Pionius' Account of Saint Polycarp's Martyrdom," in *Kyriakon Festschrift Johannes Quasten*, ed. Patrick Granfield and Josef Jungmann (Münster: Aschendorff, 1970), 192–204; Hans Freiherr von Campenhausen, "Bearbeitungen und Interpolationen des Polycarpmartyrium," in *Aus der Frühzeit des Christentums. Studien zur Kirchengeschichte des ersten und zweiten Jahrhunderts*, ed. Hans Freiherr von Campenhausen (Tübingen: Mohr Siebeck, 1963), 253–301; A. Hilgenfeld, "Das neueste Steitzianum über den Paschasreit," *Zeitschrift für wissenschaftliche Theologie* 4 (1861), 106–10, and "Der Quartodecimanismus Klein- asiens und die kanonischen Evangelien," *Zeitschrift für wissenschaftliche Theologie* 4 (1861), 285–318; Holmes, "New Testament Passion Narratives," 407–18;

W. D. Köhler, *Die Rezeption des Matthäusevangeliums in der Zeit vor Irenäus*, Wisschen-schaftliche Untersuchungen zum Neuen Testament. 2.24 (Tübingen: Mohr Siebeck, 1987).

63. *Mart. Pol.* 6.2: "καὶ ὁ εἰρήναρχος, ὁ κεκληρωμένος τὸ αὐτὸ ὄνομα, Ἡρώδης ἐπιλεγόμενος, ἔσπευδεν εἰς τὸ στάδιον αὐτὸν εἰσαγαγεῖν ἵνα ἐκεῖνος μὲν τὸν ἴδιον κλῆρον ἀπαρτίσῃ Χριστοῦ κοινωνὸς γενόμενος, οἱ δὲ προδόντες αὐτὸν τὴν αὐτοῦ τοῦ Ἰούδα ὑπόσχοιεν τιμωρίαν."

64. The identification is made stronger by calling those in his household οἱ προδόντες, the participle of the noun used to describe Judas in Luke 6:16 and Acts 7:52.

65. For a discussion of the circumstances under which Christians came to be persecuted, see Ste. Croix, "Why Were the Christians Persecuted," 105–52. Ste. Croix notes that in the Pliny-Trajan correspondence Christians are not "sought out" but instead were accused of being Christians by a *delator* (Pliny the Younger, *Ep.* 10). Eusebius gives an example of this when he relates the circumstances that lead to the martyrdom of Justin (*Hist. eccl.* 5.16.7–8).

66. *Mart. Pol.* 7.1 " Ἔχοντες οὖν τὸ παιδάριον τῇ παρασκευῇ περὶ δείπνου ὥραν ἐξῆλθον διωγμῖται καὶ ἱππεῖς μετὰ τῶν συνήθων αὐτοῖς ὅπλων ὡς ἐπὶ λῃστὴν τρέχοντες καὶ ὀψὲ τῆς ὥρας συνεπελθόντες ἐκεῖνον μὲν εὗρον ἔν τινι δωματίῳ κατακείμενον ἐν ὑπερῴῳ κἀκεῖθεν δὲ ἠδύνατο εἰς ἕτερον χωρίον ἀπελθεῖν ἀλλ' οὐκ ἠβουλήθη εἰπών, Τὸ θέλημα τοῦ θεοῦ γενέσθω. ἀκούσας οὖν αὐτοὺς παρόντας, καταβὰς διελέχθη αὐτοῖς θαυμαζόντων τῶν παρόντων τὴν ἡλικίαν αὐτοῦ καὶ τὸ εὐσταθές, καὶ εἰ τοσαύτη σπουδὴ ἦν τοῦ συλληφθῆναι τοιοῦτον πρεσβύτην ἄνδρα."

67. Ibid., 7.2–3: "εὐθέως οὖν αὐτοῖς ἐκέλευσεν παρατεθῆναι φαγεῖν καὶ πιεῖν ἐν ἐκείνῃ τῇ ὥρᾳ ὅσον ἄν βούλωνται ἐξητήσατο δὲ αὐτοὺς ἵνα δῶσιν αὐτῷ ὥραν πρὸς τὸ προσεύξασθαι ἀδεῶς, τῶν δὲ ἐπιτρεψάντων, στραθεὶς πρὸς ἀνατολὴν προσηύξατο πλήρης ὢν τῆς χάριτος τοῦ θεοῦ οὕτως ὡς ἐπὶ δύο ὥρας μὴ δύνασθαι σιωπῆσαι, καὶ ἐκπλήττεσθαι τοὺς ἀκούοντας πολλούς τε μετανοεῖν ἐπὶ τῷ ἐληλυθέναι ἐπὶ τοιοῦτον θεοπρεπῆ πρεσβύτην." Polycarp's age invites comparison with Eleazar in 2 and 4 Maccabees.

68. Ibid., 8.1: "They put him on a donkey and thus conducted him into the city. It was now a great Sabbath day." For the significance of the Sabbath, see John 19:31.

69. Ibid. 13.3–14.1:"μελλόντων δὲ αὐτῶν καὶ προσηλοῦν, εἶπεν· Ἄφετέ, με οὕτως. ὁ γὰρ δοὺς ὑπομεῖναι τὸ πῦρ δώσει καὶ χωρὶς τῆς ὑμετέρας ἐκ τῶν ἥλων ἀσφαλείας ἄσκυλτον ἐπιμεῖναι τῇ πυρᾷ. Οἱ δὲ οὐ καθήλωσαν μέν προσέδησαν δὲ αὐτόν."

70. Certain rabbinic traditions discuss the possibility that Isaac was in fact sacrificed. See *Pirqe R. El.* 31 and ibn Ezra ad Gen 22:19, which notes the tradition that Abraham actually killed Isaac and that he was later revived, but rejects it as contradicting scripture. Jon Levenson suggests that some of the midrashic material assumes that some, perhaps all, of Isaac's blood was shed on the altar, citing Mekilta de Rabbi Ishmael 7, Pseudo-Philo's Biblical Antiquities 18:5, and Mekilta de Rabbi Shimon ben Yochai, Wa'era (Jon D. Levenson, *The Death and Resurrection of the Beloved Son: The Transformation of Child Sacrifice in Judaism and Christianity* [New Haven, Conn.: Yale

University Press, 1993], 180–81, 192–93). For an evaluation of Levenson and a somewhat different view, see Alan F. Segal, "The Akedah: Some Reconsiderations," *Geschichte-Tradition-Reflexion: Festschrift für Martin Hengel zum 70. Geburtstag* Bd. 1, ed. Hubert Cancik (Tübingen: Mohr, 1996), 99–116.

71. See Heb 11:17–19; Irenaeus, *Haer.* 5.5.4.

72. See E. P. Sanders, *Jesus and Judaism* (Philadelphia: Fortress Press, 1985), chap. 11, particularly, in which he argues that this was the proverbial straw that broke the camel's back. Early scholars who argued for this include C. H. Dodd, *Historical Tradition in the Fourth Gospel* (Cambridge: Cambridge University Press, 1963), 158, and Etienne Trocmé, "L' expulsion des marchands du Temple," *New Testament Studies* 15 (1968): 1–22. This view is by no means universally accepted; see Burton L. Mack, *A Myth of Innocence: Mark and Christian Origins* (Philadelphia: Fortress Press, 1988), 88–89.

73. There is no evidence for this practice as part of the worship of Saturn. Musurillo suggests that perhaps it is related to the Sacian feast of the Persians during which criminals dressed liked kings prior to their execution. See Musurillo, *Acts of the Christian Martyrs*, 273 n. 1. The ceremony has much in common with the so-called *pharmakos* rituals in which a criminal or pauper was dressed as a king and then driven out of the city, often to die. (See the fragments of Hipponax in Tzetes, *Chil.* 5. 737–739, and Plutarch, *Quaest. conv.* 693.E.12). A number of scholars have seen the *pharmakos* rituals as providing a context for the triumphal entry and passion narratives of the gospels. See Adela Yarbro Collins, "Finding Meaning in the Death of Jesus," *Journal of Religion* 78 (1998): 175–96. Given the highly strategic use of the motif of human sacrifice in the *Mart. Dasius*, it seems possible that the author utilizes the *pharmakos* motif, perhaps recognizing its similarity to the gospel accounts, as a means of highlighting the parallels between Dasius and Jesus and to amplify the impiety of the Romans.

74. *Mart. Dasius* 11.1–2: "ὅστις ἀπερχόμενος εἰς τὴν ἔνδοξον αὐτοῦ μαρτυρίαν εἶχέν τινα προηγούμενον αὐτοῦ μετὰ ἀθεμίτου θυμιατηρίου. ὡς δὲ ἠνάγκαζον αὐτὸν προσενεγκεῖν θυσίαν τοῖς ἀκαθάρτοις δαιμόσιν, τότε λαβὼν ταῖς ἰδίαις χερσὶν ὁ μακάριος Δάσιος διεσκόρπισεν αὐτῶν τὰ θυμιάματα καὶ κατέβαλεν τὰ δυσσεβῆ καὶ ἀθέμιτα τῶν ἱεροσύλων εἴδωλα εἰς τὴν γῆν κατασύρας, ὥπλισέν τε τὸ μέτωπον αὐτοῦ τῇ σφαγῖδι τοῦ τιμίου σταυροῦ τοῦ Χριστοῦ, οὗτινος τῇ δυνάμει ἰσχυρῶς πρὸς τὸν τύραννον ἀντηγωνίσατο."

75. Nicolaus Nilles, *Kalendarium manuale utriusque ecclesiae orientalis et occidentalis* (Oeniponte: typis et sumptibus Feliciani Rauch, 1896), 1.105. In the Orthodox tradition, Theodore is revered as a general.

76. PG XLVI .74. The earliest edition of the Greek text of the *Martyrium S. Theodori Tironis* was published in Hippolyte Delehaye, *Les légendes grecques des saints militaires* (Paris: Librairie A. Picard, 1909), 227. It is considered largely interpolated.

77. See also the martyr Leo, who "dashed in pieces the lanterns and trampled the tapers underfoot, crying aloud, 'If you think that the gods have any power, let them defend themselves'" in Theodoricus Ruinart, *Acta primorum martyrum sincera et selecta* (Ratisbonae: G. Josephi Manz, 1859), 478.

78. In using the term "pagan" here, I do not mean to imply that there was a stable religious entity called "paganism" and self-identified adherents called "pagans." The use of the term here is reflective of fourth-century Christian attempts to construct "paganism" as a separate and distinct group. For a discussion of relations between "pagans" and "Christians," see Ramsay MacMullen, *Christianity and Paganism in the Fourth to Eighth Centuries* (New Haven, Conn.: Yale University Press, 1997).

79. *Sermon on the Passion of Donatus and Advocatus*, 6, trans. in Tilley, *Donatist Martyr Stories*, 57.

80. Eusebius, *Hist. eccl.* 1.32.

81. For a discussion of the legal situation during this period, see Ste. Croix, "Why Were the Early Christians Persecuted?" 105–52.

82. Mark 15:2; Matt 27:11; Luke 23:3; John 18:33. In these instances Jesus is accused of claiming to be the king of the Jews, a situation different from the execution of Symeon, who is accused of being descended from David. We can assume, however, that the issue with Davidic descent is one of kingship and claims to power. Perhaps Eusebius means to subtly extend the parallels between Jesus crucified as a monarch in Jerusalem, and Symeon crucified in Jerusalem for having a royal lineage.

83. For a discussion of the form and text history of the Acts of Peter, see the introductory sections of Christine M. Thomas, *The Acts of Peter, Gospel Literature, and the Ancient Novel: Rewriting the Past* (Oxford: Oxford University Press, 2003). See the corrections of her argument in Matthew C. Baldwin, *Whose Acts of Peter? Text and Historical Context of the Actus Vercellenses*, Wissenschaftliche Untersuchungen zum Neuen Testament 2.196 (Tübingen: Mohr Siebeck, 2005).

84. The term for "stake" here is ξύλον a somewhat ambiguous word that can mean "tree," "post," "wood," etc. (see the entry in Henry George Liddell and Robert Scott, *A Greek-English Lexicon*, 9th ed. [Oxford: Clarendon Press, 1940], 1191–92). In Acts 5:30 Peter and the apostles use the same term and a similar phrase to describe "Jesus, whom you killed by hanging on a tree" (Ἰησοῦν ὃν ὑμεῖς διεχειρίσασθε κρεμάσαντες ἐπὶ ξύλου). It would seem, therefore, that this stake or beam was associated with a cross. Against this, Vergote has argued that this term was frequently used in Christian martyrdoms to denote a specific instrument of torture. See J. Vergote, "Folterwerkzeuge," *Reallexicon für Antike und Christentum* 8 (1972): 112–41. This may well be the case, but given the way that the other martyrs see Christ in her form, it is likely that the term also contains an allusion to the cross.

85. *Lyons* 1.41: "ἡ δὲ Βλανδῖνα ἐπὶ ξύλου κρεμασθεῖσα προύκειτο βορὰ τῶν εἰσβαλλομένων θηρίων, ἣ καὶ διὰ τοῦ βλέπεσθαι σταυροῦ σχήματι κρεμαμένη, διὰ τῆς εὐτόνου προσευχῆς πολλὴν προθυμίαν τοῖς ἀγωνιζομένοις ἐνεποίει, βλεπόντων αὐτῶν ἐν τῷ ἀγῶνι καὶ τοῖς ἔξωθεν ὀφθαλμοῖς διὰ τῆς ἀδελφῆς τὸν ὑπὲρ αὐτῶν ἐσταυρωμένον, ἵνα πείσῃ τοὺς πιστεύοντας εἰς αὐτὸν ὅτι πᾶς ὁ ὑπὲρ τῆς Χριστοῦ δόξης παθὼν τὴν κοινωνίαν ἀεὶ ἔχει μετὰ τοῦ ζῶντος θεοῦ."

86. Eusebius, *Hist. eccl.* 8.7.

87. Cf. 1 Tim 2:8.

88. See, for example, Tertullian, *Or.;* Minucius Felix, *Oct.*, 29.4 and discussion of these, below.

89. The *orant* appeared as a personified virtue on the reverse of Roman coinage throughout the second and third centuries, occasionally with accompanying legends referring to piety (*pietas aug* or *pietas publica*). See Charles H. Dodd, "The Cognomen of the Emperor Antoninus Pius," *Numismatic Chronicle* 4, no. 11 (1911): 6–41. The term *pietas* itself had a significant resonance within both Roman and Christian contexts, in which it served as a rough equivalent for the Greek term *eusebeia* or, in English, "piety." In the Greco-Roman world, *pietas* conveyed not so much modern notions of religious piety as it did a sense of honor and obedience to higher authorities be they religious, civic, societal, or familial. The importance of *eusebeia* in Christian circles is exemplified in the writings and martyrdom of Justin Martyr, who constructs Christian *eusebeia* in relation to Roman notions, e.g., *1 Apol.* 3.2. We should note, with Robin Jensen, however, that the numismatic legends applied to the *orant* may have no bearing upon the meaning of the pose for early Christians. See Robin Margaret Jensen, *Understanding Early Christian Art* (London: Routledge, 2000), 32ff.

90. See, for example, the *orante* interspersed between the four-part narrative of Jonah and the whale on the dome of a cubiculum in the catacomb of Peter Marcellinus in Rome.

91. L. de Bruyne, "Les lois de l'art paléochrétien comme instrument herméneutique," *Rivista di Archeologia Cristiana* 39 (1963): 7–92; André Grabar, *Christian Iconography: A Study of Its Origins* (London: Routledge & Kegan Paul, 1969).

92. See Henri Leclercq, "Orans, Orante," *Dictionnaire d'archéologie et chrétienne et de liturgica*, 2291–322; K. Wessel, "Ecclesia Orans," *Archäologisher Anzeiger* 70 (1955): 315–34; and A. Mulhern, "L'Orante, vie et mort d'une image," *Les Dossiers de l'Archéologie* 18 (1976): 34–47.

93. See Theodor Klauser, "Studien zur Entstehungsgechichte der christlichen Kunst VII," *Jahrbuch für Antike und Christentum* 7 (1964): 67–76.

94. Minucius Felix, *Oct.* 29.6, in which Minucius compares the form of a man at prayer to the shape of the cross. These examples are cited by Robin Jensen, albeit reluctantly, in *Understanding Early Christian Art*, 32–34.

95. *Or.* 14: "Nos vero non attollimus tatum, sed etiam expandimus e dominica passione modulatum et orantes confitemur Christo." See Tertullian, *Nat.*, 1.14, in which Tertullian argues that all prayer is cruciform.

96. More generally, prayer for one's opponents was already being promoted as a kind of *imitatio Christi* in the letters of Ignatius. In Ign., *Eph.* 10.1–3, Ignatius exhorts his readers to respond to anger by offering up prayers. This response he himself ties to imitation of Christ. It may well be the case that Ignatius's words served as a preparation for martyrdom in which the readers were exhorted to pray in imitation of Christ.

97. André Grabar, *Martyrium: Recherches sur le culte des reliques et l'art Chrétien antique* (Paris: Collège de France, 1943), 2.51.

98. Ibid., 2.51, and fig. 139.

99. Fructuosus kneels in prayer, a pose slightly different from the *orans* pose previously discussed. Prayer while kneeling was also a common practice; See *Mart. Mont.* 23.6, where Flavian kneels "as if in prayer" and completes his martyrdom in the same way.

100. *Mart. Fruct.* 4.3–4: "Cumque exustae fuissent fasciolae quibus manus eorum fuerant conligatae, Fructuosus orationis diuinae et solitae consuetudinis memor gaudens positis genibus, de resurrectione securus in signo tropae Domini constitute Dominum deprecabatur."

101. See Grabar, *Martyrium*, 2.51: "On peut le reconnaître tout d'abord, chez le Christ lui-même, dans les Crucifixions archaïques où, la croix étant omise, on le voit debout et de face, les deux bras étendus et légèrement plies aux coudes: sur la porte de Saint-Sabine, sur les amphoules palestiniennes, sa silhouette est virtuellement celle d'un orante. Or, s'il en était ainsi pour le Christ, le geste de prière des martyrs, qui, par leur mort volente, renouvelèrent la passion du Christ, pouvait être interprété comme une evocation du crucifiement. Cette intention est évident sur les representations où les bras étendus du saint sont peu pliés aux coudes et forment une ligne qui s'approche de l'horizontale."

102. See Musurillo, *Acts of the Christian Martyrs*, 181. That only Fructuosus strikes the pose as he recites the *orationis diuinae* prefigures later Eucharistic liturgy in which the priest alone performs the *orans* pose at the Lord's Prayer (see *canon actionis* in the Roman missal). It is certainly possible that this is the earliest example of this liturgical element.

103. *Lyons* 1.41.

104. Both Pionius (*Mart. Pion.* 21.4) and Lawrence (Prudentius, *Peristephanon*, 2) make lighthearted jokes before their deaths, perhaps in imitation of Socrates' dying request that they sacrifice a cock to Asclepius (cf. Plato, *Phaed.*).

105. Luke 23:46: "καὶ φωνήσας φωνῇ μεγάλῃ ὁ Ἰησοῦς εἶπεν, Πάτερ, εἰς χεῖράς σου παρατίθεμαι τὸ πνεῦμά μου. τοῦτο δὲ εἰπὼν ἐξέπνευσεν."

106. Acts 7:59–60: "καὶ ἐλιθοβόλουν τὸν Στέφανον ἐπικαλούμενον καὶ λέγοντα, Κύριε Ἰησοῦ, δέξαι τὸ πνεῦμά μου. θεὶς δὲ τὰ γόνατα ἔκραξεν φωνῇ μεγάλῃ, Κύριε, μὴ στήσῃς αὐτοῖς ταύτην τὴν ἁμαρτίαν. καὶ τοῦτο εἰπὼν ἐκοιμήθη."

107. *Ac. Carpus*, Latin 4.6: "haec cum dixisset, multum supponentibus ministris ignem, aspiciens in caelum dixit: Domine Iesu Christe, suscipe spiritum meum. et sic reddidit animam."

108. *Ac. Julius*, 4.4: "te deprecor ut cum tuis sanctis martyribus spiritum meum suscipere digneris."

109. *Mart. Mont.* 14.9: "hoc enim est propter Christum pati, Christum etiam exemplo sermonis imitari et esse probationem maximam fidei. O exemplum grande credendi!"

110. For a survey of these views, see Brown, *The Gospel According to John*, 2.946–52.

111. *Lyons* 1.22: "καὶ ταῦτα μὲν ἐκαίετο, αὐτὸς δὲ παρέμενεν ἀνεπίκαμπτος καὶ ἀνέδοτος, στερρὸς πρὸς τὴν ὁμολογίαν ὑπὸ τῆς οὐρανίου πηγῆς τοῦ ὕδατος τῆς ζωῆς τοῦ ἐξιόντος ἐκ τῆς νηδύος τοῦ Χριστοῦ δροσιζόμενος καὶ ἐνδυναμούμενος·"

112. In Rev 22:1–2 the fountain appears to flow from the throne of God and the lamb that will descend from heaven in the new creation (21:1–2); this is not the understanding of the author of the *Lyons*.

113. This is by no means unique. The idea of the church continuing to be nourished by the flow of water from the side of Jesus is found elsewhere in Lyonnais

literature. Irenaeus writes, "Those who do not partake of the Spirit that is in the Church are not nourished by the stream of water that gushes from the side of Christ" (*Haer.* 3.24.1), indicating that for Christians the opposite is true.

114. *Mart. Mont.* 22.3: "quod Flauianus ipse ore suo dixit, ad hoc pluebat ut dominicae passionis exemplo aqua sanguini iungerentur"

115. Perhaps an allusion to the Sermon on the Mount (Matthew 5–7) or John 6:3.

116. See above.

117. Scholars have frequently noted the self-controlled and dispassionate nature of the Johannine Jesus. The same can be observed of Flavian, who voluntarily and calmly appears to direct the events.

118. The term "conversion" evokes a bundle of scholarly caveats and counterarguments that cannot be ignored. Our difficulty is that, in merely using the term, we unwittingly stumble into a dispute between modern Christian notions of conversion (and the inevitable pneumatological and psychological baggage it entails) and scholarly champions of philosophical conversion. Since the work of A. D. Nock, scholars have been forced to reconsider the use of the term to describe the process of becoming Christian. See Arthur Darby Nock, *Conversion: The Old and the New in Religion from Alexander the Great to Augustine of Hippo* (London: Oxford University Press, 1961). For Nock, "conversion" most appropriately describes the movement from the consideration of a number of philosophies to the selection of one. This paradigm is particularly pertinent to the conversions of intellectuals such as Justin Martyr or Augustine but fails to adequately engage with the plethora of texts recounting conversions resulting from, for example, displays of power. The work of Ramsey MacMullen has focused upon the diverse forms of conversion in the Constantinian period. See Ramsay MacMullen, *Christianizing the Roman Empire (A.D. 100–400)* (New Haven, Conn.: Yale University Press, 1984), in which he highlights the miraculous stimulant that lies behind mass conversions and the means by which imperial and local authorities attempted to force conversion upon the populace. The element of miraculous mass conversion is certainly present in some of the *acta martyrum;* however, our study is concerned with a different phenomenon—a solitary individual whose conversion is prompted by the observation of a martyrdom. Let us be clear, then, that in using the term "conversion" we imply merely a shift in allegiance and identity in which a person who was not previously recognized as a Christian is subsequently explicitly identified as such. We shall leave pneumatization to Paul and considered evaluation to Justin.

119. Since C. J. Cadoux's work on the subject, the relationship between military service and pacifism has been discussed by scholars and ethicists of the New Testament and early church alike. See Cecil John Cadoux, *The Early Christian Attitude to War: A Contribution to the History of Christian Ethics* (London: Headley Brothers, 1919). In general, scholarly attention has focused upon the extent to which all or some early Christians were pacifists. While many early soldier martyrs meet their death on account of their refusal to sacrifice or swear an oath, others refuse to engage in battle altogether. For a bibliography, see Peter Brock, *The Military Question in the Early Church: A Selected Bibliography of a Century's Scholarship* (Toronto: Network Lithographers and Composition, 1988).

120. The identification of the "military saint" as a distinct type was made by Adolf von Harnack and Hippolyte Delehaye. See Delehaye, *Les légendes grecques des saints militaires;* Adolf von Harnack, *Militia Christi: The Christian Religion and the Military in the First Three Centuries;* trans. David McInnes Gracie (Philadelphia: Fortress Press, 1981). Delehaye's work was responsible for the identification of the *état-major* as a martyrological trope. Since Delehaye's groundbreaking work, a number of more modern scholars have examined the later legends and incarnations of the military saint. See, particularly, Christopher Walter, *The Warrior Saints in Byzantine Art and Tradition* (Burlington, Vt.: Ashgate, 2003).

The evolution of the *miles Christi* draws him away from the Christly prototype toward the example of the military archangel Michael. In iconographic representation, the members of Delehaye's *état-major*, the two Theodores, Demetrius, Procopius, Mercurius, and George, are consistently assimilated and compared to Michael. They appear with wings, destroying serpents and demons with swords and lances. There is still an echo of Christ's conquest of Satan, but the overwhelming allusion is to Revelation's conquering angel. For a collection of this iconography, see Walter, *The Warrior Saints in Byzantine Art and Tradition*, plates, 1, 25, 28.

121. On the evolution of the warrior-saint, see Walter, *The Warrior Saints in Byzantine Art and Tradition*, who writes: "During the first Christian centuries, as noted already, there was no special cult of those martyrs who were to be designated later as warrior saints. However, the elements were being assembled which would later be merged to form the cult" (22–23).

122. Adolf von Harnack, *Militia Christi: The Christian Religion and the Military in the First Three Centuries*, trans. David McInnes Gracie (Philadelphis: Fortress, 1981), 89.

123. Later examples include Maximus in the *Mart. Caecilia*. An analogous conversion is found in the young lawyer Theophilius in the *Passion of Saint Dorothea*. For fourth- and fifth-century Syriac examples, see the *Mart. Simeon*, *Mart. Pusai*, and *Great Massacre of Bet-Huzaye*, all in *Biblioteca hagiographica orientalis*, and Paul Bedjan, *Acta Martyrum et Sanctorum* 7 vols. (Paris: Via dicta de Sèvres, 1890–97). For Coptic, see, for example, *Mart. Apaioule*, in E. A. E. Reymond and John W. B. Barns, *Four Martyrdoms from the Pierpont Morgan Coptic Codices* (Oxford: Clarendon Press, 1973).

124. Clement apparently had a large store of information about the apostles. Another Clementine narrative about John is also preserved in Eusebius, *Hist. eccl.* 3.23.

125. Eusebius, *Hist. eccl.* 2.9.2: "And concerning this James, Clement, in the seventh book of his Hypotyposes, relates a story which is worthy of mention; telling it as he received it from those who had lived before him. He says that the one who led James to the judgment-seat, when he saw him bearing his testimony, was moved, and confessed that he was himself also a Christian."

126. Ibid., 9.3: "They were both therefore, he says, led away together; and on the way he begged James to forgive him. And he, after considering a little, said, 'Peace be with you,' and kissed him. And they were both beheaded at the same time."

127. According to Renaudot, the phrase was used in the Alexandrian Eucharist ceremony in much the same way as it is today. See Eusèbe Renaudot, *Liturgiarum orientalium collectio* (Amersham: Gregg International, 1970).

128. See *Pass. Perp.* 21.7.

129. Eusebius, *Hist. eccl.* 6.41.16–17: "But a soldier, named Besas, who stood by them as they were led away, rebuked those who insulted them. And they cried out against him, and this most manly warrior of God was arraigned, and having done nobly in the great contest for piety, was beheaded."

130. The term "piety" was a central one for early apologists and hagiographers. See, for example, the *Ac. Just.* B 4.4; *Ac. Carp.* (Greek) 19; *First Apol.* 3.2; 12.5. The term "contest" is used of the act of martyrdom in the *Ac. Carp.*

131. For a discussion of the text-critical history of the account, see the appendix.

132. Eusebius, *Hist. eccl.* 6.5.3: " Ἅμα δὲ λόγῳ τὸν τῆς ἀποφάσεως ὅρον καταδεξαμένην ὁ Βασιλείδης, εἷς τις ὢν τῶν ἐν στρατείαις ἀναφερομένων, ἀπάγει παραλαβὼν τὴν ἐπὶ θανάτῳ. ὡς δὲ τὸ πλῆθος ἐνοχλεῖν αὐτῇ καὶ ἀκολάστοις ἐνυβρίζειν ῥήμασιν ἐπειρᾶτο, ὁ μὲν ἀνεῖργεν ἀποσοβῶν τοὺς ἐνυβρίζοντας, πλεῖστον ἔλεον καὶ φιλανθρωπίαν εἰς αὐτὴν ἐνδεικνύμενος. ἡ δὲ τῆς περὶ αὐτὴν συμπαθείας ἀποδεξαμένη τὸν ἄνδρα θαρρεῖν παρακελεύεται· ἐξαιτήσεσθαι γὰρ αὐτὸν ἀπελθοῦσαν παρὰ τοῦ ἑαυτῆς κυρίου καὶ οὐκ εἰς μακρὸν τῶν εἰς αὐτὴν πεπραγμένων τὴν ἀμοιβὴν ἀποτίσειν αὐτῷ."

133. Ibid., 6.5.5: "Οὐ μακρὸν χρόνον διαλιπὼν ὁ Βασιλείδης ὅρκον διά τινα αἰτίαν πρὸς τῶν συστρατιωτῶν αἰτηθείς, μὴ ἐξεῖναι αὐτῷ τὸ παράπαν ὀμνύναι διεβεβαιοῦτο· Χριστιανὸν γὰρ ὑπάρχειν καὶ τοῦτο ἐμφανῶς ὁμολογειν."

134. This ability can be partially explained by Eusebius's statement that Basilides was a disciple of Origen. While this is certainly plausible, the narrative itself focuses on Basilides' interaction with Potamiaena.

135. See H. W. Attridge, "Giving Voice to Jesus: Use of the Psalms in the New Testament," in *Psalms in Community: Jewish and Christian Textual, Liturgical, and Artistic Traditions*, ed. Harold W. Attridge and Margot Elsbeth Fassler (Leiden: Brill, 2004), 101–12.

136. Martyrs were generally imprisoned before arraignment or execution and had time to consider their responses and discuss their deaths with their coconfessors. The diary of Perpetua in the *Pass. Perp.* is evidence of such. Additionally, we would expect that preparation for martyrdom formed part of the early Christian catechesis, such as it was. Evidence of this preparation is found in the wealth of homiletical material concerning martyrdom (e.g., Origen, *Mart.*). The idea that Christians were prepared for martyrdom has been proposed with respect to the medieval period by Brad S. Gregory. See Brad S. Gregory, *Salvation at Stake: Christian Martyrdom in Early Modern Europe* (Cambridge, Mass.: Harvard University Press, 1999).

137. Eusebius, *Hist. eccl.* 6.5.6: "τῶν δὲ κατὰ θεὸν ἀδελφῶν ὡς αὐτὸν ἀφικνουμένων, καὶ τὴν αἰτίαν τῆς ἀθρόας καὶ παραδόξου ταύτης ὁρμῆς πυνθανομένων, λέγεται εἰπεῖν ὡς ἄρα Ποταμίαινα τρισὶν ὕστερον ἡμέραις τοῦ μαρτυρίου νύκτωρ ἐπιστᾶσα στέφανον αὐτοῦ τῇ κεφαλῇ περιθεῖσα εἴη φαίη τε παρακεκληκέναι χάριν αὐτοῦ τὸν κύριον καὶ τῆς ἀξιώσεως τετυχηκέναι, οὐκ εἰς μακρόν τε αὐτὸν παραλήψεσθαι."

138. Cf. *Pass. Perp.*, *Mart. Mar.*, *Mart. Mont.*, *Mart. Palestine.*

139. We might also note the reference to the conversion of Paul, which may resonate beneath the surface of the text here. Like the soldier-converts, Paul had

participated in the stoning of Stephen (Acts 7:58) and had converted after a vision (Acts 9). The similarities end here. Paul still seeks to "persecute" the Christians after the death of Stephen (Acts 9:1), whereas Basilides seems predisposed to favor the martyrs even at their death.

140. The significance of Potamiaena's intercession will be discussed at greater length in the section "Intercession" in chapter 4.

141. Robert Horton Gundry, *Mark: A Commentary on His Apology for the Cross* (Grand Rapids, Mich.: Eerdmans, 1993), 975.

142. J. Pobee is one of the few New Testament scholars to attempt to use the evidence of the martyrs in an analysis of the centurion's statement. Pobee uses the martyrs to support his conclusion that the centurion's statement is an admission of guilt and guarantee of Christian status. He has the evidence in hand but fails to grasp the one central point: that the martyrdoms are not just records of incidents "similar to" the centurion's acclamation, they are *modeled upon* it. See J. S. Pobee, "The Cry of the Centurion: A Cry of Defeat," in *The Trial of Jesus: Cambridge Studies in Honour of C. F. D. Moule,* ed. Ernst Bammel, Studies in Biblical Theology 13 (Naperville, Ill.: Alec R. Allenson, 1970), 99–101.

143. E.g., *Mart. Crisp.,* 4.3. A supplemental ending providing the date of the martyrdom is rejected by Cavalieri.

144. For a full discussion of the afterlife of the martyr, see chapter 4.

145. *Mart. Fruct.* 5.1–2. Musurillo's translation of this passage is markedly different from the Latin text he provides. Jan den Boeft and Jan Bremmer are correct to herald a return to Pio Franchi de' Cavlieri's text: "apertumque caelum Babylon et Migdonius fraters nostri" (providing one reads apertum caelum as an accusative or nominative absolute). See Jan den Boeft and Jan Bremmer, "Notiunculae Martyrologicae," *Vigiliae Christianae* 35 (1981): 51.

146. Like the Markan passion narrative, the accounts end with a description of the collection of the body and its burial (Mark 16:1–8; *Ac. Felix* 30; *Ac. Euplus* 3.3) although with the glaring difference that the relics of the martyr remain in their tombs administering religious power.

147. *Ac. Just.* C; *Ac. Apol.* (Armenian).

148. *Mart. Fruct.* 5–7.

149. Eusebius's edition of the *Mart. Pot.*

CHAPTER 3

1. G. E. M. De Ste. Croix, "Why Were the Early Christians Persecuted?" in *Christian Persecution, Martyrdom, and Orthodoxy,* ed. G. E. M. De Ste. Croix, Michael Whitby, and Joseph Street (Oxford: Oxford University Press, 2006), 105–52.

2. Donald W. Riddle, *Martyrs: A Study in Social Control* (Chicago: University of Chicago Press, 1931). For a more positive attempt to enter the mind of the martyr, see Jay Newman, "The Motivation of Martyrs: A Philosophical Perspective," *Thomist* 35 (1971): 581–600.

3. This is not an attempt to explore the social function of the martyr's death in the cult of the saints. While this is a fascinating point of inquiry, I am interested in the

way that the ancient audiences conceived of the martyr's death as a reading of the death of Jesus and as part of a larger plan for redemption.

4. See Anselm, *Why God Became Man*, trans. Joseph M. Colleran (Albany, N.Y.: Magi Books, 1969); Peter Abelard, et al., *Petri Abaelardi Opera Theologica*, Corpus Christianorum, Continuatio Mediaevalis (Turnhout: Typographi Brepols, 1969); Jürgen Moltmann, *The Crucified God: The Cross of Christ as the Foundation and Criticism of Christian Theology*, SCM Classics (London: SCM Press, 2001).

5. There are, of course, exceptions to this rule. Delores Williams argues forcefully against models of the atonement that focus upon the cross as the place of salvation. See Delores S. Williams, *Sisters in the Wilderness: The Challenge of Womanist God-Talk* (Maryknoll, N.Y.: Orbis, 1995), 166.

6. Young's argument that a martyr's death could in fact expiate for sin may not, as we will see, hold up to scrutiny, but her observation that the deaths of martyrs offers a window into early understandings of the death of Christ could not be more apt. Frances M. Young, *Sacrifice and the Death of Christ* (London: SPCK, 1975), 56.

7. Cordoning one theory off from another enables us to weigh the relative importance of each view more easily, but it has the effect of eradicating the nuanced ways that this imagery was interwoven.

8. Hebrews 9–10. To be sure, the author of Hebrews holds the one-and-for-all nature of the sacrifice of Christ in a delicate balance with his or her calls for imitation of the faithfulness of Christ in the lives of the audience. Hebrews nicely cordons off the work of salvation so that martyrs serve as imitators and moral exemplars, not as sacrifices. Hebrews' neat division of labor does not work for the *acta*, where the death of the martyr takes on cosmic and mythic significance.

9. See Frances M. Young, *The Use of Sacrificial Ideas in Greek Christian Writers from the New Testament to John Chrysostom*, Patristic Monograph Series 5 (Cambridge, Mass.: Philadelphia Patristic Foundation, 1979); Robert J. Daly, *Christian Sacrifice: The Judaeo-Christian Background before Origen* (Washington, D.C.: Catholic University of America Press, 1978). Cf. also the nuanced statement of Elizabeth Castelli that even though Christians saw sacrifice as something terminated by the death of Christ, they "simultaneously appropriated the language of sacrifice to describe their experience of persecution at the hands of the Romans, seeing their own deaths as parallel imitations of the death of Jesus" (*Martyrdom and Memory*, 51).

10. For every theorist on ancient sacrifice there is a theory. Most twentieth-century scholars would agree that the killing of an animal or human being is the foundation of sacrificial ritual. For most theories the killing of the victim is a vicarious action. See René Girard, *La violence et le sacré* (Paris: B. Grasset, 1972). Cf. the anthropological theory of Walter Burkert, which states that sacrificial killing in the classical world is the precondition for the preservation of society. Walter Burkert, *Homo Necans: Interpretationen Altgriechischer Opferriten und Mythen*, Religionsgeschichtliche Versuche und Vorarbeiten, Bd. 32 (Berlin: Walter de Gruyter, 1972). The same basic principle was applied to biblical texts in Hartmut Gese, "Die Sühne," in *Zur Biblischen Theologie: Altestamentliche Vorträge*, ed. Hartmut Gese (Tübingen: Mohr Siebeck, 1983), 85–106. Gese argues that in the biblical theory of atonement the person offering the sacrifice

identifies him- or herself with the sacrificial animal by placing his or her hands on it. Sin is thus transferred to the victim, which is vicariously offered in the person's place. He further argues that this is the only way to bring about the contact of the human and divine world. For a critique of Gese, see Christian A. Eberhart, "A Neglected Feature of Sacrifice in the Hebrew Bible: Remarks on the Burning Rite on the Altar," *Harvard Theological Review* 97 (2004): 485–93. For a more modern take on the notion of "dying for" someone, see Cilliers Breytenbach, *Versöhnung: Eine Studie zur Paulinischen Soteriologie*, Wissenschaftliche Monographien zum Alten und Neuen Testament 60 (Neukirchen-Vluyn: Neukirchener, 1989).

11. Young, *Use of Sacrificial Ideas*, chap. 1.

12. On this concept of "right relations," see Jonathan Klawans, *Impurity and Sin in Ancient Judaism* (Oxford: Oxford University Press, 2000).

13. For a particularly erudite study of the importance of sacrifice in Roman society, see George Heyman, *The Power of Sacrifice: Roman and Christian Discourses in Conflict* (Washington, D.C.: Catholic University of America Press, 2007). See also Nicole Kelley, "Philosophy as Training for Death: Reading the Ancient Christian Martyr Acts as Spiritual Exercises," *Church History* 75 (2006): 743.

14. Communion sacrifice, or *zebach*, involved the worshiper and the deity sharing a communal meal. In a Jewish context this term covers all the various rituals in which individuals and priests consumed part of a food offering to God. Participants in the ritual had to be in a state of ritual purity. Yahweh was invited to the meal and presumably either consumed a portion of the offering or savored its smell. The idea that God consumed food or was dependent on humans to supply nutritional needs is at odds with later biblical traditions that stress the independence and incorporeality of God. It would seem that a primitive tradition in which Yahweh consumed the offering was replaced by the Priestly author with references to God savoring the smell of the offering. Traces of the earlier idea may remain, "fossilized," as it were, in Ezekiel and the Priestly author. See Klawans, *Impurity and Sin in Ancient Judaism*; Jacob Milgrom, *Leviticus 1–16: A New Translation with Introduction and Commentary*, Anchor Bible Commentary 3 (New York: Doubleday, 1991).

15. The supreme example of the gift sacrifice was the whole burnt offering or holocaust. Roland de Vaux describes the holocaust as the primary and principal act of homage to God. See Roland de Vaux, *Les sacrifices de l'Ancien Testament*, Les Cahiers de la Revue Biblique 1 (Paris: Gabalda, 1964), 38. Temple priests would offer daily burnt offerings on behalf of the nation as a means of continual praise to God (Num 28:3–4). In early Israelite religion, the practice appears to have been used to propitiate the wrath of Yahweh in times of crisis or disaster. An example of this is seen in Genesis 8:21; after the waters of the Flood subside, Noah constructs an altar and offers sacrifice to God. Yahweh smells the odor of the sacrifice and promises never again to curse the earth. While the initial intent of the *holocaust* may have been laudatory or propitiatory, it seems likely that with the passage of time and increasing concern with cleansing of sin, the *olah* came to adopt an expiatory function. The term *holocaust* is used in the Septuagint to describe two ceremonies—the *olah* and the *kalil* (Lev 1). These terms refer to burnt offerings where the smoke of the sacrifice ascends to heaven when the

victim is burned. A similar practice took place in Greek religion. In Greek religion, however, the holocaust was an avertive sacrifice to the gods of the underworld (Lev 1:4 and 16:24).

16. The aim of the expiatory sacrifice was to remove ritual impurities and refers to both the sin-offering (*chattat*) and the guilt-offering (*asham*). The ritual requires that only specified parts of the victim were to be offered to God, but that the one in need of purification could not partake of the flesh of the sacrifice. As a result, the animal either was consumed by priests or—if the sacrifice was performed on behalf of the priest— was burned or discarded. In the expiatory sacrifice, blood ritual features more prominently than elsewhere, perhaps suggesting that blood was the most efficacious decontaminant available. Whereas the *olah* was directed toward God and was thus propitiatory, the *chattat* and *asham* were expiatory rituals that were intended to wipe away sin and would place the participant in right relation with God (See Philo, *De victimis* 4).

17. Lev 16; 23:16–32; 25:9.

18. In turning to Greek examples, Young traces out the same basic structure of communion and gift-sacrifice but argues that their underlying logic differed from biblical descriptions of sacrifice. Under the rubric of "gift-offering" she places the practice of votive offering. A votive-offering was the fulfillment of a vow to bequeath a gift to the deity providing that the deity came to one's immediate assistance. These gifts included statuettes, money, jewelry, and clothing in exchange for anything from deliverance from illness to success in battle. W. H. D. Rouse, *Greek Votive Offerings: An Essay in the History of Greek Religion* (Hildesheim: G. Olms, 1976). Like the Jews, the Greeks also offered burnt offerings to the gods. Rather than acting as sacrifices of thanksgiving, however, these appeared to serve an apotropaic or avertive function. Under the designation "communion-sacrifice" are placed communion sacrifices in which participants joined in a meal with the gods.

19. So, van Henten, *The Maccabean Martyrs as Saviours of the Jewish People*, 153.

20. John Downing argues that the historical Jesus himself saw his death as an expiatory sacrifice. Downing argues that Jesus drew upon commonplace contemporary Jewish notions about the death of the martyr. See John Downing, "Jesus and Martyrdom," *Journal of Theological Studies*, n.s., 14 (1963): 279–93.

21. 1 Cor 15:3; Rom 5:8–9; 8:3. Additionally, there is language of "dying for" something; see Gal 2:20; 2 Cor 5:14–15; Rom 8:32. See Breytenbach, *Versöhnung: Eine Studie zur Paulinischen Soteriologie*.

22. For a discussion of the various ways to interpret the term, see Heyman, *The Power of Sacrifice*, 120–22.

23. As Brown notes, the Paschal lamb was not in fact sacrificed; it is likely that the sacrifice of the lambs retained a certain sacrificial component. Raymond Edward Brown, *The Gospel According to John*, Anchor Bible Commentary 29B (Garden City, N.Y.: Doubleday, 1966), 1.63; Daly, *Christian Sacrifice*, 294.

24. We cannot be sure that the 144,000 are martyrs. Adela Collins concludes that they are just Christians in heaven. Adela Yarbro Collins, *Crisis and Catharsis: The Power of the Apocalypse* (Philadelphia: Westminster Press, 1984). The dominant interpretation

in the early church was that these were martyrs; see, for example, Augustine's Sermon on the Massa Candida of Utica (*Serm. Dom.* 306.2).

25. Cf. Num 18:12; Deut 18:4; 26:25; Exod 23:19; 34:26.

26. Cf. also Ign., *Trall.* 8.1, and Ign, *Smyrn.* 1.1. The idea of redemption through blood also appears in Justin Martyr, *1 Apol.* 32, and Clement of Alexandria *Paed.* 2.42, 49, to name but a few examples.

27. Frances M. Young, *Biblical Exegesis and the Formation of Christian Culture* (Cambridge: Cambridge University Press, 1997), 166.

28. "Τῷ δὲ θεῷ χάρις τῷ πάντοτε θριαμβεύοντι ἡμᾶς ἐν τῷ Χριστῷ καὶ τὴν ὀσμὴν τῆς γνώσεως αὐτοῦ φανεροῦντι δι' ἡμῶν ἐν παντὶ τόπῳ· ὅτι Χριστοῦ εὐωδία ἐσμὲν τῷ θεῷ ἐν τοῖς σῳζομένοις καὶ ἐν τοῖς ἀπολλυμένοις, οἷς μὲν ὀσμὴ ἐκ θανάτου εἰς θάνατον, οἷς δὲ ὀσμὴ ἐκ ζωῆς εἰς ζωήν. καὶ πρὸς ταῦτα τίς ἱκανός"

29. The processional aspect of this passage has been discerned in Harold W. Attridge, "Making Scents of Paul," in *Early Christianity and Classical Culture: Essays in Honor of Abraham Malherbe*, ed. John Fitzgerald (Leiden: Brill, 2003), 71–88.

30. Cf. 2 Tim 4:6, where pseudo-Paul describes his suffering and death using the libation image. The truly Pauline letter is relatively modest; the libation is upon the sacrifice of faith of the Philippian community.

31. See, for example, *2 Clem.* 1.3, 5; 9.7; 15.2, which describe praise, repayments, and fruits owed to God. These may be allusions to the fruits and debt of sacrifice owed to God but delivered, in Clement's letter, in the form of praise.

32. Once again, we should be wary of cordoning off different forms of sacrifice from one another (this is especially true in the case of Eucharistic practices, which varied widely from place to place). The purpose of doing so here is to demonstrate the different ways that sacrifice functions rhetorically.

33. 1 Cor 10.

34. Justin Martyr, *1 Apol.* 65–66; Justin Martyr, *Dial.* 117–118; Hippolytus, *Trad. ap.* 14. 19–20; Irenaeus, *Haer.* 9.17.5; Clement of Alexandria, *Paed.* 2.4.43–44; Origen, *Cels.* 8.33–34.

35. This interpretation seems confined to the institution narratives in the gospel accounts. See Mark 14: 24 and Matt 26:28. We should note that Origen does not include the Eucharist among his list of sacrifices for sin (*Hom Lev.* 2.4).

36. Ign., *Eph.* 13.

37. See the much later Cyril of Jerusalem, *Catechetical Lectures*, 5.8–10.

38. Robin Darling Young, *In Procession before the World: Martyrdom as Public Liturgy in Early Christianity* (Milwaukee, Wis.: Marquette University Press, 2001), 2.

39. For a discussion of the Roman imperial cult, see S. R. F. Price, *Rituals and Power: The Roman Imperial Cult in Asia Minor* (Cambridge: Cambridge University Press, 1984).

40. R. L. Gordon, "The Veil of Power: Emperors, Sacrificers, Benefactors," in *Pagan Priests*, ed. Mary Beard and John North (Ithaca, N.Y.: Cornell University Press, 1993) 201–31.

41. Heyman, *The Power of Sacrifice*, 203–17.

42. Heyman's decision to cordon off New Testament texts from other early church writings (Ignatius, et al) is, to my mind, ill-justified.

43. Heyman, *The Power of Sacrifice*, 95–159, 203–18.

44. See Robert J. Daly, *The Origins of the Christian Doctrine of Sacrifice* (Philadelphia: Fortress Press, 1987), 102–4.

45. See Young, *Use of Sacrificial Ideas*, 107–11, 129–34, 223–38.

46. Ign., *Rom.* 2.2; cf. Phil 2:17.

47. Ign., *Rom.* 4.2; Ign., *Eph.* 21.1; Ign., *Smyrn.* 10.2; Ign., *Pol.* 2.3; 6.1.

48. I prefer to date the account to the middle of the third century. See the appendix for details.

49. *Mart. Pol.* 14.1–3: "Οἱ δὲ οὐ καθήλωσαν μέν, προσέδησαν δὲ αὐτόν. ὁ δὲ ὀπίσω τὰς χεῖρας ποιήσας καὶ προσδεθεὶς ὥσπερ κριὸς ἐπίσημος ἐκ μεγάλου ποιμνίου εἰς προσφοράν, ὁλοκαύτωμα δεκτὸν τῷ θεῷ ἡτοιμασμένον, . . . καθὼς προητοίμασας καὶ προεφανέρωσας καὶ ἐπλήρωσας ὁ ἀψευδὴς καὶ ἀληθινὸς θεός διὰ τοῦτο καὶ περὶ πάντων σὲ αἰνῶ, σὲ εὐλογῶ, σὲ δοξάζω διὰ τοῦ αἰωνίου καὶ ἐπουρανίου ἀρχιερέως Ἰησοῦ Χριστοῦ."

50. For a discussion of the allusion to *akedah* tradition and the intersection between this and *imitatio*, see the section "Narrative Mirroring of the Passion Narrative" in chapter 2.

51. Although there is by no means agreement on the matter, a number of scholars have suggested that Polycarp's prayer betrays a familiarity with tripartite anaphoric prayer, most probably that of *The Apostolic Tradition*. For a discussion of the prayer in *Mart. Pol.*, see the excellent excursus in Buschmann, *Martyrium des Polykarp*, 241–57; Enrico Mazza and Ronald E. Lane, *The Origins of Eucharistic Prayer* (Collegeville, Minn.: Liturgical Press, 1995), 154–55.

52. *Mart. Conon* 6.7.

53. Gese, "Die Sühne," 85–106. Many scholars have followed Gese, yet there are some notable exceptions; see Gary A. Anderson, *Sacrifices and Offerings in Ancient Israel: Studies in Their Social and Political Importance*, Harvard Semitic Monographs 41 (Atlanta, Ga.: Scholars Press, 1987). On the priority of the *olah*, see James W. Watts, "'Olah: The Rhetoric of Burnt Offerings," *Vetus Testamentum* 61 (2006): 125–37.

54. Eberhart, "A Neglected Feature of Sacrifice in the Hebrew Bible," 485–93. Eberhart observes that the burning ritual dominates the landscape of Israelite sacrificial practice as a vital part of all Israelite offerings (*corban*), including the much neglected grain offering (*minchah*).

55. Ibid., 491.

56. Although it is not an expiatory sacrifice, the opening of *Mart. Pol.* indicates that Polycarp's death is effective in the sense that it puts an end to the persecution.

57. The argument of Frances Young, then, that the martyr's death could atone for sin does not stand up to scrutiny. Within her own typology, the death of Polycarp is a burnt offering. Young, *Sacrifice and the Death of Christ*, 56. Elsewhere, she acknowledges that "the sacrifice [in *Mart. Pol.*] is nowhere claimed to have expiatory significance," so we have to wonder on what she bases her numerous statements to the contrary. See Young, *Use of Sacrificial Ideas*, 130.

58. *Lyons* 1.38–39.

59. On a separate occasion in the account, the sweet smell of the martyrs utilizes the language of 2 Cor 2:15. See 1.34–35. Here, in 1.39, however it is associated with the beastly rage of the mob.

60. *Mart. Dasius* 5.2:" Ἐπειδὴ ἐπὶ τὸ τοιοῦτον μυσαρὸν ἀναγκάζετέ με, κρεῖττόν μοί ἐστιν οἰκείᾳ προαιρέσει τῷ δεσπότῃ Χριστῷ θυσία γενέσθαι ἢ τῷ Κρόνῳ ὑμῶν τῷ εἰδώλῳ ἐπιθῦσαι ἐμαυτόν."

61. See, for example, *Ac. Just.* Recension B 2.

62. These examples fit well into Heyman's analysis of the rhetorical function of ideologies of sacrifice. He does not, unfortunately, engage them.

63. *Ac. Euplus* 2.6: "Euplius answered, 'I sacrifice myself now to Jesus Christ my God'" (Euplius dixit: Sacrifico modo Christo Deo me ipsum); The Latin version includes a different spelling of Euplus's name. As with Dasius, the sacrificial language serves a rhetorical purpose, being placed in antithesis with a command to sacrifice to the emperor.

64. *Ac. Felix* 30: "I bend my neck as a sacrifice for you, who abide for ever" (tibi ceruicem meam ad uictiam flecto, qui permanes in aeternum);. We should note that the appendix to this account removes this phrase. See Theodoricus Ruinart, *Acta primorum martyrum sincera et selecta* (Ratisbonae: G. Josephi Manz, 1859), 390–91.

65. *Mart. Arcadius* 2.3: "Arcadius, surveying his scattered limbs all around him said, 'Happy members, now dear to me, as you at last truly belong to God, being all made a sacrifice to him.'"

66. Pace W. H. C. Frend, *Martyrdom and Persecution in the Early Church* (Oxford: Blackwell, 1965), chap. 1. This is not to say that the Maccabean literature was not influential on Christians, merely that it was not influential in this respect. The notion that Polycarp's death "puts an end" to the persecution would appear to recall the function of the deaths of the Maccabees, as does the idea that the martyrs of *Lyons* fill up the number of the martyrs although, in the case of the latter the idea of filling up the number of the martyrs seems closer to Revelation 6:11.

67. Despite the dearth of sacrificial language, we might wish to argue that sacrificial logic underlies the *acta martyrum*, particularly with respect to the way in which martyrdom could remove sin. A number of scholars have pointed to the ever-present belief among Christians that suffering for Christ counteracted and washed away the effects of sin. The *Shepherd of Hermas* illustrates the point that those who suffer for the faith, presumably by dying, have their sins forgiven. This belief is frequently linked to the ideas surrounding expiatory or purificatory sacrifice. Yet the language used here is not sacrificial. Nowhere in the *Shepherd of Hermas* is sacrificial language used to describe this kind of death. The same observation can be made of the martyr acts; sacrificial language is never used to describe the removal of the martyrs' sins. In those few instances that sacrificial language is used, expiation, propitiation, and purification are noticeably absent. For the use of sacrificial language in the *acta* to describe worship, see *Mart. Iren.* 4.2; the Greek version of *Ac. Phileas* 39–43; *Pass. Maxima* 5. Arguably, the forgiveness of sins in the *Shepherd of Hermas* may be tied to the notion of suffering and death as punishment, but there is nothing in the text to

support this interpretation. Furthermore, the connection between suffering and sinfulness is absent from the acts of the martyrs and Christian ideologies of martyrdom in general. Martyrdom is not a punishment for the sinful; it is a blessing for the pious. Moreover, for members of the early churches, sacrifice was not the only way to remove sin. In fact, the primary means of removing sin was through baptism. Given that martyrdom is frequently described as a form of baptism, it is premature to jump to the conclusion that just because martyrdom cleanses from sin it is a type of sacrifice. Tertullian, *Bapt.* 16.2; Origen, *Comm. Matt.* 16.6; Cyril of Jerusalem, *On the Words Crucified and Buried*, Lecture 13.21.

68. The conviction that martyrdom is a form of expiatory sacrifice is pervasive and ill justified. The linch pin in the whole enterprise is the Ignatian-Polycarp tradition. Scholarly constructions fixate upon this tradition as the prime example and originating source for this idea. The unanimous acceptance of this model is indicative of the disproportionate place *Mart. Pol.* occupies in the minds of modern scholars. An example of this is Frances Young, who in her chapter on the deaths of the martyrs exclusively uses the *Mart. Pol.* and Ignatian traditions. She refers to only one other example, Blandina from *Lyons*, and in this case to refer to the sufferings of the martyrs, not their sacrificial deaths. She does not even refer to *Mart. Conon* or *Mart. Dasius* to support her argument. In the writings of other authors, such as George Heyman and Robin Darling Young, the martyr's death as sacrifice is assumed more than it is proved. Amid his brilliant observations on the way in which martyrdom accounts construct their protagonists as male, counterimperial, exemplary heroes, Heyman can cite only one example—*Mart. Pol.*—in which sacrificial language is used (Heyman, *The Power of Sacrifice*, 193–94).

69. Gustaf Aulén, *Christus Victor: An Historical Study of the Three Main Types of the Idea of Atonement*, trans. A. G. Hebert (New York: Macmillan, 1969).

70. See the opening sentence in Aulén's preface to the paperback edition: "The central idea of *Christus Victor* is the view of God and the Kingdom of God as fighting against evil powers ravaging in mankind." Ibid. ix.

71. We should note that Aulén's theory, like that of Anselm and Abelard before him, is an exercise in constructive theology. It is an attempt to make sense of biblical and ecclesiastical language about the work and person of Christ. This much is evident in the flow of his work, which runs from Irenaeus to Augustine before it returns to the New Testament texts that preceded them. Chapter 2 concerns Irenaeus, chapter 3 deals with the fathers in the East and West, and chapter 4 discusses the New Testament.

72. The likely source for the militarized imagery of battle with Satan is likely to be the product of an apocalyptic mind-set fueled by the language of Revelation, especially Rev 12:10–12. For a discussion of the origins of the combat myth, see Adela Yarbro Collins, *The Combat Myth in the Book of Revelation*, Harvard Dissertations in Religion 9 (Missoula, Mont.: Scholars Press, 1976), 79–83. For a discussion of the importance of cosmic battle in the acts of the martyrs, see Paul Middleton, *Radical Martyrdom and Cosmic Conflict in Early Christianity*, Library of New Testament Studies 307 (London: T & T Clark, 2006).

73. Lieu, *Neither Jew nor Greek?* 220, and the excellent book-length treatment of cosmic battle in Middleton, *Radical Martyrdom and Cosmic Conflct in Early Christianity*.

74. See, for example, Heb 2:14 and Revelation 12.

75. *Ac. Phileas* should not be confused with the Greek *Letter of Phileas*.

76. *Ac. Phileas*, Latin 9.1.

77. *Ac. Apol.* 47.

78. For a discussion of the textual history of the *Ac. Apol.*, see the appendix.

79. The division and categorization of the manuscripts of the *Ac. Just.* into three recensions were achieved by Pio Franchi de' Cavalieri, "Gli Atti di S. Giustino," *Studi e Testi* 8 (1902): 33–36; F. C. Burkitt, "The Oldest Manuscript of St. Justin's Martyrdom," *Journal of Theological Studies* 11 (1909): 61–66; and Giuseppi Lazzati, "Gli Atti di S. Giustini Martire," *Aevum* 27 (1953): 473–97. See also the appendix and the discussion in Gary A. Bisbee, *Pre-Decian Acts of the Martyrs and Commentarii*, ed. Margaret R. Miles and Bernadette J. Brooten, Harvard Dissertations in Religion 22 (Philadelphia: Fortress Press, 1988).

80. *Ac. Just.*, Recension C: 1.1–2: " Ἀντωνίνου τοῦ δυσσεβοῦς τῆς Ῥωμαϊκῆς ἀρχῆς τὰ σκῆπτρα διέποντος Ῥούστικος ὁ ἔχιστος ἔπαρχος τῆς Ῥώμης ἐτύγχανε, δεινὸς ἀνὴρ καὶ λοιμὸς καὶ πάσης μεστὸς ἀσεβείας. τούτῳ γοῦν ἐπὶ βήματός ποτε προκαθίσαντι στῖφος ἁγίων προσάγονται δέσμιοι, ἑπτὰ τὸν ἀριθμόν. τοῦτο γὰρ περισπούδαστον ἦν τοῖς ὑπηρέταις τοῦ σατανᾶ τὸ συλλαμβάνεσθαι τούτους πικραῖς τε βασάνοις δίδοσθαι καὶ οὕτω καθυπάγεσθαι τῷ διὰ ξίφους θανάτῳ."

81. Ibid., 4.4: "And what person of sound mind . . . would choose to turn from piety to impiety, from light to darkness, and from the living God to soul-destroying demons?"

82. In his own writings, Justin himself speaks of the Greek gods as demons, so the incorporation of this idea may be part of the redactor's program to make the Justin of the *acta* appear more like the Justin of the *Apologia*.

83. E.g., *Mart. Agape* 2.4.

84. The strong link between apocalypticism and persecution in the scholarly imagination has long been established. In an early and very pejorative evaluation of apocalypticism, Donald W. Riddle uses psychology of religion to account for its appearance in situations of persecution; Donald W. Riddle, "The Physical Basis of Apocalypticism," *Journal of Religion* (1924): 174–91. Less daming explanations are offered by more modern scholars who nonetheless explain that apocalyptic literature, at least, tends to be produced by communities experiencing oppression. See the introduction to John Joseph Collins, Bernard McGinn, and Stephen J. Stein, eds., *The Encyclopedia of Apocalypticism* (New York: Continuum, 1999). While apocalyptic literature and the apocalyptic mind-set no doubt arise in the majority of cases from experiences of real or perceived persecution, we should nonetheless entertain the possibility that some individuals merely enjoyed the flourish of its literary style.

85. Some would go so far as to state that Irenaeus is the putative author of the letter. See Judith Perkins, *The Suffering Self: Pain and Narrative Representation in the Early Christian Era* (New York: Routledge, 1995), 121.

86. An example of this general involvement is the statement that the "Gaolers [were] aroused and filled with the Devil" (*Lyons* 1.27).

87. Ibid., 23: "τὸ δὲ σωμάτιον μάρτυς ἦν τῶν συμβεβηκότων, ὅλον τραῦμα καὶ μώλωψ καὶ συνεσπασμένον καὶ ἀποβεβληκὸς τὴν ἀνθρώπειον ἔξωθεν μορφήν, ἐν ᾧ πάσχων Χριστὸς μεγάλας ἐπετέλει δόξας, καταργῶν τὸν ἀντικείμενον καὶ εἰς τὴν τῶν λοιπῶν ὑποτύπωσιν ὑποδεικνύων ὅτι μηδὲν φοβερὸν ὅπου πατρὸς ἀγάπη μηδὲ ἀλγεινὸν ὅπου Χριστοῦ δόξα."

88. The same term is used in 1 Tim. 1:16 and 2 Tim. 1:13. Here pseudo-Paul uses the term of the person and words of the apostle, which are a pattern for those seeking eternal life. In this instance, however, the virtues that serves as the ὑποτύπωσις are patience, faith, and love. The idea of fearlessness in the love of the Father is more reminiscent of the argument of John 16:33, where courage and Christ's triumph are similarly linked, particularly in light of the frequent allusions to John throughout the *Lyons*. See chapter 1, above.

89. See discussion of the moral exemplar model, below. Martyrs inspiring other Christians is a theme both in martyrdoms more generally and in *Lyons*. Later in the account, the deaths of the martyrs are described as strengthening the resolve of confessors: "When the others saw this, their resistance was stiffened, and those who were arrested straightaway confessed the faith without one thought for the Devil's arguments" (*Lyons* 1.35).

90. "There was a woman named Biblis among those who had denied Christ, and the Devil thought that he had already devoured her; hoping further to convict her as a slanderer, he brought her to the rack and tried to force her to say impious things about us, thinking she was a coward and easily broken" (*Lyons* 1.25).

91. *Lyons* 1.42: "εἰς ἄλλον ἀγῶνα τηρουμένη ἵνα διὰ πλειόνων γυμνασμάτων νικήσασα τῷ μὲν σκολιῷ ὄφει ἀπαραίτητον ποιήσῃ τὴν καταδίκην, προτρέψηται δὲ τοὺς ἀδελφοὺς ἡ μικρὰ καὶ ἀσθενὴς καὶ εὐκαταφρόνητος, μέγαν καὶ ἀκαταγώνιστον ἀθλητὴν Χριστὸν ἐνδεδυμένη, διὰ πολλῶν κλήρων ἐκβιάσασα τὸν ἀντικείμενον καὶ δι' ἀγῶνος τὸν τῆς ἀφθαρσίας στεψαμένη στέφανον."

92. For a discussion of the origins of this motif, see Collins, *Combat Myth in the Book of Revelation*, 76–79; Richard J. Clifford, "The Roots of Apocalypticism in Near Eastern Myth," in *The Encyclopedia of Apocalypticism*, ed. John J. Collins (London: Continuum, 1998), 1.3–38.

93. *Lyons* 2.6: "καὶ αὖθίς φασι μεθ' ἕτερα· οὗτος γὰρ καὶ μέγιστος αὐτοῖς πρὸς αὐτὸν ὁ πόλεμος ἐγένετο διὰ τὸ γνήσιον τῆς ἀγάπης ἵνα ἀποπνιχθεὶς ὁ θὴρ οὓς πρότερον ᾤετο καταπεπωκέναι ζῶντας ἐξεμέσῃ."

94. Aulén, *Christus Victor*, 52.

95. Gregory of Nyssa, *Great Catechism* 24–26.

96. Aulén, *Christus Victor*, 51–53. Aulén also notes the idea of deceiving Satan in Augustine. See page 53, especially.

97. Gregory of Nyssa, *Great Catechism*, 24 (*NPNF* 5.494).

98. John of Damascus, *An Exposition of the Orthodox Faith*, 3.2 (*NPNF* 9.72).

99. Gregory of Nyssa, *Great Catechism*, 23 (*NPNF* 5.494).

100. See the work of J. A. Thompson, "The Alleged Persecution of the Christians at Lyons in 177," *American Journal of Theology* 16 (1912): 359–84, in which he suggests that the account is a pious third-century forgery. He was viciously attacked by Harnack

and Allard for this assertion and responded in J. A. Thompson, "The Alleged Persecution of the Christians at Lyons in 177: A Reply to Certain Criticisms," *American Journal of Theology* 17 (1913): 249–58.

101. Even Thompson's theory, rejected as it is, postulated a third-century composition at the latest: "The account of Eusebius is of third-century, not second century, origin" Thompson, "The Alleged Persecution of the Christians at Lyons in 177," 360. A number of other factors suggest that Gregory of Nyssa was influenced by the letter. Foremost is Gregory's own affinity for the cult of the martyrs; he delivered impassioned homilies in honor of Saint Stephen, the Forty Martyrs, and Theodore the Martyr and exhorted his fellow bishops to celebrate local martyrs in Cappadocia. See James C. Skedros, "The Cappadocian Fathers on the Veneration of Martyrs," in *Studia Patristica: Papers Presented at the Thirteenth International Conference on Patristic Studies held in Oxford 1999*, ed. M. F. Wiles and E. J. Yarnold (Leuven: Peters, 2001), 294–300.

102. For a discussion of the fish of Jonah in funerary art, see Stephen J. Davis, "Jonah in Early Christian Art: Allegorical Exegesis and the Roman Funerary Context," *ARS Review* 13 (2000): 72–83.

103. More often than not, theological metaphors and ideas are attributed to the genius of a particular intellectual figure rather than an interpretative tradition.

104. Aulén, *Christus Victor*, 22.

105. The dating of *Mart. Pol.* to the Decian period doubtless raises some eyebrows. I refer the readers to the appendix, where the arguments for a later dating are laid out in full. Even if the readers will disagree with me regarding the dating of the martyrdom account, I hope they will be convinced that it is remarkably different from other second-century *acta*.

106. A largely rhetorical, rather than cosmological, oberservation.

107. *Mart. Pol.* 17: " Ὁ δὲ ἀντίζηλος καὶ Βάσκανος καὶ πονηρός, ὁ ἀντικείμενος τῷ γένει τῶν δικαίων, ἰδὼν τό τε μέγεθος αὐτοῦ τῆς μαρτυρίας καὶ τὴν ἀπ' ἀρχῆς ἀνεπίληπτον πολιτείαν, ἐστεφανωμένον τε τὸν τῆς ἀφθαρσίας στέφανον καὶ βραβεῖον ἀναντίρρητον ἀπενηνεγμένον, ἐπετήδευσεν ὡς μηδὲ τὸ σωμάτιον αὐτοῦ ὑφ' ἡμῶν ληθῆναι, καίπερ πολλῶν ἐπιθυμούντων τοῦτο ποιῆσαι καὶ κοινωνῆσαι τῷ ἁγίῳ αὐτοῦ σαρκίῳ. ὑπέβαλεν γοῦν Νικήτην τὸν τοῦ Ἡρώδου πατέρα, ἀδελφὸν δὲ Ἄλκης, ἐντυχεῖν τῷ ἄρχοντι ὥστε μὴ δοῦναι αὐτοῦ τὸ σῶμα·"

108. This is but one of many places where the narrative of *Mart. Pol.* follows that of the Gospel of John. For others, see the section "Narrative Mirroring of the Passion Narrative" in chapter 2.

109. Cf. *Mart. Marinus*, *Ac. Marcellus*, and *Ac. Julius*, in which the refusal to swear an oath leads to the martyr's unmasking as a Christian.

110. *Mart. Dasius* 3.2–4: " ἐν γὰρ τῇ ἡμέρᾳ τῶν καλανδῶν Ἰαννυαρίων μάταιοι ἄνθρωποι τῷ ἔθει τῶν Ἑλλήνων ἐξακολουθοῦντες Χριστιανοὶ ὀνομαζόμενοι μετὰ παμμεγέθους πομπῆς προέρχονται ἐναλλάττοντες τὴν ἑαυτῶν φύσιν καὶ τὸν τρόπον καὶ τὴν μορφὴν τοῦ διαβόλου ἐνδύονται."

111. Ibid., 4.1: "ταύτην ὁ μακάριος Δάσιος ματαίαν παράδοσιν εἶναι ἐπιγνοὺς κατεπάτησεν τὸν κόσμον σὺν ταῖς ἀπάταις αὐτοῦ καὶ κατέπτυσεν τὸν διάβολον σὺν ταῖς πομπαῖς αὐτοῦ καὶ ὑπέζευξεν ἑαυτὸν τῷ σταυρωθέντι Χριστῷ καὶ κατὰ

τῆς τοῦ διαβόλου ἀτιμίας νικητὴς προῆλθεν." Emended translation from Herbert Musurillo, *Acts of the Christian Martyrs* (Oxford: Clarendon Press, 1972), 275.

112. Cf. the Latin traditions below.

113. "By it [confession of trinity] I can quickly conquer and overthrow the Devil's madness." *Mart. Dasius* 8.2.

114. *Mart. Agape* 1.1:" Ἐπὶ τῆς παρουσίας καὶ ἐπιφανείας τοῦ δεσπότου καὶ σωτῆρος ἡμῶν Ἰησοῦ Χριστοῦ . . . ἀόρατοι ἐχθροὶ νικῶνται, ἀφανεῖς δαιμόνων ὑποστάσεις πυρὶ παραδίδονται ὑπὸ γυναικῶν καθαρῶν καὶ σεμνῶν, πνεύματος ἁγίου πληρουμένων." (my translation).

115. *Mart. Agape* 2.4: " ἵνα διὰ πυρὸς προσκαίρου τοὺς αὐτῷ πειθομένους νικήσασαι διάβολον καὶ πᾶσαν αὐτοῦ τὴν ὑπ' οὐρανῶν δαιμόνων στρατιάν." (modified translation).

116. All these examples date from the turn of the third century onward.

117. For example, "And so the Devil's servant struck the blessed martyr with a sword and brought his life to an end" (*Ac. Julius* 4.5); "magistrates of Cirta, priests of the Devil" (*Mart. Mar.* 5.1).

118. *Ac. Julius* 2.6.

119. "Καὶ ἐγένετο πόλεμος ἐν τῷ οὐρανῷ, ὁ Μιχαὴλ καὶ οἱ ἄγγελοι αὐτοῦ τοῦ πολεμῆσαι μετὰ τοῦ δράκοντος. καὶ ὁ δράκων ἐπολέμησεν καὶ οἱ ἄγγελοι αὐτοῦ, καὶ οὐκ ἴσχυσεν οὐδὲ τόπος εὑρέθη αὐτῶν ἔτι ἐν τῷ οὐρανῷ. καὶ ἐβλήθη ὁ δράκων ὁ μέγας, ὁ ὄφις ὁ ἀρχαῖος, ὁ καλούμενος Διάβολος καὶ ὁ Σατανᾶς, ὁ πλανῶν τὴν οἰκουμένην ὅλην, ἐβλήθη εἰς τὴν γῆν, καὶ οἱ ἄγγελοι αὐτοῦ μετ' αὐτοῦ ἐβλήθησαν. καὶ ἤκουσα φωνὴν μεγάλην ἐν τῷ οὐρανῷ λέγουσαν, Ἄρτι ἐγένετο ἡ σωτηρία καὶ ἡ δύναμις καὶ ἡ βασιλεία τοῦ θεοῦ ἡμῶν καὶ ἡ ἐξουσία τοῦ Χριστοῦ αὐτοῦ, ὅτι ἐβλήθη ὁ κατήγωρ τῶν ἀδελφῶν ἡμῶν, ὁ κατηγορῶν αὐτοὺς ἐνώπιον τοῦ θεοῦ ἡμῶν ἡμέρας καὶ νυκτός. καὶ αὐτοὶ ἐνίκησαν αὐτὸν διὰ τὸ αἷμα τοῦ ἀρνίου καὶ διὰ τὸν λόγον τῆς μαρτυρίας αὐτῶν καὶ οὐκ ἠγάπησαν τὴν ψυχὴν αὐτῶν ἄχρι θανάτου."

120. *Pass. Perp.* 4.3–7: "et erat sub ipsa scala draco cubans mirae magnitudinis, qui ascendentibus insidias praestabat, et exterrebat ne ascenderent. ascendit autem Saturus prior, qui postea se propter nos ultro tradiderat, (quia ipse nos aedificauerat) et tunc cum adducti sumus, praesens non fuerat: et peruenit in caput scalae, et conuertit se ad me et dixit mihi: «Perpetua, sustineo te. Sed uide ne te mordeat draco ille.» . . . et desub ipsa scala, quasi timens me, lente eiecit caput: et quasi primum gradum calcarem, calcaui illi caput et ascendi."

121. Cf. *Mart. Pion.* 12.3; also Irenaeus, *Haer.* 5.24.4: "The Word of God, who is creator of all things, overcame him [the devil] through man, and branded him as an apostate, and made him subject to man. See, says the Word, I give you power to tread upon serpents and scorpions, and upon all the power of the enemy."

122. See, for example, "From there we returned to the prison, victorious over the Devil whom we laid low, and we were to be saved for another victory" (*Mart. Mont.* 6.4). Translated in Maureen A. Tilley, *Donatist Martyr Stories: The Church in Conflict in North Africa* (Liverpool: Liverpool University Press, 1996), 218.

123. *Pass. Perp.* 10.13–14: "et experrecta sum. et intellexi me non ad bestias, sed contra diabolum esse pugnaturam; sed sciebam mihi esse uictorum."

124. *Mart. Mar.* 2.4–5: "For the madness of a blind and bloodthirsty prefect was hunting out all of God's beloved by means of bands of soldiers with a vicious and savage spirit. . . . the Devil stretched forth his insatiate hand as well against those who, though earlier driven into exile, had become martyrs in spirit."

125. Ibid., 5.4: "How novel, and how cleverly invented by the Devil's poisoned mind and the tricks by which he tries to destroy!"

126. Ibid., 2.2: "the onslaughts of persecution surged like the waves of this world and the fury of the ravening Devil gaped with hungry jaws to weaken the faith of the just"

127. For the martyrs, see 10.3. For Christ, see 5.10. The reference to Christ's triumph before the description of the deaths of the martyrs sets up a frame of reference for the listener who connects the later triumphs of the martyrs with those of Christ.

128. *Mart. Mont.* 4.4–5: "quo enim temptatio grandis est, eo maior est ille qui eam uincit in nobis. et non est pugna, quia est domino protegente uictoria. nam et occidi seruis Dei leue est, et ideo mors nihil est, cuius aculeos comminuens contentionemque deuincens dominus per trophaeum crucis triumphauit."

129. In both the North African tradition and *Lyons*, death and the devil are used interchangeably.

130. Aulén cites Irenaeus, *Haer.* 3.16.9: "per passionem reconcilivat nos Deo" in support of his claim, but we should note the term "cross" is never used in such contexts by Irenaeus; Aulén, *Christus Victor*, 30–31, especially footnote 26.

131. *Mart. Mar.* 13.5: "qui in hoc quoque paterna indulgentia semper operator ut in nos et hoc ipsum, quod in nostro sanguine rependi credimus, conferatur ab ominpotente Deo."

132. λύτρον Mark 10:45; ἀπολύτρωσις Eph 1:7; ἀντίλυτρον 1 Tim 2:6; λύτρωσις Heb 9:12.

133. See, for example, Origen, *Comm. Matt.*, 14.8.

134. See chapter 2, "Martyrdom as *Imitatio* and Fulfillment of Biblical Command."

135. For a full discussion of these, see chapter 1.

136. *Pass. Perp.* 1.1–2: "si uetera fidei exempla, et Dei gratiam testificantia et aedificationem hominis operantia, propterea in litteris sunt digesta, ut lectione eorum, quasi repensitatione rerum, et Deus honoretur et homo confortetur, cur non et noua documenta aeque utrique causae convenientia et digerantur? uel quia et haec uetera futura quandoque sunt et necessaria posteris, si in praesenti suo tempore minori deputantur auctoritati propter praesumptam uenerationem antiquitatis."

137. *Mart. Mont.* 3.4: "And it was not difficult for those of faith to believe that modern marvels could equal those of old, in view of the Lord's promise through the spirit."

138. For a discussion of this phenomenon in North African literature, see Maureen A. Tilley, *The Bible in Christian North Africa: The Donatist World* (Minneapolis, Minn.: Fortress Press, 1997), 40–46.

139. *Mart. Maximian* 18: "Ad uos nunc, fratres, cuncta iam redeunt quae eos ad regna caelestia deduxerunt. Vos exempla ista compellunt, quae illos primo per uos ad has glorias compulerunt. Magistros uos illis confessionum frequentia crebis opinionibus

fecerat et ipsi nunc uobis de martyrio suggerunt. Similiter documenta uestra uos adhortantur quae alios adhortata sunt. Tendunt ad uos e caelo iam brachia opperientes tempus quo uobis occurrant." Jean-Lous Maier, *Le dossier de donatisme* (Berlin: Akademie-Verlag, 1987), 275, translated in Tilley, *Donatist Martyr Stories*, 74–75.

140. Tertullian, *Apol.* 1.

141. See, for example, Lucius in the *Acts of Ptolemaeus and Lucius*, Basilides in the *Martyrdom of Potamiaena and Basilides*, and the prison guard who becomes sympathetic in the *Passion of Perpetua and Felicitas*. For a discussion of this theme and its relation to gospel accounts of the centurion at the cross in Mark 14, see the section "Conversion of the Centurion at the Cross" in chapter 2.

142. *Mart. Mar.* 4.1: "Denique ita proficiscentes illi Marianum et Iacobum exemplo et magisterio suo dispositos reliquerunt ut recentissima gloriae suae uestiga dimitterent secuturis."

143. Given the close literary ties between this text and the *Passion of Perpetua and Felicitas*, we might reasonably suppose that Marian and James modeled their conduct on that of Perpetua and Felicitas.

144. See Mark 10:21 and discussion in chapter 1.

145. *Mart. Mont.* 23.7: o martyrum gloriosa documenta!

146. *Ac. Abit.* 1: "aggredior, inquam, ex actis publicis scribere non tam ingenio praeditus quam ciuico illis amore coniunctus, consulto quidem hoc faciens duplici sciliet modo, ut imitatoribue eorum ad martyrium animos praeparemus et, quos uiuere in perpetuum atque cum domino Christo regnare confidimus." Text Maier, *Le dossier de donatisme*, 60; translated in Tilley, *Donatist Martyr Stories*, 28. This section is absent in Ruinart's edition.

147. *Mart. Pol.* 18.3.

148. *Ac. Phileas* col. VII lines 5–6:

Φιλέας εἶπεν· Ἤι]δει ὅτι ταις τ[. . .]
ὅτ[ι] μαστιγωθ[ήσε
[ται και]ὶ ῥα[πί]ζεται κα[ὶφ . . . . .]
[. . . . κ]αὶ ἐξ ἀκάνθω[ν σ]τέφαν[ον
φορε[ῖ] καὶ [θ]άνατον [π]άσχε[ι],
ὑπό[δ]ειγμα τῆς σω[τηρί]α[ς ἡμῖν]

149. Methodius of Sicilly's description of Agatha: "Agatha, her goodness coincides with her name and her way of life. . . . She teaches them by her example to hasten with her to the true Good, God alone." *Homily on St Agatha* in *Anal. Boll* 68 (1950): 76–78.

150. *Mart. Mar.* 9.4: "In this way the blessed martyrs as they were preparing for their death won many more witnesses for god by the record of their conduct"

151. *Mart. Pol.* 1.2: "περιέμενεν γὰρ ἵνα παραδοθῇ ὡς καὶ ὁ κύριος ἵνα μιμηταὶ καὶ ἡμεῖς αὐτοῦ γενώμεθα μὴ μόνον σκοποῦντες τὸ καθ' ἑαυτούς ἀλλὰ καὶ τὸ κατὰ τοὺς πέλας ἀγάπης γὰρ ἀληθοῦς καὶ βεβαίας ἐστιν μὴ μόνον ἑαυτὸν θέλειν σώζεσθαι ἀλλὰ καὶ πάντας τοὺς ἀδελφούς."

152. The command to love one another is found in Mark 12:33; Matt 19:19; and Luke 10:27.

153. John 15:13: "μείζονα ταύτης ἀγάπην οὐδεὶς ἔχει, ἵνα τις τὴν ψυχὴν αὐτοῦ θῇ ὑπὲρ τῶν φίλων αὐτοῦ."

154. See, for example, *Mart. Mont.* 22.3; *Sermon on the Passion of Donatus and Advocatus* 11.

155. *Mart. Pol.* 2.2: "τὸ γὰρ γενναῖον αὐτῶν καὶ ὑπομονητικὸν καὶ φιλοδέσποτον τίς οὐκ ἂν θαυμάσειεν; . . . . τοὺς δὲ καὶ εἰς τοσοῦτον γενναιότητος ἐλθεῖν, ὥστε μήτε γρύξαι μήτε στενάξαι τινὰ αὐτῶν, ἐπιδεικνυμένους ἅπασιν ἡμῖν, ὅτι ἐκείνῃ τῇ ὥρᾳ βασανιζόμενοι τῆς σαρκὸς ἀπεδήμουν οἱ μάρτυρες τοῦ Χριστοῦ, μᾶλλον δὲ ὅτι παρεστὼς ὁ κύριος ὡμίλει αὐτοῖς."

156. Ibid., 17.3: "τοῦτον μὲν γὰρ υἱὸν ὄντα τοῦ προσκυνοῦμεν, τοὺς δὲ μάρτυρας ὡς μαθητὰς καὶ μιμητὰς τοῦ κυρίου ἀγαπῶμεν ἀξίως ἕνεκα εὐνοίας ἀνυπερβλήτου τῆς εἰς τὸν ἴδιον βασιλέα καὶ διδάσκαλον, ὧν γένοιτο καὶ ἡμᾶς κοινωνούς τε καὶ συμμαθητὰς γενέσθαι."

157. Ibid., 19.1–2: "οὐ μόνον διδάσκαλος γενόμενος ἐπίσημος ἀλλὰ καὶ μάρτυς ἔξοχος, οὗ τὸ μαρτύριον πάντες ἐπιθυμοῦσιν μιμεῖσθαι κατὰ τὸ εὐαγγέλιον Χριστοῦ γενόμενον. διὰ τῆς ὑπομονῆς καταγωνισάμενος τὸν ἄδικον ἄρχοντα καὶ οὕτως τὸν τῆς ἀφθαρσίας στέφανον ἀπολαβών."

158. I am extremely grateful to Meghan Henning for allowing me to read, in advance, her persuasive argument for the relationship between Pauline virtues, Thessalonians, and this martyrdom account. Her paper posits that the personification of the virtues in the martyrs was related to a particular reading of Thessalonians by the community that produced the account. Meghan Henning, "The Intersection of Performance, Power and Pain in the *Martyrdom of Saints Agape, Irene and Chione*" (paper presented at the South Eastern Conference of the Society of Religion, Atlanta, Georgia, March 8, 2008).

159. "This then is what it means to suffer for Christ, to imitate Christ even in his words, and to give the greatest proof of one's faith. What a marvelous example he was of belief!"; *Mart. Mont.* 14.9. Peace is also highlighted in the person of Irene in *Mart. Agape*.

160. *Lyons* 2.3; *Mart. Mont.* 13.6; *Mart. Mar.* 12.8.

161. *Lyons* 2.2.

162. Ibid., 1.23: "τὸ δὲ σωμάτιον μάρτυς ἦν τῶν συμβεβηκότων, ὅλον τραῦμα καὶ μώλωψ καὶ συνεσπασμένον καὶ ἀποβεβληκὸς τὴν ἀνθρώπειον ἔξωθεν μορφήν, ἐν ᾧ πάσχων Χριστὸς μεγάλας ἐπετέλει δόξας, καταργῶν τὸν ἀντικείμενον καὶ εἰς τὴν τῶν λοιπῶν ὑποτύπωσιν ὑποδεικνύων ὅτι μηδὲν φοβερὸν ὅπου πατρὸς ἀγάπη μηδὲ ἀλγεινὸν ὅπου Χριστοῦ δόξα."

163. *Mart. Mar.* 12.8: "qua praedicatione non tantum gentilibus insultabat fides martyris, sed etiam fratribus incentiuum aemulandae uirtutis et quasi classicum praecanebat, ut inter tantas saeculi plagas a iustis Dei tam bonae atque pretiosae mortis raperetur occasio."

164. At the end of his appendix, Abelard promises his readers an extended discussion of redemption in his *Tropology*, a work either lost or never written. See Abelard, et al., *Petri Abaelardi Opera Theologica*, 154–56.

165. For the relevant passages in Abelard, see ii17–18.

166. Delores S. Williams, "Black Women's Surrogacy Experience and the Christian Notion of Redemption," in *Cross Examinations: Reading on the Meaning of the Cross Today*, ed. Marie Trelstad (Minneapolis, Minn.: Fortress Press, 2006), 19–22, 279–89.

167. See, for example, Rita Nakashima Brock and Rebecca Ann Parker, *Proverbs of Ashes: Violence, Redemptive Suffering, and the Search for What Saves Us* (Boston: Beacon Press, 2001).

168. *Mart. Pol.* 2.1 and *Letter of Phileas;* cf. 1 John 4:18.

169. *Lyons* 1.23. See discussion above.

170. *Ac. Just.*, B. 2–4; *Mart. Pol.* 2.2, 4; 3.1; 19.2; *Lyons* 1.4, 6, 7, 16, 20, 27, 36, 39, 45, 51, 54, 56; *Mart. Dasius* 4.4. The theme of endurance is similarly prominent in 4 Maccabees 1:11, 5: 23; 7:9; 9:8, 30; 15:30; 16:8; 17:4, 12, 17, 23.

171. Crispina in *Mart. Crisp.* and Chione in *Mart. Agape.*

172. For the former, see the Donatist martyrdoms, in particular. For the latter, see the topos of bold speech in *Mart. Pol.*, 10–11; *Ac. Just.* B. 5; *Ac. Apol.*, 32.

CHAPTER 4

1. From the beginning of prophetic visions of the heavenly realm, a distinct hierarchy emerges. In the visions of Micaiah (1 Kings 22:19) and Isaiah (Isa 6), God is depicted as enthroned in a heavenly court surrounded by heavenly attendants. The focal point of these visions is the singular enthroned deity attended and encircled by the non-enthroned "living beings." Even in early, simplified depictions of the heavenly court, the hierarchy is clearly articulated. It does not take the close analysis of the ritual theorist to identify the enthroned being as the locus of power and the attendant beings as his or her subordinates. In Second Temple Jewish literature, descriptions of heaven and its inhabitants grew increasingly complex. The singular courtly heaven was enlarged to three or seven heavens, each heaven a discrete realm with concrete purposes. (For a discussion of the origins of the idea of seven heavens and its relationship to the planets, see Adela Yarbro Collins, "The Seven Heavens in Jewish and Christian Apocalypses," in *Death, Ecstasy and Other Worldly Journeys*, ed. John J. Collins and Michael Fishbane (Albany: State University of New York Press, [1995], 59–93) Just as the number of heavens multiplied, so also did the classes and orders of their angelic inhabitants (to fill up all the space, presumably). To the plebeian class of angels was added the exalted angelic mediator, or the archangel. In Daniel there are two exalted angels: Michael, one of the chief princes and protector of Israel (Dan 10:13, 21; 12:1), and Gabriel the *angelus interpres* of the visionary (8:15–26). In addition to the elevation of Michael and Gabriel, we find groups of select angels—usually four or seven—who perform special tasks such as administering divine punishment (Ezekiel 9) or transmitting the prayers of the holy ones (Tob 12:12). *1 En.* 9 lists four archangels—Michael, Sariel/Uriel, Raphael, and Gabriel. The expansion of the ranks of angels was gaining momentum.

Never ones to have too much of a good thing, apocalyptic writers continued to magnify the classes of angels. In *1 En.* 71.7 the *opannim* (the hubs) of the throne-chariot of God have evolved into their own angelic class, and together with the *cherubim and seraphim*, they guard the glorious throne. The emergence of manifold classes of angelic beings demanded stratification and taxonomic description. Take, for example, the first-century apocalyptic work *T. Levi* 3:1–8, which describes multiple classes of divine beings, from the "powers of the hosts" in the third heaven (3:3) to the "thrones and authorities" in the fourth heaven (3:8) to the angels in the fifth heaven (3:7). Of the greatest importance are the "angels in the presence of the Lord" (3:5), whose residence in the sixth heaven and physical proximity to the Lord mark them as superior to the beings in the lesser heavens. Division and categorization along the lines of relative importance is the underlying principle of angelology.

The interest in angelic hierarchies extends into the Jesus movement, whose authors note the different categories of angels in the heavens. The structure and details of these hierarchies are not elaborated upon, but the existence of different categories of angelic beings presumes distinctions, and thus hierarchical divisions, among the angels. The Pauline and Deutero-Pauline epistles, for instance, describe the rulers, angels, thrones, powers, principalities, and authorities that coexist in the heavens. For the related issue of anthropomorphic deities and divine beings and their relation to humans, see Esther J. Hamori, *"When Gods Were Men": The Embodied God in Biblical and Near Eastern Literature* (Berlin: Walter de Gruyter, 2008).

2. In some cases, the heavenly hierarchy may have been related to earthly hierarchies. Take, for instance, the fourth-century *Hierarchia coelestis* of Pseudo-Dionysius, where the relationship of angels to God was modeled on that of the imperial court.

3. For a discussion of modern Christian expectations of postmortem equality, see Alister E. McGrath, *Christianity: An Introduction*, 2d ed. (Oxford: Blackwell, 2006), 291–92.

4. See, for example, the coterminus use of "angels" and "saints" (of which martyrs are a subset) in modern-day Roman Catholic liturgy. Cardinal Arinze stated to a synod of U.S. bishops that "we [Roman Caholics] celebrate the Mass in union with the Blessed Virgin Mary, the Angels and the Saints." Cardinal Arinze, "The Holy Eucharist Unites Heaven and Earth," address at Eucharistic Congress, Basilica of the Immaculate Conception, Washington, D.C (2004). The presentation of saints and angels as analogous in status is typical of Roman Catholic liturgical performance.

5. See Larry W. Hurtado, *One God, One Lord: Early Christian Devotion and Ancient Jewish Monotheism*, 2d ed. (Edinburgh: T & T Clark, 1998), although Hurtado has a pious commitment to Nicene Christology that prevents him taking this comparison to its logical conclusions.

6. In my use of the category of the "special dead," I am indebted to Adela Yarbro Collins, "The New Age and the Other World in the Letters of Paul," in *The Other World and Its Relations to This World*, ed. E. Eynikel, et al., Journal for the Study of Judaism Supplement Series. (Leiden: Brill, forthcoming). For further discussion of this category as it relates to the martyrs, see the discussion of resurrection below.

7. Following Jonathan Z. Smith, I maintain that the task of academic comparison is more properly taken in triadic than dyadic terms. In this case, martyrs are more like Christ than angels with respect to certain functions. This methodology is, to my

mind, a superior heuristic tool in general and a particularly useful approach here, when the subjects and terms are so closely related and in some cases indistinguishable. This theme reverberates throughout Smith's work, although this passage summarizes its strengths: "'x resembles y more than z with respect to . . . ;' or, 'x resembles y more than w resembles z with respect to . . . ' That is to say, the statement of comparison is never dyadic, but always triadic; there is always an implicit 'more than,' and there is always a 'with respect to.' In the case of an academic comparison, the 'with respect to' is most frequently the scholar's interest, be this expressed in a question, a theory, or a model, recalling, in the case of the latter, that a model is useful precisely when it is different from that to which it is being applied"; Jonathan Z. Smith, *Drudgery Divine: On the Comparison of Early Christianities and the Religions of Late Antiquity*, Jordan Lectures in Comparative Religion 14 (London: School of Oriental and African Studies; Chicago: University of Chicago Press, 1990), 51.

8. Christopher Rowland, *The Open Heaven: A Study of Apocalyptic in Judaism and Early Christianity* (New York: Crossroad, 1982), 94–113. Here, Rowland builds upon the earlier work of Martin Werner, who argued that angelic Christology was the earliest form of Christology to emerge in the Jesus movement. See Martin Werner, *Die Entstehung des christlichen Dogmas: Problemgeschichtlich dargestellt* (Bern-Leipzig: P. Haupt, 1941). Werner's argument has been criticized, most forcefully by Wilhelm Michaelis, who played down the importance of this idea in the development of early Christology, and Joseph Barbel, see below. See Wilhelm Michaelis, *Zur Engelchristologie im Urchristentum: Abbau der Konstruktion Martin Werners* (Basel: Heinrich Majer, 1942); Joseph Barbel, *Christos Angelos: die Anschauung von Christus als Bote und Engel in der Gelehrten und Volkstümlichen Literatur des Christlichen Altertums* (Bottrop: W. Postberg, 1941). Even those, such as Michaelis and Barbel, who reject the priority of angelic Christology admit that this kind of thinking played a key role in the development of later Arianism.

Rowland's work has been challenged by Larry Hurtado, who argues that Jewish interest in angelic or intermediary figures reflects "traditional Jewish concern for the uniqueness of God." He argues that the glorious depictions of angelic figures was a creative attempt to demonstrate the majesty conferred upon the angel as God's agent. For Hurtado, the only anomaly in this scheme of divine agency is the development of Christological ideas that transformed Jesus into the object of devotion. See Hurtado, *One God, One Lord*, 38; Larry W. Hurtado, *How on Earth Did Jesus Become a God? Historical Questions about Earliest Devotion to Jesus* (Grand Rapids, Mich.: Eerdmans, 2005). It has also been expanded and applied by his students to other texts, including Luke-Acts. See, for example, Crispin H. T. Fletcher-Louis, *Luke-Acts: Angels, Christology, and Soteriology*, Wissenschaftliche Untersuchungen zum Neuen Testament 2. 94 (Tübingen: Mohr Siebeck, 1997).

9. Rowland, *Open Heaven*, 111. Rowland situates his idea in opposition to that of Alan Segal. See Alan F. Segal, *Two Powers in Heaven: Early Rabbinic Reports about Christianity and Gnosticism*, Studies in Judaism in Late Antiquity 25 (Leiden: Brill, 1977), 182–219.

10. Rowland, *Open Heaven*, 112–13.

11. See Rev 14:14–16, where the vision of the "one like a son of man" precedes the introduction of the subject of the next vision as "another angel" in 14:17.

12. While some scholars have argued that the "one like a son of man" in Daniel is a messianic or collective figure, the identification of the figure as an angel has gained widespread critical recognition. This view is in keeping with the Hebrew Bible's use of human figures for angels (cf. Gen 18:2; Josh 5:13; Ezek 8:2). Cf. the "Animal Apocalypse" (1 En. 85–90), in which animals are humans and men are angels. See Patrick A. Tiller, A Commentary on the Animal Apocalypse of1 Enoch, Early Judaism and its Literature 4 (Atlanta, Ga.: Scholars Press, 1993), and the allusion to Dan 7:13–14 in the "Similitudes of Enoch" (1 En. 37–41) and in 4 Ezra 13. In these works the manlike figure of Daniel is the Messiah but also appears to be a heavenly being. Within Daniel itself, the interpretation of the being as a messianic figure jars with the themes of the work as a whole, which makes no reference to a Davidic monarchy. The collective interpretation relies upon two levels of speculative interpretation: the equation of the "one like a son of man" with the holy ones and the equation of the holy ones with the Jewish people. For a survey of the strengths and weaknesses of all three positions, see John J. Collins, Daniel: A Commentary on the Book of Daniel, ed. Frank Moore Cross, Hermeneia: A Critical and Historical Commentary on the Bible (Minneapolis, Minn.: Fortress Press, 1993), 304–10.

13. Although we should note the instances in which the author of Revelation seeks to modify the presence of angelic Christology by specifying that the angel of the Lord was not the subject of human worship (Rev 19:10; 20:8). For a detailed discussion of the presence of angelomorphic Christology in the book of Revelation, see Loren T. Stuckenbruck, Angel Veneration and Christology: A Study in Early Judaism and in the Christology of the Apocalypse of John, Wissenschaftliche Untersuchungen zum Neuen Testament 2.70 (Tübingen: J. C. B. Mohr, 1995); Peter R. Carrell, Jesus and the Angels: Angelology and the Christology of the Apocalypse of John (Cambridge: Cambridge University Press, 1997).

14. For the assumption of the heavenly name of God by Metatron, cf. 3 En. 12.15. For the transformation of an elect person into a kind of "son of God," see the heavenly consecration of Levi in T. Levi 4.2.

15. So, Rowland, Open Heaven, 111. Also, Otto Michel, Der Brief an die Hebräer, Kritisch-exegetischer Kommentar über das Neue Testament Bd. 13 (Göttingen: Vandenhoeck & Ruprecht, 1984), 105; Hugh Montefiore, A Commentary on the Epistle to the Hebrews, Harper's New Testament Commentaries (New York: Harper & Row, 1964), 35. For a discussion of Jewish and Christian polemics against the worship of angels, see Stuckenbruck, Angel Veneration and Christology, 47–149.

A more nuanced version of this theory is fleshed out in Attridge, Hebrews, 51–53. Attridge suggests that while Hebrews may be in dialogue with the kinds of speculative angelological traditions described here, the Christological picture of Hebrews—as it is elaborated upon later in the epistle—is a motivating factor. By stating at the outset the superiority of Christ to the angels, Hebrews heads off at the pass any interpretation of the heavenly high priest Christ in light of the kinds of angelic high priests found in the Qumran literature (11QMelch).

A variety of alternative theories have been put forward to account for Hebrews' anxiety over angels. One view, first advanced by Windisch, builds upon the admonition in Colossians 2:18 against angelic worship and supposes that Hebrews' audience might have been engaged in some kind of worship of angels. See Hans Windisch, *Der Hebräerbrief*, Handbuch zum Neuen Testament 14 (Tübingen: J. C. B. Mohr, 1931), 17. Given the absence of a direct citation, the certainty of this interpretation is by no means assured.

16. This interpretation is further advanced by the theory of Craig Koester that Heb 1:5–14 recalls scenes of imperial adoption in which the emperor acclaims his successor as his son. If, as Koester implies, adoptionism on account of sacrificial death is the criterion for exaltation, the martyrs are strong candidates for promotion in the cosmological hierarchy. See Craig R. Koester, *Hebrews: A New Translation with Introduction and Commentary*, Anchor Bible Commentary 36 (New York: Doubleday, 2001), 201.

17. For a discussion of this issue, see Carolyn Osiek, *Shepherd of Hermas: A Commentary*, ed. Helmut Koester, Hermeneia: A Critical and Historical Commentary on the Bible (Minneapolis, Minn.: Fortress Press, 1999).

18. Justin Martyr, *1 Apol.* 62–63; Justin Martyr, *Dial.* 34.2; 58; 61; 75–86.

19. *Gos. Thom.*, Logion 13 (34, 34).

20. Hippolytus, *Haer.* 9.8. Here the male angel in Elchasai's vision is identified as the Son of God.

21. See also the description of Jesus as the "angel of the church" in *Ascen. Isa.* 3.15.

22. Norbert Brox, *Der Hirt des Hermas*, Kommentar zu den Apostolischen Vätern 7 (Göttingen: Vandenhoeck & Ruprecht, 1991), 490–92.

23. All four canonical gospels record Jesus' use of this term. The development and origins of the designation "son of man" is one of the most controversial topics in New Testament studies. The question of whether this term was used by the historical Jesus himself and for what purposes is hotly contested. Regardless of how Jesus himself may or may not have used the term, it seems clear that after his death a number of his followers began to identify him with the figure in Daniel 7:13, presumably on the basis of his heavenly exaltation. Thus the identification of Jesus with the son of man occurred in one of the earliest stages of the development of the Jesus movement. For a discussion of the origins of the term, see Adela Yarbro Collins, "The Origin of the Designation of Jesus as 'Son of Man,'" *Harvard Theological Review* 80 (1987): 391–407. For a summary of the various critical difficulties in the study of the son of man tradition, see Adela Yarbro Collins, "The Influence of Daniel on the New Testament," in John J Collins, *Daniel: A Commentary on the Book of Daniel*, Hermeneia: A Critical and Historical Commentary on the Bible (Minneapolis, Minn.: Fortress Press, 1993), 90–112.

24. This became a controversial point during the Reformation, in which period the abolition of purgatory forced Protestants in Germany to confront the uncomfortable truth about death, burial, and the eschaton. See Craig Koslofsky, *The Reformation of the Dead: Death and Ritual in Early Modern Germany, 1450–1700*, Early Modern History (New York: St. Martin's Press, 2000).

25. 1 Thess 4:13–18; 1 Cor 15:23–24.

26. The diversity of views are surveyed in Outi Lehtipuu, *The Afterlife Imagery in Luke's Story of the Rich Man and Lazarus*, Supplements to Novum Testamentum, vol. 123 (Leiden: Brill, 2006), 55–162.

27. Phil 3:10–11; 1 Cor 15:3–5; Rom 1:4; 6:5; Matt 27:53; Acts 1:22; 1 Pet 1:3, to name but a few passages articulating this belief. For a discussion of the various traditions and interpretations of the significance of the resurrection, see Dale C. Allison, *Resurrecting Jesus: The Earliest Christian Tradition and Its Interpreters* (New York: T & T Clark, 2005).

28. This is not to say that the belief in the general resurrection went unchallenged. If we presume that the epistles of Paul, Clement of Rome, Ignatius, and Polycarp envision actual communal problems, then we can only conclude that certain passages are designed to counteract doubts about the resurrection (cf. 1 Cor 15:12; 1 *Clem.* 25–26; 2 *Clem.* 9.1–5; Pol., *Phil.* 2.1–2).

29. Alfred Stuiber, *Refrigerium Interim*, Theophaneia, 11 (Bonn: P. Hanstein, 1957); Jeffrey R. Asher, *Polarity and Change in 1 Corinthians 15: A Study of Metaphysics, Rhetoric, and Resurrection*, Hermeneutische Untersuchungen zur Theologie 42 (Tübingen: Mohr Siebeck, 2000).

30. 1 Thess 4:14–18: "εἰ γὰρ πιστεύομεν ὅτι Ἰησοῦς ἀπέθανεν καὶ ἀνέστη, οὕτως καὶ ὁ θεὸς τοὺς κοιμηθέντας διὰ τοῦ Ἰησοῦ ἄξει σὺν αὐτῷ. Τοῦτο γὰρ ὑμῖν λέγομεν ἐν λόγῳ κυρίου, ὅτι ἡμεῖς οἱ ζῶντες οἱ περιλειπόμενοι εἰς τὴν παρουσίαν τοῦ κυρίου οὐ μὴ φθάσωμεν τοὺς κοιμηθέντας· ὅτι αὐτὸς ὁ κύριος ἐν κελεύσματι, ἐν φωνῇ ἀρχαγγέλου καὶ ἐν σάλπιγγι θεοῦ, καταβήσεται ἀπ' οὐρανοῦ καὶ οἱ νεκροὶ ἐν Χριστῷ ἀναστήσονται πρῶτον, ἔπειτα ἡμεῖς οἱ ζῶντες οἱ περιλειπόμενοι ἅμα σὺν αὐτοῖς ἁρπαγησόμεθα ἐν νεφέλαις εἰς ἀπάντησιν τοῦ κυρίου εἰς ἀέρα· καὶ οὕτως πάντοτε σὺν κυρίῳ ἐσόμεθα. Ὥστε παρακαλεῖτε ἀλλήλους ἐν τοῖς λόγοις τούτοις."

31. 1 *Clem.* 24.1–2: "We should consider, loved ones, how the Master continuously shows us the future resurrection that is about to occur, of which he made the Lord Jesus Christ the first fruit by raising him from the dead."

32. 1 *Clem.* 50.3–4: "All the generations from Adam till today have passed away, but those perfected in love through the gracious gift of God have a place among the godly. And they will be revealed when the kingdom of Christ appears. For it is written, 'Come into the inner rooms for just a short while, until my anger and wrath pass by; and I will remember a good day and raise you up from your tombs.'"

2 *Clem.* 19.3–4: "And so we should practice righteousness, that we may be saved in the end. How fortunate are those who obey these commandments! Even if they suffer ill for a brief time in this world, they will reap the imperishable fruit of the resurrection. And so the one who is pious should not be despondent over miseries suffered at present. A more fortunate time awaits him! When he is restored to life with our ancestors he will be jubilant, in an age removed from sorrow."

33. Irenaeus, *Haer.* 5.31.1–2.

34. Justin Martyr, *Dial.* 80. See Pistis Sophia 2.99, which interprets Revelation similarly.

35. That Rev 20:4–6 describes a partial resurrection of the just is disputed. For a discussion of the problem of the thousand-year reign, see Alfred Wilkenhauser, "Das Problem des tausendjährigen Reiches in der Johannes-apokalypse," *Römische Quartalschrift für christliche Altertumskunde und Kirchengeschichte* 45 (1937): 13–25; David Edward Aune, *Revelation*, Word Biblical Commentary, vol. 52 (Dallas, Tex.: Word Books, 1997), 3.1089–90.

36. See below.

37. *Did.* 16.6–8.

38. For a list of cross-references between the *Did.* 16 and Matthew, see Bart D. Ehrman, *The Apostolic Fathers*, Loeb Classical Library 24–25 (Cambridge, Mass.: Harvard University Press, 2003), 441–43. Strangely, with respects to the phrase "all of his holy ones with him," Ehrman notes only Zech 14: 5 and 1 Thess 3:13, not Matt 27:51–53.

39. See Pol., *Phil.* 2.2. This view is also ascribed to Papias by Irenaeus, *Haer.* 5.33.3 and Eusebius, *Hist. eccl.* 3.39.11–13.

40. The *Didache* breaks off sharply after 16.8. Two pieces of evidence point to the possibility of a lost ending: the eight blank lines at the end of the Byrennios manuscript and the longer ending supplied in *The Apostolic Constitutions*. A number of scholars have taken the blank space to indicate that there was a longer ending and have supplied their own suggestions for what would originally have been found here. We should remember, however, that blank space on a manuscript does not have the properties of a blank Scrabble tile and cannot be used to supply what is missing in the hypothesis of a scholar. The later edition of the *Didche* found in *The Apostolic Constitutions* 7.32.4 reads that after the Lord and the holy ones arrive, the enthroned Christ will judge the deceiver and repay each person according to one's deeds with either eternal punishment or eternal life. Both the mention of the burning process and the selective resurrection are removed. As Milavec observes, individual judgment is necessitated by the more general resurrection. Aaron Milavec, "The Saving Efficacy of the Burning Process in Did. 16.5," in *The Didache in Context: Essays on Its Text, History and Tradition*, ed. Clayton N. Jefford, Supplements to Novum Testamentum (Leiden: Brill, 1995), 153.

41. Ibid., 131–55.

42. Ign., *Trall.* 9.2: "He was also truly raised from the dead, his Father having raised him. In the same way his Father will also raise us in Christ Jesus, we who believe in him, apart from whom we do not have true life."

43. It has been suggested to me by Adela Collins that Paul subscribed to a belief in the "special dead" of which he considered himself a part. The idea of a "special dead" would certainly lay the groundwork, religiously, for Paul's somewhat audacious claim. It would also establish a precedent for the exceptionally speedy resurrection of the martyr. See Collins, "The Other World and the New Age in the Letters of Paul," 11–13.

44. Matt 27:51–53: "Καὶ ἰδοὺ τὸ καταπέτασμα τοῦ ναοῦ ἐσχίσθη ἀπ᾽ ἄνωθεν ἕως κάτω εἰς δύο καὶ ἡ γῆ ἐσείσθη καὶ αἱ πέτραι ἐσχίσθησαν, καὶ τὰ μνημεῖα ἀνεῴχθησαν καὶ πολλὰ σώματα τῶν κεκοιμημένων ἁγίων ἠγέρθησαν, καὶ

ἐξελθόντες ἐκ τῶν μνημείων μετὰ τὴν ἔγερσιν αὐτοῦ εἰσῆλθον εἰς τὴν ἁγίαν πόλιν καὶ ἐνεφανίσθησαν πολλοῖς."

45. See W. D. Davies and Dale C. Allison, *A Critical and Exegetical Commentary on the Gospel According to Saint Matthew*, International Critical Commentary (Edinburgh: T & T Clark, 1988); Ulrich Luz, *Matthew: A Commentary*, ed. Helmut Koester, trans. James E. Crouch (Minneapolis, Minn.: Fortress Press, 2001), 561ff.

46. For a discussion of the biblical use of the term, see Otto Procksch, "Hagios," in *Theological Dictionary of the New Testament*, ed. Gerhard Kittel (Grand Rapids, Mich.: Eerdmans, 1964), 88–110.

47. Luke 22:42–43: "καὶ ἔλεγεν, Ἰησοῦ, μνήσθητί μου ὅταν ἔλθῃς εἰς τὴν βασιλείαν σου.καὶ εἶπεν αὐτῷ, Ἀμήν σοι λέγω, σήμερον μετ' ἐμοῦ ἔσῃ ἐν τῷ παραδείσῳ."

48. Luke describes Jesus' ascent on Easter Sunday, and Acts describes his ascent forty days later. It may well be the case that Luke, like John, regards the postcrucifixion Jesus as a commuter, who ascends on multiple occasions.

49. Cf. the story of the rich man and Lazarus in Luke. In this account Lazarus goes to the equivalent of paradise immediately after his death. On this passage and on Lukan eschatology more generally, see Lehtipuu, *Afterlife Imagery in Luke's Story of the Rich Man and Lazarus*, 243–94. On the belief in the immediate resurrection see W. Rordorf, "L' espérance des Martyrs chrétiens," in *Forma Futuri: Studi in onore del Cardinale Michele Pellegrino* (Turin: Bottega d'Erasmo, 1975), 445–61.

50. Alan F. Segal, *Life after Death: A History of the Afterlife in the Religions of the West* (New York: Doubleday, 2004). Segal essentializes, solidifies, and polarizes "Orthodoxy" and "Gnosticism" in the first and second centuries, a period when neither group had yet forged concrete identities or manifestos (if they ever did).

51. *Gos. Thom.*, Logia 50–51.

52. Elaine H. Pagels, *The Gnostic Gospels* (New York: Random House, 1979); Gregory J. Riley, *Resurrection Reconsidered: Thomas and John in Controversy* (Minneapolis, Minn.: Fortress Press, 1995), 127–75.

53. *Testament of Truth* 31.22–32.8 and 33.25–34.26, cited in Segal, *Life after Death*, 551–52.

54. *Ac. Apol.* 37.

55. *1 En.* 27.2, translated in George W. E. Nickelsburg, *1 Enoch: A Commentary on the Book of 1 Enoch*, Hermeneia: A Critical and Historical Commentary on the Bible (Minneapolis, Minn.: Fortress Press, 2001), 317. All translations of *1 Enoch* are taken from Nickelsburg.

56. *1 En.* 22.3–5; translation, Ibid., 300.

57. These verses of *1 En.* 22 pose a distinct textual problem. For a summary of the textual difficulties and the religious background of this passage, see Ibid.

58. *Ascen. Isa.*, 9.7–18. Translated by M. A. Knibb in James H. Charlesworth, *Old Testament Pseudepigrapha* (Garden City, N.Y.: Doubleday, 1983), 2.164–76.

59. Robin Lane Fox, *Pagans and Christians* (New York: Knopf, 1987), 435. In some early Jewish texts it is not clear that Abraham's bosom is an intermediary step. As a result, Outi Lehtipuu has argued that Abraham's bosom can be read ambiguously

as conferring familiarity with the patriarch (see Lehtipuu, *Afterlife Imagery in Luke's Story of the Rich Man and Lazarus*, 219, 294). In early church constructions of heaven, "Abraham's Bosom" was understood more concretely as a specific place. In his reply to Vigilantius, Jerome counters the view that martyrs were either in their tombs, in the place of refreshment, or in Abraham's bosom, arguing that they can travel from place to place at ease (Jerome, *Vigil.* 6). Jerome's argument hinges on the idea that Abraham's bosom is both a place and a place distinct from other heavenly places.

60. *Ac. Scil.* 15: "Hodie martyres in caelis sumus."

61. The notion of being received the same day into heaven is also found in *Mart. Pol.* 14.2–3. The implication of immediate receipt into heaven is found in *Ac. Ptole.* 19; *Mart. Fruct.* 3.3; *Lyons* 2.7; *Mart. Pion.* 22.1; *Mart. Maximilian* 2.11; *Ac. Abit.* 13 Cf. Also John Chrysostom, *Ign.* 17.

62. *Lyons* 2.7: "ζωὴν ᾐτήσαντο καὶ ἔδωκεν αὐτοῖς· ἣν καὶ συνεμερίσαντο τοῖς πλησίον, κατὰ πάντων νικηφόροι πρὸς θεὸν ἀπελθόντες . . . μετ᾽ εἰρήνης ἐχώρησαν πρὸς θεόν." cf. Sir 44: 14.

63. A peculiar feature of literary accounts of the martyr's death is that martyrs are frequently referred to as martyrs "in heaven." This seems to imply that the status is one held in heaven, and that to be a martyr one must reside there. For example, Cyprian of Carthage is described as such in Prudentius, *Crowns of Martyrdom* 2.579; 6.145; 13.106.

64. *Mart. Pol.* 14.2–3: "λαβεῖν μέρος ἐν ἀριθμῷ τῶν μαρτύρων, ἐν τῷ ποτηρίῳ τοῦ Χριστοῦ σου εἰς ἀνάστασιν ζωῆς αἰωνίου ψυχῆς τε καὶ σώματος ἐν ἀφθαρσίᾳ πνεύματος ἁγίου, ἐν οἷς προσδεχθείην ἐνώπιόν σου σήμερον ἐν θυσίᾳ πίονι καὶ προσδεκτῇ, καθὼς προητοίμασας καὶ προεφανέρωσας καὶ ἐπλήρωσας ὁ ἀψευδὴς καὶ ἀληθινὸς θεός διὰ τοῦτο καὶ περὶ πάντων σὲ αἰνῶ, σὲ εὐλογῶ, σὲ δοξάζω διὰ τοῦ αἰωνίου καὶ ἐπουρανίου ἀρχιερέως Ἰησοῦ Χριστοῦ."

65. See discussion of Mark 10:37–40 in chapter 1.

66. The use of sacrificial language is, however, typical of *Mart. Pol.* For a full discussion of sacrificial language and imagery in the acts of the martyrs, see the section "Martyrdom as Sacrifice" in chapter 3.

67. *Mart. Pion.* 22.1

68. Cf. Mygdonia, a convert of Thomas in the *Apocryphal Acts* who prays to quickly depart from life. Cited in Judith Perkins, *The Suffering Self: Pain and Narrative Representation in the Early Christian Era* (New York: Routledge, 1995), 27.

69. *Mart. Pion.* 21.4: "Διὰ τοῦτο σπεύδω ἵνα θᾶττον ἐγερθῶ, δηλῶν τὴν ἐκ νεκρῶν ἀνάστασιν."

70. Cf. *Mart. Fruct.* 3.3.

71. This curious phrase could be read otherwise as implying that the sooner he dies, the sooner he awakes. And certainly an element of this idea is present here. It may still remain, however, that Pionius believes that he will awake more quickly than others on account of the mode of his death.

72. *Mart. Fruct.* 3.3

73. Ibid., 4.3.

74. Ibid., 5.1: "Post haec solita Domini non defuere magnalia, apertumque caelum, Babyla et Mygdonio fratres nostri ex familia Aemiliani praesidis, filiae eius, dominae suae carnali, ostendebant Fructuosus cum diaconibus suis, adhuc stipitibus quibus ligati fuerant permanentibus, ad caelum ascendentes coronatos."

75. Cf. Luke 24:51.

76. See the section "Eschatological Resurrection," above.

77. *Testament of the Forty Martyrs* 3.4: "ψυχῇ δὲ καὶ πνεύματι θείῳ εὐχόμεθα, ὅπως τύχωμεν ἅπαντες τῶν αἰωνίων τοῦ θεοῦ ἀγαθῶν καὶ τῆς βασιλείας αὐτοῦ νῦν καὶ εἰς τοὺς αἰῶνας τῶν αἰώνων."

78. Ibid., 1.5: " ἐὰν δὲ διαφυλαχθῇ ἀβλαβὴς τῇ τοῦ Χριστοῦ χάριτι καὶ ἔτι ἐν τῷ κόσμῳ ἐξετάζοιτο, σχολάζειν αὐτὸν μετ᾽ ἐλευθερίας τῷ μαρτυρίῳ ἡμῶν παραγγέλλομεν καὶ τὰς ἐντολὰς τοῦ Χριστοῦ φυλάττειν παρακαλοῦμεν, ἵνα ἐν τῇ μεγάλῃ τῆς ἀναστάσεως ἡμέρᾳ τῆς μεθ᾽ ἡμῶν ἀπολαύσεως τύχῃ."

79. Eunoicus is, technically speaking, a confessor who was arrested and tried with the martyrs. If he does not die, however, he will be judged on account of his good works, *not his profession of Christian identity*. For the community of the *Testament of the Forty Martyrs*, salvation for non martyrs is a question of works, not faith.

80. *Pass. Perp.* 4.3–4: "uideo scalam aeream mirae magnitudinis pertigentem usque ad caelum et angustam, per quam nonnisi singuli ascendere possent, et in lateribus scalae omne genus ferramentorum infixum. erant ibi gladii, lanceae, hami, machaerae, ueruta, ut si quis neglegenter aut non sursum adtendens ascenderet, laniaretur et carnes eius inhaererent ferramentis."

81. *Mart. Mar.* 6.6–10. For a further discussion of this passage, see the discussion of judgment, below.

82. *Mart. Mont.* 4.2: "et ad summum ascendebamus locum poenarum quasi ascenderemus in caelum."

83. *Mart. Iren.* 5.4: "Domine Iesu Christe, qui pro mundi salute pati dignatus es, pateant caeli tui, ut suscipiant angeli spiritum serui tui Irenaei, qui propter nomen tuum et plebem tuam productam de ecclesia tua catholica Sirmiensium haec patior. Te peto, tuamque deprecor misericordiam, ut et me suscipere et hos in fide tua confirmare digneris."

84. *Lyons* 2.7; *Mart. Maximilian* 2.11.

85. *Mart. Mont.* 7.4: "Dic illis quia Gloriosiorem coronam habebitis, necnon Ad deum suum spiritus properat, et anima iam proxima passioni sedes suas requisiuit." See Eccl. 12:7.

86. For the presence of angels, see "they might overcome those that are devoted to fire, that is, the Devil and all his heavenly host of demons, and, attaining the incorruptible crown of glory, they might endlessly praise along with the angels the God who had showered this grace upon them" (*Mart. Agape* 2.4); see also *Mart. Symph.* For reception by Christ into heaven, see *Ac. Marcellus* N, 5.2; *Mart. Conon* 6.4. For cohabitation with the members of the Trinity, see *Mart. Fruct.* 7.2.

87. "Maximillian replied: 'I shall not perish, and if I depart from this world, my soul lives with Christ my Lord'"; *Ac. Maximillian* 2.11

88. *Mart. Pol.* 14.2–3.

89. *Mart. Fruct.* 3.3: "He was hastening joyfully and confidently to break his fast with the martyrs and prophets in heaven, which the Lord has prepared for those who love him."

90. *Mart. Mar.* 11.8: "For by it [the sentence] Marian and James and the rest of the clergy were at last restored to the patriarchs in glory and were delivered from the distress of this world." The idea of joining the patriarchs in heaven is also found in 4 Maccabees 7:19; 13:17; 16:25.

91. *Mart. Dasius* 4.4.

92. LXX Ps. 88:8: "ὁ θεὸς ἐνδοξαζόμενός ἐν βουλῇ ἁγίων, μέγας καὶ φοβερὸς ἐπὶ πάντας τοὺς περικύκλῳ αὐτοῦ."

93. In critical scholarship, this was first proposed by Otto Procksch, "Der Menschensohn als Gottessohn," *Christentum und Wissenschaft* 3 (1927): 425–43, 473–81. His view was challenged by Martin Noth, "The Holy Ones of the Most High," in *The Laws in the Pentateuch and Other Studies* (Philadelphia: Fortress Press, 1966), 215–28. Nonetheless, this theory has been generally accepted by modern scholars. For a survey of the debate, see the excursus on the "Holy Ones" in Collins, *Daniel: A Commentary*, 313–17.

94. Job 5:1; 15:15; Zech 14:5; Dan 7:18 are the most generally accepted. In a review of literature from Qumran, Brekelmans identified at least thirteen passages in which, he argued, the term "holy ones" is indisputably used to refer to angels: 1QM 1:16; 10:11–12; 12:1, 4, 7; 15:14; 1QS 11:7–8; 1QH 3:21–22; 10:35; 1QDM 4:1; 1QSb 1:5; 1Q 36:1; 1QapGen 2:1. See C. H. W. Brekelmans, "The Saints of the Most High and Their Kingdom," *Old Testament Studies* 14 (1965): 305–29.

95. E.g., Rom 1:7; 8:27; 15:31; 16:2, 15; 1 Cor 1:2; 6:1; 2 Cor 1:1. Cf. Matt 27:52–53, where Matthew uses the term, possibly to refer to prophets of Israel.

96. 1 Cor 6:2–3: " ἢ οὐκ οἴδατε ὅτι οἱ ἅγιοι τὸν κόσμον κρινοῦσιν; καὶ εἰ ἐν ὑμῖν κρίνεται ὁ κόσμος, ἀνάξιοί ἐστε κριτηρίων ἐλαχίστων; οὐκ οἴδατε ὅτι ἀγγέλους κρινοῦμεν, μήτι γε βιωτικά;"

97. Henri Leclercq, "Hagios," *Dictionnaire d'archéologie chrétienne et de liturgie*, ed. Fernand Cabrol and Henri Leclercq (Paris: Librairie Letouzey et Ané, 1936), 373–462.

98. *Ac. Julius* 3.6: "Iulius respondit: Elegi mori ad tempus ut in perpetuum uiuam cum sanctis" (emended translation).

99. *Mart. Conon* 6.4: "Κύριε Ἰησου Χριστέ, δέξαι τὴν ψυχήν μου καὶ ῥῦσαί με ἀπὸ τῶν αἱμοβόρων κυνῶν καὶ ἀνάπαυσόν με μετὰ πάντων τῶν δικαίων σου τῶν πεποιηκότων τὸ θέλημά σου."

100. Matt 23:35; Heb 1:14; 1 John 3:12.

101. Matt 13:17; 23:29.

102. Matt 23:35.

103. Luke 1:16; 2:25; 10:22.

104. Jer 23:5, 6; 33:15; Zech 9:9. In Matt 27:19 the term is used of Jesus by Pilate's wife.

105. "There they gave themselves to prayer: though their bodies resided on a mountain top, their souls lived in heaven"; *Mart. Agape* 1.3.

106. A similar idea appears in the North-African *Mart. Mont.*, where the martyr Flavian has already become a man of heaven even before his execution: "Thus it

seemed as though some opposing spirit had sealed it shut in witness of the fact that Flavian, for whom a heavenly mansion was being made ready, was unworthy to be soiled by the filth of a prison. But because the Lord had worthy reasons for postponing his crown, the prison at last unwillingly admitted this man now of heaven and of God"; *Mart. Mont.* 17. In this case, we should note that the phrase "man of heaven and God" does not necessarily entail residence in heaven. It could equally denote his good character and ethical fortitude as a "man of God." We should also note that this martyrdom was composed in Carthage during the Donatist controversy and in the midst of developing ideas about the importance of confessors as authorities in the church. This idea seems to be reflected in the martyrdom's portrayal of Flavian's character.

107. See Carol Newsom, *Songs of the Sabbath Sacrifice: A Critical Edition* (Atlanta, Ga.: Scholars Press, 1985), on the relationship between the liturgy at Qumran and the heavenly liturgy see 11QMelch.

108. *Mart. Mar.* 11.3: "ad Agapii ceterorumque martyrum beatissimorum pergo conuiuium." Later in the account the martyrs are told by another martyr, this time a young boy, that they will "dine" with him in heaven the next day (11.6).

109. *Mart. Fruct.* 3.3.

110. *Testament of the Forty Martyrs* 1.5.

111. Lawrence H. Schiffman, *The Eschatological Community of the Dead Sea Scrolls: A Study of the Rule of the Congregation* (Atlanta, Ga.: Scholars Press, 1989), 53–67. Schiffman refers primarily to 1QSa 2.11–22 and 1QS 6:2–6. Schiffman's analysis of this material and particularly his categorization of the meal as "messianic" have been challenged. See the review by Ben Zion Wacholder in *Journal of Biblical Literature* 110 (1991): 147–48.

112. Schiffman, *The Eschatological Community of the Dead Sea Scrolls*, 56.

113. Luke 22:30.

114. Matt. 22:1–14; 25:10.

115. Examples of this are the meal scene in the Capella Graeca of the Catacomb of Priscilla, banquet scenes in the Catacombs of Callistus, the depiction of a banquet on a sarcophagus fragment now in the Vatican Museo Pio Cristiano, and a banquet scene found in the small catacomb of Vibia on the Via Appia Antica in Rome.

116. See Josef Wilpert, *Fractio Panis* (Freiburg im Breisgau: Herder, 1895). For the interpretation of the scene as a reference to the Eucharist, see Richard H. Hiers and Charles A. Kennedy, "The Bread and Fish Eucharist in the Gospels and Early Christian Art," *Perspectives in Religious Studies* 3, no. 1 (1976): 21–48. The categorization of the meal as a eucharist seems bizarre given that fish form part of the meal and only five or seven people attend. The designation of the meal as a representation of the Last Supper seems likewise flawed by the small number of attendees. In its depiction of the Last Supper, the church of Sant' Apollinare Nuovo in Ravenna displays Jesus reclining with all the apostles. For the relationship to pagan funerary practices, see Elisabeth Jastrzebowska, "Les scènes de banquet dans les peintures et sculptures chrétiennes des 3e et 4e siècles," *Recherches Augustiniennes* 14 (1979): 3–90. On Hellenistic banquets as the backdrop to Christian practices in general, see Dennis Edwin Smith,

From Symposium to Eucharist: The Banquet in the Early Christian World (Minneapolis, Minn.: Fortress Press, 2003).

117. In the *Odyssey* the thirsty dead crowd around Odysseus to drink the spilled blood (*Od.* xi.36–37); cf. Orphic tablets B10 and B11; Aristophanes, *Ran.* 504 (although Aristophanes may be lampooning Greek symposia); and Virgil, *Aen.* 5.75–78. For a discussion of the motif of the thirsty dead in ancient Greek thought. see Radcliffe G. Edmonds, *Myths of the Underworld Journey: Plato, Aristophanes, and the "Orphic" Gold Tablets* (Cambridge: Cambridge University Press, 2004), 47–49.

118. For the archaeological evidence. see J. M. C. Toynbee, *Death and Burial in the Roman World*, Aspects of Greek and Roman Life (London: Thames & Hudson, 1971), 51–52. Ancient authors referring to libations offered to the dead include Lucian, *On Mourning* 9; Aeschylus, *Per.* 607–15; and Euripides, *Iph. taur.* 157–166. For further discussion on libations, see Robert Garland, *The Greek Way of Death* (Ithaca, N.Y.: Cornell University Press, 1985), 113–15.

119. Robin M. Jensen proposes a variation on this theme when she writes that "the Christian Banquet paintings portray a combination of the post-resurrectional meal described in John 21, a meal in Paradise granted to the baptized, and an actual funerary banquet held in honor of the deceased." See Robin M. Jensen, "Dining in Heaven," *Bible Review* 15, no. 5 (1998): 49. Jensen argues that the idea of the postresurrectional meal is derived from John 21 and is connected to the idea of an eschatological banquet following the resurrection at the end of the world. With regard to martyrs, Jensen argues that Christian martyrs envisioned the afterlife as a kind of primordial garden populated by saints and angels (38). For this she cites *Pass. Perp.* She fails to note the prevalence of the idea of a banquet of martyrs among the other *acta*. For a lengthier discussion of this view, see Robin M. Jensen, *Understanding Early Christian Art* (London: Routledge, 2000), 52–59.

120. For example, at Qumran; see discussion above.

121. For the possibility that the scenes depict the eschatological banquet, see Jensen, "Dining in Heaven," 32–39, and Jensen, *Understanding Early Christian Art*, 59, in which she cites Tertullian, *Nat.* 1.13, and Tertullian, *Marc.* 5.4.

122. Andrew McGowan, *Ascetic Eucharists: Food and Drink in Early Christian Ritual Meals*, Oxford Early Christian Studies (Oxford: Clarendon Press, 1999); McGowan, "Discipline and Diet: Feeding the Martyrs in Roman Carthage," *Harvard Theological Review* 94 (2003): 455–76.

123. The role of the angel as a heavenly tour guide is a topos in the genre of heavenly ascent. For example, *3 Baruch*; *Ascen. Isa.* 7.11; *Apoc. Zeph.*; *Apoc. Jas.* For a discussion of this phenomenon, see Martha Himmelfarb, *Ascent to Heaven in Jewish and Christian Apocalypses* (New York: Oxford University Press, 1993).

124. Heb 1:14 (the angels are "sent forth" as ministering spirits); *Pass. Perp.* 11.7.

125. Angels guard the throne of God (*1 En.* 71:7), the Garden of Eden (Gen 3:24; *1 En.* 32), and the gates of heaven (*Ascen. Isa.*; *T. Levi* 5.1).

126. Rev 4:9–11; 5:11–12; 7:11–12; 11:16–18.

127. E.g., Songs of the Sabbath Sacrifice 4Q405 21–22:10–11.

128. *Pass. Perp.* 12.2.

129. *Mart. Agape* 2.4.

130. In late antique martyrdoms of the fifth and sixth centuries, this idea becomes standard. See, for example, the *Theban Legion* and *Pass. Serge*, where repeated statements compare the martyrs to angels and, in the case of the latter, describe Bacchus's transformation into an angel. The consistent portrayal of the martyrs as angels may be tied to the importance of angels in Monophysite Christianity. See Jonathan Bardhill, "The Church of Saints Sergius and Bacchus in Constantinople and the Monophysite Refugees," *Dumbarton Oaks Papers* 54 (2000): 1–11.

131. Pace Jensen, "Dining in Heaven," who writes that the paradisiacal garden was the dominant way that martyrs viewed heaven. Instances of this motif are limited to *Pass. Perp.* and her literary dependents. With respect to iconographic depictions, Jensen is very accurate. Despite the scant use of the paradisiacal garden imagery in other *acta*, the image of Jesus as Good Shepherd and heaven as a garden dominates the iconography of Christian funerary art. See Jensen, *Understanding Early Christian Art*, 37–41. We should beware of concluding that funerary art is somehow a more substantial indication of Christian belief than the *acta*. After all, the cross does not make an appearance in the earliest Christian art, and the image of a suffering Jesus is very much a marginalized figure in artistic representation. See Graydon F. Snyder, *Ante Pacem: Archaeological Evidence of Church Life before Constantine*, rev ed. (Macon, Ga.: Mercer University Press, 2003), 14. The concept of suffering, arguably the most important premise of the ideology of martyrdom, is underrepresented in the artistic record. As such, we should be careful about using artistic representations as the gauge for the popularity of certain key martyrological themes.

132. *Pass. Perp.* 4.8–9: "et uidi spatium immensum horti et in medio sedentem hominem canum in habitu pastoris, grandem, oues mulgentem. et circumstantes candidati milia multa. et leuauit caput et aspexit me et dixit mihi: Bene venisti *teknon*."

133. *Mart. Mar.* 6.12–13: "iter autem nobis erat per locum pratis amoenum et uirentium nemorum laeta fronde uestitum, opacum cupressis consurgentibus in excelsum et pinis pulsantibus caelum, ut putares eum locum per omnem circuitus ambitum lucis uirentibus coronatum. sinus autem in medio perlucidi fontis uberantibus uenis et puris liquoribus redundabat."

We should admit some overlap in the description of the paradisiacal heaven and the heavenly court in *Mart. Mar.* While the martyr wanders through the garden and past streams of living waters, the eventual destination is the palace of the judge, which, we can assume, contains a court or throne room.

134. *1 En.* 32 and also the statement of the Lukan Jesus to his crucifixion companion that "today you will be with me in paradise" (Luke 23:43). In *1 En.* heaven is at the ends of the earth.

135. Peter Brown, *The Cult of the Saints: Its Rise and Function in Late Antiquity* (Chicago: University of Chicago Press, 1981).

136. See Eusebius, *Hist. eccl.* 5.4–5.

137. Cf. Mark 15:39. For a full discussion see chapter 2, above.

138. *Mart. Pot.* 6 (Eusebius, *Hist. eccl.* 6.5.6): "λέγεται εἰπεῖν ὡς ἄρα Ποταμίαινα τρισὶν ὕστερον ἡμέραις τοῦ μαρτυρίου νύκτωρ ἐπιστᾶσα στέφανον αὐτοῦ τῇ

κεφαλῇ περιθεῖσα εἴη φαίη τε παρακεκληκέναι χάριν αὐτοῦ τὸν κύριον καὶ τῆς ἀξιώσεως τετυχηκέναι, οὐκ εἰς μακρόν τε αὐτὸν παραλήψεσθαι."

139. Cf. *Mart. Fruct.* 4.1: "coronam immarcescibilem"; *Mart. Mar.* 7.1; *Mart. Mont.* 2; *Ac. Euplus* 2.4.

140. *Pass. Perp.* 7.4–9: "uideo Dinocraten exeuntem de loco tenebroso ubi et conplures errant, aestuantem ualde et sitientem, sordido cultu et coloe pallido; et uulunus in facie eius, quod cum moreretur habuit. hic Dinocrates fuerat frater meus carnalis, annorum septem, qui per infirmitatem facie cancerata male obiit ita ut mors eius odio fuerit omnibus hominibus. pro hoc ergo orationem feceram; et inter me et illum grande erat diastema ita ut uterque ad inuicem accedere non possemus. erat deinde in illo loco ubi Dinocrates erat piscine plena aqua altiorem marginem habens quam erat statura pueri; et extendebat se Dinocrates quasi bibiturus. ego dolebam quod et piscina illa aqam habebat et tamen propter altitudinem marginis bibiturus non esset. et experrecta sum, et cognoui fratrem meum laborare."

141. While drinking from a cup is frequently a symbol of martyrdom (cf. *Mart. Isa.* 5:13, *Mart. Pol.* 14:2; *Mart. Mar.* 6.13–15), here the boy is already dead. We must surmise that he died before baptism. The overlap between baptismal and martyrological language and the presentation of martyrdom as a kind of baptism means that we cannot exclude either possibility entirely.

142. *Pass. Perp.* 8.1–4: "uideo locum illum quem retro uideram et Dinocraten mundo corpore bene uestitum refrigerantem; et ubi erat uulnus uideo cicatricem, et piscinam illam, quam retro uideram, summisso margine usque ad umbilicum pueri; et aquam de ea trahebat sine cessatione. et super marginem fiala aurea plena aqua. et accessit Dinocrates et de ea bibere coepit; quae fiala non deficiebat. et satiatus accessit de aqua ludere more infantium gaudens. et experrecta sum. tunc intellexi translatum eum esse de poena."

143. For metaphors of cleanliness and washing as linked to baptism, see 1 Cor 6:11; Eph 5:26; Heb 10:22. The putting on of clean white robes is also a metaphor of postmortem reception by God in Rev 6:11. Drinking (of the spirit) as a metaphor for baptism is found in 1 Cor 12:13.

144. *Mart. Mar.* 11.1–2: "Tunc Agapius, qui iamdudum martyrio suo consummatae fidei sacramenta perfecerat, qui et ipse, cum pro puellis duabus, Tertulla et Antonia, quas sibi carissimas ad uicem pignerum diligebat, repetitis frequenter precibus oraret ut secum et illae dei dignatione martyres fierent, retulerat meritorum suorum tali reuelatione fiduciam. cui dictum est: Quid assidue petis quod una oratione meruisti?"

145. This notion has profound ramifications for our view of martyrs who pray to be martyred. Ordinarily, these prayers are seen as the feverish requests of ardent confessors desperate for martyrdom. In light of this idea, however, these prayers serve a serious purpose in securing from God the grace and favor that was martyrdom. The abstract idea that God wants people to be martyred becomes concrete. For the Carthaginians, God does not merely allow, desire, or permit martyrdom, he enables and bestows it. This underscores one of the chief differences between modern constructions of martyrdom and ancient ones. In modern constructions, definitions of

martyrdom focus on the agency of the martyr. In ancient constructions, the agency of God was also a factor.

146. This evidence is supported by literary references describing the efficacy of the prayers of the martyrs. See, for example, Gregory of Nyssa: "In this way one implores the martyr who intercedes on our behalf and is an attendant of God for imparting those favors and blessings which people seek." *Praise of Blessed Theodore the Great Martyr*, trans. John P. Cavarnos, Gregorii Nysseni Opera, Sermones (Leiden: Brill, 1990), 2.10.61–71.

147. Duane F. Watson, "Angels," in *Anchor Bible Dictionary*, ed. David Noel Freedman (New York: Doubleday, 1992), 248–53.

148. An exception to this can be noted in the case of Satan in Job who acts as an accuser against humanity. This role has much in common with intercession, but intercession was not the generally accepted role of the angel. We should further note the intercessory role of Enoch and angels in 1 *En.* 1–36.

149. E.g., Heb 7:25: "Consequently he is able for all time to save those who approach God through him, since he always lives to make intercession for them." (ὅθεν καὶ σώζειν εἰς τὸ παντελὲς δύναται τοὺς προσερχομένους δι' αὐτοῦ τῷ θεῷ, πάντοτε ζῶν εἰς τὸ ἐντυγχάνειν ὑπὲρ αὐτῶν).

150. Rom 8:34: "τίς ὁ κατακρινῶν; Χριστὸς [ιησοῦς] ὁ ἀποθανών, μᾶλλον δὲ ἐγερθείς, ὃς καί ἐστιν ἐν δεξιᾷ τοῦ θεοῦ, ὃς καὶ ἐντυγχάνει ὑπὲρ ἡμῶν."

151. 1 Tim 2:5: "εἷς γὰρ θεός, εἷς καὶ μεσίτης θεοῦ καὶ ἀνθρώπων, ἄνθρωπος Χριστὸς Ἰησοῦς, "

152. " ὃς γὰρ ἐὰν ἐπαισχυνθῇ με καὶ τοὺς ἐμοὺς λόγους ἐν τῇ γενεᾷ ταύτῃ τῇ μοιχαλίδι καὶ ἁμαρτωλῷ, καὶ ὁ υἱὸς τοῦ ἀνθρώπου ἐπαισχυνθήσεται αὐτόν, ὅταν ἔλθῃ ἐν τῇ δόξῃ τοῦ πατρὸς αὐτοῦ μετὰ τῶν ἀγγέλων τῶν ἁγίων."

153. " ὁ ἀθετῶν ἐμὲ καὶ μὴ λαμβάνων τὰ ῥήματά μου ἔχει τὸν κρίνοντα αὐτόν· ὁ λόγος ὃν ἐλάλησα ἐκεῖνος κρινεῖ αὐτὸν ἐν τῇ ἐσχάτῃ ἡμέρᾳ."

154. Ign., *Smyrn.* 6.1 "Judgment is prepared even for the heavenly beings, for the glory of the angels, and for the rulers both visible and invisible, if they do not believe in the blood of Christ."

155. "For they kept before their eyes the knowledge that they were escaping that eternal fire never to be extinguished"; *Mart. Pol.* 2.3; also, "Let us endure all things looking forward to the judgment seat of truth"; *Act. Carp.* 40.

156. The *Ac. Apol.* does the same and may well have been originally set in Rome, but extant traditions place it in Asia.

157. *Mart. Pion.* 4.24.

158. The idea of periodic conflagration of the world is attributed to Zeno of Cittum. See Jaap Mansfeld, "Resurrection Added: The Interpretatio Christiana of a Stoic Doctrine," *Vigiliae Christianae* 37 (1983), 218–33.

159. 2 Cor 6:2–3: " ἢ οὐκ οἴδατε ὅτι οἱ ἅγιοι τὸν κόσμον κρινοῦσιν; καὶ εἰ ἐν ὑμῖν κρίνεται ὁ κόσμος, ἀνάξιοί ἐστε κριτηρίων ἐλαχίστων; οὐκ οἴδατε ὅτι ἀγγέλους κρινοῦμεν, μήτιγε βιωτικ" cf. *Ascen. Isa.* 1.5, where Isaiah learns of the future judgment of the angels.

160. 1 Cor 6:1; 14:33; 2 Cor 9:12; Rom 8:27; 12:13; 15:26; 16:2.

161. See "Eschatological Resurrection," above.

162. *Mart. Mar.* 6.6–11: "Ostensum est, inquit, mihi fraters, tribunalis excelsi et candidi nimium, sublime fastigium, in quo ad uicem praesidis iudex satis decora facie praesidebat. illic era catasta, non humili pulpitu nec uno tantum ascensibilis gradu, sed multis ordinata gradibus et longe sublimis ascensu. et admouebantur confessorum singulae classes quas ille iudex ad gladium duci iuebat. uentum est et ad me. tunc exaudiur mihi uox clara et inmensa dicentis: Marianum applica. et scendebam in illam catastam et ecce ex improusio mihi sedens ad dextera eius iudicis Cyprianus apparuit et porrexit manum et leuauit me in altiorem catastae locum et arrisit et ait: Veni, sede mecum. et factum est ut audirentur aliae classes, me quoque assidente."

163. This seems further implied by "me quoque assidente," which suggests that he sits with Cyprian. Musurillo's translation "I formed part of the audience" pushes both the language and the logic of the passage too far. Apart from the judge and Cyprian, there is no one else there. For a discussion of the meaning of the *assideo*, see *Oxford Latin Dictionary*, 188.

164. The idea of reigning with Christ may have developed out of Revelation 20:4.

165. *Mart. Mont.* 10.4–8: "nec alio modo uitam aeternam accipere et cum Christo regnare poterimus, nisi fecerimus quod praecipit faciendum, qui et uitam promisit et regnum. eos denique hereditatem Dei consequi, qui pacem cum fratribus tenuerint, suo magisterio ipse dominus denuntiat dicens: Beati pacifici quoniam filii Dei uocabuntur. quod exponens apostolus ait: sumus filii Dei si autem filii, et heredes; heredes quidem Dei coheredes autem Christi siquidem conpatiamur ut et conglorificemur. si heres esse non potest nisi fillius, fillius autem non est nisi pacificus, hereditatem Dei habere non poterit qui pacem Dei rumpit. et hoc non quasi non admoniti dicimus aut sine diuina ostensione suggerimus." Cf. Matt 5:9 and Rom 8:16–17.

166. *Mart. Mont.* 22.2: "Sic regnaturum cum Deo martyrem iam spiritu ac mente regnatem, etiam itineris tota dignitas exprimebat." Cf. Rev 3:21.

167. They are similarly absent in Revelation.

CHAPTER 5

1. See Robin Darling Young, *In Procession before the World: Martyrdom as Public Liturgy in Early Christianity* (Milwaukee, Wis.: Marquette University Press, 2001), 56–81, who refers to patristic authors to describe the martyr's postmortem functions.

2. A number of scholars have argued that the imagery of enthronement is derived from an ancient Israelite liturgical event, the "festival of Yahweh" celebrated at the New Year. References to the enthronement of the King in the so-called enthronement or royal psalms are, it is argued, part of this practice. For the classification of the psalms, see Hermann Gunkel, *Die Psalmen*, Handkommentar zum Alten Testament, Abt. 2, Bd. 2, 4. Aufl. (Göttingen: Vandenhoeck & Ruprecht, 1926). For the argument that these psalms are part of a New Year festival, see Sigmund Mowinckel, *The Psalms in Israel's Worship* (Grand Rapids, Mich.:Eerdmans, 2004), 106–29. Mowinckel locates the origins of this festival in Canaanite myth and practice (130–82). The dating of the royal/enthronement psalms to the First Temple period is by no means universally accepted.

See Otto Eissfeldt, *The Old Testament: An Introduction, Including the Apocrypha and Pseudepigrapha* (New York: Harper and Row, 1965). For the enthronement of messianic figures in the Second Temple period, see 1 *En.* 51:3; 55:4; 61:8; 62:5; 69:27, 29.

3. See chapter 1, above.

4. See the comment of Adela Collins that "the one who wishes to have a high rank in the messianic kingdom must be ready to suffer," in Adela Yarbro Collins, *Mark: A Commentary*, Hermeneia: A Critical and Historical Commentary on the Bible (Minneapolis, Minn.: Fortress Press, 2007), 496.

5. Mark 14:62: "ὁ δὲ Ἰησοῦς εἶπεν, Ἐγώ εἰμι, καὶ ὄψεσθε τὸν υἱὸν τοῦ ἀνθρώπου ἐκ δεξιῶν καθήμενον τῆς δυνάμεως καὶ ἐρχόμενον μετὰ τῶν νεφελῶν τοῦ οὐρανοῦ."

6. For a discussion of Markan modifications of contemporary understandings of the Messiah, see Collins, *Mark: A Commentary*, 53–72, 705.

7. Heb 1:1–4: "Πολυμερῶς καὶ πολυτρόπως πάλαι ὁ θεὸς λαλήσας τοῖς πατράσιν ἐν τοῖς προφήταις ἐπ᾽ ἐσχάτου τῶν ἡμερῶν τούτων ἐλάλησεν ἡμῖν ἐν υἱῷ, ὃν ἔθηκεν κληρονόμον πάντων, δι᾽ οὗ καὶ ἐποίησεν τοὺς αἰῶνας· ὃς ὢν ἀπαύγασμα τῆς δόξης καὶ χαρακτὴρ τῆς ὑποστάσεως αὐτοῦ, φέρων τε τὰ πάντα τῷ ῥήματι τῆς δυνάμεως αὐτοῦ, καθαρισμὸν τῶν ἁμαρτιῶν ποιησάμενος ἐκάθισεν ἐν δεξιᾷ τῆς μεγαλωσύνης ἐν ὑψηλοῖς, τοσούτῳ κρείττων γενόμενος τῶν ἀγγέλων ὅσῳ διαφορώτερον παρ᾽ αὐτοὺς κεκληρονόμηκεν ὄνομα."

8. The term used to describe this saving act (καθαρισμὸν) is rare in the New Testament. The notion that the death of Christ provides a cleansing of sin, however, is much more common; cf. Rom 3:25; 5:8; Acts 15:91; John 1:29.

9. For a discussion on the importance of this psalm more generally, see David M. Hay, *Glory at the Right Hand: Psalm 110 in Early Christianity* (Nashville, Tenn.: Abingdon Press, 1973).

10. See Attridge, *Hebrews*, 46.

11. See Ibid., 47–48; cf. Phil 2:9–11.

12. For a discussion of angelic Christology, the theological structure that may lie behind this text, see discussion in the previous chapter.

13. Rev 3:21: "ὁ νικῶν δώσω αὐτῷ καθίσαι μετ᾽ ἐμοῦ ἐν τῷ θρόνῳ μου, ὡς κἀγὼ ἐνίκησα καὶ ἐκάθισα μετὰ τοῦ πατρός μου ἐν τῷ θρόνῳ αὐτοῦ."

14. Cf. Rev 1:6; 5:10; 20:4, 6; 22:5.

15. "ὑμεῖς δέ ἐστε οἱ διαμεμενηκότες μετ᾽ ἐμοῦ ἐν τοῖς πειρασμοῖς μου· κἀγὼ διατίθεμαι ὑμῖν καθὼς διέθετό μοι ὁ πατήρ μου βασιλείαν, ἵνα ἔσθητε καὶ πίνητε ἐπὶ τῆς τραπέζης μου ἐν τῇ βασιλείᾳ μου, καὶ καθήσεσθε ἐπὶ θρόνων τὰς δώδεκα φυλὰς κρίνοντες τοῦ Ἰσραήλ."

16. "ὁ δὲ Ἰησοῦς εἶπεν αὐτοῖς, Ἀμὴν λέγω ὑμῖν ὅτι ὑμεῖς οἱ ἀκολουθήσαντές μοι ἐν τῇ παλιγγενεσίᾳ, ὅταν καθίσῃ ὁ υἱὸς τοῦ ἀνθρώπου ἐπὶ θρόνου δόξης αὐτοῦ, καθήσεσθε καὶ ὑμεῖς ἐπὶ δώδεκα θρόνους κρίνοντες τὰς δώδεκα φυλὰς τοῦ Ἰσραήλ."

17. "εἰ ὑπομένομεν, καὶ συμβασιλεύσομεν·"

18. "ὁ νικῶν δώσω αὐτῷ καθίσαι μετ᾽ ἐμοῦ ἐν τῷ θρόνῳ μου, ὡς κἀγὼ ἐνίκησα καὶ ἐκάθισα μετὰ τοῦ πατρός μου ἐν τῷ θρόνῳ αὐτοῦ."

19. Another example is found in Herm., *Vis.* 3.1.9. In this passage, the old lady (the Church) tells Hermas that sitting on the right is an honor reserved for those who have suffered for the name.

20. *Mart. Mont.* 10.4.

21. Ibid., 22.4.

22. Origen *Mart.* 14.28; Cyprian, *Fort.* praef. 4; 5.11; 12.1–8; Cyprian, *On the Glory of Martyrdom* 11.2.

23. André Grabar, "Le trône des martyrs," *Cahiers Archéologiques* 6 (1952): 31–41.

24. Grabar hypothesizes that in their enthronement, martyrs replace Christ, presiding over earthly affairs and, in particular, the agape meal: "Le martyr surtout peut être appelél à cette présidence, parce que son propre sacrifice l'a fait participer à la passion du Christ que renouvellent les agapes mystiques de chaque messe. Il remplace en quelque sorte le Christ, dans ce rôle de president" Grabar, "Le trône des martyrs," 40; André Grabar, *Martyrium: Recherches sur le culte des reliques et l'art Chrétien antique* (Paris: Collège de France, 1943), 2:51, 69.

25. G. W. Clarke, *The Letters of St. Cyprian of Carthage* (New York: Newman Press, 1984), 194.

26. *Mart. Mont.* 10.4–8: "nec alio modo uitam aeternam accipere et cum Christo regnare poterimus, nisi fecerimus quod praecipit faciendum, qui et uitam promisit et regnum. eos denique hereditatem Dei consequi, qui pacem cum fratribus tenuerint, suo magisterio ipse dominus denuntiat dicens: Beati pacifici quoniam filii Dei vocabuntur. Quod exponens apostolus ait: sumus filii Dei si autem filii et heredes heredes quidem Dei coheredes autem Christi siquidem conpatimur ut et conglorifice-mur. Si heres esse non potest nisi fillius fillius autem non est nisi pacificus, heredi-tatem Dei habere non poterit qui pacem Dei rumpit. et hoc non quasi non admoniti dicimus aut sine diuina ostensione suggerimus." Cf. Matt 5:9 and Rom 8:16–17.

27. *Mart. Mar.* 5.8

28. *Ac. Phileas* Latin 6.1: "Omnium spirituum nostrorum saluator est dominus Iesus Christus, cui ego uinctus seruio. Potens est ipse qui me uocauit in hereditatem gloriae suae et hanc uocare."

29. Ibid., 8.2: "ego autem magnam ago gratiam regibus et praesidatui quoniam coheres factus sum Christi Iesu."

30. " ἔφη ὁ Ἰησοῦς, Ἀμὴν λέγω ὑμῖν, οὐδείς ἐστιν ὃς ἀφῆκεν οἰκίαν ἢ ἀδελφοὺς ἢ ἀδελφὰς ἢ μητέρα ἢ πατέρα ἢ τέκνα ἢ ἀγροὺς ἕνεκεν ἐμοῦ καὶ ἕνεκεν τοῦ εὐαγγελίου, ἐὰν μὴ λάβῃ ἑκατονταπλασίονα νῦν ἐν τῷ καιρῷ τούτῳ οἰκίας καὶ ἀδελφοὺς καὶ ἀδελφὰς καὶ μητέρας καὶ τέκνα καὶ ἀγροὺς μετὰ διωγμῶν, καὶ ἐν τῷ αἰῶνι τῷ ἐρχομένῳ ζωὴν αἰώνιον." As a matter of interest, D(it) augments the Greek text here so that the English translation reads, "He who has left house and sisters and brothers and mother and children and farms with persecution will receive eternal life in the age to come." The reading focuses the reader's attention on the postmortem heavenly rewards of following Jesus. See Collins, *Mark: A Commentary*, 475 n.k.

31. Collins, *Mark: A Commentary*, 481. Given that Mark is willing to advocate martyrdom to all who follow after Jesus, it does not seem to me particularly extraordi-nary that he would propose abandoning one's non-Christian biological family.

32. *Mart. Iren.* 4.6–7: "Irenaeus respondit: Praeceptum est domini mei Iesu Christi dicentis, Qui diligit patrem aut matrem aut uxorem aut filios aut fratres aut parentes super me, non est me dignus. itaque ad Deum in caelum adspiciens et ad eius promissiones intendens, omnia despiciens nullum parentem absque eo se nosse atque habere fatebatur."

33. Irenaeus's behavior here may owe much to the depiction of Socrates in the *Crito*, but he explicitly cites scriptural traditions in support of his behavior.

34. 1 John 4:20.

35. *Testament of the Forty Martyrs* 2.4: "καὶ γὰρ διὰ τοῦ ὁρωμένου ἀδελφοῦ ὁ ἀόρατος τιμᾶται θεός· καὶ πρὸς μὲν τοὺς ὁμομητρίους ἀδελφοὺς ὁ λόγος, πρὸς δὲ πάντας τοὺς φιλοχρίστους ἡ γνώμη. καὶ γὰρ ὁ ἅγιος ἡμῶν σωτὴρ καὶ θεὸς ἐκείνους ἔφασκεν ἀδελφοὺς εἶναί, τοὺς οὐχὶ τῇ φύσει κοινωνοῦντας ἀλλήλοις, ἀλλὰ τῇ ἀρίστῃ πράξει πρὸς τὴν πίστιν συναπτομένους καὶ τὸ θέλμα ἐκπληροῦντας τοῦ πατρὸς ἡμῶν τοῦ ἐν τοῖς οὐρανοῖς." The translation of ὁμομητρίους as "biological" does not do justice to the matriarchal focus of the term but has the additional benefit of avoiding the implicit comparison between biological maternal family ties and the better spiritual patriarchal family of God. Musurillo's translation "true brothers" seems to reinforce the modern bias toward biological children and seems to completely miss the point of this passage, in which spiritual siblings are the "true" siblings. Herbert Musurillo, *Acts of the Christian Martyrs* (Oxford: Clarendon Press, 1972), 359.

36. Cf. 1.5–6 and discussion in the section "Heavenly Banquet" in chapter 4.

37. The gendered nature of participation in the Christian family is debated. For the view that the Christian family is predicated upon patriarchal notions of fathers and sons, see Lone Fatum, "Brotherhood in Christ: A Gender Hermeneutical Reading of 1 Thessalonians," in *Constructing Early Christian Families: Family as Social Reality and Metaphor*, ed. Halvor Moxnes (London: Routledge, 1997), 183–97. For a broader discussion of gender in early Christianity, see Ross Shepard Kraemer and Mary Rose D'Angelo, *Women and Christian Origins* (New York: Oxford University Press, 1999); Patricia Cox Miller, *Women in Early Christianity: Translations from Greek Texts* (Washington, D.C.: Catholic University of America Press, 2005); Dale B. Martin and Patricia Cox Miller, *The Cultural Turn in Late Ancient Studies: Gender, Asceticism, and Historiography* (Durham, N.C.: Duke University Press, 2005).

38. *Ac. Phileas* 6.4: "Aduocati et officium una cum curatore et cum omnibus propinquis eius pedes ipsius complectebantur rogantes eum ut respectum haberet uxoris et curam susciperet liberorum. ille uelut si saxo immobili unda adilderetur, garrientium dicta respuere, Deum in oculis habere, parentes et propinquos apostolos et martyres ducere."

39. Irenaeus tells Probus that his sons have the same God as he does (4.8).

40. "ὁ γὰρ διὰ τὸ ὄνομα Κυρίου τοῦ Θεοῦ καταδικαζόμενος, οὗτος μάρτυς ἅγιος, ἀδελφὸς τοῦ Κυρίου, υἱὸς τοῦ ὑψίστου, δοχεῖον τοῦ εὐαγγελίου ἔλαθεν ἕκαστος τῶν πιστῶν ἐν τῷ καταξιωθῆναι τοῦ ἀφθάρτου στεφάνου καὶ τῆς μαρτυρίας τῶν παθημάτων αὐτοῦ καὶ τῆς κοινωνίας τοῦ αἵματος αὐτοῦ, συμμορφωθῆναι τῷ θανάτῳ τοῦ Χριστοῦ εἰς υἱοθεσίαν." Text, Marcel Metzger, *Les constitutions apostoliques* (Paris: Editions du Cerf, 1985), 2.202–4.

41. Francis Xavier Funk, *Didascalia et Constitutiones Apostolorum* (Padernorn: Schoeningh, 1905).

42. Cuthbert H. Turner, "A Primitive Edition of the Apostolic Constitutions and Canons," *Journal of Theological Studies* 15 (1913): 54–61; Bernard Capelle, "Le texte du 'gloria in excelsis,'" *Revue de Histoire Eccléstiastique* 44 (1949): 439–57.

43. Origen, *Mart.* 14, trans. Rowan A. Greer, *Origen*, Classics of Western Spirituality (New York: Paulist Press, 1979), 53–54.

44. Robin Darling Young sees the family of martyrs as part of the blessings of martyrdom. See Young, *In Procession before the World*, 58.

45. In addition to the passages we have discussed, it also appears in the catena of scriptural passages cited in Cyprian, *Fort.* 12.6. Additionally, he relates, in *On the Glory of Martyrdom* 15, a story of a man who is unswayed by the demands of family and material possessions: "I indeed have known it, and I am not deceived in the truth of what I say, when the cruel hands of the persecutors were wrenching asunder the martyr's limbs, and the furious torturer was ploughing up his lacerated muscles, and still could not overcome him. I have known it by the words of those who stood around. 'This is a great matter. Assuredly I know not what it is—that he is not subdued by suffering, that he is not broken down by wearing torments.' Moreover, there were other words of those who spoke: 'A And yet I believe he has children: for he has a wife associated with him in his house; and yet he does not give way to the bond of his offspring, nor is he withdrawn by the claim of his family affection from his steadfast purpose. This matter must be known, and this strength must be investigated, even to the very heart; for that is no trifling confession, whatever it may be, for which a man suffers, even so as to be able to die'" (*ANF* 5.583).

46. Young, *In Procession before the World*, 29.

47. J. Duncan M. Derrett, "Scripture and Norms in the Apostolic Fathers,"*ANRW* 27.1.649–99.

48. *Mart. Pol.* 2.3.

49. Tertullian, *Mart.* 3.

50. Robin Darling Young, for instance, interprets the declaration of the Scillitan martyrs that "today we are martyrs in heaven" in the following way: "They [the Scillitan martys] are also saying that they belong already to the ordered angelic society of the heavenly court, they are recognized by many authors as being, already, angelic in status. Their predecessors were numerous: Enoch, Jacob, Moses; Jesus, Paul, Stephen" (Young, *In Procession before the World*, 13). Young does not explicitly cite Origen here, but she does elsewhere. I remain curious as to how she compiles her list of the "predecessors" of the Scillitan martyrs given that they are nowhere mentioned in the account itself.

51. "Dicebat autem et Hebraeus magister quod duo illa Seraphim, quae in Esaia senis alis describuntur clamantia adinuicem et dicentia: *Sanctus sanctus sanctus dominus Sabaoth*, de unigenito filio dei et de spiritu sancto esset intellegendum. Nos uero putamus etiam illud, quod in cantico Ambacum dictum est: *In medio duorum animalium* (uel *duarum uitarum*) *cognosceris*, de Christo et de spiritu sancto sentiri debere." Origen, *Princ.* I.iii.4 p. 148 in *SC* 252, trans. Joseph W. Trigg, "The Angel of

Great Counsel: Christ and the Angelic Hierarchy in Origen's Theology," *Journal of Theological Studies* 42 (1991): 38. This passage of *First Principles* survives only in Rufinus and Justinian. For a discussion of Rufinus's translation, see Nicola Pace, *Ricerche sulla traduzione di Rufino del "De principiis" di Origene* (Firenze: La Nuova Italia, 1990). For a discussion of Rufinus's role in the Origenist controversy, see Elizabeth A. Clark, *The Origenist Controversy: The Cultural Construction of an Early Christian Debate* (Princeton, N.J.: Princeton University Press, 1992).

52. Even popular works trace the roots of Arianism and the Arian controversy to Origen. See, for example, Justo L. González, *The Story of Christianity* (San Francisco: Harper & Row, 1984), 1.159–61.

53. For the importance of this idea in the charges laid against Origen, see Justinian's *Letter to Menas* and Pierre Nautin, *Origène: Sa vie et son œuvre*, Christianisme Antique 1 (Paris: Beauchesne, 1977), 132–33. Nautin discusses how, according to Photius, Origen was charged with teaching that "the cherubim are *epinoiai* of the son." Origen's tendency to use angelic terminology to describe the Son has caused manifold problems for theologians who wish to rehabilitate Origen for Christian theology. Consequently, a number of scholars have labored to demonstrate that while Origen speaks of the Son as an angel, there are a number of ways in which this language may operate:

"(a) Sometimes 'angel' is a bare title whose implications are not apparent. (b) A second way could be called 'functional,' where the Son is an 'angel' because of this function as a 'messenger' of God. . . . (c) A third way could be called 'dispensational,' where the Son's taking on angelic nature corresponds to taking on human nature in the Incarnation. (d) A fourth way could be called 'natural,' where it is taught that the Son has an angelic (not a divine) nature." Trigg, "The Angel of Great Counsel," 37.

Trigg, who offers this range of interpretations, is correct to direct us to the nuances in language and its application. Other scholars offering a defense of Origen against charges of angelic Christology include Joseph Barbel, *Christos Angelos: Die Anschauung von Christus als Bote und Engel in der Gelehrten und Volkstümlichen Literatur des Christlichen Altertums* (Bottrop: W. Postberg, 1941). Comparisons between two discernible groups (e.g., martyrs and angels, or Christ and angels) necessitate careful and sophisticated analysis. We should note, however, that the subtle and nuanced way that scholars approach comparisons between Christ and other beings is nowhere to be found in statements about martyrs. Attempting to do justice to Origen's thought should be the primary task of the scholar, but this endeavor should be evenhanded.

54. For a full discussion and list of references, see the section "Angelomorphic Christology" in chapter 4. Origen is cited in a number of works on angelic Christology, including Werner, who sees Origen as the link between angelic Christology and Arius's subordinationanism. See Martin Werner, *Die Entstehung des christlichen Dogmas: Problemgeschichtlich dargestellt* (Bern-Leipzig: P. Haupt, 1941).

55. The capitalization of "Gods" here may raise some eyebrows. Given that debates about the status of the martyrs involve Christians and Christian theology, it is only appropriate to treat the martyrs as potential Christian deities.

56. Theological discussions of *theosis* frequently import the categories of later theological debate into an earlier period. In writing of Ignatius of Antioch, Vladimir

Kharlamov argues that "[Ignatius's] identification with Christ, or christification, is not spelled out in an ontological sense," mistakenly assuming that ontological categories are an important part of second-century discussions of imitating Christ (see Vladimir Kharlamov, "Emergence of the Deification Theme in the Apostolic Fathers," in *Theosis: Deification in Christian Theology*, ed. Stephen Finlan and Vladimir Kharlamov, Princeton Theological Monograph Series 52 (Eugene, Ore.: Pickwick, 2006), 65. We cannot assume, therefore, that the category of essence or *ousia* was an operative concept for Christians in the second or even third century. The absence of this term is not evidence either for or against an idea of ontological deification. The absence of the term merely demonstrates that these were not operative categories for the communities that produced these texts.

57. Even in those instances where Christians understood martyrs as equal to Christ in status, we cannot say that the martyrs were viewed as Gods. In these instances, sharing the status of Christ does not say anything (positively or negatively) about ontological deification.

58. For a discussion of imitation and theosis in pilgrimage, dress, and other rituals in Egypt, see Stephen J. Davis, *Coptic Christology in Practice: Incarnation and Divine Participation in Late Antique and Medieval Egypt*, Oxford Early Christian Studies (Oxford: Oxford University Press, 2008).

59. A. A. R. Bastiaensen, "Quelques observations sur la terminologie du martyre chez saint Augustin," in *Signum Pietatis: Festgabe für Cornelius Petrus Mayer OSA zum 60. Geburtstag*, (ed. Adolar Zumkeller; Würzburg: Augustinus-Verlag, 1989), 201–16.

60. A. Dupont, "Imitatio Christi, Imitatio Stephani: Augustine's Thinking on Martyrdom Based on his Sermons on the Protomartyr Stephen," *Augustiniana* 56 (2006) 33. Following Victor Saxer, *Morts, martyrs, reliques en Afrique chrétienne aux premiers siècles. Les témoignages de Tertullien, Cyprien et Augustin à la lumière de l'archéologie africaine*, Théologie historique 55 (Paris: Beauchesne, 1980), 124.

61. Of the 546 extant *sermons* of Augustine, 102 are dedicated to the feast days of saints and martyrs. In addition, his *Enarrat. Ps.*, *Tract. Ev. Jo.*, and *Tract. ep. Jo.* all deal with martyrdom at length.

62. *Serm. Dom.* 273.7, translated in Augustine, *Serm. 273–305A*, ed. John E. Rotelle, trans. Edmund Hill, The Works of Saint Augustine 3 (New York: New City Press, 1994) 18 (PLXXXVIII 1251).

63. *Serm. Dom.* 273. 9; *NPNF* 1.8.4.350 (PL XXXVIII.1252).

64. Ibid.

65. Ibid.

66. Hans Freiherr von Campenhausen, *Die Idee des Martyriums in der alten Kirche* (Göttingen: Vandenhoeck & Ruprecht, 1936), 101–6.

67. Dupont, "Imitatio Christi, Imitatio Stephani" 33.

68. Augustine, *Faust.* 20.4; 20.21.

69. Augustine employs a number of other strategies to undermine the influence of the martyrs. He focuses on the linguistic meaning of the term *martys* as "witness," thereby broadening its applicability and reference. Additionally, he conflates the meaning of *sanctus* and *martys* so that the two become exchangeable and compares the

veneration of martyrs to the veneration of living men. See Bastiaensen, "Quelques observations sur la terminologie du martyre chez saint Augustin," 201–16. I am grateful to Christine Luckritz Marquis for allowing me to read her paper, "Augustine's Martyr Complex" (unpublished paper, Duke University, 2008).

70. A number of scholars have observed that Augustine becomes considerably more accepting of the cult of the saints once he comes to control the relics of Stephen.

71. All translations of Victricius are taken from Gillian Clark, "Victricius of Rouen: Praising the Saints," *Journal of Early Christian Studies* 7 (1999): 365–99 (PL XX.449).

72. Victricius, *De Laude Sanctorum* 6.34–35.

73. Ibid., 7.44–8.5.

74. Ibid., 8.19–20.

75. Clark, "Victricius of Rouen," 367.

76. John of Damascus, *Exact Exposition of the Orthodox Faith*, 4.15 (*NPNF* 2.9.87).

77. While we must be wary of assuming that John of Damascus opposes a realized rather than accused or potential misunderstanding, his defense of the saints indicates that this kind of interpretation was at the very least possible and threatening.

78. *Pass. Perp.* 11.7.

CONCLUSION

1. Ramsay MacMullen suggests that as little as 5 percent of the population of a given town or city would have been able to attend an individual church service. His findings radically alter our understanding of the religious lives of ancient Christians. If MacMullen is correct, then the "average" Christian may have been more familiar with the feast days of martyrs than the homilies of their bishops. See, Ramsay MacMullen, *The Second Church: Popular Christianity A.D. 200–400*, Writings from the Greco-Roman World Supplements (Atlanta, Ga.: Society of Biblical Literature, 2009).

Bibliography

Abelard, Peter, E. M. Buytaert, C. J. Mews, Mary Romig, and Charles Burnett. *Petri Abaelardi Opera Theologica*. Corpus Christianorum, Continuatio Mediaevalis. Turnhout: Typographi Brepols, 1969.

Achtemeier, Paul J. *1 Peter: A Commentary on First Peter*. Edited by Eldon J. Epp. Hermeneia: A Critical and Historical Commentary on the Bible. Minneapolis, Minn.: Fortress Press, 1996.

Aland, Barbara, et al., eds. *Novum Testamentum Graecae*. 27th ed. Stuttgart: Deutsche Bibelgesellschaft, 1993.

Aland, Kurt, Barbara Aland, and Erroll F. Rhodes. *The Text of the New Testament: An Introduction to the Critical Editions and to the Theory and Practice of Modern Textual Criticisms*. Grand Rapids, Mich.: Eerdmans, 1987.

Allison, Dale C. *Resurrecting Jesus: The Earliest Christian Tradition and Its Interpreters*. New York: T & T Clark, 2005.

Anderson, Gary A. *Sacrifices and Offerings in Ancient Israel: Studies in Their Social and Political Importance*. Harvard Semitic Monographs 41. Atlanta, Ga.: Scholars Press, 1987.

Anselm. *Why God Became Man*. Translated by Joseph M. Colleran. Albany, N.Y.: Magi Books, 1969.

Argyle, A. W. "The Greek of Luke and Acts." *New Testament Studies* 20 (1973–74): 441–45.

Arinze, Cardinal Francis. "The Holy Eucharist Unites Heaven and Earth." Address at Eucharist Congress, Basilica of the Immaculate Conception, Washington, D.C., 2004.

Asher, Jeffrey R. *Polarity and Change in 1 Corinthians 15: A Study of Metaphysics, Rhetoric, and Resurrection*. Hermeneutische Untersuchungen zur Theologie 42. Tübingen: Mohr Siebeck, 2000.

Attridge, Harold W. *The Epistle to the Hebrews: A Commentary on the Epistle to the Hebrews*. Edited by Helmut Koester. Hermeneia: A Critical and Historical Commentary on the Bible. Philadelphia: Fortress Press, 1989.

―――. "Giving Voice to Jesus: Use of the Psalms in the New Testament." Pages 101–12 in *Psalms in Community: Jewish and Christian Textual, Liturgical, and Artistic Traditions*. Edited by Harold W. Attridge and Margot Elsbeth Fassler. Leiden: Brill, 2004.

―――. "Making Scents of Paul." Pages 71–88 in *Early Christianity and Classical Culture: Essays in Honor of Abraham Malherbe*. Edited by John Fitzgerald. Leiden: Brill, 2003.

Attridge, Harold W., and Margot Elsbeth Fassler. *Psalms in Community: Jewish and Christian Textual, Liturgical, and Artistic Traditions*. Leiden: Brill, 2004.

Aulén, Gustaf. *Christus Victor: An Historical Study of the Three Main Types of the Idea of Atonement*. Translated by A. G. Hebert. New York: Macmillan, 1969.

Aune, David E. "Following the Lamb: Discipleship in the Apocalypse." Pages 269–84 in *Patterns of Discipleship in the New Testament*. Edited by Richard N. Longenecker. Grand Rapids, Mich.: Eerdmans, 1996.

―――. *Revelation*. 3 vols. Word Biblical Commentary 52. Dallas, Tex.: Word Books, 1997.

Baldwin, Matthew C. *Whose Acts of Peter? Text and Historical Context of the Actus Vercellenses*. Wissenschaftliche Untersuchungen zum Neuen Testament 2.196. Tübingen: Mohr Siebeck, 2005.

Bammel, C. P. "Ignatian Problems." *Journal of Theological Studies*, n.s., 33 (1982): 62–97.

Barbel, Joseph. *Christos Angelos: Die Anschauung von Christus als Bote und Engel in der Gelehrten und Volkstümlichen Literatur des Christlichen Altertums*. Bottrop: W. Postberg, 1941.

Bardhill, Jonathan. "The Church of Saints Sergius and Bacchus in Constantinople and the Monophysite Refugees." *Dumbarton Oaks Papers* 54 (2000): 1–11.

Barrett, C. K. *Commentary on the Second Epistle to the Corinthians*. New York: Harper & Row, 1973.

―――. "Imitatio Christi in Acts." Pages 251–62 in *Jesus of Nazareth: Lord and Christ. Essays on the Historical Jesus and New Testament Christology*. Edited by Joel B. Green and Max Turner. Grand Rapids, Mich.: Eerdmans, 1994.

Barnard, Leslie W. "In Defense of Pseudo-Pionius' Account of Saint Polycarp's Martyrdom." Pages 192–204 in *Kyriakon Festschrift Johannes Quasten*. Edited by Patrick Granfield and Josef Jungmann. Münster: Aschendorff, 1970.

Baslez, Marie-Françoise. *Les persecutions dans l'Antiquité: Victimes, heroes, martyrs*. Paris: Fayard, 2007.

Bastiaensen, A. A. R. "Quelques observations sur la terminologie du martyre chez saint Augustin." Pages 201–16 in *Signum Pietatis: Festgabe für Cornelius Petrus Mayer OSA zum 60. Geburtstag*. Edited by Adolar Zumkeller. Würzburg: Augustinus-Verlag, 1989.

Bastiaensen, A. A. R., A. Hilhorst, and C. H. Kneepkens, eds. *Fructus Centesimus: Mélanges Gerard J. M. Bartelink*. Instrumenta Patristica 19. Steenbrugge and Dordrecht: Kluwer, 1989.

Bastiaensen, A. A. R., A. Hilhorst, G. A. A. Kortekaas, A. P. Orban, and M. M. van Assendelft. *Atti e Passioni dei Martiri*. Milan: Mondadori, 1987.

Bauckham, Richard. "For Whom Were the Gospels Written?" Pages 9–48 in *The Gospels for All Christians: Rethinking the Gospel Audiences*. Edited by Richard Bauckham. Grand Rapids, Mich.: Eerdmans, 1997.

———. *God Crucified: Monotheism and Christology in the New Testament*. Grand Rapids, Mich.: Eerdmans, 1998.

Baumeister, Th. *Die Anfänge der Theologie des Martyriums*. Münster: Aschendorff, 1980.

Beare, Francis Wright. *The First Epistle of Peter*. Oxford: Blackwell, 1947.

Bedjan, Paul. *Acta Martyrum et Sanctorum*. 7 vols. Paris: Via dicta de Sèvres, 1890–97.

Bell, Catherine M. *Ritual Theory, Ritual Practice*. New York: Oxford University Press, 1992.

Belleville, Linda L. "Imitate Me, Just as I Imitate Christ: Discipleship in the Corinthian Correspondence." Pages 120–41 in *Patterns of Discipleship in the New Testament*. Edited by Richard N. Longenecker. Grand Rapids, Mich.: Eerdmans, 1996.

Ben-Porat, Ziva. "The Poetics of Literary Allusion." *PTL: A Journal for Descriptive Poetics and Theory of Literature* 1 (1970): 105–28.

Benham, William. *The Imitation of Christ: Four Books*. London: J. C. Nimmo & Bain, 1882.

Betz, Hans Dieter. *2 Corinthians 8 and 9: A Commentary on Two Administrative Letters of the Apostle Paul*. Edited by George W. MacRae. Hermeneia: A Critical and Historical Commentary on the Bible. Philadelphia: Fortress Press, 1985.

———. *Nachfolge und Nachahmung Jesu Christi im Neuen Testament*. Beiträge zur Historischen Theologie 37. Tübingen: Mohr Siebeck, 1967.

———. "Spirit, Freedom and the Law." *Svensk exegetisk årsbok* 39 (1974): 145–60.

Bhabha, Homi. *The Location of Culture*. London: Blackburn, 1994.

Birdsalll, J. Neville. "The Western Text in the Second Century." Pages 3–17 in *Gospel Traditions in the Second Century: Origins, Recensions, Text, and Transmission*. Edited by William L. Petersen. Christianity and Judaism in Antiquity 3. Notre Dame, Ind.: University of Notre Dame Press, 1989.

Bisbee, Gary A. *Pre-Decian Acts of the Martyrs and Commentarii*. Edited by Margaret R. Miles and Bernadette J. Brooten. Harvard Dissertations in Religion 22. Philadelphia: Fortress Press, 1988.

Boeft, Jan den. "Martyres sunt hominess fuerunt." Pages 115–24 in *Fructus Centesimus: Mélanges Gerard J. M. Bartelink*. Edited by A. A. R. Bastiaensen, A. Hilhorst, and C. H. Kneepkens. Instrumenta Patristica 19. Steenbrugge and Dordrecht: Kluwer, 1989.

Boeft, Jan den, and Jan N. Bremmer. "Notiunculae Martyrologicae." *Vigiliae Christianae* 35 (1981): 43–56.

———. "Notiunculae Martyrologicae IV." *Vigiliae Christianae* 45 (1991): 105–22.

Bolin, Thomas M. "A Reassessment of the Textual Problem of Luke 23.34a." *Proceedings of the Eastern Great Lakes and Midwestern Biblical Society* 12 (1992): 131–44.

Bollandus, Jean, et socii. *Acta Sanctorum*. 71 vols. Brussels: Société des Bollandistes, 1642–1906.

Borchardt, Brian. *Two Saints: The Martyrdom of St. Sergius & St. Bacchus*. Fond du Lac, Wis.: Seven Hills Press, 2004.

Bowersock, G. W. *Martyrdom and Rome*. Cambridge: Cambridge University Press, 1995.

Boyarin, Daniel. *Dying for God: Martyrdom and the Making of Christianity and Judaism*. Stanford, Calif.: Stanford University Press, 1999.

Bradshaw, Paul F., Maxwell E. Johnson, and L. Edward Phillips. *The Apostolic Tradition: A Commentary*. Hermeneia: A Critical and Historical Commentary on the Bible. Minneapolis, Minn.: Fortress Press, 2002.

Branscomb, Bennett Harvie. *The Gospel of Mark*. The Moffat New Testament Commentary Series 2. New York: Harper, 1937.

Brekelmans, C. H. W. "The Saints of the Most High and Their Kingdom." *Old Testament Studies* 14 (1965): 305–29.

Bremmer, Jan N. "The Motivation of Martyrs: Perpetua and the Palestinians." Pages 535–54 in *Religion im kulturellen Diskurs. Festschrift für Hans G. Kippenberg zu seinem 65. Geburtstag*. Edited by B. Luchesi and K. von Stuckrad. Berlin: Walter de Gruyter, 2004.

———. *The Rise and Fall of the Afterlife*. London: Routledge, 2002.

Breytenbach, Cilliers. *Versöhnung: Eine Studie zur Paulinischen Soteriologie*. Wissenschaftliche Monographien zum Alten und Neuen Testament 60. Neukirchen-Vluyn: Neukirchener, 1989.

Brock, Peter. *The Military Question in the Early Church: A Selected Bibliography of a Century's Scholarship*. Toronto: Network Lithographers and Composition, 1988.

Brock, Rita Nakashima, and Rebecca Ann Parker. *Proverbs of Ashes: Violence, Redemptive Suffering, and the Search for What Saves Us*. Boston: Beacon Press, 2001.

Broeck, R. van den. "Popular Religious Practices and Ecclesiastical Policies in the Early Church." Pages 11–54 in *Official and Popular Religion: Analysis of a Theme for Religious Studies*. Edited by P. H. Vrijoh and Jean Jacques Waardenburg. Berlin: Mouton de Gruyter, 1979.

Brown, Peter. *The Cult of the Saints: Its Rise and Function in Late Antiquity*. Chicago: University of Chicago Press, 1981.

Brown, Raymond E. *The Death of the Messiah: From Gethsemane to the Grave, A Commentary on the Passion Narratives in the Four Gospels*. 2 vols. Anchor Bible Reference Library. New York: Doubleday, 1994.

———. *The Gospel According to John*. 2 vols. Anchor Bible Commentary 29–29B. Garden City, N.Y.: Doubleday, 1966.

Brox, Norbert. *Der erste Petrusbrief*. Evangelisch-katholischer Kommentar zum Neuen Testament. Zürich: Benziger Verlag, 1979.

———. *Der Hirt des Hermas*. Kommentar zu den Apostolischen Vätern 7. Bd. Göttingen: Vandenhoeck & Ruprecht, 1991.

———. *Zeuge und Märtyrer: Untersuchungen zur frühchristlichen Zeugnis-Terminologie*. Studien zum Alten und Neuen Testament 5. Munich: Kösel-Verlag, 1961.

Bruyne, L. de. "Les lois de l'art paléochrétien comme instrument herméneutique." *Rivista di Archeologia Cristiana* 39 (1963): 7–92.

Bultmann, Rudolf Karl. *The History of the Synoptic Tradition*. 2d ed. Oxford: Blackwell, 1963.

Burkert, Walter. *Homo Necans: Interpretationen Altgriechischer Opferriten und Mythen.* Religionsgeschichtliche Versuche und Vorabeiten. Bd. 32. Berlin: Walter de Gruyter, 1972.

Burkitt, F. C. "The Oldest Manuscript of St. Justin's Martyrdom." *Journal of Theological Studies* 11 (1909): 61–66.

Burridge, Richard A. *What Are the Gospels? A Comparison with Graeco-Roman Biography.* 2d ed. Grand Rapids, Mich.: Eerdmans, 2004.

Burrus, Virginia, ed. *Late Ancient Christianity.* A People's History of Christianity 2. Minneapolis, Minn.: Fortress Press, 2005.

Buschmann, Gerd. *Das Martyrium des Polykarp.* Kommentar zu den Apostolischen Vätern 6. Göttingen: Vandenhoeck & Ruprecht, 1998.

Cadoux, Cecil John. *The Early Christian Attitude to War: A Contribution to the History of Christian Ethics.* London: Headley Brothers, 1919.

Campenhausen, Hans Frieherr von. "Bearbeitungen und Interpolationen des Polycarpmartyrium." Pages 253–301 in *Aus der Frühzeit des Christentums. Studien zur Kirchengeschichte des ersten und zweiten Jahrhunderts.* Edited by Hans Freiherr von Campenhausen. Tübingen: Mohr Siebeck, 1964.

———. *Die Idee des Martyriums in der alten Kirche.* Göttingen: Vandenhoeck & Ruprecht, 1936.

Capelle, Bernard. "Le texte du 'gloria in excelsis.'" *Revue de Histoire Eccléstiastique* 44 (1949): 439–57.

Capes, David A. "*Imitatio Christi* and the Early Worship of Jesus." Pages 293–307 in *The Jewish Roots of Christological Monotheism: Papers from the St. Andrews Conference on the Historical Origins of the Worship of Jesus.* Edited by Carey C. Newman, James R. Davila, and Gladys S. Lewis. Leiden: Brill, 1999.

Cardas, G. R. "A Pentateuchal Echo in Jesus' Prayer on the Cross: Intertextuality between Numbers 15.22–31 and Luke 23.34a." Pages 605–16 in *The Scriptures in the Gospels.* Edited by C. M. Tuckett. Leuven: Leuven University Press, 1997.

Carrell, Peter R. *Jesus and the Angels: Angelology and the Christology of the Apocalypse of John.* Cambridge: Cambridge University Press, 1997.

Castelli, Elizabeth A. *Imitating Paul: A Discourse of Power.* Literary Currents in Biblical Interpretation. Louisville, Ky.: Westminster John Knox Press, 1991.

———. *Martyrdom and Memory: Early Christian Culture Making.* Gender, Theory, and Religion Series. New York: Columbia University Press, 2004.

Catholic Church and the International Committee on English in the Liturgy. *General Instruction of the Roman Missal.* Liturgy Documentary Series 2. Washington, D.C.: United States Conference of Catholic Bishops, 2003.

Cavalieri, Pio Franchi de'. "Gli Atti di S. Giustino." *Studi e Testi* 8 (1902): 33–36.

Cavarnos, John P. *Gregorii Nysseni Opera, Sermones.* Leiden: Brill, 1990.

Charlesworth, James H. *Old Testament Pseudepigrapha.* 2 vols. Garden City, N.Y.: Doubleday, 1983.

Clark, Elizabeth A. *The Origenist Controversy: The Cultural Construction of an Early Christian Debate.* Princeton, N.J.: Princeton University Press, 1992.

Clark, Gillian. "Victricius of Rouen: Praising the Saints." *Journal of Early Christian Studies* 7 (1999): 365–99.

Clifford, Richard J. "The Roots of Apocalypticism in Near Eastern Myth." Pages 3–38 in *The Encyclopedia of Apocalypticism.* Edited by John J. Collins. London: Continuum, 1998.

Cobb, L. Stephanie. *Dying to Be Men: Gender and Language in Early Christian Martyr Texts.* New York: Columbia University Press, 2008.

Collins, Adela Yarbro. *The Combat Myth in the Book of Revelation.* Harvard Dissertations in Religion 9. Missoula, Mont.: Scholars Press, 1976.

———. *Crisis and Catharsis: The Power of the Apocalypse.* Philadelphia: Westminster Press, 1984.

———. "Dating the Apocalypse of John." *Biblical Research* 26 (1981): 33–45.

———. "Finding Meaning in the Death of Jesus." *Journal of Religion* 78 (1998): 175–96.

———. "The Influence of Daniel on the New Testament." Pages 90–112 in John J. Collins, *Daniel: A Commentary on the Book of Daniel.* Hermeneia: A Critical and Historical Commentary on the Bible. Minneapolis, Minn.: Fortress Press, 1993.

———. *Mark: A Commentary.* Edited by Harold W. Attridge. Hermeneia: A Critical and Historical Commentary on the Bible. Minneapolis, Minn.: Fortress Press, 2007.

———. "Myth and History in the Book of Revelation: The Problem of Its Date." Pages 377–403 in *Traditions in Transformation: Turning Points in the Biblical Faith.* Edited by Baruch Halpern and Jon D. Levenson. Winona Lake, Ind.: Eisenbrauns, 1981.

———. "The Origin of the Designation of Jesus as 'Son of Man.'" *Harvard Theological Review* 80 (1987): 391–407.

———. "The New Age and the Other World in the Letters of Paul." In *The Other World and Its Relations to This World.* Edited by E. Eynikel, F. García Martinez, T. Nicklas, and J. Verheyden. Journal for the Study of Judaism Supplement Series. Leiden: Brill, Forthcoming.

———. "The Seven Heavens in Jewish and Christian Apocalypses." Pages 59–93 in *Death, Ecstasy and Other Worldly Journeys.* Edited by John J. Collins and Michael Fishbane. Albany: State University of New York Press, 1995.

Collins, John J. *Daniel: A Commentary on the Book of Daniel.* Edited by Frank Moore Cross. Hermeneia: A Critical and Historical Commentary on the Bible. Minneapolis, Minn.: Fortress Press, 1993.

———. "The Genre Apocalypse in Hellenistic Judaism." In *Apocalypticism in the Mediterranean World and the Near East: Proceedings of the International Colloquium on Apocalypticism, Uppsala, August 12–17, 1979.* Edited by David Helholm. Tübingen: Mohr Siebeck, 1983.

Collins, John J., Bernard McGinn, and Stephen J. Stein, eds. *The Encyclopedia of Apocalypticism.* 3 vols. New York: Continuum, 1998–2000.

Constitutions of the Holy Apostles. Vol. 7 of *The Ante-Nicene Fathers.* Translated by James Donaldson. Edited by Alexander Roberts and James Donaldson. Grand Rapids, Mich.: Eerdmans, 1979.

Conzelmann, Hans. *Acts of the Apostles: A Commentary on the Acts of the Apostles.* Translated by James Limburg. Edited by Eldon J. Epp. Hermeneia: A Critical and Historical Commentary on the Bible. Philadelphia: Fortress Press, 1987.

————. *1 Corinthians: A Commentary on the First Epistle to the Corinthians.* Translated by James W. Leitch. Edited by George W. MacRae. Hermeneia: A Critical and Historical Commentary on the Bible. Philadelphia: Fortress Press, 1975.

Cranfield, C. E. B. *The Gospel According to Saint Mark: An Introduction and Commentary.* Cambridge Greek Testament Commentary. Cambridge: Cambridge University Press, 1959.

Crouzel, Henri. "L'imitation et la 'suite' de Dieu et du Christ dans les premiers siècles chrétiens: sources gréco-romaines et hébraïques." *Jahrbuch für Antike und Christentum* 21 (1978): 7–41.

Daly, Robert J. *Christian Sacrifice: The Judeo-Christian Background before Origen.* Washington, D.C.: Catholic University of America Press, 1978.

————. *The Origins of the Christian Doctrine of Sacrifice.* Philadelphia: Fortress Press, 1978.

Davies, W. D., and Dale C. Allison. *A Critical and Exegetical Commentary on the Gospel According to Saint Matthew.* 3 vols. International Critical Commentary. Edinburgh: T & T Clark, 1988.

Davis, Philip. "Christology, Discipleship and Self-Understanding in the Gospel of Mark." Pages 101–19 in *Self-Definition in Early Christianity: A Case of Shifting Horizons: Essays in Appreciation of Ben F. Meyer from His Former Students.* Edited by David Hawkin and Tom Robinson. Lewiston, Maine: Melen, 1990.

Davis, Stephen J. *Coptic Christology in Practice: Incarnation and Divine Participation in Late Antique and Medieval Egypt.* Oxford Early Christian Studies. Oxford: Oxford University Press, 2008.

————. "Jonah in Early Christian Art: Allegorical Exegesis and the Roman Funerary Context." *ARS Review* 13 (2000): 72–83.

Dawson, David. *Allegorical Readers and Cultural Revision in Ancient Alexandria.* Berkeley: University of California Press, 1992.

De Boer, Willis Peter. *The Imitation of Paul: An Exegetical Study.* Kampen, Netherlands: J. H. Kok, 1962.

Dehandschutter, Boudewijn. *Martyrium Polycarpi: Ein literair-kittisch studie.* Bibliotheca ephemeridum theologicarum lovaniensium 52. Leuven: Leuven University Press, 1979.

————. "The Meaning of Witness in the Apocalypse." Pages 283–88 in *L'apocalypse johannique et l'apocalyptique dans le nouveau testament.* Edited by Jan Lambrecht. Leuven: Leuven University Press, 1980.

————. "The New Testament and the *Martyrdom of Polycarp.*" Pages 395–406 in *Trajectories through the New Testament and the Apostolic Fathers.* Edited by Andrew F. Gregory and Christopher M. Tuckett. Oxford: Oxford University Press, 2005.

Deissmann, Adolf, and A. J. Grieve. *Bible Studies: Contributions, Chiefly from Papyri and Inscriptions, to the History of the Language, the Literature, and the Religion of Hellenistic Judaism and Primitive Christianity.* Edinburgh: T & T Clark, 1901.

Delehaye, Hippolyte. *Les légendes grecques des saints militaries.* Paris: Librairie A. Picard, 1909.

————. *L'œuvre des bollandistes à travers trios siècles, 1615–1915.* Subsidia Hagiographica 13A. Brussels: Société des Bollandistes, 1959.

Delobel, Joël. "Luke 23.34a: A Perpetual Text-Critical Crux?" Pages 25–36 in *Sayings of Jesus Canonical and Non-canonical: Essays in Honor of Tjitze Baarda*. Edited by William L. Petersen, Johan S. Vos, and Henk J. de Jonge. New York: Brill, 1997.

Derrett, J. Duncan M. "Scripture and Norms in the Apostolic Fathers." *ANRW* 27.1: 649–99. Part 2, Principat 27.1 Edited by H. Temporini and W. Haase. New York: de Gruyter, 1993.

Dinkler, Erich. "Jesu Wort vom Kreuztragen." Pages 110–29 in *Neutestamentliche Studien für Rudolf Bultmann zu seinem 70. Geburtstag am 20. August 1954*. Edited by Walter Eltester. Berlin: A. Töpelmann, 1954.

Dodd, C. H. "The Cognomen of the Emperor Antoninus Pius." *Numistmatic Chronicle* 4, no. 11 (1911): 6–41.

———. *Historical Tradition in the Fourth Gospel*. Cambridge: Cambridge University Press, 1963.

Donahue, John R., and Daniel J. Harrington. *The Gospel of Mark*. Collegeville, Minn.: Liturgical Press, 2002.

Donfried, Karl P. "The Cults of Thessalonica and the Thessalonian Correspondence." *New Testament Studies* 31 (1985): 336–56.

Downing, John. "Jesus and Martyrdom." *Journal of Theological Studies*, n.s., 14 (1963): 279–93.

Drewery, Benjamin. "Deification." Pages 35–62 in *Christian Spirituality: Essays in Honour of Gordon Rapp*. Edited by Peter Brooks. London: SCM Press, 1975.

Droge, Arthur J., and James D. Tabor. *A Noble Death: Suicide and Martyrdom among Christians and Jews in Antiquity*. San Francisco: HarperCollins, 1992.

Dupont, A. "Imitatio Christi, Imitatio Stephani: Augustine's Thinking on Martyrdom Based on His Sermons on the Protomartyr Stephen." *Augustiniana* 56 (2006): 29–61.

Eberhart, Christian A. "A Neglected Feature of Sacrifice in the Hebrew Bible: Remarks on the Burning Rite on the Altar." *Harvard Theological Review* 97 (2004): 485–93.

Edmonds, Radcliffe G. *Myths of the Underworld Journey: Plato, Aristophanes, and the 'Orphic' Gold Tablets*. Cambridge: Cambridge University Press, 2004.

Ehrman, Bart D. *The Apostolic Fathers*. 2 vols. Loeb Classical Library 24–25. Cambridge, Mass.: Harvard University Press, 2003.

Eissfeldt, Otto. *The Old Testament: An Introduction, Including the Apocrypha and Pseudepigrapha*. New York: Harper & Row, 1965.

Elliott, John Hall. *1 Peter: A New Translation with Introduction and Commentary*. Anchor Bible Commentary 37B. New York: Doubleday, 2000.

Else, Gerald. "'Imitation' in the Fifth Century." *Classical Philology* 73 (1958): 73–90.

Epp, Eldon Jay. "The 'Ignorance Motif' in Acts and Anti-Judaic Tendencies in Codex Bezae." *Harvard Theological Review* 55 (1962): 51–62.

Evans, Craig A. *Mark 8:27–16:20*. Word Biblical Commentary 34B. Nashville, Tenn.: T. Nelson, 2001.

Farkasfalvy, M., and William R. Farmer. *The Formation of the New Testament Canon: An Ecumenical Approach*. Mahwah, N.J.: Paulist Press, 1983.

Fatum, Lone. "Brotherhood in Christ: A Gender Hermeneutical Reading of 1 Thessalonians." Pages 183–97 in *Constructing Early Christian Families: Family as Social Reality and Metaphor*. Edited by Halvor Moxnes. London: Routledge, 1997.

Fee, Gordon D. *The First Epistle to the Corinthians*. Grand Rapids, Mich.: Eerdmans, 1987.

Finlan, Stephen, and Vladimir Kharlamov. *Theosis: Deification in Christian Theology*. Princeton Theological Monograph Series. Eugene, Ore.: Pickwick Press, 2006

Fletcher-Louis, Crispin H. T. *Luke-Acts: Angels, Christology, and Soteriology*. Wissenschaftliche Untersuchungen zum Neuen Testament 2.94. Tübingen: Mohr Siebeck, 1997.

Flusser, David. "Sie wissen nicht, was sie tun." Pages 179–96 in *Kontinuitaet und Einheit: Fuer Franz Mussner*. Edited by Paul Mueller and Werner Stenger. Freiburg: Herder, 1981.

Fowl, S. E. "Imitation." Pages 428–31 in *Dictionary of Paul and His Letters*. Edited by Gerald F. Hawthorne, Ralph P. Martin, and D. G. Reid. Downers Grove, Ill.: InterVarsity Press, 1993.

Frend, W. H. C. *The Donatist Church: A Movement of Protest in Roman North Africa*. Oxford: Clarendon Press, 1952.

———. *Martyrdom and Persecution in the Early Church*. Oxford: Blackwell, 1965.

Freud, Sigmund. *The Standard Edition of the Complete Psychological Works of Sigmund Freud*. Edited by James Strachey et al. London: Hogart Press, 1953.

Funk, Francis Xavier. *Didascalia et Constitutiones Apostolorum*. 2 vols. Padernorn: Schoeningh, 1905.

Gamble, Harry Y. *Books and Readers in the Early Church: A History of Early Christian Texts*. New Haven, Conn.: Yale University Press, 1995.

Garland, Robert. *The Greek Way of Death*. Ithaca, N.Y.: Cornell University Press, 1985.

Gebhardt, Otto von. *Acta Martyrum Selecta. Ausgewählte Martyreracten und andere Urkunden aus der Verfolgungszeit der christlichen Kirche*. Berlin: A. Dunker, 1902.

Gese, Hartmut. "Die Sühne." Pages 85–106 in *Zur Biblischen Theologie: Altestamentliche Vorträge*. Edited by Hartmurt Gese. Tübingen: Mohr Siebeck, 1983.

Gibson, E. Leigh. "The Jews and Christians in the *Martyrdom of Polycarp:* Entangled or Parted Ways?" Pages 145–58 in *The Ways That Never Parted: Jews and Christians in Late Antiquity and the Early Middle Ages*. Edited by Adam H. Becker and Annette Yoshiko Reed. Tübingen: Mohr Siebeck, 2003.

Girard, René. *La violence et le sacré*. Paris: B. Grasset, 1972.

Givens, Terryl L. *When Souls Had Wings: Pre-Mortal Existence in Western Thought*. New York: Oxford University Press, 2009.

Glare, P. G. W. *Oxford Latin Dictionary*. Oxford: Clarendon Press, 1982.

González, Justo L. *The Story of Christianity*. 2 vols. San Francisco: Harper & Row, 1984.

Gordon, R. L. "The Veil of Power: Emperors, Sacrificers, Benefactors." Pages 201–31 in *Pagan Priests*. Edited by Mary Beard and John North. Ithaca, N.Y.: Cornell University Press, 1993.

Grabar, André. *Christian Iconography: A Study of Its Origins*. London: Routledge & Kegan Paul, 1969.

———. *Martyrium: Recherches sur le culte des reliques et l'art Chrétien antique*. 2 vols. Paris: Collège de France, 1943.

———. "Le trône des martyrs." *Cahiers Archéologiques* 6 (1952): 31–41.

Grant, Robert McQueen. *Greek Apologists of the Second Century*. Philadelphia: Westminster Press, 1988.

Greene, W. C. "Plato's View of Poetry." *Harvard Studies in Classical Philology* 29 (1918): 1–75.

Greer, Rowan A. *Origen*. Classics of Western Spirituality. New York: Paulist Press, 1979.

Gregory, Andrew F., and Christopher M. Tuckett, eds. *The Reception of the New Testament in the Apostolic Fathers*. Oxford: Oxford University Press, 2005.

———. *Trajectories through the New Testament and the Apostolic Fathers*. Oxford: Oxford University Press, 2005.

Gregory, Brad S. *Salvation at Stake: Christian Martyrdom in Early Modern Europe*. Cambridge, Mass.: Harvard University Press, 1999.

Grig, Lucy. *Making Martyrs in Late Antiquity*. London: Duckworth Press, 2004.

Guillaumin, M.-L. "En marge du 'Martyre de Polycarpe': Le discernment des allusions scripturaires." Pages 462–69 in *Forma Futuri: Studi in onore del Cardinale Michele Pellegrino*. Turin: Bottega d'Erasmo, 1975.

Gundry, Robert Horton. *Mark: A Commentary on His Apology for the Cross*. Grand Rapids, Mich.: Eerdmans, 1993.

Gunkel, Hermann. *Die Psalmen*. Handkommentar zum Alten Testament. Abt. 2 Bd. 2, 4. Aufl. Göttingen: Vandenhoeck & Ruprecht, 1926.

Hamori, Esther J. *"When Gods Were Men": The Embodied God in Biblical and Near Eastern Literature*. Berlin: Walter de Gruyter, 2008.

Hanson, R. P. C. *Allegory and Event: A Study of the Sources and Significance of Origen's Interpretation of Scripture*. Louisville, Ky.: Westminster John Knox Press, 2002.

Harnack, Adolf von. *Militia Christi: The Christian Religion and the Military in the First Three Centuries*. Translated by David McInnes Gracie. Philadelphia: Fortress Press, 1981.

———. *Studien zur Geschichte des Neuen Testaments und der Alten Kirche*. Berlin: Walter de Gruyter, 1931.

Hawthorne, Gerald. "The Imitation of Christ: Discipleship in Philippians." Pages 168–78 in *Patterns of Discipleship in the New Testament*. Edited by Richard Longenecker. Grand Rapids, Mich.: Eerdmans, 1996.

Hay, David M. *Glory at the Right Hand: Psalm 110 in Early Christianity*. Nashville, Tenn.: Abingdon Press, 1973.

Hays, Richard B. *Echoes of Scripture in the Letters of Paul*. New Haven, Conn.: Yale University Press, 1989.

Heintz, Michael. "*Mimetes Theou* in the *Epistle to Diognetus*." *Journal of Early Christian Studies* 12 (2004): 107–119.

Hengel, Martin. *Studies in the Gospel of Mark*. Philadelphia: Fortress Press, 1985.

Henning, Meghan. "The Intersection of Performance, Power and Pain in the *Martyrdom of Saints Agape, Irene and Chione*." Paper presented at the South Eastern Conference of the Society of Religion, Atlanta, Georgia, March 8, 2008.

Henten, Jan Willem van. "Archangel." Pages 80–82 in *Dictionary of Deities and Demons*. Edited by K. van der Toorn, Bob Becking, and Pieter Willem van der Horst. Leiden: Brill, 1999.

————. *The Maccabean Martyrs as Saviours of the Jewish People: A Study of 2 and 4 Maccabees*. Supplements to the Journal for the Study of Judaism 57. Leiden: Brill, 1997.

Henten, Jan Willem van, and Friedrich Avemarie, eds. *Martyrdom and Noble Death: Selected Texts from Graeco-Roman, Jewish and Christian Antiquity*. London: Routledge, 2002.

Heyman, George. *The Power of Sacrifice: Roman and Christian Discourses in Conflict*. Washington, D.C.: Catholic University of America Press, 2007.

Hiers, Richard H., and Charles A. Kennedy. "The Bread and Fish Eucharist in the Gospels and Early Christian Art." *Perspectives in Religious Studies* 3 (1976): 21–48.

Hilgenfeld, A. "Das neueste Steitzianum über den Paschasreit," *Zeitschrift für wissenschaftliche Theologie* 4 (1861): 106–10.

————. "Der Quartodecimanismus Kleinasiens und die kanonischen Evangelien," *Zeitschrift für wissenschaftliche Theologie* 4 (1861): 285–318.

Himmelfarb, Martha. *Ascent to Heaven in Jewish and Christian Apocalypses*. New York: Oxford University Press, 1993.

Holmes, Michael W. *Apostolic Fathers: Greek Texts and English Translations*. 2d ed. Grand Rapids, Mich.: Baker Books, 2007.

————. "The *Martyrdom of Polycarp* and the New Testament Passion Narratives." Pages 407–32 in *Trajectories through the New Testament and the Apostolic Fathers*. Edited by Andrew F. Gregory and Christopher M. Tuckett. Oxford: Oxford University Press, 2005.

Hurtado, Larry W. "Following Jesus in the Gospel of Mark—and Beyond." Pages 9–29 in *Patterns of Discipleship in the New Testament*. Edited by Richard Longenecker. Grand Rapids, Mich.: Eerdmans, 1996.

————. *How on Earth Did Jesus Become a God? Historical Questions about Earliest Devotion to Jesus*. Grand Rapids, Mich.: Eerdmans, 2005.

————. "Jesus as Lordly Example in Philippians 2:5–11." Pages 113–26 in *From Jesus to Paul: Studies in Honour of Francis Wright Beare*. Edited by J. C. Hurd and G. P. Richardson. Waterloo, Ontario: Wilfred Laurier University Press, 1984.

————. *One God, One Lord: Early Christian Devotion and Ancient Jewish Monotheism*. 2d ed. Edinburgh: T & T Clark, 1998.

Irwin, William. "What Is an Allusion?" *Journal of Aesthetics and Art Criticism* 59 (2001): 287–97.

Jackson, H. Latimer. *The Problem of the Fourth Gospel*. Cambridge: Cambridge University Press, 1918.

Jastrzebowska, Elisabeth. "Les scènes de banquet dans les peintures et sculptures chrétiennes des 3e et 4e siècles." *Recherches Augustiniennes* 14 (1979): 3–90.

Jensen, Robin M. "Dining in Heaven." *Bible Review* 15, no. 5 (1998): 32–39, 48–50.

————. *Understanding Early Christian Art*. London: Routledge, 2000.

Jewett, Robert. "The Agitators and the Galatian Congregation." *New Testament Studies* 17 (1971): 198–212.

Joly, Robert. *Le dossier d'Ignace d'Antioche*. Brussels: Éditions de l'Université de Bruxelles, 1979.

Jungmann, Josef A. *The Mass of the Roman Rite: Its Origins and Development (Missarum sollemnia).* 2 vols. New York: Benziger, 1951.

Käsemann, Ernst. "Critical Analysis of Philippians 2:5–11." *Journal for Theology and the Church* 5 (1968): 45–88.

Keller, Catherine. *God and Power: Counter-apocalyptic Journeys.* Minneapolis, Minn.: Fortress Press, 2005.

Kelley, Nicole. "Philosophy as Training for Death: Reading the Ancient Christian Martyr Acts as Spiritual Exercises." *Church History* 75 (2006): 723–47.

Kempis, Thomas à. *Opera omnia.* Freiburg: Herder, 1902.

Ketter, Peter. *Hebräerbrief, Jakobusbrief, Petrusbrief, Judasbrief.* Die Heilige Schrift für das Leben erklärt. Bd 16/1. Freiburg: Herder, 1950.

Kharlamov, Vladimir. "Emergence of the Deification Theme in the Apostolic Fathers." Pages 51–66 in *Theosis: Deification in Christian Theology.* Edited by Stephen Finlan and Vladimir Kharlamov. Eugene, Ore.: Pickwick Press, 2006.

King, J. Christopher. *Origen on the Song of Songs as the Spirit of Scripture: The Bridegroom's Perfect Marriage-Song.* Oxford Theological Monographs. Oxford: Oxford University Press, 2005.

Kingsbury, Jack Dean. *Conflict in Mark: Jesus, Authorities, Disciples.* Minneapolis, Minn.: Fortress Press, 1989.

Klauser, Theodor. "Studien zur Entstehungsgeschichte der christlichen Kunst VII." *Jahrbuch für Antike und Christentum* 7 (1964): 67–76.

Klawans, Jonathan. *Impurity and Sin in Ancient Judaism.* Oxford: Oxford University Press, 2000.

Klawiter, Frederick, C. "The Eucharist and Sacramental Realism in the Thought of St. Ignatius of Antioch." *Studia Liturgica* 37 (2007): 129–63.

———. "The Role of Martyrdom and Persecution in Developing the Priestly Authority of Women in Early Christianity: A Case Study of Montanism." *Church History* 49 (1990): 251–62.

Knopf, R. G. Krüger, and G. Ruhbach. *Ausgewählte Märtyrerakten.* 4th ed. Tübingen: Mohr, 1965.

Koester, Craig R. *Hebrews: A New Translation with Introduction and Commentary.* Anchor Bible Commentary 36. New York: Doubleday, 2001.

Köhler, W. D. *Die Rezeption des Matthäusevangeliums in der Zeit vor Irenäus.* Wisschenschaftliche Untersuchungen zum Neuen Testament. 2.24. Tübingen: Mohr Siebeck, 1987.

Koller, Hermann. *Die Mimesis in der Antike: Nachahmung, Dastellung, Ausdruck.* Bernae: A. Francke, 1954.

Koslofsky, Craig. *The Reformation of the Dead: Death and Ritual in Early Modern Germany, 1450–1700.* Early Modern History. New York: St. Martin's Press, 2000.

Kraemer, Ross Shepard, and Mary Rose D'Angelo. *Women and Christian Origins.* New York: Oxford University Press, 1999.

Kümmel, Werner Georg. *Introduction to the New Testament.* Nashville, Tenn.: Abingdon Press, 1975.

Kurz, William S. "Kenotic Imitation of Paul and of Christ in Philippians 2 and 3."
Pages 103–25 in *Discipleship in the New Testament*. Edited by Fernando F. Segovia.
Philadelphia: Fortress Press, 1985.

Lanata, G. *Gli atti dei martiri come documenti processuali*. Milan: Giuffre, 1973.

Lane Fox, Robin. *Pagans and Christians*. New York: Knopf, 1987.

Layton, Bentley. *The Gnostic Scriptures: A New Translation with Annotations and Introductions*. Garden City, N.Y.: Doubleday, 1987.

Lazzati, Giuseppi. "Gli Atti di S. Giustini Martire." *Aevum* 27 (1953): 473–97.

———. *Gli Sviluppi della letteraturs sui martiri nei primi quattrosecoli*. Turin: Società Editrice Internazionale, 1956.

Leclercq, Henri. "Orans, Orante." Pages 2291–322 in *Dictionnaire d'archéologie chrétienne et de liturgie*. Edited by Fernand Cabrol and Henri Leclercq. Paris: Libraire Letouzey et Ané, 1936.

———. "Saint." Pages 373–462 in *Dictionnaire d'archéologie chrétienne et de liturgie*. Edited by Fernand Cabrol and Henri Leclercq. Paris: Libraire Letouzey et Ané, 1950.

Lehtipuu, Outi. *The Afterlife Imagery in Luke's Story of the Rich Man and Lazarus*. Supplements to Novum Testamentum vol. 123. Leiden: Brill, 2006.

Levenson, Jon D. *The Death and Resurrection of the Beloved Son: The Transformation of Child Sacrifice in Judaism and Christianity*. New Haven, Conn.: Yale University Press, 1993.

Liddell, Henry George, and Robert Scott. *A Greek-English Lexicon*. 9th ed. Oxford: Clarendon Press, 1940.

Lietzmann, Hans, and Werner Georg Kümmel. *An Die Korinther I–II*. Handbuch zum Neuen Testament 9. Tübingen: Mohr Siebeck, 1949.

Lieu, Judith M. *Image and Reality: The Jews in the World of the Christians in the Second Century*. Edinburgh: T & T Clark, 1996.

———. *Neither Jew nor Greek? Constructing Early Christianity*. Studies of the New Testament and Its World. London: T & T Clark, 2005.

Lightfoot, Joseph Barber. *The Apostolic Fathers*. London: Macmillan, 1885.

Lohmeyer, Ernst. *Die Briefe an die Philipper, an die Kolosser und an Philemon*. Göttingen: Vandenhoeck & Ruprecht, 1930.

———. *Galiläa und Jerusalem*. Göttingen: Vandenhoeck & Ruprecht, 1936.

———. *Kyrios Jesus: Eine Untersuching zu Phil 2, 5–11*. Sitzungsberichte der Heidelberger Akademie der Wissenschaften. Philosophisch-Historische Klasse. Bd. 18. Bericht 4. Heidelberg: Carl Winter, 1928.

Lueken, Wilhelm. *Der Erzengel Michael in der Überlieferung der Judentums*. Marburg: E. A. Huth, 1898.

Luz, Ulrich. *Matthew: A Commentary*. Translated by James E. Crouch. Edited by Helmut Koester. 3 vols. Hermeneia: A Critical and Historical Commentary on the Bible. Minneapolis, Minn.: Fortress Press, 2001.

Mach, Michael. *Entwicklungsstadien des jüdischen Engelglaubens in vorrabbinischer Zeit*. Texte und Studies zum antiken Judentum 34. Tübingen: Mohr Siebeck, 1992.

Mack, Burton L. *A Myth of Innocence: Mark and Christian Origins*. Philadelphia: Fortress Press, 1988.

MacMullen, Ramsay. *Christianity and Paganism in the Fourth to Eighth Centuries*. New Haven, Conn.: Yale University Press, 1997.

———. *Christianizing the Roman Empire (A.D. 100–400)*. New Haven, Conn.: Yale University Press, 1984.

———. *The Second Church: Popular Christianity A.D. 200–400*. Writings from the Greco-Roman World Supplements. Atlanta, Ga.: Society of Biblical Literature, 2009.

Maier, Jean Louis. *Le dossier du donatisme*. 2 vols. Berlin: Akademie-Verlag, 1987.

Malherbe, Abraham J. *The Letters to the Thessalonians: A New Translation with Introduction and Commentary*. Anchor Bible Commentary 32B. New York: Doubleday, 2000.

———. *Moral Exhortation: A Greco-Roman Sourcebook*. Library of Early Christianity 4. Philadelphia: Westminster Press, 1986.

Mansfeld, Jaap. "Resurrection Added: The Interpretatio Christiana of a Stoic Doctrine." *Vigiliae Christianae* 37 (1983): 218–33.

Marcus, Joel. *Mark 1–8: A New Translation with Introduction and Commentary*. Anchor Bible Commentary Series 27. New York: Doubleday, 1999.

Martin, Dale B., and Patricia Cox Miller. *The Cultural Turn in Late Ancient Studies: Gender, Asceticism, and Historiography*. Durham, N.C.: Duke University Press, 2005.

Martin, Ralph P. *A Hymn of Christ: Philippians 2:5–11 in Recent Interpretation and in the Setting of Early Christian Worship*. Downer's Grove, Ill.: InterVarsity Press, 1997.

Maunder, A. S. D. "The Date and Place of Writing of the Slavonic Book of Enoch." *Observatory* 41 (1918): 309–16.

McGowan, Andrew. *Ascetic Eucharists: Food and Drink in Early Christian Ritual Meals*. Oxford Early Christian Studies. Oxford: Clarendon Press, 1999.

———. "Discipline and Diet: Feeding the Martyrs in Roman Carthage." *Harvard Theological Review* 94 (2003): 455–76.

McGrath, Alister E. *Christianity: An Introduction*. 2d ed. Oxford: Blackwell, 2006.

McKeon, Richard. "Literary Criticism and the Concept of Imitation in Antiquity." *Modern Philology* 34 (1936): 1–35.

Menzies, Allan. *The Earliest Gospel: A Historical Study of the Gospel According to Mark*. London: Macmillan, 1901.

Metzger, Bruce Manning. *A Textual Commentary on the Greek New Testament*. Corrected edition. London: United Bible Societies, 1975.

Metzger, Marcel. *Les constitutions apostoliques*. 3 vols. Paris: Editions du Cerf, 1985.

Michaelis, Wilhelm. *Zur Engelchristologie im Urchristentum: Abbau der Konstruktion Martin Werners*. Basel: Heinrich Majer, 1942.

Michel, Otto. *Der Brief an die Hebräer*. Kritisch-exegetischer Kommentar über das Neue Testament. Bd. 13 Göttingen: Vandenhoeck & Ruprecht, 1984.

Middleton, Paul. *Radical Martyrdom and Cosmic Conflict in Early Christianity*. Library of New Testament Studies 307. London: T & T Clark, 2006.

Milavec, Aaron. "The Saving Efficacy of the Burning Process in Did. 16.5." Pages 131–55 in *The Didache in Context: Essays on Its Text, History and Tradition.* Edited by Clayton N. Jefford. Supplements to Novum Testamentum. Leiden: Brill, 1995.

Milgrom, Jacob. *Leviticus 1–16: A New Translation with Introduction and Commentary.* Anchor Bible Commentary 3. New York: Doubleday, 1991.

Miller, Patricia Cox. *Women in Early Christianity: Translations from Greek Texts.* Washington, D.C.: Catholic University of America Press, 2005.

Mingana, Alphonse. *Commentary of Theodore of Mopsuestia on the Lord's Prayer and on the Sacraments of Baptism and the Eucharist.* Cambridge: W. Heffer, 1933.

Moltmann, Jürgen. *The Crucified God: The Cross of Christ as the Foundation and Criticism of Christian Theology.* SCM Classics. London: SCM Press, 2001.

Montefiore, Hugh. *A Commentary on the Epistle to the Hebrews.* Harper's New Testament Commentaries. New York: Harper & Row, 1964.

Moule, C. F. D. *The Birth of the New Testament.* Harper New Testament Commentaries. New York: Harper & Row, 1962.

Mowinckel, Sigmund. *The Psalms in Israel's Worship.* Grand Rapids, Mich.: Eerdmans, 2004.

Mulhern, A. "L'orante, vie et mort d'une image." *Les Dossiers de l'Archéologie* 18 (1976): 34–47.

Murray, Robert P. R. "Some Themes and Problems of Early Syriac Angelology." Pages 143–53 in *Symposium Syriacum V, Katholieke Universiteit, Leuven, 29–31 août 1988.* Edited by René Lavenant. Rome: Pontifical Institute Orientalium Studiorum, 1990.

Musurillo, Herbert. *Acts of the Christian Martyrs.* Oxford: Clarendon Press, 1972.

Nasrallah, Laura S. "Empire and Apocalypse in Thessaloniki: Interpreting the Early Christian Rotunda." *Journal of Early Christian Studies* 13 (2005) 465–508.

Nautin, Pierre. *Origène: Sa vie et son œuvre.* Christianisme Antique 1. Paris: Beauchesne, 1977.

Neuss, W. "Die Oranten in der altchristlicher Kunst." Pages 130–49 in *Festschrift zum sechzigsten Geburtstag von Paul Clemens.* Bonn: Schwann, 1926.

Newman, Jay. "The Motivation of Martyrs: A Philosophical Perspective." *Thomist* 35 (1971): 581–600.

Newsom, Carol. *Songs of the Sabbath Sacrifice: A Critical Edition.* Atlanta, Ga.: Scholars Press, 1985.

Nickelsburg, George W. E. *1 Enoch: A Commentary on the Book of 1 Enoch.* Hermeneia: A Critical and Historical Commentary on the Bible. Minneapolis, Minn.: Fortress Press, 2001.

Nilles, Nicolaus. *Kalendarium manuale utriusque ecclesiae orientalis et occidentalis.* 2 vols. Oeniponte: Typis et sumptibus Feliciani Rauch, 1896.

Nock, Arthur Darby. *Conversion: The Old and the New in Religion from Alexander the Great to Augustine of Hippo.* New York: Oxford University Press, 1961.

Noth, Martin "The Holy Ones of the Most High." Pages 215–28 in *The Laws in the Pentateuch and Other Studies.* Philadelphia: Fortress Press, 1966.

———. *Überlieferungsgeschichtliche Studien.* Halle: M. Niemeyer, 1943.

Oden, Thomas C., and Christopher A. Hall. *Mark*. Ancient Christian Commentary on Scripture, New Testament 2. Downer's Grove, Ill.: InterVarsity Press, 1998.

Orr, William F., and James Arthur Walther. *I Corinthians: A New Translation*. Anchor Bible Commentary 37. Garden City, N.Y.: Doubleday, 1976.

Osiek, Carolyn. *Shepherd of Hermas: A Commentary*. Edited by Helmut Koester. Hermeneia: A Critical and Historical Commentary on the Bible. Minneapolis, Minn.: Fortress Press, 1999.

Pace, Nicola. *Ricerche sulla traduzione di Rufino del "De principiis" di Origene*. Firenze: La Nuova Italia, 1990.

Pagels, Elaine H. *The Gnostic Gospels*. New York: Random House, 1979.

Perkins, Judith. *The Suffering Self: Pain and Narrative Representation in the Early Christian Era*. New York: Routledge, 1995.

Petzer, Jacobus H. "Anti-Judaism and the Textual Problem of Luke 23.34." *Filologia Neotestamentaria* 5 (1993): 199–203.

Pobee, J. S. "The Cry of the Centurion: A Cry of Defeat." Pages 91–102 in *The Trial of Jesus: Cambridge Studies in Honour of C. F. D. Moule*. Edited by Ernst Bammel. Studies in Biblical Theology 13. Napperville, Ill.: Alec R. Allenson, 1970.

Preiss, Theodor. "La mystique de l'imitation du Christ et de l'unité chez Ignace d'Antioche." *Revue d'histoire et de philosophie religieuses* 17 (1938): 197–241.

Price, S. R. F. *Rituals and Power: The Roman Imperial Cult in Asia Minor*. Cambridge: Cambridge University Press, 1984.

Procksch, Otto. "Hagios." Pages 88–110 in *Theological Dictionary of the New Testament*. Edited by Gerhard Kittel. Grand Rapids, Mich.: Eerdmans, 1964.

———. "Der Menschensohn als Gottessohn." *Christentum und Wissenschaft* 3 (1927): 425–43, 473–81.

Pucci, Joseph. *The Full-Knowing Reader: Allusion and the Power of the Reader in the Western Literary Tradition*. New Haven, Conn.: Yale University Press, 1998.

Rajak, Tessa. "Talking at Trypho: Christian Apologetics as Anti-Judaism in Justin's Dialogue with Trypho the Jew." Pages 59–80 in *Apologetics in the Roman Empire: Pagans, Jews and Christians*. Edited by Mark Edwards, Martin Goodman, and Simon Price. Oxford: Oxford University Press, 1999.

Reardon, Patrick Henry. "The Cross, Sacraments and Martyrdom: An Investigation of Mark 10: 35–45." *St. Vladimir's Theological Quarterly* 36 (1992): 103–15.

Reitzenstein, R. *Die Nachrichten über den Tod Cyprians*. Heidelberg: Winter, 1913.

Renaudot, Eusèbe. *Liturgiarum orientalium collectio*. 2 vols. Amersham: Gregg International, 1970.

Reymond, E. A. E., and John W. B. Barns. *Four Martyrdoms from the Pierpont Morgan Coptic Codices*. Oxford: Clarendon Press, 1973.

Riddle, Donald W. *Martyrs: A Study in Social Control*. Chicago: University of Chicago Press, 1931.

———. "The Physical Basis of Apocalypticism." *Journal of Religion* 4 (1924): 174–91.

Riley, Gregory J. *Resurrection Reconsidered: Thomas and John in Controversy*. Minneapolis, Minn.: Fortress Press, 1995.

Rius-Camps, Josep. *The Four Authentic Letters of Ignatius, the Martyr*. Orientalia Christiana Analecta 213. Rome: Pontificium Institutum Orientalium Studiorum, 1980.

Robertson, Archibald, and Alfred Plummer. *A Critical and Exegetical Commentary on the First Epistle of St. Paul to the Corinthians*. 2d ed. International Critical Commentary. Edinburgh: T & T Clark, 1971.

Robinson, John A. T. *Redating the New Testament*. London: SCM Press, 1976.

Robinson, Stephen E. *The Testament of Adam: An Examination of the Syriac and Greek Traditions*. Society of Biblical Literature Dissertation 52. Atlanta, Ga.: Scholars Press, 1982.

Rordorf, W. "L' espérance des Martyrs chrétiens." Pages 445–61 in *Forma Futuri: Studi in onore del Cardinale Michele Pellegrino*. Turin: Bottega d'Erasmo, 1975.

Rotelle, John E., ed. *The Works of Saint Augustine*. Translated by Edmund Hill. New York: New City Press, 1994.

Rouse, W. H. D. *Greek Votive Offerings: An Essay in the History of Greek Religion*. Hildesheim: G. Olms, 1976.

Rowland, Christopher. *The Open Heaven: A Study of Apocalyptic in Judaism and Early Christianity*. New York: Crossroad, 1982.

Ruinart, Theodoricus. *Acta primorum martyrum sincera et selecta*. Ratisbon: G. Josephi Manz, 1859.

Russell, Norman. *The Doctrine of Deification in the Greek Patristic Tradition*. Oxford: Oxford University Press, 2004.

Sanders, B. "Imitating Paul: 1 Cor 4:16." *Harvard Theological Review* 74 (1981): 353–63.

Sanders, E. P. *Jesus and Judaism*. Philadelphia: Fortress Press, 1985.

Sanders, Jack T. *The New Testament Christological Hymns: Their Historical Religious Background*. Cambridge: Cambridge University Press, 1971.

Saxer, Victor. *Bible et hagiographie: Textes et thèmes bibliques dans les actes des martyrs authentiques des premiers siècles*. Bern: Peter Lang, 1986.

———. "The Influence of the Bible in Early Christian Martyrology." Pages 342–74 in *The Bible in Greek Christian Antiquity*. Edited by Paul M. Blowers. Notre Dame, Ind.: University of Notre Dame Press, 1997.

———. *Morts, martyrs, reliques en Afrique chrétienne aux premiers siècles. Les témoignages de Tertullien, Cyprien et Augustin à la lumière de l'archéologie africaine*. Théologie historique 55. Paris: Beauchesne, 1980.

Schaff, Philip, and Henry Wace. *Nicene and Post-Nicene Fathers of the Christian Church*. Ser. 2. New York: Christian Literature Company, 1890–.

Schiffman, Lawrence H. *The Eschatological Community of the Dead Sea Scrolls: A Study of the Rule of the Congregation*. Atlanta, Ga.: Scholars Press, 1989.

Schmidt, Traugott. *Der Leib Christi eine Untersuchung zum urchristlichen Gemeindegedanken*. Leipzig: A. Deichert, 1919.

Schmitz, Otto. *Die Christus-Gemeinschaft des Paulus im Lichte seines Genetivgebrauchs*. Neutestamentliche Forschungen. Reihe 1. Paulusstudien. Heft 2. Gütersloh: C. Bertelsmann, 1924.

Schoedel, William R. *Ignatius of Antioch: A Commentary on the Letters of Ignatius of Antioch*. Edited by Helmut Koester. Hermeneia: A Critical and Historical Commentary on the Bible. Philadelphia: Fortress Press, 1985.

Schweizer, Eduard. *The Good News According to Mark*. Translated by Donald Harold Madvig. Richmond, Va.: John Knox Press, 1970.

Seeley, David. "Was Jesus Like a Philosopher? The Evidence of Martyrological and Wisdom Motifs in Q, Pre-Pauline Traditions and Mark." Pages 540–49 in *Society of Biblical Literature Seminar Papers*. Edited by D. J. Lull. Atlanta, Ga.: Scholars Press, 1989.

Segal, Alan F. "The Akedah: Some Reconsiderations." Pages 99–116 in *Geschichte-Tradition-Reflexion: Festschrift für Martin Hengel zum 70. Geburtstag* Bd. 1. Edited by Hubert Cancik. Tübingen: Mohr, 1996.

———. *Life after Death: A History of the Afterlife in the Religions of the West*. New York: Doubleday, 2004.

———. *Two Powers in Heaven: Early Rabbinic Reports about Christianity and Gnosticism*. Studies in Judaism in Late Antiquity 25. Leiden: Brill, 1977.

Semler, Johann Salomo. *Abhandlung von freier Untersuchung des Canon*. Halle, 1771–75.

Shaw, Brent D. "Body/Power/Identity: Passions of the Martyrs." *Journal of Early Christian Studies* 4 (1996): 269–312.

Skedros, James C. "The Cappadocian Fathers on the Veneration of Martyrs." Pages 294–300 in *Studia Patristica: Papers Presented at the Thirteenth International Conference on Patristic Studies Held in Oxford 1999*. Edited by M. F. Wiles and E. J. Yarnold. Leuven: Peeters, 2001.

———. *Saint Demetrios of Thessaloniki: Civic Patron and Divine Protector*. Harrisburg, Pa.: Trinity Press International, 1999.

Smith, Dennis Edwin. *From Symposium to Eucharist: The Banquet in the Early Christian World*. Minneapolis, Minn.: Fortress Press, 2003.

Smith, Jonathan Z. *Drudgery Divine: On the Comparison of Early Christianities and the Religions of Late Antiquity*. Jordan Lectures in Comparative Religion 14. London: School of Oriental and African Studies; Chicago: University of Chicago Press, 1990.

Snyder, Graydon F. *Ante Pacem: Archaeological Evidence of Church Life before Constantine*. Rev. ed. Macon, Ga.: Mercer University Press, 2003.

Ste. Croix, G. E. M. De "Why Were the Early Christians Persecuted?" Pages 105–52 in *Christian Persecution, Martyrdom, and Orthodoxy*. Edited by G. E. M. De Ste. Croix, Michael Whitby, and Joseph Street. Oxford: Oxford University Press, 2006.

Strathmann, H. "Martus, etc." Pages 477–520 in *Theological Dictionary of the New Testament*. Edited by Gerhard Kittel. Stuttgart: W. Kohlhammer, 1939.

Stuckenbruck, Loren T. *Angel Veneration and Christology: A Study in Early Judaism and in the Christology of the Apocalypse of John*. Wissenschaftliche Untersuchungen zum neuen Testament 2.70. Tübingen: J. C. B. Mohr, 1995.

Stuiber, Alfred. *Refrigerium Interim*. Theophaneia 11. Bonn: P. Hanstein, 1957.

Styler, G. M. "The Priority of Mark." Pages 285–316 in *The Birth of the New Testament*. Edited by C. F. D. Moule. London: Black's, 1981.

Tannehill, Robert C. *The Narrative Unity of Luke-Acts: A Literary Interpretation*. 2 vols. Foundations and Facets. Philadelphia: Fortress Press, 1986.

Tate, J. "'Imitation' in Plato's Republic." *Classical Quarterly* 22 (1928): 16–23.

———. "Plato and Imitation." *Classical Quarterly* 26 (1932): 161–69.

Theissen, Gerd. *The Gospels in Context: Social and Political History in the Synoptic Tradition*. Minneapolis, Minn.: Fortress Press, 1991.

Thomas, Christine M. *The Acts of Peter, Gospel Literature, and the Ancient Novel: Rewriting the Past.* Oxford: Oxford University Press, 2003.

Thompson, J. A. "The Alleged Persecution of the Christians at Lyons in 177." *American Journal of Theology* 16 (1912): 359–84.

———. "The Alleged Persecution of the Christians at Lyons in 177: A Reply to Certain Criticisms." *American Journal of Theology* 17 (1913): 249–58.

Thompson, Leonard. "The Martyrdom of Polycarp: Death in the Roman Games." *Journal of Religion* 82 (2002): 27–52.

Tiller, Patrick A. *A Commentary on the Animal Apocalypse of I Enoch.* Early Judaism and Its Literature 4. Atlanta, Ga.: Scholars Press, 1993.

Tilley, Maureen A. *The Bible in Christian North Africa: The Donatist World.* Minneapolis, Minn.: Fortress Press, 1997.

———. *Donatist Martyr Stories: The Church in Conflict in North Africa.* Liverpool: Liverpool University Press, 1996.

———. "The Passion of Perpetua and Felicity." Pages 387–97 in *Religions of Late Antiquity in Practice.* Edited by Richard Valantasis. Princeton, N.J.: Princeton University Press, 2000.

Tinsley, E. J. "The *Imitatio Christi* in the Mysticism of St. Ignatius of Antioch." *Studia Patristica* 64 (1957): 553–60.

———. *The Imitation of God in Christ: An Essay on the Biblical Basis of Christian Spirituality.* The Library of History and Doctrine. Philadelphia: Westminster Press, 1960.

Torrance, Thomas Forsyth. *The Doctrine of Grace in the Apostolic Fathers.* Edinburgh: Oliver & Boyd, 1948.

Toynbee, J. M. C. *Death and Burial in the Roman World.* Aspects of Greek and Roman Life. London: Thames & Hudson, 1971.

Trigg, Joseph W. "The Angel of Great Counsel: Christ and the Angelic Hierarchy in Origen's Theology." *Journal of Theological Studies* 42 (1991): 35–51.

Trocmé, Etienne, "L'expulsion des marchands du Temple." *New Testament Studies* 15 (1968): 1–22.

Tuckett, Christopher M. *The Revival of the Griesbach Hypothesis: An Analysis and Appraisal.* Cambridge: Cambridge University Press, 1983.

Turner, Cuthbert H. "A Primitive Edition of the Apostolic Constitutions and Canons." *Journal of Theological Studies* 15 (1913): 53–65.

Vaux, Roland de. *Les sacrifices de l'Ancien Testament.* Les Cahiers de la Revue Biblique 1. Paris: Gabalda, 1964.

Vergote, J. "Folterwerkzeuge." *Reallexicon für Antike und Christentum* 8 (1972): 112–41.

Völker, Walther. *Der wahre Gnostiker nach Clemens Alexandrinus.* Berlin: Akademie-Verlag, 1952.

Vrijoh, P. H., and Jean Jacques Waardenburg, eds. *Official and Popular Religion: Analysis of a Theme for Religious Studies.* Berlin: Mouton de Gruyter, 1979.

Walter, Christopher. *The Warrior Saints in Byzantine Art and Tradition.* Burlington, Vt.: Ashgate Press, 2003.

Watson, Duane F. "Angels." Pages 248–53 in *Anchor Bible Dictionary.* Edited by David Noel Freedman. New York: Doubleday, 1992.

Watts, James W. "*'Olah:* The Rhetoric of Burnt Offerings." *Vetus Testamentum* 61 (2006): 125–37.

Weijenborg, Reinoud. *Les lettres d'Ignace d'Antioche, étude de critique littéraire et de théologie: Mis en français par Barthélemy Héroux.* Leiden: Brill, 1969.

Weiss, Johannes, Rudolph Knopf, Fredrick C. Grant, Arthur Hare Forster, Paul Stevens Kramer, and Sherman E. Johnson. *The History of Primitive Christianity.* New York: Wilson-Erikson, 1937.

Welborn, Lawrence L. "On the Date of 1 Clement." *Biblical Research* 29 (1984): 35–54.

Werner, Martin. *Die Entstehung des christlichen Dogmas: Problemgeschichtlich dargestellt.* Bern-Leipzig: P. Haupt, 1941.

Wessel, K. "Ecclesia Orans." *Archäologisher Anzeiger* 70 (1955): 315–34.

Whitlark Jason A., and Mikeal C. Parsons. "The 'Seven' Last Words: A Numerical Motivation for the Insertion of Luke 23.34a." *New Testament Studies* 52 (2006): 188–204.

Wilken, Robert Louis, Angela Russell Christman, and Michael J. Hollerich. *Isaiah: Interpreted by Early Christian and Medieval Commentators.* Church's Bible. Grand Rapids, Mich.: Eerdmans, 2007.

Wilkenhauser, Alfred. "Das Problem des tausendjährigen Reiches in der Johannes-apokalypse." *Römische Quartalschrift für christliche Altertumskunde und Kirchengeschichte* 45 (1937): 1–24.

Williams, Delores S. *Sisters in the Wilderness: The Challenge of Womanist God-Talk.* Maryknoll, N.Y.: Orbis, 1995.

Wilpert, Josef. *Fractio Panis.* Freiburg im Breisgau: Herder, 1895.

Wilson, J. C. "The Problem with the Domitianic Date of Revelation." *New Testament Studies* 39 (1993): 587–605.

Windisch, Hans. *Der Hebräerbrief.* Handbuch zum Neuen Testament 14. Tübingen: J. C. B. Mohr, 1931.

Young, Frances M. *Biblical Exegesis and the Formation of Christian Culture.* Cambridge: Cambridge University Press, 1997.

———. "Greek Apologists of the Second Century." Pages 81–104 in *Apologetics in the Roman Empire: Pagans, Jews and Christians.* Edited by Mark Edwards, Martin Goodman, and Simon Price. Oxford: Oxford University Press, 1999.

———. *Sacrifice and the Death of Christ.* London: SPCK Press, 1975.

———. *The Use of Sacrificial Ideas in Greek Christian Writers from the New Testament to John Chrysostom.* Patristic Monograph Series 5. Cambridge, Mass.: Philadelphia Patristic Foundation, 1979.

Young, Robin Darling. *In Procession before the World: Martyrdom as Public Liturgy in Early Christianity.* Milwaukee, Wis.: Marquette University Press, 2001.

———. "Martyrdom as Exaltation." Pages 70–92, 293–94 in *Late Ancient Christianity.* Edited by Virginia Burrus. Minneapolis, Minn.: Fortress Press, 2005.

Zahn, Theodor. *Ignatius von Antiochien.* Gotha: Friedrich Andreas Perthes, 1873.

Subject Index

Ancient Authors Index